A QUEST FOR
A THEOLOGY OF JUDAISM

The Divine, the Human
and the Ethical Dimensions
in the Structure-of-Faith of Judaism

Essays in Constructive Theology

Studies in Judaism

A QUEST FOR
A THEOLOGY OF JUDAISM

The Divine, the Human
and the Ethical Dimensions
in the Structure-of-Faith of Judaism

Essays in Constructive Theology

Manfred H. Vogel

UNIVERSITY
PRESS OF
AMERICA

LANHAM • NEW YORK • LONDON

"Some Reflections on the Concept of God" © 1977 Consilium Foundation
"Man and Creation According to the Religious Tradition of Judaism"
© 1978 SIDIC
"The Jewish Image of Man and Its Relevance for Today"
© 1969 B'nai Brith Hillel Foundation
"Some Reflections on the Question of Jewish Identity" © 1970
American Academy of Religion
"The Dilemma of Identity for the Emancipated Jew" © 1966 SIDIC
"The Distinctive Expression of the Category of Worship in Judaism"
© 1982 Bijdragen
"Hebrew Scripture and Social Action" © 1969 SIDIC
"The Link Between People, Land and Religion in the Structure-of-Faith
of Judaism © 1975 SIDIC
"Toward Reformulating Zionist Ideology" © 1983 Folkertsma Foundation
"Kierkegaard's Teleological Suspension of the Ethical" © 1984 UPA

Library of Congress Cataloging-in-Publication Data

Vogel, Manfred H.
A quest for a theology of Judaism.

(Studies in Judaism)
Includes index.
1. Judaism—Doctrines   I. Title.   II. Series.
BM601.V64   1987   296.3   87-19042
ISBN 0-8191-6593-X (alk. paper)
ISBN 0-8191-6594-8 (pbk. : alk. paper)

For

Susan, Evan and Henry

and the threefold cord will
not readily be broken
Ecclesiastes 4:12

CONTENTS

Acknowledgements ix

Introduction xi

Part One
THE THEOLOGICAL POLE
Concerning Matters Pertaining to the Divine Domain

1. Some Reflections on the Concept of God 3

2. Man and Creation According to the Religious Tradition of
    Judaism 11

3. Some Reflections on the Question of Divine Providence When
    Viewed in the Context of Mainstream Judaism 41

Part Two
THE ANTHROPOLOGICAL POLE
Concerning Matters Pertaining to the Human Domain

4. The Jewish Image of Man and Its Relevance for Today.......65

5. Some Reflections on the Question of Jewish Identity.........77

6. The Dilemma of Identity for the Emancipated Jew...........109

7. Some Reflections on Death and Immortality in Mainstream
    Judaism 121

8. The Distinctive Expression of the Category of Worship in
    Judaism 141

Part Three
THE SOCIAL POLE
Concerning Matters Pertaining to the Domain Between Man and Fellow-man

9. Hebrew Scripture and Social Action................................173

10. The Link Between People, Land and Religion in the Structure-of-
    Faith of Judaism 181

11. Toward Reformulating Zionist Ideology...........................205

12. The Separation of State and Church and the Rise of Civil Religion
Viewed from the Vantage Point of Jewry and Judaism 225

13. The Social Dimension of the Structure of Faith in Judaism...............245

Part Four
THE ETHICAL PERSPECTIVE

14. Kierkegaard's Teleological Suspension of the Ethical – Some
Reflections from a Jewish Perspective 257

Index 287

Acknowledgements

The Northwestern University Research Grants Committee has provided partial support for the publication of this book. The University Press of America gratefully acknowledges this assistance.

Introduction

The fourteen essays presented in this volume have been composed over a period of about twenty years. Originally these essays were composed disjointly and independently of each other without there being any overarching conception of a whole into which they could be embedded as links in a progressive chain, or as chapters in a book, connected to each other in such a way as to allow a single pattern, a unified thesis to emerge. Indeed, in most cases the impetus for writing these essays came from the outside – an invitation to contribute an article addressing a particular issue to one or another journal, or an assignment to prepare a paper on a proposed topic for one or another conference or symposium (the one exception being the sixth essay in this collection entitled "The Dilemma of Identity for the Emancipated Jew").[1] In view of this the question arises only naturally as to what possible consideration might have motivated us to collect these essays and republish them together in a single volume.

To start with, there were three considerations that entered the picture. First, it was quite evident that all of these essays, notwithstanding the original circumstances of their composition, did in fact share a common denominator as far as their content was concerned inasmuch as the content of all these essays clearly impinges on the domain of theology, more specifically, on the domain of Jewish theology. This is so inasmuch as all the essays presented here are concerned with one or another aspect of the constitution, life and beliefs of the community of faith of Judaism and in that this concern expresses itself specifically in the intention to analyze, delineate, clarify and explicate these aspects doing this in full cognizance of (and, as much as possible, in full accordance with) the classical sources and the main interpretive strands of the tradition.[2]

Secondly, and even more poignantly, it became evident on closer inspection that all these essays share a common denominator not only by virtue of their doing Jewish theology but even more specifically by virtue of their doing *constructive* Jewish theology. For clearly the essays here, while they are certainly concerned to explicate and represent, in as authentic a manner as possible, the distinctive mainstream formulations of the community of faith of Judaism as these were articulated in the past, they do not stop with this concern. Just as much, if not more, they are concerned to see Judaism articulate formulations that are meaningful and acceptable in the present. And this is precisely the sense by which we mean to say that the essays here do a *constructive* theology of Judaism rather than a theology of Judaism pure and simple. Namely, inasmuch as the essays here undertake to explicate the various aspects of the constitution, life and beliefs of the community of faith of Judaism not only with the intention of clarifying them in harmony with the classical sources and the main interpretive strands of the tradition but also with the intention of clarifying them in harmony with our *Zeitgeist,* and inasmuch as the explication wants to go beyond the mere accommodation of past interpretive authorities of the tradition to grasp the very inner-logic operating in the structure-of-faith of the tradition and on the latter basis interpret the various aspects of the constitution, life and beliefs of the community of faith in a way that would make them meaningful for us today (even if at times this may mean going in new directions or even in contradiction to previous interpretations), in other words, inasmuch as the interpretation here is for the sake of accommodating not only the past but also the present, being not only an act of clarification and harmonization but an act of creativity and innovation, the enterprise is one of constructive theology rather than of theology pure and simple. It is in this sense, then, that the essays collected here manifest another common denominator – they are all committed in principle to do a constructive theology of Judaism.

Lastly, and most significantly in our judgment, there was the third consideration which impinged not on the content but on the methodological approach which characterizes these essays; namely, in terms of this consideration one goes beyond the general characterization of the approach as theological (signifying thereby that the approach is basically one of interpretation, explication and clarification) to ask for the specific set of criteria, the specific perspective, in terms of which such explication and clarification (and, indeed, also evaluation) can be carried out. And when one does that, one is led to encounter, we would submit, a decisive common denominator underlying the various essays of this collection. For upon closer scrutiny one will come to see that they all resort, in the last analysis, to the same basic perspective, the same fundamental set of criteria, in the light of which they undertake to interpret, explicate, clarify and evaluate the various aspects of the constitution, life and beliefs of the community of faith of Judaism. Thus, the concrete content may be disparate, the underlying method of approach operating in all these essays is one and the same – and it is the same not only in the rather loose and general sense of being theological but in the very specific sense of utilizing one and the same perspective, one and the same set of criteria, in carrying out its assignment.

Briefly stated, this unified method of approach underlying the various essays presented here is an approach which grounds itself in the Buberian bifurcation between the It-domain and the Thou-domain; namely, the perspective, the set of criteria, which directs and determines the approach here is constituted by the It-Thou bifurcation in all its many implications (of course, as understood by us). Thus, these essays undertake to explicate the signification and rationale of the various tenets and categories of the structure-of-faith of Judaism on the basis of the inner logic operating in the It and the Thou domain respectively; even more, on this basis they undertake not only to explicate but to actually reformulate the signification and rationale of some of these tenets and categories so as to make them more meaningful and acceptable to the temper and orientation of our *Zeitgeist*. In other words, not only is the theological enterprise of these essays determined by this common criterion, but also their *constructive* theological enterprise is so determined as well.[3]

As said, these considerations seemed to us at first to provide a solid enough justification and rationale for collecting these essays and republishing them, so to speak, under one roof, namely, in one single volume. For after all, as regards the first two considerations presented above (namely, the claim that all the essays assembled here manifest the theological enterprise and the even more specific claim that they manifest the enterprise of a constructive theology), it is not as if the domain of Jewish theology, let alone the domain of constructive Jewish theology, is already overly saturated with works. If anything, it is amazing how little has been done in these domains and this even though we live at a time when Judaism is being shaken to its very foundations and when, therefore, reflection in the domain of theology and even more pressingly in the domain of constructive theology would be (so one would have thought) sorely needed. But this is not the case and consequently any offering in these domains should have at least an *a priori* presumption for justification. And as regards the third consideration presented above (namely, the claim that all the essays here manifest the same methodological approach, i.e., the methodological approach of dialogical theology), surely there should be great advantage in presenting all these essays together in one unit. For in order to fully appreciate the potential of this methodological approach (as, indeed, of any other methodological approach) one would clearly want to see it applied cumulatively, namely, see it operate again and again with respect to as many different theological categories as possible. Bringing therefore these various essays together in one volume should greatly help us to better appreciate the value of this methodological approach.

These then were the considerations that originally motivated us to undertake this collection. However, when the scheme by which the various essays were to be ordered emerged, a fourth and by far the most instructive consideration for collecting these essays into a single unit suggested itself. For once the scheme of presentation was introduced, it became evident that these essays are after all linked by their very content; that, indeed, when seen from the vantage point of their content a pattern, a system does emerge which, in turn, means that these essays do succeed in constituting a meaningful whole. It became clear, although we in no way so intended it initially, that the essays presented here do trace, by their very content, an outline of a systematic presentation of a theology of Judaism. This is so inasmuch as their respective topics touch upon themes which constitute strategic junctures in the structure-of-faith of Judaism thus allowing for the general contour of the structure-of-faith to become manifest. As such, we are no longer faced with a potpourri of disconnected themes albeit of a theological nature, but with a sketch of a systematic outline of a theology of Judaism; and correspondingly, we can have now a rationale for collecting these essays in one volume which no longer need be delineated exclusively in terms of their method of approach but which, once again, can also be delineated – and just as validly if not, indeed, more so – in terms of their content. Let us attempt to briefly illustrate and explicate this outline.

In the main, the essays presented here divide themselves into three headings (the fourth heading which indeed includes only a single essay is really but an addendum whose significance will be made clear presently). These three headings correspond to the three domains which, we would submit, constitute the essential structure-of-faith in the distinctive mainstream expression of Judaism;[4] namely, they correspond respectively to the domain of the divine, to the domain of man and to the domain of the in-between man and man, i.e., to the domain of the social. As such, the essays in this collection do indeed cover the full extent of the structure-of-faith which characterizes Judaism.

Now, that the structure-of-faith encompasses here the first two domains, i.e., the domain of the divine and the domain of man, should not be surprising at all. Indeed, we should expect these two domains to be present in the structure-of-faith of each and every religious phenomenon seeing that the religious orientation by its very essence must impinge upon both the divine and the human. It must impinge on the divine inasmuch as the religious orientation is by its very essence an orientation which, in the last analysis, is concerned with the dimension of ultimacy, of absoluteness, and the essential signification of the divine is nothing else but the signification of ultimacy and absoluteness; in the last analysis, what the notion of the divine signifies is but the notion of the ultimate, the absolute – that which is ultimate, absolute, is divine. As such, we cannot really have a religion without the realm of the divine (it clearly would not make sense) and Judaism is certainly no exception to this. But the religious orientation must also impinge on the human. For in contradistinction to the orientation of philosophy (philosophy, at least in its more traditional metaphysical garb, it being the other orientation which is concerned with ultimacy and absoluteness), the concern of the orientation of religion in the ultimate, the absolute, is never for its own sake but always, in the last analysis, for the sake of man. Thus, while philosophy, specifically, the philosophy of religion, is basically concerned with the divine as it is in itself (for example, whether or not it exists and what attributes it may or may not possess), religion in its authentic expression is concerned with the divine only as it relates to man, with the divine as it is for-man.[5]

As such, the phenomenon of religion is just as much concerned with man as it is concerned with the divine. It is a phenomenon which by its very essence establishes itself not in any one single category but in the axis that combines two categories; it is a phenomenon which builds itself on the divine-human axis. Neither the divine-in-itself nor man-as-such constitutes the foundation; rather, the foundation is constituted by the divine-human axis. And this, in turn, means, of course, that probably in all, and certainly in most, structures-of-faith we would encounter at least two subdivisions – one pertaining to the divine and the other pertaining to man. Consequently, if our collection of essays is indeed to trace the main outline of the structure-of-faith of Judaism, we should not be in the least surprised that the two opening sections of our collection are constituted by essays relating to the divine and to man respectively.[6]

But while the structure-of-faith of many a religious phenomenon may well be completed in all essential respects by this two-fold subdivision, this is not the case with respect to the structure-of-faith of Judaism. Namely, while in many a religious phenomenon the divine-human relationship is encompassed in all essential respects by the direct interaction between the two, this is not the case in Judaism. Indeed, it is a distinctive characteristic of Judaism that in it the divine-human interaction is, so to speak, refracted through a third domain – the domain of the world or, more precisely, the domain of the human world, i.e., of society. Here, the divine-human interaction does not oscillate directly along a single axis combining two poles, the human and the divine. A third pole, the pole of the fellow-man, intrudes into the picture through which the interaction is, in a most significant and essential sense, refracted or, to change the metaphor, detoured. Namely, the address from the divine to man and, even more significantly, the response from man to the divine, is refracted through the world, specifically, through the human world, the world of society, of the fellow-man. The vertical relation between man and the divine is refracted here through the horizontal relation between man and fellow-man. Thus, while many a structure-of-faith may be aptly represented by the symbol of the cross, the direct intercrossing between two lines, the divine which is vertical and the human which is horizontal, the structure-of-faith of Judaism is more aptly represented by the symbol of the triangle – the connection between two points which goes through a third.[7] And, of course, any systematic theological outline of such a structure-of-faith would of necessity have to articulate itself through a tripartite rather than through the more standard two-fold subdivision; namely, in addition to the standard subdivision into the domain of the divine and the domain of man, a third domain, the domain of the in-between man and fellow-man will have to be introduced. In addition to the first axis, the vertical axis, which is constituted by the two poles, that of the divine and that of man, a second axis, the horizontal axis, which is constituted by the two poles, that of man and that of fellow-man, will have to be included here. As such, this means that the whole horizontal domain between man and fellow-man in all its manifold dimensions, i.e., the political, the social and the economic, which is usually relegated to the secular realm and thus essentially banished from the context of theological concern, is here fully and directly incorporated into the religious domain and consequently must be fully articulated in any theological representation of that domain.[8]

We would suggest that the rationale which would explain this remarkable intrusion of the horizontal into the structure-of-faith of Judaism (and, indeed, its full appropriation by this structure-of-faith) is to be located in the fact that, in contradistinction to other manifestations of the religious phenomenon, in Judaism (more specifically, in that Judaism which is constituted by the prophetic and by the non-mystical halachic expressions) the fundamental concern is not with the ontological predicament but rather with the ethical predicament of man. Namely, in the last analysis, the rationale lies in the fact that Judaism, in the main, constitutes itself in response to the ethical problematic rather than to the ontological problematic of man. For as such, it is readily understandable that Judaism should formulate itself so predominantly in the horizontal domain seeing that the ethical dimension arises precisely in this domain, i.e., in the horizontal domain; indeed, strictly speaking, the ethical can arise only in the context of the relations which subsist between man and fellow-man. Thus, if Judaism is concerned with the ethical problematic, it per force must formulate itself in the context of the horizontal domain and this, in turn, means that the many issues connected with this domain, i.e., the various issues belonging to the political, social and economic dimensions, issues which in so many other religious formulations are relegated to the secular and thus excluded from the religious concern, are here thoroughly infused with religious significance. The social, the economic, the political – in the context of Judaism they all provide *bona fide* material for the theological grist.

Indeed, so overpowering is the ethical concern in Judaism that it, so to speak, overspills its proper boundaries within the horizontal domain and injects itself into the vertical domain. The ethical which, strictly speaking, impinges exclusively on the horizontal axis, on the domain of man, is referred here back to the vertical axis, to the domain of the divine. Not only man but the divine too is to be subjected to the ethical, even though the ethical here may well be capable of expressing itself only in the form of a challenge and nothing more – "Is the Judge of all the earth not to do justice?" Namely, while with regard to man the ethical can and does express itself categorically and didactically, with regard to the divine it may well be capable of expressing itself only in the form of a question, a challenge.

Still, it is precisely in the possibility of raising such a challenge, rather than in providing the conclusive answer for it, that Judaism is essentially characterized and this, of course, means that any theological representation of Judaism, if it is to have any pretense of being adequate, must address itself to this issue. Indeed, this is precisely what we try to do when in the fourth and last section of this collection of essays we shift our concern from how the ethical dimension impinges upon the horizontal domain of man to how it impinges upon the vertical domain of the divine. As such, we round off our outline of the theological presentation of Judaism and bring it to a fitting conclusion. Indeed, we come full circle back to the beginning, to the vertical, to the divine. And it is the ethical consideration, the very consideration which is the responsible factor for starting, so to speak, the movement by propelling the theological concern from the divine realm to the human realm, that is now also the responsible factor for bringing the movement to a close by extracting it from its refraction in the horizontal domain of man and returning it to the vertical domain of the divine. Clearly, the ethical consideration provides the impetus both for the "lowering" of the religious dimension into the horizontal domain (for its incarnation, so to speak, in the horizontal domain) and for "raising" it back from the horizontal to the vertical domain. In other words, it provides the motor-power that drives the circle from the divine to the human realm and back again to the divine realm. Thus, it is the ethical consideration which brings about the movement – the movement from the divine to man and back again to the divine.

In a way, of course, one may feel that all this movement is sham, that it does not really go anywhere, that it is truly circular, seeing that it begins with the divine and ends with the divine. Yet, like the Hegelian synthesis (at which the thesis arrives through its movement via the anti-thesis back to itself), the notion of the divine to which we come at the end is a greatly enriched and deepened notion as compared to the notion of the divine with which we start – we start with the notion of the divine merely in its ontological signification but end up with a notion of the divine infused with ethical signification. Thus, we do have movement here in a significant sense after all – true, not so much in terms of the reality involved (here we begin and end with one and the same reality, i.e., the divine) but in terms of its signification.

Thus, the division of the essays collected here into the four major sub-divisions, i.e., sections, of this volume clearly retraces the major, rather gross, movements of the inner-logic as it operates in the structure-of-faith of Judaism (namely, the movements which proceed from the divine to man, from man to fellow-man and finally from fellow-man back to the divine) and in doing this it sketches out the main outline of what a systematic presentation of a theology of Judaism would look like. What we have to do now is go back and examine the particular order by which the individual essays are arranged within each of the four sections in order to show how this order traces the smaller, more refined movements of the inner-logic as it operates in the structure-of-faith of Judaism thus sketching out in greater detail the contours of the outline presented here.

Turning to our first section, the section dealing with the domain of the divine, we begin logically enough in the essay "Some Reflections on the Concept of God in the Religious Tradition of Judaism" with the attempt to delineate the essential signification of the notion of the divine as it operates in mainstream Judaism. In the main, we attempt to show here that for Judaism the very essence of the divine lies in its being constituted as a personal being, a being-of-consciousness, a Thou-God. Of course, it should not be too difficult to show that from this it follows that such a divine being cannot, by its very essence, exist in-itself but only in-relation, specifically, only in a relation that is an I-Thou relation. For *qua* a Thou-being such a divine being can arise only from within a relation, specifically, only from within an I-Thou relation. By itself or, indeed, in any other relation outside the I-Thou relation it must perforce disintegrate. This being the case, we should not expect to encounter in the structure-of-faith of Judaism God as he is in-himself but rather as he is in-relation, even more specifically, as he is in the I-Thou relation; correspondingly, we should not expect the theological enterprise in Judaism to deal with the various aspects of God as he is in-himself but rather with the aspects of God as he is in-relation, specifically, in the I-Thou relation.[9]

In view of this it should not be surprising that the remaining essays in this section should impinge exclusively upon aspects connected with the divine as it is in-relation and not at all upon aspects connected with the divine as it is in-itself. For after all, as we have seen, from a god constituted as a person, i.e., as a Thou, there can be no other way to proceed except to a god who is in-relation. And consequently, in the theology of Judaism, where the very essence of the enterprise lies in encountering a god who is a Thou, the only legitimate dealings regarding the divine can be those dealings which impinge upon the divine as it is in-relation. Thus, we are clearly following the dictates of the inner-logic operating here when, after the opening essay which deals with the kind of divine being one encounters in Judaism, we concentrate in the rest of the essays of this section exclusively on the divine as it is in-relation, dealing with its involvement first in the relation of creation (dealt with in the essay "Man and Creation According to the Religious Tradition of Judaism") and then in the relation of providence (dealt with in the essay "Some Reflections on the Question of Divine Providence").

Now, it should not be too difficult to see the further rationale for following this particular order. For one would obviously want to start with the most extensive, inclusive and, indeed, fundamental relation in which the divine is involved and this clearly is the relation of creation – the relation of the divine to the world as a whole, to all that is. But given the fundamental thrust of the methodology characterizing the theological approach reflected in the essays of this collection, namely, the commitment to consistently draw and apply the implications of the Thou-dimension and correspondingly at the same time to consistently limit and circumscribe all elements belonging to the It-dimension, we can readily understand that our theological enterprise does not linger too long with the relation of creation and, indeed, is propelled to move on to the relation of providence. For the notion of creation in its common traditional signification (namely, in its signification of making things or of bringing things into physical existence) implicates a relation that is inescapably an I-It relation and an I-It relation could not possibly involve a Thou-god. Thus, quite evidently the notion of creation in its traditional signification is not too fruitful a notion in our context seeing that the god implicated in this context is constituted as a Thou-god. Indeed, as a Thou-god this god can be involved only in an I-Thou relation. Now, it is precisely the notion of providence (particularly given the way we are using it here) that can provide us with the I-Thou relation. As such, it is understandable that in the context of the structure-of-faith of Judaism a momentum would be, so to speak, generated propelling one from the relation of creation to the relation of providence. Indeed, in the last analysis, it is not really the relation of creation but the relation of providence which is really significant to the structure-of-faith of Judaism.

Let us briefly enlarge on our argument. In particular, it is our delineation of the two notions involved, i.e., the notion of creation and the notion of providence, that may require some further explication. Thus, we said that the notion of creation implicates an I-It relation. This is so for two reasons: first, the object of the relation implicated here is comprised overwhelmingly of beings constituted as It-beings. For after all the relation implicated by the notion of creation, in being directed to the world as a whole, is being directed mainly to inanimate physical nature and its projection into the vegetable and animal realms, all of which presents us with It-beings. As such, the overwhelming burden of the relation implicated by the notion of creation is directed to It-beings which, of course, means that the relation in these circumstances can only be an I-It relation seeing that the only relation possible with an It-being is the I-It relation. The one exception in the inventory of the world, and obviously, it is a most minimal exception, is man – the one being that may allow an I-Thou relation. But even here with regard to man the relation implicated by the notion of creation would fail to realize itself as an I-Thou relation and this because of our second reason which maintains that the traditional signification of the notion of creation as making things or bring them into physical existence necessarily implies that the relation implicated by the notion of creation is an I-It relation. For in terms of this signification creation inevitably becomes, in one way or another, a transaction in Power. To make things, to bring them into physical existence, is clearly a one-way relation that utilizes Power and as such it can only be an I-It relation.[10]

We also said that it is the notion of providence which can provide us with the needed I-Thou relation and the reason for this lies in the fact that the notion of providence implicates a relation that subsists essentially between the divine and man.[11] For, as observed above, inasmuch as man is the only being of all the beings constituting the inventory of the world with which the divine can enter into an I-Thou relation, the relation implicated by the notion of providence, in contradistinction to the relation implicated by the notion of creation, can meet the need of the Thou-god to be in a relation that is specifically an I-Thou relation. But let us note that what we say is that the relation implicated by the notion of providence *can* provide the I-Thou relation, not that it must or that it inevitably does. For after all, man is this distinctive being which is constituted as an It-Thou being and which as such can participate in either an I-Thou or an I-It relation. Thus, it is possible to establish with man not only an I-Thou relation but also an I-It relation. Still, in the context of the structure-of-faith of Judaism, precisely because the divine is constituted as a pure Thou-being, we should expect the relation implicated by the notion of providence to be exclusively an I-Thou relation; namely, while man's participation in the relation makes it only possible for the relation to be an I-Thou relation, it is the divine participation which dictates that it be exclusively so.[12] But as such, as implicating an I-Thou relation, the notion of providence does indeed provide a relation which is an authentic expression and thus a fitting locus, a final resting-point, for the divine in-relation.

Furthermore, the relation implicated by the notion of providence, coming as it does after the relation implicated by the notion of creation, provides a fitting conclusion to this section. For inasmuch as the subject matter of this section is the divine in-relation, the section can be satisfactorily concluded only when the gamut of possible relations implicating the divine is covered, which is indeed what the two relations presented here – the relation implicated by the notion of creation and the relation implicated by the notion of providence – succeed in accomplishing. For after all, the relation implicated by the notion of creation, as used by us here, would encompass all the relations which the divine may have with the world, i.e., primarily with the physical-material aspect of the world, while the relation implicated by the notion of providence, as used by us here, would encompass all the relations which the divine may have with man, i.e., primarily with the affairs of the human community. As such, the former relation clearly covers nature while the latter relation covers history or, even more comprehensively, the former relation covers space while the latter relation covers time, and surely this would delineate the maximum extent to which the relation implicating the divine can be stretched. For what else beyond the physical-material world and man, nature and history, space and time, is there to which the divine can relate?[13]

The relation implicated by the notion of providence, however, does not only constitute a fitting conclusion to our first section, i.e., the section concerned with matters pertaining to the divine, but seeing that it is a relation which proceeds from the divine to man, it also constitutes a fitting transition to our next section, i.e., the section concerned with matters pertaining to man. For in linking the divine with man, indeed, in moving from the divine to man, the relation already points beyond matters pertaining to the divine towards matters pertaining to man thus propelling us from our first to our second section.

Moving to our second section, we begin with the essay entitled "The Jewish Image of Man and Its Relevance for Today" where we attempt to establish the essential constitution of the entity which serves as the linchpin of this section, namely, man. Thus, our starting point in this section parallels our starting point in the previous section. In both sections we start with the attempt to establish the essential identity of the entity with which we are going to deal (the divine in the previous and man in the present section) – a procedure that appears to us to be eminently logical. But while the procedure is the same, the results are, as to be expected, quite different. Indeed, in contradistinction to having established above that in the view of Judaism the divine is constituted by its very essence as a pure Thou-being, the very point of the essay here is to establish that in the view of Judaism the man by his very essence is constituted as an inextricable It-Thou being.

We must realize however, that in the context of the religious phenomenon or, even more specifically, in the context of the theological enterprise, namely, in the context of articulating a theology for any particular concrete manifestation of the religious phenomenon, one cannot stop with providing merely the identity of man in general, of man as such. One has to provide also the more specific and concrete identity of man as a member of the community of faith of the religion with which one is dealing – for example, one must provide the more specific and concrete identity of man *qua* Jew, *qua* Christian or *qua* Moslem. For the religious context man in general is concretized as a member of a specific community of faith – man as such becomes a Jew, a Christian, a Moslem, etc. We can perhaps put the matter more accurately by saying that the notion of man as such finds its place within the religious discourse mainly when the discourse addresses itself to the issue of the predicament, of the problematic of man (the overcoming of which being, of course, the very vocation of religion); but as soon as the discourse addresses itself to formulating the solution, the answer, to the predicament, i.e., to articulating the redemptive dimension (or in those religions which do not articulate themselves in terms of the redemptive dimension, as soon as the discourse addresses itself to formulating its ideal of optimal man), the notion of man as such is replaced by the much more specific and concretized notion of man as a member of the community of faith. Thus, for example, in the covenantal relation which expresses the divine-human relation in the context of the redemptive dimension (and as such constituting indeed the very foundation of the structure-of-faith in such biblical faiths as Judaism and Christianity), the human pole of the relation is not occupied by man as such but rather by man as a member of the community of faith – for example, the covenantal relation as it expresses itself in the context of Judaism formulates itself primarily as a relation between god and the people of Israel while the convenantal relation as it expresses itself in the context of Christianity formulates itself primarily as a relation between God and the Christian (by the way, note that in the former instance the human pole is represented primarily by the collectivity while in the latter instance it is represented primarily by the individual). Thus, to the extent that we are attempting to delineate here the main contours of a theology of Judaism, and to the extent that in such a delineation one cannot stop with the aspect of the predicament but must move on to the redemptive aspect, we cannot stop with the formulation of the identity of man as such but must instead move to the formulation of the identity of the Jew. What constitutes the identity of the Jew is of fundamental importance in the theology of Judaism in the same way, indeed, that what constitutes the identity of the Christian is of fundamental importance in a theology of Christianity. We are, therefore, following the inner-logic operating in the structure-of-faith of Judaism when pursuant to the essay "The Jewish Image of Man and Its Relevance for Today" we present the essay "Some Reflections on the Question of Jewish Identity" which addresses itself to the task of delineating the essential identity of the Jew.[14]

The same, alas, cannot be claimed for our next move when persuant to our essay "Some Reflections on the Question of Jewish Identity" we introduce the essay "The Dilemma of Identity for the Emancipated Jew." Indeed, the very inclusion of this essay must seem rather puzzling. For the essay in no way impinges upon any topic which can constitute itself as a category in the structure-of-faith of Judaism. As the title clearly indicates, this essay undertakes to deal with the problematic situation which the Emancipation ushered in by the French Revolution precipitates for Jewry and Judaism. As such, the topic of this essay is clearly historical and contingent – in no way does it impinge upon any inherent, permanent feature or aspect of the phenomenon of Judaism. Thus, if our aim in presenting these essays was to trace the main contours of the structure-of-faith which operates in Judaism and as such delineate the outline of a theology of Judaism (as, indeed, is the case), then the inclusion of this essay must be perplexing. Indeed, we must concede that in turning our attention from the notions which constitute the permanent categories of the structure-of-faith to the problematic of a situation that is historical and thus contingent we are veering away from our task. Yet, so radical is this problematic, signaling for Judaism the very shaking of its foundations, that it is difficult to imagine that any attempt to construct a theology of Judaism in modern times would not feel itself compelled to address this topic. And since the problematic devolves, again as the title of the essay clearly indicates, upon the question of Jewish identity it is quite understandable that we should place it after the essay which undertakes to delineate for us what that identity of the Jew is.[15]

Returning from this brief yet important detour to our main task, one may well be perplexed by the fact that the next essay in our outline is the essay "Some Reflections on Death and Immortality in Mainstream Judaism." Many would wonder why the theme of death and after-life should have been selected as the next issue following the determination of the essential identity of man in general and of the Jew in particular; indeed, some, no doubt, would wonder why the theme of death and after-life is included at all in a mere sketch of a theology, let alone the position where it may be placed. Clearly, the route that we propose to take here does not parallel the route taken in the preceding section where we moved directly from establishing the essential identity of the divine to the divine as it is in-relation. For quite obviously the theme of death and after-life does not seem to implicate man in-relation (quite the contrary, if anything, death would seem to be the instance par excellence where man is completely by himself). But then, a moment's reflection will show us that the inner-logic operating in the case of man is by no means identical with the inner-logic operating in the case of the divine. For after all the inner-logic which dictated above that the divine be in-relation was derived from the fact that the divine was constituted as a pure Thou-being (it being the Thou-dimension which necessarily implicates being in relation) – the divine being constituted exclusively as a Thou, it necessarily must be in-relation; it cannot be otherwise. But with man it can be otherwise. For in man, unlike the divine, there is an alternative seeing that he is not constituted as a pure Thou-being but rather as an inextricable It-Thou being. For surely it is only the Thou-aspect but not the It-aspect of man's constitution that would necessarily implicate his being in-relation.[16]

Thus, man can be in-relation but he can also be not in-relation and whether he is or not will depend, it would seem, on whether he expresses himself in the context of the Thou-dimension or in the context of the It-dimension. More precisely, we should say that whether or not man is viewed as a being in-relation would depend on the specific context in which the perception of his ultimate predicament is formulated, namely, whether it is perceived to be formulated in the context provided by the Thou-dimension or in the context provided by the It-dimension. For, we would submit that what is perceived as man's ultimate predicament constitutes the very foundation on which the whole structure-of-faith is built; indeed, the whole structure-of-faith may be seen as but the formulation of the answer to the problematic which the ultimate predicament presents, as but the delineation of the way to overcome it. As such, that which is perceived as the ultimate predicament evidently becomes the factor which determines everything else in the structure-of-faith. Thus, if the perceived ultimate predicament formulates itself in the context of the It-dimension, the structure-of-faith as a whole would formulate itself in the It-dimension and this, in turn, would mean that its various entities (and specifically, as regards our concern here, man), would not be constituted as entities in-relation; on the other hand, if the perceived ultimate predicament formulates itself in the context of the Thou-dimension, the structure-of-faith as a whole would formulate itself in the Thou-dimension and this, in turn, would mean that its various entities (and specifically man) would indeed be constituted as entities in-relation.

In view of these considerations the rationale for turning to an essay which deals with the issue of death and, indeed, of turning to it at this particular juncture in the outline, should become clear. For, we would suggest that in bringing up the issue of death we bring up nothing less than the issue of the ultimate predicament. Indeed, the issue of death is so central and pervasive in the history of religions (so much so, that some people have identified the very essence of the phenomenon of religion with the concern with death) precisely because for so many religions it articulates the perception of the ultimate predicament. Thus, inasmuch as we need to determine what the perception of man's ultimate predicament is once his essential identity is established (seeing that this determination would, in turn, determine how we are to proceed with our outline of the structure-of-faith of Judaism) and inasmuch as the ultimate predicament is so prevalently perceived in terms of the event of death, it is understandable that immediately after establishing Judaism's perception of the essential identity of man in general and of the Jew in particular we should undertake to establish Judaism's perception of man's ultimate predicament and that we should attempt to do it by undertaking to investigate Judaism's evaluation of and response to the event of death.

Indeed, turning to the issue of death does prove, in the last analysis, to be a crucial turn in our outline, a turn which determines in a most significant way the whole subsequent direction of our outline.[17] For as we have just seen in the preceding footnote, the essay establishes that Judaism formulates itself from the perspective of the Thou-dimension and, even more specifically, that within this perspective it formulates itself in terms of the ethical domain and clearly these two considerations must influence very profoundly and materially the direction which the structure-of-faith of Judaism would take towards its completion as we shall try to show in the remainder of this introduction.

Thus, to the extent that Judaism formulates itself from the perspective of the Thou-dimension it necessarily implicates that man or, more precisely, optimal man (i.e., man as he ought to realize himself) be a being in-relation. For as we have seen, the inner-logic of the Thou-dimension dictates that all beings within the dimension be in-relation; indeed, and this is what is really significant here, it dictates that they be not just in any relation but specifically in the I-Thou relation. Thus, we are back here to the situation encountered in the former section with respect to the divine being. For as was the situation there, where the divine being was established as necessarily a being in-relation, so optimal man here is also established as a being in-relation. Furthermore, as in the former section, after establishing the essential identity of the divine we were propelled to move to the divine as it is in-relation, specifically, as it is in the I-Thou relation, so also here, after establishing the essential identity of man we are propelled to move to man as he is in-relation, and again specifically, as he is in the I-Thou relation. Lastly, given that our context here is the context of religion and that, as observed above, the religious enterprise is essentially concerned with the divine-human relation, it is to be expected that as in the former section where the establishing of the divine as a being in-relation propelled us to move to a divine who is specifically in-relation to man so also here the establishing of man as a being in-relation would propel us to move to man who is specifically in-relation to the divine. Indeed, this is precisely what happens when we move to our next essay entitled "The Distinctive Expression of the Category of Worship in Judaism." For as the title indicates we clearly take up in this essay the subject of man's relation to the divine grasping this relation in its all-inclusive signification (this being precisely what the category of worship signifies to us) although, sure enough, the reality of Jewish religious life soon leads us to focus our attention on one particular expression of this category, namely, on the expression of prayer, which not surprisingly is precisely the expression that articulates itself specifically in the context of the I-Thou relation. Thus, in moving to this essay we satisfy all the requirements that still remain outstanding for this section, to wit, the requirement to deal with man as a being in-relation, more specifically, the requirement to have the relation thus implicated directed to the divine and, even more specifically, to have this relation be an I-Thou relation. In this way this essay provides a fitting conclusion to the second section in our outline.

Indeed, in a sense this essay, in bringing to a close the second section, could have also signaled in a very fitting way the end of our whole outline. For, as noted above, generally the concern of the phenomenon of religion centers on the relation which subsists between the divine and man (this relation constituting the proper domain for the religious interest) and consequently having dealt with the divine and with man (i.e., with the two poles of the relation) or, even more precisely, having dealt with both the divine as it relates to man and with man as he relates to the divine, our outline could have been brought to an end. In other words, in having traced the relation from the divine to man and back again from man to the divine the religious circle could have been completed – the circle originating with the divine could have been brought to a close with its return to the divine.

That this is not the case here is due to the other consideration which emerged from our previous essay dealing with the theme of death, namely, the consideration that Judaism formulates itself not only in the context of the Thou-dimension but also more specifically in terms of the ethical domain. It is this consideration which compels us to redirect the orientation of man's being in-relation from orienting itself exclusively in a vertical fashion to the divine to orienting itself also in a horizontal fashion to the fellow-man. For, as we have already noted above, the ethical perspective impinges essentially upon the domain of the in-between man and man and consequently, inasmuch as Judaism formulates itself in terms of the ethical perspective, the vertical relation to the divine must be, so to speak, refracted here through the horizontal relation to the fellow-man – the direct relation to the divine must take a detour and arrive at the divine through the mediation of the fellow-man. Thus, the ethical consideration clearly prevents us from bringing our outline to a close at this point and instead propels us to our third section, the section concerned with the social domain, the domain of the in-between man and man (evidently "social" is used here in its broadest sense to include all aspects of the relation between man and man as, for example, the economic and the political).[18]

In turning now to the third section, one soon realizes that, in contradistinction to the previous two sections, it is difficult to locate here an inherent rationale for the selection of the specific topics (i.e., which topics to include and which to exclude) and, even more so, for their arrangement in any specific order of progression. For essentially any topic that impinges on the horizontal dimension of life in its human context, i.e., any topic that impinges on the social-economic-political domain, should qualify. Thus, the rationale does not emerge from the nature of the subject matter but is imposed from the outside by us. Let us, therefore, briefly delineate the rationale which the essays presented here manifest to us.

The section opens with the essay "Hebrew Scripture and Social Action" which undertakes to examine the relation between religion and social ethics (thus coming to deal with one of the most fundamental values in the tradition, the value of justice) in the context of its original formulation, namely, in the context of its formulation within the Prophetic writings and the Pentateuchal legislation of Hebrew Scripture. It is fitting that the section should open with an examination of this fundamental theme, and that this theme should be pursued in terms of its original formulation, particularly since this formulation is also viewed by most people as providing the classical expression for it. For surely nowhere else in the tradition can one find a clearer, fuller and more poignant expression of this linkage between religion and social ethics, a linkage which, as we had occasion to suggest in many of the essays presented here, constitutes the very essence of the distinctive, mainline strand within Judaism, the strand to which we referred above as the "prophetic-halachic" strand.

The next three essays proceed to deal with three particular, concrete issues that arise in the social-political arena. Thus, in contradistinction to the foregoing essay which dealt with a fundamental pervasive theme belonging to the social-economic sphere, we proceed to deal with the specific issues belonging to the social-political arena. But by what criteria were these issues selected? A quick glance at the headings should readily indicate that they all deal with issues that are very prominent on the agenda of Jewish life today. Clearly, the criterion of selection here was the contemporary relevancy of the issues.[19]

Thus, the first essay "The Link Between People, Land and Religion in the Structure-of-Faith of Judaism" addresses itself to the issue of the relationship between the structure-of-faith of Judaism on the one hand and the categories of nationhood, homeland and sovereignty on the other, an issue which the renaissance of national consciousness in this century and, even more so, the re-establishment of the state of Israel have clearly brought to the fore.[20] The second essay, "Toward Reformulating Zionist Ideology," addresses itself to the crisis precipitated for Zionism as regards its *raison d'être* which the re-establishment of the state brings about.[21] And the third essay, "The Separation of State and Church and the Rise of Civil Religion Viewed from the Vantage Point of Jewry and Judaism," addresses itself to the issue of the relation that ought to exist between religion and the body politic according to the view of Judaism, an issue which is very much on the agenda of the two largest Jewish communities today, i.e., the Jewish community in the United States and in

Israel.[22] Clearly, all three essays deal with issues that are of great significance in contemporary Jewish life. The section is brought to a close with the essay, "The Social Dimension of the Structure-of-Faith of Judaism," where some of the important points made disparately in the previous essays are gathered together as we attempt to restate in a systematic yet concise way the very essence of the position of Judaism towards the horizontal dimension of life.

Finally, as already pointed out above, the inclusion of the fourth section as a closing addendum to our outline not only expresses explicitly what is implicit all along, namely, that the movement originating from the divine can culminate and be brought to an end only in its return to the divine (in other words, that the detour into the horizontal dimension does not stop with fellow-man but leads ultimately back to the divine, that Judaism's interest in the horizontal is ultimately not for its own sake but for the sake of the vertical, for the sake of heaven), but it also manifests how fundamental and pervasive is the ethical perspective in the structure-of-faith of Judaism so much so that it, so to speak, spills over its proper boundaries within the horizontal dimension, the human domain, to impinge upon the vertical dimension, upon the divine. In this latter aspect it precipitates the challenge that is so characteristic and fundamental to Judaism, i.e., the challenge of theodicy. This challenge was already encountered by us before when the movement from the divine to man was being traced in our essay on providence. Now, when the movement is returning to the divine we encounter it again, this time in our closing essay "Kierkegaard's Teleological Suspension of the Ethical – Some Reflections from a Jewish Perspective." But while in the former instance we encounter the challenge in terms of God's responsibility in the face of the evil occurring in the world, in this instance we encounter the challenge in terms of God's ultimacy, namely, in terms of the question of which, in the last analysis, constitutes the true ultimate, the divine or the ethical?[23] Is the divine bound to observe the ethical, thus limiting its freedom and indeed conceding ultimacy to the ethical, or is the divine free to do what it pleases, even to do evil, thus safeguarding its ultimacy and sovereignty but undermining the ethical? Using Kierkegaard's famous formulation as a springboard we try in this our last essay to put forth a solution to this dilemma along lines that we believe would be congenial to the structure-of-faith of Judaism.[24]

Given the task which it sets for itself, this essay not only comes to grips with what is really at stake in this section (namely, with what is really at stake in the intrusion of the ethical into the divine realm), but for all intents and purposes it preempts the section of any further issue or problematic – given the intrusion of the ethical into the divine realm, the only significant issue, the only important problematic, is the clash between the ethical constraint and the divine free will. This means, of course, that this section really requires only this essay (which, indeed, is the case) and as such that this essay is not only the opening essay of the section but at the same time also the essay that brings the section to a close. And, of course, in bringing this section to a close it brings our entire outline to a close – with this essay the movement of theology returns to the divine and the circle is closed. Indeed, this essay provides us with a most fitting conclusion to our attempt to present an outline of the structure-of-faith of Judaism seeing that it impinges on a theme that captures in the most poignant way the distinct spirit and nature of Judaism, namely, the theme which articulates the challenge of theodicy, which raises the question "Is the judge of all the earth not to do justice?" For clearly this is a question that captures the very essence of Judaism in a more profound way than any other question or statement in the religious discourse of Judaism; it is certainly a question which Judaism has been raising continuously and persistently from its inception to our day. Indeed, it is in the very raising of this question (rather than in providing a satisfactory answer to it which, by the way, Judaism may not be able to do) that Judaism expresses its ultimate act of witnessing, for in raising this question Judaism establishes the two most fundamental tenets of its faith, to wit, that the ultimate, that God, is a Thou, a person (thus that ultimately one encounters free will, the free will of God, and not necessity) and that the ethical enterprise is the ultimate vocation not only for man and the world but also for God.

---

[1] As such, much of this material (albeit by no means all) has already appeared in previous publications either in the form of journal articles or in the form of book chapters. This then might be as convenient a point as any to acknowledge these original sites of publication (wherever, of course, it may apply). Thus, "Some Reflections on the Concept of God" originally appeared in *Concilium* vol. 103; "Man and Creation According to the Religious Tradition of Judaism" in *Sidic,* vol. XII, Nos. 1-2; "The Jewish Image of Man and Its Relevance for Today" in *Tradition and Contemporary Experience* edited by A. Jospe, 1970; "Some Reflections on the Question of Jewish Identity" in *Bijdragen* Vol. 31, No. 1; "The Dilemma of Identity for the Emancipated Jew" in *The Journal of Bible and Religion,* vol. XXXIV, No. 3; "The Distinctive Expression of the Category of Worship in Judaism in *Bijdragen,* vol. 43, No. 4; "Hebrew Scripture and Social Action" in *Sidic,* vol. II, No. 3; "The Link Between People, Land and Religion in the Structure-of-Faith of Judaism" in *Sidic* vol. VIII, No. 2; "Toward Reformulating Zionist Ideology" in *Sjaloom* edited by M. de Kruijf and H. Van der Sandt, 1983; and lastly, "Kierkegaard's Teleological Suspension of the Ethical – Some Reflections from a Jewish Perspective; in *The Georgetown Symposium on Ethics* edited by R. Porreco, 1984.

[2] Clearly, the notion of theology is used here not in its narrow pedantic signification, i.e., in its literal signification, according to which it is to be a body of propositional statements (thus a corpus of knowledge) referring to the divine being. Rather, it is used in its broader and somewhat looser signification (yet of fairly widespread usage) according to which it is a body of interpretive and explicatory statements referring to all aspects connected with the constitution, life and beliefs of a community of faith.

[3] By the way, a most interesting and significant by-product of this approach is the emergence from the. working of the inner-logic operating in the Thou-domain of a new and distinctive way of doing theology, to wit, the emergence of what we may call dialogical theology (in contradistinction both to natural and to revelatory theology). This way of doing theology has its starting-point and is grounded in the "in-between," i.e., in the relation between the divine and man, rather than in man (or, more comprehensively, in nature) as in natural theology or in the divine, i.e., in the divine impartation to man, as in revelatory theology. We would submit that such a way of doing theology may prove of great value to biblical religions generally and to Judaism in particular – it may well illumine new significations in the

structure of faith involved here and thus point to new possibilities in reconstructing their traditional interpretations.

[4]We would argue below in some of the essays of this volume that the distinctive mainstream expression of Judaism is to be seen as being basically constituted in terms of the prophetic articulation in the context of Hebrew Scriptures and in terms of the non-mystical, halachic articulation in the context of Rabbinic Judaism (the latter articulation, by the way, being in its essential features a continuation of the former articulation).

In this connection we should perhaps attempt to briefly deal with a question that is bound to arise, namely how can we maintain the position that the non-mystical halachic expression is to be viewed as a continuation of the prophetic expression and as such, indeed, as an expression of the Thou-dimension and at the same time claim to appropriate and follow Buber's stance seeing that Buber's stance in this respect is diametrically opposed to ours, i.e., viewing the halachic expression as breaking with the prophetic expression and as being an expression of the It-dimension. How is one to explain the fact that even though we are obviously greatly influenced by Buber's dialogical stance, we still can arrive at opposite ends to him in the perception and evaluation of the non-mystical halachic expression of Rabbinic Judaism? Although the full answer is rather complex and multi-faceted and as such we obviously cannot deal with it here in full measure, its main thrust is fundamentally this: Buber's negative evaluation of the halachic expression and, indeed, his viewing it as an expression of the I-it dimension result in the main from the fact that he views the halachic expression as being a closed system. To him this aspect occupies center stage and reveals the very essence of the halachic expression which as such inescapably constitutes itself as an expression of the It-dimension. We, on the other hand, while not denying that the halachic expression is indeed in principle a closed system, see this as but the accommodation of Rabbinic Judaism to diaspora existence, i.e., to existence outside the flux of history. As such, however, this aspect becomes merely a contingent and external but not an essential aspect of the halachic expression. In its essence, in terms of its very *Weltanschauung,* of what it has to say, the halachic expression remains in our view very much an expression of the Thou-dimension though, admittedly, an expression which, because of the impact of certain aspects of diaspora-existence (the existence to which it is subjected), is compromised by the It-dimension. Thus, we can appropriate Buber's basic dialogical orientation and yet differ from him in the perception and evaluation of the halachic expression.

[5]The concern with the divine as it relates to the world at large, specifically to the physical world, which may also be present here, takes place, however, only because and to the extent that it impinges on the fortunes of man. Of course, the concern with the relation of the divine to the world may also characterize the philosophic approach (thus allowing both approaches to share this concern). But in contrast to the religious approach, the philosophic approach may become involved in this concern only because and to the extent that the notion of the divine implicates its involvement in the world. Thus, the distinction between the philosophic approach being concerned with God in-Himself and the religious approach being concerned with God for-man remains also here. Indeed, this is the fundamental distinction between the philosophic and the religious approach to the divine – the former is theoretical and motivated by curiosity while the latter is pragmatic and motivated by existential concerns such as the desire, or more accurately, the need to improve the lot of man.

[6]By the way, one can either start with the section pertaining to the divine to be followed by the section pertaining to man, or conversely, one can start with the section pertaining to man which would lead to the section pertaining to the divine. Whether one chooses the former or the latter form of presentation may depend on any number of different considerations such as, for example, whether the systematic or the phenomenological, the didactic or the analytical manner of approach is to be emphasized. Evidently, we have opted here for a form of presentation which would emphasize the systematic-didactic approach. As such, it makes sense to start with the *locus de Deo* seeing that the divine signifies ultimacy and absoluteness.

[7]As Franz Rosenzweig (borrowing the idea, it would seem, from Rosenstock-Heussy) has so nicely shown, the Star of David which has come to symbolize Judaism is but the putting together of two triangles – the imposition of one triangle over another.

[8]When we say that the horizontal domain is "usually" relegated to the secular realm we evidently have in mind all those structures-of-faith which constitute themselves on the basis of a two-fold subdivision, i.e., the subdivision into the domain of the divine and the domain of man. For as such, these structures are constituted exclusively by the vertical axis which, in turn, means that the religious realm is defined exclusively in vertical terms thus relegating by definition the horizontal domain to the realm of the secular. Of course, these structures may further divide themselves into those where the vertical and the horizontal are to have nothing to do with each other and those where the vertical, while being clearly separated and distinguished from the horizontal, is nonetheless brought to bear in various ways upon the horizontal thus allowing after all the horizontal domain to be appendaged to their theological representation though only in this special rather extraneous sense, namely, in the sense where the horizontal is incorporated not as a domain constituting the religious but merely as a domain upon which some of the implications of the religious may impinge. For us, however, it is important to note that the structure-of-faith in Judaism is clearly different not only from the former alternative but also from the latter alternative. For in the case of the structure-of-faith of Judaism the horizontal is incorporated precisely as a domain which constitutes the religious.

[9]Thus, this means, for example, that the whole gamut of questions regarding divine attributes or God's existence are not really, in the last analysis, legitimate for Jewish theology; indeed, it means that much of natural theology should be excluded as far as Jewish theology is concerned.

Also, it should be clear that the relational aspect of the divine established here is quite different from that introduced above on the basis of the religious enterprise. For while here the relational aspect of the divine is derived from the fact that the divine is constituted as a Thou-being and a Thou-being is a being which can arise and subsist only in the context of a relation (specifically, only in the context of an I-Thou relation), in the case of the religious enterprise the relational aspect of the divine is derived from the fact that the religious enterprise, in contra-distinction to the philosophical enterprise, is not interested in the divine as it is in-itself but only as it impinges upon human life, only as it is for-man. But this means, of course, that while it is also the case that in the instance where the relational aspect is brought about by the religious enterprise the divine involved can be only a god in relation, the kind of god and the kind of relation involved are left, on the other hand, quite open. God need not be a Thou-god nor need the relation be an I-Thou relation; from the vantage point of the interest characterizing the religious enterprise the relation may just as well be an I-It relation and the god involved an It-god, i.e., an impersonal, unconscious being, a being constituted exclusively in terms of power. Indeed, a good case can be made that the god-in-relation with which most religions deal is an It-god and the relation involved is an I-It relation; that only in a very few instances, specifically, only in the instances comprised by biblical faiths, would one encounter a Thou-god who as such would, of course, relate to man only in an I-Thou relation.

By the way, this being the case, it means that the essay here, articulating the orientation of the structure-of-faith of Judaism, is not merely presenting us with yet another factor to account for the relational aspect of the divine (to wit, that the relational aspect of the divine is due not only to the interest of the religious enterprise in the god-for-man but also to the constitution of the divine as a Thou-being) but that it presents us with the factor which constitutes the most fundamental division possible in our field, the division underlying all other divisions including the one presented above between the god-in-itself and the god-for-us which separates the philosophic from the religious interest. Namely, we are suggesting that the most fundamental division facing us in our field is the division between the Thou-god and the It-god and that this division does not run between the religious and the philosophic domain relegating the former to the Thou-god (the god of Abraham, Isaac and Jacob) and the latter to the It-god (the god of the philosophers) but rather that it runs right through the religious domain itself placing on the one side, the side of the Thou-god, biblical faiths while on the other side, the side of the It-god, it places all other non-biblical religions and the philosophical domain. The real fundamental division is not between the religious and the philosophic domain but between biblical faiths on the one side and all other religions plus the philosophic domain on the other side. Indeed, we can now see that the other division suggested here, the division between the religious and the philosophic domain based on the distinction between the notion of god-in-itself and that of god-for-man, is secondary and rather partial in its application. For this distinction between the notion of god-in-itself and the notion of god-for-man can arise only with respect to a god constituted as an It-god – it is excluded by the very essence of the god constituted as a Thou-god. Thus, the division between the religious and the philosophic domain arises secondarily and only within the more fundamental domain of the It-god which, in turn, arises by its division from the domain of the Thou-god. To be more precise, therefore, we should realize that as regards all non-biblical religions when we speak of the division between religion and philosophy (on the basis of the distinction between god-in-itself and god-for-man) this division is grounded in a more fundamental commonality which they share with the philosophic enterprise, namely, the commonality derived from the fact that both they and the philosophic enterprise relate to a god constituted as an It-god. At the same time, when we lump together biblical faiths and non-biblical religions as sharing in the same religious orientation constituted by the exclusive interest in god-for-man, we should realize that the two, biblical faiths and non-biblical religions, differ radically as regards the constitution of the divine and consequently as regards the kind of relation which they establish between the divine and man – biblical faiths establishing a Thou-god and consequently a relation that is exclusively an I-Thou relation while non-biblical religions establish an It-god and consequently the only relation available to them is an I-It relation.

[10] Of course, as claimed above, an I-It relation cannot really apply to a god who is constituted exclusively as a Thou-being. Indeed, the very thrust of our essay on creation is to argue that the proper signification of the notion of creation in the context of the structure-of-faith of Judaism, which is to say its signification as it articulates itself in the formulation of *creatio ex nihilo*, is not to be construed in terms of bringing things into physical existence; in other words, we argue that the notion of creation should not be taken as if it intended to account for how the world came into existence. For in terms of this signification, the notion really belongs in the scientific and not in the religious enterprise – it transforms religion into a science or, more accurately, into a pseudo-science. Furthermore, in terms of this signification the relation which the notion introduces is inescapably an I-it relation, a relation which is totally unacceptable to the structure-of-faith of Judaism. Rather, we suggest that in the context of religion, specifically, in the context of the structure-of-faith of Judaism, the proper signification must be in terms of value and meaningfulness which means that the notion is to be understood as coming to constitute value and meaningfulness with respect to the various entities constituting the world, and thus to delineate the way one is to relate to them, more specifically, delineate the way in which responsibility towards them may be established. In this context, of course, the notion establishes a relation that is an I-thou relation and clearly this is the relation acceptable to the structure-of-faith of Judaism.

[11] Clearly we are using the notion of providence in its more limited signification. Namely, the signification here excludes its impingement upon nature (i.e., it excludes the relation implicated by the notion of providence from connecting the divine with nature) confining it exclusively to man. And even with respect to man (as is manifested only too clearly in our essay on providence) there is a further limitation inasmuch as its impingement is directed to the collectivity, i.e., to the national community, rather than to the individual person. Thus, the notion of providence as it is used here signifies essentially a relation between the divine and national communities which, in turn, means that it signifies essentially the impingement of the divine upon history seeing that history is but the life-story of national communities.

This two-fold limitation, however, is not completely capricious or arbitrary. A good case can be made for it. For surely, the distinctive signification of the notion does not lie in the impingement of the divine upon nature but in its impingement upon man (indeed, in terms of the impingement of the divine upon nature, the notion of providence would seem to coalesce, in the last analysis, with the notion of creation, certainly with the notion of continuous creation); and while the notion in terms of the impingement of the divine upon the individual person certainly found expression within mainstream Judaism, and not just on the popular level but also on the literary-philosophical level (see, for example, the book of Job), surely the burden of the tradition deals with the notion mainly in terms of the impingement of the divine upon the national community, i.e., upon the nation of Israel (see, for example, classical prophecy). By the way, we would suggest that the clear emphasis on formulating the notion in terms of the impingement of the divine on the national community rather than on the individual is brought about by the fundamental ethical orientation which characterizes Judaism seeing that it is the ethical which requires the collectivity – a point which we had occasion to discuss above. In any case, there is no denying that the central and distinctive formulation of the notion of providence in mainstream Judaism is in terms of the national collectivity and consequently our use of the notion in this specific signification is very much in accord with the basic orientation of Judaism.

[12]Indeed, the very point of our essay on providence is 1) to show that the traditional formulation of the notion in terms of divine rule, divine governance, i.e., in terms of the divine being in charge of things and running, so to speak, the show, inevitably establishes the relation implicated by the notion of providence as an I-It relation which as such should make it, in the last analysis, invalid in the context of Judaism and 2) to formulate the notion in such a way that it would indeed implicate a relation that is an I-Thou relation. Thus, the thrust of this essay parallels that of the essay on creation. Namely, in both the thrust is to argue against that formulation of the notions which constitutes them in terms of the I-It relation and provide an alternative formulation which would constitute them in terms of the I-Thou relation.

[13]Of course, the objection may be raised that our presentation contains a glaring omission in that it does not address itself to the relation implicated by the notion of revelation. In brief, our answer is that since in the structure-of-faith of Judaism the relation implicated by the notion of revelation is not directed essentially to the individual but to the national collectivity and since, because of the constraints placed upon it by the fact that it is constituted as an I-thou relation, it cannot transmit any content from the divine to man, the relation implicated by the notion of revelation does, in the last analysis, coalesce here with the relations implicated by the notions of creation and providence (of course, when these are constituted, as indeed we argued above they should be, as an I-thou and not as an I-It relation). As such we can say that the notion of revelation manifests itself in the notions of creation and providence or, put conversely, that the notions of creation and providence are but expressions of the notion of revelation – creation being the divine revealing itself through nature and providence being the divine revealing itself through history (and given the ethical orientation of the structure-of-faith of Judaism, it is to be expected that the coalescence of revelation with providence, i.e., the encounter of the divine in history, should play a far more authentic and incisive role in Jewish theology than the coalescence of revelation with creation, i.e., the encounter of the divine in nature). Furthermore, these observations would seem to indicate that the notion of revelation is of a different order than the other two notions. It is a generic notion which encompasses any and all relations from the divine to man but, precisely as such, does not articulate itself in the refraction of time as a specific expression on an equal footing with, though distinct from, the other expressions refracted in time. This can actually be seen in the common identification of creation with an orientation to the past and providence with an orientation to the future as against revelation which is orientated to the present. For the present to which revelation is oriented is not a moment or a collection of moments in the flux of time as the past or the future is, rather, it is a stepping out of the flux of time altogether into eternity. Thus, inasmuch as when speaking of the question of the extension of the divine-human relation one necessarily speaks in terms of the expressions of this relation in the flux of time, revelation cannot affect this question of extension since it itself is not such a refracted expression. The notion of revelation may well express the depth of the divine-human relation but it cannot affect in any way its extension.

[14]It may be worth noting, perhaps, that the delineation of the essential identity of the Jew offered in this essay – namely, a delineation in terms of an inextricable union between the ethnic and the religious, the Jew being inextricably both a member of an ethnic-national collectivity and a member of a community of faith (this delineation being established, by the way, on the basis that it corresponds to the objective reality of Jewish history, to the consensus of the world at large in how it views Jewry and to the halachic definition of who is a Jew, thus, to the traditional self-understanding of the Jewish community) – parallels very neatly the delineation of the essential identity of man as such offered in the preceding essay, namely, the delineation of man as belonging inextricably to both the It and the Thou

dimensions. Indeed, we can see very clearly how the delineation of the essential identity of the Jew as belonging inextricably to both the ethnic-national and the religious dimension is but a concretization, a specification, of the delineation of the essential identity of man as such as an It-Thou being. For the ethnic category, i.e., the ethnic-national collectivity, is universally constituted as but a concrete, specific expression of the It dimension (seeing that it constitutes itself in terms of power) while the religious category, i.e., the structure-of-faith, at least in the case of Judaism, is but a concrete, specific expression of the Thou dimension (seeing that it constitutes itself in Judaism in terms of the ethical dimension, thus, in terms of spirit, of consciousness). Thus, the Jew's belongingness to an ethnic-national collectivity is but an expression of his ontic capacity to participate in the It dimension while his belongingness to a community of faith is but an expression of his ontic capacity to participation in the Thou dimension.

[15]Indeed, the very intention of this essay is to show that the problematic is precipitated in no small measure precisely because of the kind of identity that the Jew possesses viz., the identity delineated in the preceding essay. Thus, the essay tries to delineate and analyze the seriousness of the problematic for both Jewry and Judaism that the Emancipation precipitates when it arises in the context of diaspora-existence and to further show that given the kind of identity the Jew possesses and the kind of new circumstances which the Emancipation introduces, the prognosis for Jewish survival in the context of diaspora-existence is not too bright.

[16]As we have already seen, unlike the Thou-dimension, there is nothing in the signification of the It-dimension that would posit the relation as the primary ontological reality from which the particular entities arise, thus necessarily implicating their being in-relation. The relation which arises in the It-dimension is secondary and, indeed, external to the particular entities. As such, the entities may enter relations but they do not necessarily have to be in relation. Furthermore, as a result of this the kind of relation involved in the It-dimension would, of course, be quite different from the kind of relation involved in the Thou-dimension. But this is a different matter and does not concern us here.

[17]By the way, at first glance this would not at all appear to be the case. If anything, it would appear that, whatever the case may be with most other religions, in the case of Judaism the turn to the issue of death is a clear bust, a turn that quickly leads to a dead-end yielding no significant observations. For as many people would be quick to point out, and as our essay readily admits, the issue of death does not occupy a central and all-absorbing place in the mind of Judaism and quite evidently does not constitute for it the ultimate predicament. As such, therefore, a turning to the issue of death in the context of Judaism should have proven to be a futile and unjustified move. But this is not really so. Our examination of the issue of death yields some very significant insights into the structure-of-faith of Judaism even though death does not constitute for Judaism the ultimate predicament. It is only that these insights are gained indirectly through inference, through a *via negativa,* rather than through a direct, positive exposition. Indeed, the very thrust of our essay here is to depict the basis on which the inferences can be made and then to show how some of the more far-reaching inferences are actually drawn from this basis.

Thus, the essay establishes the equation between death and the finitude of being and on the basis of this equation it draws its inferences. Namely, it argues that death signifies in the most striking manner the finitude of being seeing that it is the most radical manifestation of such finitude of being; consequently, when death is taken up as the ultimate predicament, this can be translated into saying that finitude of being is the ultimate predicament. It then further argues that with this equation at hand two important inferences can be drawn from the observation that death does not constitute the ultimate predicament for Judaism. For on the basis of this equation this can be translated to say that finitude of being does not constitute the ultimate predicament for Judaism and this, in turn, would yield the double inference that for Judaism the ultimate predicament formulates itself neither in the ontological domain nor in the more comprehensive It-dimension (seeing that in the ontological domain, and even more decisively and comprehensively, in the It-dimension the ultimate predicament would have to constitute itself, according to the dictates of the inner logic operating here, in terms of the finitude of being). Of course, this means that in place of the rejected It-dimension, the ultimate predicament must formulate itself for Judaism in the Thou-dimension (there being no other alternative dimension). And in place of the rejected ontological domain, since here a number of possible replacements are theoretically available, the essay resorts to inferring its answer from the way Judaism "officially" formulates its response to the event of death; namely, it resorts to inferring its answer from the fact that "officially" Judaism responds to the event of death in terms of resurrection and not in terms of immortality, and even more specifically, that the resurrection for Judaism is explicitly for the purpose of facing the Last Day of Judgment and not for the purpose of prolonging life. In this way the essay arrives at the conclusion that for Judaism it is the ethical domain which provides the matrix in which the ultimate predicament formulates itself. Thus, this essay does indeed contain very significant and far-reaching implications for our outline seeing that it provides us with two fundamental insights, to wit, first that for Judaism the ultimate predicament and, therefore, the structure-of-faith as a whole formulate themselves in terms of the Thou-dimension and secondly, that within this context, they formulate themselves, even more specifically, in terms of the ethical domain.

[18]Indeed, this move from the vertical to the horizontal orientation is already intimated in our essay on worship. For the act of prayer which in its own terms clearly constitutes itself exclusively in the direct vertical relation to the divine, it being a relation of direct address to the divine, assumes in Judaism a number of characterizations that seem to transform it into an act in the horizontal domain. Thus, as the essay attempts to show, the impact of the ethical perspective on the category of worship as it expresses itself in the context of Judaism manifests itself not only in extending the category horizontally to encompass the social relations between man and fellow-man, but in introducing into the very vertical expression of the category, i.e., into its expression in prayer, elements from the horizontal domain. By the way, in view of this we can say that the essay on worship serves not only as a fitting conclusion to the second section (seeing that it deals with man as he is in-relation to the divine) but it also serves as a very suitable transition to the third section (seeing that it intimates the move from the vertical to the horizontal). Evidently, the situation here parallels the situation that was obtained with respect to the essay on providence where the essay served both as a conclusion to the first section and as a transition to the second section.

[19]It may be worthwhile pointing out that this consideration of contemporary relevancy comes to the fore only in this section and not in any of the other sections. The only exception is the essay "The Dilemma of Identity for the Emancipated Jew." But then, as noted above, this essay was clearly an intrusion from the outside.

[20]That a structure-of-faith may be concerned with such categories as land, nationhood and sovereignty or, to put the matter differently, that these categories can constitute a proper subject matter for theological reflection and clarification, may appear strange to many readers in the West where under the influence of some trends within Christianity religion is perceived as relegated exclusively to the perpendicular dimension and where therefore theology can have no interest or, at most, only a secondary interest in categories belonging to the horizontal dimension. To clarify and, hopefully, remove, such perplexity and discomfiture we must refer the reader to our discourse above where we attempted to show that with respect to this point Judaism presents a quite different kind of a structure-of-faith – indeed, it presents a structure-of-faith where the horizontal dimension is very much incorporated into the religious enterprise and where, therefore, categories like sovereignty, nationhood and land, i.e., categories belonging to the horizontal dimension, are very proper subjects for the reflection of theology.

[21]Although this essay addresses itself quite clearly to a different issue from the one to which the preceding essay addressed itself, the two essays are at one in making the following point: in terms of its structure-of-faith, mainstream Judaism's link to the nation is essential, primary and inextricable while its link to the land is only secondary, derived from its need for sovereignty, a need which itself is required only for the optimal expression of Judaism but not for its very existence as its long survival in diaspora clearly shows (although, as we have tried to indicate in the essay "The Dilemma of Identity for the Emancipated Jew," the need does become essential for its very survival when Judaism finds itself in the context of the Emancipation). This point may not sit well with much of current Jewish sentiment. Certainly, it goes against some recent trends in Jewish apologetics which invest the very land

of Israel with special, extra sanctity (and then certain places within the land with even more sanctity) and consequently see the link to the land as being as primary and essential, if, indeed, not more so, as the link to the nation. Such apologetic may be understandable given the circumstances of our time but it is not supported by the inner-logic operating in the structure-of-faith of distinctive, mainstream Judaism, i.e., in the structure-of-faith of what we referred to as the "prophetic-halachic" strand. Indeed, it seems clear that this apologetic derives its ammunition, so to speak, from the structure-of-faith of a rival strand, i.e., from the structure-of-faith of what we referred to as the "priestly-mystical" strand.

[22]Our analysis of what the structure-of-faith of Judaism implies with respect to this issue (and this in clear contradistinction to what individual Jews, particularly in the United States where this issue is a particularly sensitive issue, may wish the case to be) may be rather provocative and unsettling; in many respects it certainly goes against the well-established and long-held position of the preponderant majority of emancipated Jewry, certainly of American Jewry. But perhaps precisely as such, this essay may render some good by inviting us to take another look at this all-important issue.

[23]Indeed, it is understandable that in the context where the divine is implicated in the world, as in the case of providence, the challenge of theodicy should express itself in terms of how to exonerate the divine in the face of the evil occurring in the world; on the other hand, in a context where the ethical, being all-pervasive and all-encompassing, intrudes into the very realm of the divine, it is understandable that the challenge of theodicy should express itself in terms of how to safeguard the ultimacy and sovereignty of the divine in the face of the challenge coming from the ethical side.

[24]Thus, essentially the essay suggests that the structure-of-faith of Judaism implicates a position in this matter which comes down on the side of Kierkegaard in his concern to safeguard God's absolute freedom and thus His ultimacy and sovereignty. Indeed, only in this way can Judaism avert the danger of losing its authentic character as a religion and being reduced to a mere ethical system. Yet, unlike Kierkegaard, it is not prepared to pay the price of suspending the ethical (more accurately, given its nature it cannot pay this price). For it is essential to the structure-of-faith of Judaism that the ethical be kept, namely, Judaism cannot accept that at any time or under any circumstance God would not act ethically. Thus, the essay further suggests that Judaism offers an alternative solution to the problematic involved here according to which God is, indeed, absolutely free to do whatever He wishes including the unethical yet Judaism lives in the *trust* that God will never act unethically. This is the abiding fundamental faith in which Judaism lives. In this way Judaism succeeds in preserving the ultimacy and sovereignty of God without compromising the pervasiveness and efficacy of the ethical dimension.

Part One

THE THEOLOGICAL POLE

Chapter One

Some Reflections on the Concept of God

Our subject matter is clearly in the domain of theology; that is to say, in the rational interpretive superstructure that a religious tradition provides for its faith. As such, it should not really be all that surprising to ascertain that as a matter of historical fact more than one concept of God found articulation within the theology of the tradition. For no concrete historical religious tradition is monolithic in its intellectual understanding of its faith. An historical religious tradition is bound by common memories, symbols, celebrations, rituals and texts, but it almost invariably presents a spectrum of views when it comes to interpreting their meaning and signification. This is true particularly of Judaism, where the thrust of the structure of faith is towards the deed rather than the intellectual confession, towards *Halacha* rather than dogma, and where consequently the striving for uniformity is directed towards *halachic* practice while a fairly wide leeway is tolerated as regards the philosophic-theological interpretation of the faith. Still, we would want to argue that amidst the variety of views which arose in the course of time in different quarters there is a view that is normative, particularly as regards the concept of God, seeing that this concept is so fundamental in the structure of the tradition of faith. (We use the notion of normative here not only in the sense of being a view that is distinctive, widely and consistently held but also in the sense that where different views are held, such views are mitigated as much as possible to meet the requirements of this view.)

Most scholars would most probably agree that such a normative view of God in the religious tradition of Judaism would assert the following: (a) that God is one – one in the sense that there is only one divine being (arithmetical oneness), or in the sense that God in constituted as an uncompounded and simple substance or, in the more general sense, that God's being is in some qualitative sense unique (either in the aforementioned sense or in some other sense); (b) that God is transcendent to man and the world, thus making it, in principle, impossible for either apotheosis or incarnation to ever take place: in short, that the view of God is thoroughly theistic; (c) that God by his very essence is ethical; and (d) that the relation of man to God is a relation of prayer, of address, and not of use and manipulation. We would submit, however, that by far the most fundamental assertion, the assertion constituting the very essence of the normative view, and indeed, the assertion from which all the previous assertions follow, is the assertion that God *qua* ultimate being is a person – a living being endowed with awareness and the spontaneity of free will. The ultimate is encountered by man as consciousness, concern, and not as an impersonal power moving blindly by inexorable necessity; in other words God is encountered as a Thou and not as an It.

The Essence of the Normative View: God as a Thou

With the exception of the "arithmetical oneness" characterization which follows from the consideration that God is encountered here as the ultimate being rather than from the consideration that He is constituted as a Thou (ultimacy necessarily implicates arithmetical oneness and as such, indeed, an It-God when viewed as ultimate would equally be arithmetically one), all the above characterizations – and the many other, albeit less fundamental, characterizations of the normative view not mentioned here – would, as said, follow necessarily from the inner logic of the consideration that God is constituted as a Thou and would receive their rationale from this consideration.

Thus, to briefly delineate what we have in mind, the characterization of the being of God as uncompounded and simple (that is, undifferentiated and indivisible) is necessitated by his Thouness. For division and multiplicity are feasible only with respect to matter, to corporeality, to a being extended in the space-time continuum. But these are all inescapable determinants of the manifestation of power and therefore of an It-being. A Thou-God on the other hand, being the expression of consciousness and not of power, is by its very constitution not subject to these determinants and consequently compoundness and differentiation are in principle inapplicable to it.

Similarly, a Thou-God is necessarily unique inasmuch as every Thou is by its very constitution necessarily unique. Each person *qua* person is unique – non-duplicable and irreplaceable. Uniqueness here is not merely quantitative and contingent; it is qualitative and essential. Each Thou-being, in contradistinction to an It-being, is constituted as a unique being. As such, uniqueness is applicable not only to God but to any being that is a Thou and is grounded in the very constitution of the being as a Thou. This is not the case in the It-realm. An It-being is not constituted as unique and consequently when uniqueness is applied to an It-God, its status and rationale are quite different. It cannot be grounded in its very constitution as an It but only in such distinctions which are ultimately reducible to the infinite-finite distinction – a distinction which, in the last analysis, is merely quantitative. As such, uniqueness here can only be a uniqueness of quantity or configuration but not, as is the case with the Thou-being, one of essence.

These distinctions are further clarified and buttressed by the additional all-important characterization of the Thou-God as necessarily theistic in contradistinction to the It-God which necessarily gravitates towards being pantheistic. A Thou-God is necessarily theistic because he is a being of consciousness, and consciousness by its very essence is always and necessarily structured as a consciousness of something, thus necessarily implicating on the one hand a something, an other, and, on the other hand, a "gap," an over-againstness, between itself and this other. A Thou-God, therefore, by virtue of his being a being-of-consciousness, necessarily implicates an other over against himself and consequently is necessarily a theistic, transcending God. Pantheism cannot provide the relational matrix for a Thou-God. For pantheism is based on the oneness of a continuum whereas consciousness is based on the duality of an over-againstness. Consciousness cannot be constituted within a continuum, and consequently a Thou-God cannot be, in principle, embedded with a continuum: which is to say, that in principle a Thou-God cannot be pantheistic. A Thou-God linked to pantheism is possible only at the price of inconsistency. No wonder that normative Judaism has consistently and strenuously rejected pantheism. The situation is reversed, however, regarding the It-God, the ultimate being-of-power. The inner logic of the It domain necessarily pulls the It-God towards pantheism. For power in manifesting itself constitutes itself as a continuum, and consequently the ensuing oneness is integral to a being-of-power. In such a context where a continuum and quantitative gradation inextricably characterize the being-of-power, the It-God *qua* ultimate must manifest maximal power which, in turn, requires that the totality of manifested power be included in it: that is, that it be a pantheistic God.

The case for the remaining two characterizations can be made briefly. Ethical considerations can be applied only to a Thou-God. For only a being endowed with awareness and free will can carry responsibility and therefore be subject to ethical demands and judgment. As against this, it simply does not make sense to raise the ethical in regard to an It-God, a being devoid of awareness and acting blindly with inexorable necessity. Only in regard to a Thou-God can one ask: "Is the judge of all the earth not to do justice?" or raise the Jobian challenge; it is senseless to do so with regard to blind power. Similarly, addressing the other in the second person is feasible only with regard to a being endowed with awareness: that is, a Thou-God; to address a being devoid of awareness, an It-God, is simply senseless. One can relate to an It-God only in the third person – describing, manipulating, predicting (thus introducing respectively, in the context of the religious discourse, the categories of natural theology, magic and divination), relations which are excluded by the very essence of the ontological constitution of a Thou.

Does a Thou View Imply a Utilitaristic Individualism?

Clearly, in the whole question of formulating the concept of God, the fundamental parting of the way – the basic alternative – is whether God is viewed as Thou or as It. All other issues are ultimately clarified by reference to one or the other of these basic characterizations and the inner logic they respectively imply. Let us briefly illustrate this by referring to the following intriguing question: "Does a personalist-theistic view, in contradistinction to an impersonalist-pantheistic view, imply a utilitaristic individualism?"

What are we to say to this? First, our analysis above should clearly justify the linking of the personalist view, i.e., the Thou-God, with theism and the impersonalist view, i.e., the It-God, with pantheism. Thus the formulation of the question is legitimate and consequently in order to secure the proper answer to it we must first and foremost follow the implications of the Thou-God and the It-God respectively. Here, we must grant that a Thou-God does indeed imply individualism. A Thou-God requires that the man who is placed in relation to him, i.e., that the man who authentically expresses his being, be also a Thou; and as a Thou, such a man necessarily preserves his particularity, uniqueness and irreplaceability over-against his fellow-man, nature and God. Thus, the necessarily implied theism would imply, in turn, individualism. By the same score, on the other hand, the It-God in its implication of pantheism would indeed abrogate the possibility of individualism. Ultimately, all individuation is illusory – all individuals are in essence one and the same. Thus, ontologically speaking, while the theistic Thou-God would necessitate individualism, the pantheistic It-God would exclude it.

It is a different matter, however, when we come to consider the utilitaristic aspect of the contention, namely, that aspect which contends that the Thou-God in precipitating individuation would precipitate also a utilitaristic relationship between the individuals involved (the argument consisting essentially in making the point that in being distinct and unique the individuals involved would be self-centered and consequently utilitaristic in relating to the other). For this aspect of the contention is clearly untenable. After all, the Thou-individual by his very constitution can arise only in relation (specifically, only in relation to another Thou), and consequently the Thou-individual is always and necessarily in relation; he cannot be self-enclosed, in isolation, "monadic." The Thou must be embedded in a relation. But moreover, and most tellingly, not every relation would do. The Thou can arise only in a relation of address – of calling forth, of confirming, the other as a Thou. And this means that the Thou can arise only in a relation of giving, of self-impartation (either in the form of self-presentation or in the form of challenge) and such a relation clearly cannot be self-centered, egotistical; in its very essence it is other-centered. Even more to the point, inasmuch as the calling forth, the confirming, is of the other in his otherness, this means that the Thou can arise only in relating to the other as an end-in-itself, as a subject; by its very constitution it cannot relate to the other as a means, as an object. But this clearly implies that a Thou cannot subsist in a utilitaristic relation, seeing that the very essence of a utilitaristic relation consists of relating to the other as a means.

The Thou cannot be constituted as a being-in-itself or as a being-for-itself. By its very essence it is constituted as a being-towards-another and for-another and as such its relation can be neither self-centered nor utilitaristic. The theistic

Thou-God view does indeed precipitate individuation, but it is an individuation that necessarily implies communion – caring and responsibility for the other in his otherness.

Strange as it may seem, it is the pantheistic It-God view which, although abrogating ontological individualism, can nonetheless give rise to a self-centered and utilitaristic relating. Briefly stated, the rationale for this is as follows: as we have seen, on the most fundamental level, individuation in this view is ultimately only apparent. Ultimately, there is only one all-encompassing being. As such, therefore, there can be, strictly speaking, no other-centered relation here. For the all-encompassing has no other over against it; and the apparent individuals are all but constituents of one and the same being and, therefore, no genuine otherness exists here either – all action of the apparent individual, both on behalf of self and on behalf of the other, is ultimately one and the same; to wit, action on behalf of the one, all-encompassing being. But this rationale establishes only that there can be no other-centered action here. It does not establish that a utilitaristic relating is possible, and indeed takes place here. Indeed, if anything, the rationale would lead to the opposite conclusion. For inasmuch as there is no genuine, real other available here, the entity that could serve as an object or as a means (which is necessary in order to constitute the utilitaristic equation) would be missing here; namely, without a genuine other that could thus be constituted as an object, as a means, to serve the designs or the needs of another, a utilitaristic relating cannot arise.

But if a rationale for a utilitaristic relating could not be gotten as long as we viewed things on the most fundamental level, such a rationale would readily present itself if we but move to a secondary, more relativistic, level, i.e., to the level of the apparent individual. Namely, if we but shift our view of things from the vantage-point of the underlying, all-encompassing, unitary substance to the vantage-point of the various particular apparent individual entities that are abstracted from the underlying unitary substance, a rationale not only for self-centered action but equally for a utilitaristic relating readily presents itself. For in this context the necessary other is made available in the multiplicity of the apparent individual entities and from the viewpoint of the apparent individual, its relation to such other apparent individuals would clearly tend to be self-centered and utilitaristic. This is so inasmuch as the all-encompassing being of which the apparent individual is but a manifestation is an It-being, a being-of-power, and consequently the apparent individual would manifest the characterizations of a being-of-power, the essential characterization being self-aggrandizement towards the concentration of maximal power. A being-of-power is "imperialistic;" striving to increase the manifestation of power in itself to the maximum level (hence the tendency to pantheism). It is thus constituted as a being-for-itself, and consequently its relation to all other entities is self-centered and utilitaristic; that is, using the other as a means to increase its manifestation of power. Thus, on this level, the pantheistic It-God view would give rise not only to self-centered action but also to a utilitaristic relating.

We have contended that the view of God as a theistic Thou-God is normative and deeply embedded in Judaism. The overwhelming witness of the Bible (excepting possible Wisdom literature) and of rabbinic literature clearly testifies to this. But, as we have also noted above, no historical religious tradition is monolithic. Not surprisingly, we encounter variations and differences in the further elaboration of this basic view. What is somewhat more surprising, however, is the fact that we also encounter views which implicate a pantheistic It-God.

Thus, most of the philosophic formulations within Judaism (e.g., Aristotelianism and neo-Platonism in the Middle Ages or idealism and naturalism in modern times) implicate an It-God. This is actually readily understandable. For, inasmuch as man is the starting point and reason is the ultimate criterion of the philosophic enterprise, such an enterprise would only naturally lead to an It-God. Furthermore, the philosophic enterprise, by its very essence, consists of description, demonstration or evaluation, and as such its object (in this instance God) is necessarily an It-being. But although the God of Jewish philosophy is, in the last analysis, definitely an It-God, the interesting aspect of this enterprise lies in the attempts made to ascribe characterizations of the Thou-God to him and in the glossing over of the various problematic implications which an It-God inescapably introduces. Thus, for example, see the sustained efforts by medieval Jewish Aristotelianism to ascribe providence to a God viewed as First Cause; the strong emphasis by nineteenth-century Jewish idealism on the ethical and free-will aspects of the divine viewed as Spirit (and although the divine is viewed here as Spirit it is nevertheless, in the last analysis, an It-God, as indeed is the case with the view of God as First Cause); the efforts of Jewish neo-Platonism to gloss over and conceal the necessary pantheistic implications of its philosophy for Kant and the later Schelling (where a theistic dimension is present) over undiluted Hegelianism (where an uncompromised pantheism is expressed). Clearly, even in formulations where the view of God is unmistakably that of an It-God, the impact of the normative view of a Thou-god is strongly felt.

But an even more striking and intriguing instance of this phenomenon is encountered in the mystical enterprise which, by the way, pervades Judaism much more extensively and significantly than the philosophic enterprise. Of course, the mystical expression within Judaism is but an instance of the universal expression of the phenomenon of mysticism and as such it partakes of the essential structure which characterizes the mystical phenomenon in its universal manifestation. Now, the essential thrust of this structure, we would submit, is a striving for oneness. Namely, mysticism perceives the ultimate predicament to lie in separation, division (thus in alienation), and correspondingly the salvation it yearns for lies in the complete overcoming of all separation and distinction represented so poignantly in its notion of the *unio mystica*. Clearly, the inner logic of such a structure would necessarily implicate the pantheistic formulation and the notion of an It-God. But again, it is interesting to note how Jewish mysticism strives to accommodate itself to the normative view by mitigating the pantheism and the It-God which are implied in its structure. Not only does it often resort to using language that obscures and hides the implicated It-God and the pantheistic view, but it actually alters the very substance of the mystical structure, so as to mitigate some of the implications which the normative view is bound to consider problematic.

A striking instance of this last observation can be seen in the introduction by Jewish mysticism of the notion of *D'vekut* (i.e., a notion signifying, so to speak, the gluing of the mystic to the divine) as the ultimate goal for the mystic's strivings, thus replacing the notion of *unio mystica* (i.e., a notion signifying the complete absorption, the complete disappearance of the mystic within the divine) which most mystical expressions take as their ultimate goal. Thus, *D'vekut,* as the consummation of mystical strivings, brings the Jewish mystic as close and near to the divine as possible short of allowing his disappearance within the divine. In this way the notion approaches as close as possible the notion of *unio mystica* but with the all important difference that it safeguards a distinction, no matter how minimal, between the mystic and the divine. As such, the pantheistic oneness necessarily implicated by the notion of *unio mystica* is clearly mitigated by the notion of *D'vekut* towards a theistic dualism.

Another instance of the above observation can be seen in the way Jewish mysticism deals with the concept of the divine. For while there is no escaping the fact that for Jewish mysticism the divine *qua* ultimate being (what it refers to as the *Ein-Sof,* i.e., the infinite) is constituted as an It-being, seeing that it is perceived as the maximal, uncompromised expression of a being in-itself and for-itself (these being characteristics which are simply inapplicable to a Thou-being but are the characteristics *par excellence* of an It-being), it is most significant to note that, by and large, Jewish mysticism does not direct its active concern (intellectual or spiritual) to this aspect of the divine, i.e., to the divine as the *Ein-Sof.* Rather, it directs its main concern to that aspect of the divine which is constituted by the *sefirot,* i.e., the realm of divine emanations. As such, its concern is centered not on the notion of the divine as it is in itself but on the notion of the divine as it relates itself to the world. And here, in the realm of the *sefirot,* it obviously can (and actually does) introduce any number of the characteristics of the Thou-God. Thus, although for Jewish mysticism the divine as it is in itself is an It-God, an impersonal being, the divine with which it mainly deals has many of the characteristics of a Thou-God, of a personal being.

But Jewish mysticism (in some of its expressions) goes even further in attempting to mitigate the presence of its It-God in the direction of the Thou-

God. For it not only shifts its interest from one aspect of the divine to another, from the divine as it is in-itself, the It-God, to the divine as it impinges on the world, the apparent Thou-God; it actually attempts to introduce characteristics of the Thou-God into the divine as it is in-itself, namely, it attempts to introduce elements of the Thou-God into its It-God. Thus, in some formulations, the *sefirot* are placed ontologically within the *Ein-Sof* while in some other formulations the act of *Zimzum* (the act of divine contraction making room for its emanations) is seen not as a mechanical, blind act but as a free, volitional act on the part of the *Ein-Sof* (indeed, some refer to the *Ein-Sof* as *Baal Ha-Razon,* the possessor of will).

Evidently, we have in the above instances a most intriguing attempt to combine an It-God with a Thou-God in one and the same being (or, to put it more precisely, to introduce elements of the Thou-God into a divinity that is an It-God). Whether such an attempt is legitimate or, indeed, feasible is a different matter which we cannot enter into here. What is, however, of great significance and bears, therefore, repeated stress is the observation that whatever else these instances may or may not establish they clearly indicate the great pull that the concept of the Thou-God exercises within Judaism and thus establish that the concept of the Thou-God is the normative concept of God in Judaism. That God is a Thou-God, a personal conscious being, is the most fundamental, most essential, normative statement about God in Judaism. From this, all else follows.

Chapter Two

Man and Creation According to the Religious Tradition of Judaism

In the religious discourse, certainly in the religious discourse of biblical faiths, the term "creation" stands for the notion of the world or, even more specifically, for the notion of nature – creation is nature. This being the case, the title of this paper actually suggests that we are to deal with man and nature, or to put it even more explicitly, it proposes that we examine the relation of man to nature in the context of the religious tradition of Judaism. The issue before us here, then, is to ascertain what kind of relation between man and nature is feasible in terms of the structure-of-faith of Judaism.[1]

Before entering, however, into our discussion of this issue it may be significant to observe that the relation of man to nature does not stand at the very core of the religious structure of Judaism. This is so because nature does not occupy a central place in the religious drama of Judaism. The religious drama of Judaism does not take place between man and nature; it takes place between man and his fellow-man. In other words, the predicament and, commensurate to this, the salvation are anchored in the social dimension and not in nature, and correspondingly, therefore, God is encountered primarily not in nature but in history (seeing that it is history and not nature which is constituted by the social, political and economic relations between man and his fellow-man). Thus, it is history and not nature which constitutes the matrix in which the religious drama unfolds. In brief, Judaism is not a "nature religion." Still, inasmuch as the religious drama of Judaism is by its very essence this-worldly, nature of necessity enters the picture. It is the inescapable stage (though not the matrix!) on which the religious drama – played between man and his fellow-man, between man and God, in the matrix of history – takes place. The this-worldly aspect of Judaism necessitates the presence of nature. But nature is present (and this is all that the this-worldly aspect of Judaism would require) only as background, as the passive agent bearing and suffering the action of man and God.[2] Nonetheless, inasmuch as nature is present, even though its role is passive and contingent on man's action, the issue of man's relation to nature does arise and demands a response from the religious tradition of Judaism.

In trying to determine and explicate the stance that Judaism takes with regard to the issue of man's relation to nature, the primary and all-important question is: What kind of being is attributed to nature? This question bears heavily on the issue before us inasmuch as the answer to it will fundamentally determine the kind of relation that is feasible vis-à-vis nature and, indeed, will provide the "key" to the inner logic that operates and determines the stance that Judaism takes as regards man's relation to nature. We would suggest that in answering this question we are in essence confronted with the alternative of two (and only two) qualitatively different kinds of being. We are confronted with the alternative between a personal being, a being endowed with awareness, a being that is the expression of Consciousness, i.e., a being-of-Consciousness, on the one hand, and an impersonal being, a being devoid of awareness, a being that is the expression of blind Power, i.e., a being-of-Power, on the other hand. Using Buberian terminology as a shorthand, we would say that we are confronted with the unbridgeable alternative between an It-being and a Thou-being.

I-Thou vs. I-It

Now this ontological bifurcation clearly implicates, in turn, the relational, behavioral bifurcation described by Buber in terms of the I-It and the I-Thou relations. For evidently vis-à-vis an impersonal being-of-Power the only relation feasible is a relation of utilization and manipulation; one can relate to a being-of-Power only as an object (an object as an ontological, not a grammatical, category), only as a means to some further end. In short, the only relation that is feasible here is the I-It relation. This is so inasmuch as the relation here is of necessity a transaction in blind power and such a transaction inescapably implicates utilization and manipulation; such a transaction is inescapably caught in an unending network of causation. As against this, vis-à-vis a personal being-of-Consciousness the only relation feasible is a relation of address and affirmation; one can relate to a being-of-Consciousness only as a subject (here again, a subject as an ontological, not a grammatical category), only as an end in itself. Here, the only relation that is feasible is the I-Thou relation. This is so inasmuch as the relation here is a transaction in consciousness – an act of the confirmation of being and the bestowal of meaningfulness – and such a transaction implicates exclusively the mere presence of consciousness and its address to the others as an end in itself. Thus, a being constituted as an It-being of necessity implicates a relation towards itself that is qualitatively and radically different from the relation which a being constituted as a Thou would of necessity implicate towards itself. A Thou-being would of necessity implicate an I-Thou relation towards itself and correspondingly an It-being would of necessity implicate an I-It relation towards itself. For it simply would not make sense to relate to a being-of-Power in an I-Thou relation (it simply would not make sense to address a being devoid of consciousness), nor would it be feasible to relate to a being-of-Consciousness in an I-It relation without, in so doing, reducing the being-of-Consciousness to an It-being. Thus, the kind of being attributed to nature would determine the kind of relation that is feasible towards it.[3]

There is one further consideration that is implicated by this ontological bifurcation between an It-being and a Thou-being to which we must turn briefly as it is of special significance to our topic here. Namely, the ontological bifurcation between an It-being and a Thou-being not only determines the kind of relation that is feasible, it also determines whether accountability and responsibility can be exacted. We would want to contend that an It-being can neither exact accountability and responsibility for action directed towards itself nor can it be held accountable and responsible for the action it directs towards other beings. Accountability and responsibility make sense and are feasible only in the context of the relations, the actions between Thou-beings; they do not make sense and are not feasible in the context of the relations, the actions, between It-beings. For to exact responsibility for action directed towards oneself, i.e., to challenge an other with regards to its action towards oneself, requires that the recipient of the action be a being endowed with consciousness, i.e., a Thou-being. A being devoid of consciousness, i.e., an It-being, cannot question or challenge. Thus, for example, it simply would not make sense and, indeed, would not be feasible to suppose that a rock can challenge me for having hit it, saying in effect, "Why did you do this to me? You should not have done this." And to be a bearer of responsibility, i.e., to be answerable for one's actions, requires that the agent who is the subject of the action be free, i.e., capable of having acted differently. Such freedom to act differently is available, however, only to a being endowed with consciousness, i.e., a Thou-being. For only in the context of Consciousness is there spontaneity and choice; in the context of Power there is only causality and determinism. A being devoid of consciousness, an It-being, is therefore inextricably caught in a network of deterministic causality and cannot be held responsible for its actions. Thus, to use the example of the rock again, it would not make sense to hold responsible for its actions a rock that fell and killed an innocent child. It would not make sense to say to the rock, "This is despicable; you should not have done it." Only a being endowed with consciousness, i.e., a Thou-being, can challenge the action directed towards itself exacting accountability from its perpetrator; and likewise, only a being endowed with consciousness, i.e., a Thou-being, is a free agent (in the sense of having the capacity to have acted differently) and consequently responsible for its actions towards others. With regard to a being devoid of consciousness, i.e., an It-being (a being-of-Power), the notions of accountability and responsibility simply do not make sense.

Man and Nature: I-It

Now, in terms of this ontological bifurcation between the It-being and the Thou-being and the kind of relation they respectively implicate with regard to themselves, we can now proceed to answer the two basic questions posed above, namely, what kind of being does Judaism attribute to nature and, corresponding to this, what kind of relation does nature implicate with regard to itself. We would submit that the answer to the first question is quite definite and unambiguous – Judaism (though quite obviously not expressing itself in our terminology) views nature as being constituted as an It-being. For clearly nature is not viewed as a being endowed with consciousness; it is not seen as a personal being.[4] Very poignantly and in clear contradistinction to man, nature is not characterized as a bearer of the divine image. Indeed, not only is nature not a bearer of the divine image, i.e., constituted in itself as a Thou-being, it also does not serve as an abode for the divine, i.e., for a Thou-being. The divine does not dwell in nature; he may encounter man through the agency of nature here and there as, for example, in the burning bush, but he does not reside permanently in any part of nature. Here, indeed, lies the very reason for the observation above that Judaism is not a "nature religion." For the very essence of "nature religion" is that the divine does reside permanently in one or another part of nature; inasmuch as it is precisely this that is excluded in the structure of faith of Judaism, Judaism is not a "nature religion." Thus, in Judaism nature is desacralized from the very start inasmuch as it is never sacralized to begin with (sacralized, of course, in the sense of being constituted as a divine being or as a permanent abode for the divine being). But the divine being implicated in the discussion here is clearly divine by virtue of being a Thou-being and this, therefore, means that in Judaism nature from the very start is not constituted as a Thou-being or, to put the point in the affirmative, that from the very start and by its very essence nature in Judaism is constituted as an It-being.[5] Indeed, the description above of the role assigned to nature in the structure of faith of Judaism, namely, the passive role of serving as the stage and background to the religious drama (which drama is carried out in terms of the encounter between man and God), clearly corresponds to and reflects our contention that nature is viewed in Judaism as being constituted as an It-being.

But this, in turn, means that in this context man's relation to nature must be an I-It relation. For nature constituted as an It-being would of necessity implicate an I-It relation towards itself, namely, it would of necessity implicate towards itself a relation of utilization and manipulation, a relation in which nature cannot exact accountability and responsibility for the action directed towards itself. We would contend that this is indeed the case in Judaism. The relation of man towards nature is essentially seen as being at its core an I-It relation which thus allows the utilization and manipulation of nature. Indeed, this is clearly and explicitly expressed in Genesis 1:28-30 and in Genesis 9:2-3. Man is given dominion and rule over nature to utilize and manipulate it for his needs. True, it would not be legitimate to resolve such an issue on the basis of one or two references. No doubt, in such an old and rich tradition as Judaism, one could find references to support practically any conceivable view. Still, Genesis 1:28-30 and Genesis 9:2-3 are the only references where the relation is delineated with respect to the totality of nature rather than with respect to any particular class of entities within nature. Furthermore, they are placed in a conventional framework clearly indicating that they are meant to be taken as the basic normative delineation of man's relation to nature; indeed, in the rabbinic-halakhic tradition they were taken as the normative source providing the basic guidelines for the tradition's more detailed formulation of the relationship. Thus, these passages in Genesis can be taken as the *locus classicus* for the delineation of man's relation towards nature, and quite clearly the delineation encountered here is of an I-It relation.[6]

Creation "Ex Nihilo"

But this is not the whole story. While we would want to contend that nature is indeed constituted as an It-being and therefore the relation to it can only be an I-It relation (the possibility of an I-Thou relation being definitely excluded), this I-It relation, however, is significantly circumscribed in Judaism. This circumscription is introduced by the tenet of Creation, i.e., by the fact that nature is viewed as a created being. Namely, the circumscription is introduced not by impinging on the ontological constitution of nature but by impinging upon its status. Nature remains constituted as an It-being but its status is that of a created It-being. Here, in the last analysis, lies the true signification of the tenet of creation for Judaism. Indeed, this is clearly seen in the fact that the tenet of creation formulates itself in Judaism as *creatio ex nihilo* and that it is specifically as such that is assumes its importance and centrality in the structure of faith of Judaism. For Judaism creation signifies *creatio ex nihilo* and the signification of *creatio ex nihilo* clearly impinges on the question of the status of nature (inasmuch as its signification is to assert that the being of nature is not eternal and therefore not coeval with the divine or, to put it in the affirmative, that the being of nature is contingent and dependent).

It must be admitted, however, that it is not all that clear that the formulation of the tenet of creation as *creatio ex nihilo* finds explicit expression prior to the middle ages. Thus, for example, it is dubious whether a formulation of *creatio ex nihilo* is actually expressed in the Bible. Certainly, those passages describing God's battle with the primordial *tanin* or with some other primordial animals[7] do not bear a view of creation as *creatio ex nihilo*. These passages are clearly remnants, albeit truncated and impoverished by the monotheistic refraction, of the rich and imposing myths of creation found in ancient Sumer, Babylon, Assyria and Ugarit, and these myths by their very essence exclude *creatio ex nihilo*. Indeed, if anything, these passages, far from intimating a *creatio ex nihilo*, clearly exclude such a view. They clearly suggest the presence of a primordial being, e.g., the *tanin*, of whose body the world, i.e., nature, is created, and this is simply not compatible with *creatio ex nihilo*. Evidently, these passages would not support the claim of *creatio ex nihilo*.

Nor would those passages where the monotheistic refraction is carried out in a much more thorough manner support, in the last analysis, the claim of *creatio ex nihilo*. One has in mind those passages in which God is represented as placing the cornerstone of the world with the angels singing, or in which God is represented as measuring the water and the mountains and stretching the heavens above.[8] Here, the more thorough monotheistic refraction is clearly seen in the absence of a primordial, coeval divine being, thus leaving God as the sole actor in the act of creation. Evidently, these passages are more congenial to the monotheistic viewpoint as they eliminate any rival divine beings. But what about the view of creation as *creatio ex nihilo?* Here, it is not at all clear that these passages implicate a view of *creatio ex nihilo.* If anything, they seem to implicate the pre-existence of the water, the mountains and the heavens prior to God's creative acts, i.e., prior to his acts of measuring and stretching. Indeed, it would seem that the view of creation emerging from these passages is patterned after the model of the artisan creating, i.e., fashioning, his artifact, and such a view certainly excludes a *creatio ex nihilo.* In any event, these passages are really but fleeting references to creation and do not yield much substance that impinges on the question before us regarding the status of nature.

Creation Account in Genesis

The main source in biblical literature that impinges on the question before us regarding the status of nature is of course the creation narrative in the opening chapter of Genesis (Gen 1-2:7).[9] Any determination of whether or not the view of *creatio ex nihilo* is reflected in the Bible must devolve on this account. Now this narration too, in all probability, is a truncated remnant of the creation epic current in the ancient Near East. It is, however, in contradistinction particularly to the references of God's battle with the primordial animal mentioned above, much more thoroughly refracted by the monotheistic viewpoint. The monotheistic hallmark of the refraction of this narration lies in the fact that creation here is brought about through the sole agency of God's word. Thus, the creation story in the opening chapter of Genesis is not only the most substantial treatment of our subject in biblical literature, but it is also the treatment that is most thoroughly refracted by the monotheistic viewpoint.[10]

The burden of the narrative here, however, is on the "how" question, namely, the narration deals in the main with how the world, i.e., nature, in its various parts is constituted, and this unfortunately does not impinge on the issue that concerns us.[11] What concerns us is the "what" question, namely, what kind of being, what status is accorded to nature in the scheme of things. In its original setting, i.e., in its status as a full-fledged myth in the context of paganism, the "how" may indeed have been the main intention and thrust of the myth of creation. In the context of paganism myth may indeed serve as a pseudo-science, and thus it is to be expected that the myth of creation would undertake to account for how the world, i.e., nature, in its various parts was constituted. But in the context of the distinctive biblical faith, the scientific concern, i.e., the concern with the "how," is not the real concern or indeed even a legitimate concern. Here, the religious concern cannot be identified with the scientific concern; the religious concern impinges mainly (one is tempted to say exclusively) on the "what" question, i.e., what kind of being, what status, does nature possess.

Inasmuch, however, as the Genesis narrative, despite its monotheistic refraction, continues to dwell largely on the "how" question and does not address itself explicitly to the "what" question, the answer to the "what" question can be ascertained only through inference. It is interesting that the pronouncement which suggests itself for such inference is the pronouncement which affects the monotheistic refraction, namely, the monotonously repetitive formula "And God said let there be ... and it was so." According to this formula, nature is brought into existence by the mere agency of God's speech. This may suggest the view of *creatio ex nihilo* – prior to God's speech there is nothing. Indeed, later tradition was inclined to understand the signification of this formula in this way. But the Genesis narrative, taken in its own terms, does not really state this. A careful reading clearly shows that what is brought into existence by the mere agency of God's speech are the particular entities of nature but not the very being of nature itself, i.e., the matter of which these particular entities are constituted. The formula does not exclude the pre-existence of some primordial matter out of which the specific entities of nature are fashioned and brought into existence by the agency of God's speech. Indeed, the opening of the Genesis account would seem to support precisely such a state of affairs – the pre-existence of some primordial being or beings. Genesis 1:2 taken literally and in its own terms would seem to suggest the existence prior to the act of creation of a body of primordial water, of darkness (which, by the way, is not mentioned subsequently as being created), and of *tohu* and *vohu*. Furthermore, if Genesis 1:1 reading "In the beginning God created" (thus suggesting a *creatio ex nihilo* view which indeed was widely utilized by the later tradition to support its claim that the view of *creatio ex nihilo* is already expressed in the Bible) is by mere change of vocalization emended to read "When God was initially creating," as indeed it seems the text should read, then we have here an adverbial clause clearly suggesting a creation in time which, in turn, implicates an existence of matter prior to the act of creation and consequently the absence of a *creatio ex nihilo* view.[12] Thus, a critical reading of the Genesis narrative in its own terms would not support the claim the narrative reflects a *creatio ex nihilo* view. Indeed, if anything, the narrative here suggests once again a notion of creation that is modeled after the artisan fashioning his artifact (a model that clearly excludes the view of *creatio ex nihilo*). The only distinction of the Genesis narrative lies in the fact that here the act of creation is in a sense "spiritualized" inasmuch as the creation, i.e., the fashioning, of the artifact is not by concrete, mechanical action but by pure speech alone.[13] But the signification of this "spiritualization" implicated by the notion of creation by speech alone impinges on the aspect of the creator, i.e., on the question of what kind of God is implicated in the creation here, rather than on the aspect of the created, i.e., on the *creatio ex nihilo*. Thus, this notion of creation by speech alone further strengthens the already thorough monotheistic refraction characterizing the Genesis narrative. It does not, however, implicate a view of creation as *creatio ex nihilo*.

Creation in Other Biblical Literature

The further expression of the creation motif in biblical literature, i.e., its expression in the Davidic royal theology, in wisdom literature and in later prophecy, does not essentially change the picture as regards the issue before us. That is, the various expressions of the creation motif in these sources do not imply, let alone state explicitly, a view of creation as *creatio ex nihilo*. Indeed, the signification given to the notion of creation here is a signification that is commonly met in the creation myths of paganism. Creation signifies here the introduction of order into chaos; it is the establishment of order into what previously was chaos, the molding of chaos into cosmos. As such the signification here clearly excludes a *creatio ex nihilo* view. For it suggests a creation that reflects the model of the artisan fashioning his artifact and commensurate with this it suggests the pre-existence of matter prior to creation.[14]

What is of special significance, however, in these expressions is the fact that creation thus understood, i.e., understood as the transformation of chaos into order, is applied here not in the metaphysical domain but in the historical and ethical domains (Davidic royal theology and prophecy apply it in the historical domain while wisdom literature applies it in the ethical domain). Namely, the creation motif is articulated here not with regard to its metaphysical implications but rather with regard to its historical and ethical implications. Thus, Davidic royal theology, in order to establish the firmness and eternity of God's covenant with the House of David, links this covenant with the primary covenant of creation whereby an ordered world is established out of chaos. "The royal theologians in Jerusalem laid the foundations of the Davidic dynasty in firmer soil than in the problematic and conditional grounds of the Mosaic covenant ... This invited God's eternal commitment to the dynasty of David, a commitment as firmly established as God's creation of an ordered world."[15] Prophecy (especially deutero-Isaiah) likewise links creation, again seen as signifying the establishment of order, i.e., as the slaying of Rahab representing chaos, with the succeeding mighty acts of God such as the dividing of the sea of reeds, the conquest of Canaan, and the new exodus from Babylonian captivity about to take place.[16] Creation is but the first redemptive act of God; it is but the first event in the consequent succession of redemptive events constituting the *heilsgeschichte*.[17] The creative and the redemptive are linked together: "Creator and Savior or Redeemer are one and the same God."[18] Lastly, in wisdom literature where the concern is with "practical, prudential, moral knowledge of what is best for daily life," creation, which is seen here too as the establishment of order, provides the guarantee for the possibility of the ethical life. "This world is created in such a way that man can have confidence that the ethical life is rooted in the very creation itself."[19]

Clearly, creation is converted here from a metaphysical category to an ethical or historical category. This indeed reflects the basic posture of biblical thought – deep involvement in the historical and ethical domains but hardly any concern with the metaphysical domain. This absence of interest in the metaphysical domain is distinctive of biblical thought, and it is most significant for our consideration here as it bears heavily on the biblical handling of the creation motif. Thus, it may well account for the lack of explicit concern in biblical thought with the question of *creatio ex nihilo*. For the question of *creatio ex nihilo* versus the existence of coeval matter is a thoroughly metaphysical question and as such it can arise only in a context of metaphysical concern. Indeed, it may also account for the lack of sensitivity in biblical thought to the borrowed elements of pagan creation mythology which imply a view of creation that excludes *creatio ex nihilo* as, for example, the view of creation that is patterned after the model of the artisan fashioning his artifact, or the view of creation as the establishment of order out of chaos. True, their views exclude the *creatio ex nihilo* view clearly and explicitly only when their signification is articulated in the metaphysical context, as indeed is the case in paganism,[20] and in the Bible they are not articulated in the metaphysical context. Still, these views when not articulated in the metaphysical context do continue nonetheless to exclude the *creatio ex nihilo* view, though now only implicitly, and yet the Bible is tolerant of them. This is all the more remarkable when compared to the jealousy which the Bible manifests with regard to those borrowings from pagan mythology which impinge on the monotheistic aspect. Here the biblical tendency is clearly to refract the pagan borrowings so as to remove any allusion that may compromise the monotheistic aspect. That the Bible is not equally sensitive to the aspect of *creatio ex nihilo* and thus does not refract with equal zeal the pagan borrowings impinging upon it can be accounted for only on the basis that biblical thought is not metaphysically oriented. Thus, it is because of this lack of metaphysical orientation that biblical thought, as we have seen, does not articulate the signification of its tenet of creation in the metaphysical domain (articulating it rather in the historical and ethical domains), and that consequently it can avoid dealing explicitly with the aspect of *creatio ex nihilo*. Moreover, this lack of metaphysical orientation desensitizes biblical thought to the implicit negating of a *creatio ex nihilo* view which is contained in its borrowings from the pagan creation myths. Their half-way "neutralization" or "suppression" due to the fact that the tenet of creation is articulated in the historical and ethical rather than the metaphysical domain, seems sufficient for biblical thought, so that a more thorough refraction to eliminate this implicit negation of a *creatio ex nihilo* view is not undertaken by it.

And yet when the metaphysical aspect is, so to speak, forced from the outside upon the Bible, the biblical response, now impinging much more clearly on the metaphysical aspect, is quite suggestive of a *creatio ex nihilo* view. True, we have only one instance that exemplifies this. It is to be found in deutero-Isaiah 45:7 where the prophet declares that God created not only light but also darkness (thus supplementing a glowing omission in the Genesis account, namely, the omission of the creation of darkness). This declaration is clearly methaphysical in its signification and as such it of course impinges on the issue of *creatio ex nihilo*. Indeed, the declaration here is very suggestive of affirming a *creatio ex nihilo* view inasmuch as it clearly negates the pre-existence of a being other than God, i.e., inasmuch as it negates the pre-existence of darkness as a primordial, coeval being with God. But it seems quite clear that this declaration by deutero-Isaiah is precipitated as a reaction against dualistic formulations which in all probability used the omission in the Genesis account as a telling point in their arsenal of argumentation. Thus, deutero-Isaiah provides us with an instance where a *creatio ex nihilo* view is strongly suggested, but this instance is provided only because the issue is precipitated from the outside. When confronted with a dualistic formulation, deutero-Isaiah articulates the creation motif in the metaphysical context and, indeed, in a way that is congenial to the *creatio ex nihilo* view.

Still, even though deutero-Isaiah is the sole instance that articulates a view that is clearly suggestive of *creatio ex nihilo,* it may be taken nonetheless as reflecting what ought to be the tendency of biblical thought. For a case can be made that in spite of all that was said above, the thrust of biblical thought by its very inner logic ought to tend towards a view of creation that would implicate a *creatio ex nihilo*. This is so inasmuch as the negation of a *creatio ex nihilo* view may be taken as impinging negatively on the monotheistic aspect. That is, the negation of the *creatio ex nihilo* view may well suggest the existence of more than one divine being – divine in the specific sense of being an absolute, i.e., a non-dependent, non-contingent being.[21] For clearly the negation of the *creatio ex nihilo* view necessarily implicates the existence of another primordial coeval being beside the being of God. It thus necessarily establishes the existence of two absolute, i.e., divine, beings and as such, it clearly impinges negatively on the monotheistic aspect. It should be noted, however, that this conclusion that biblical thought ought to affirm a *creatio ex nihilo* view is not derived from a direct consideration of the tenet of creation. Rather it is derived from the consideration of the monotheistic aspect – it follows as an implication of the monotheistic aspect. Thus, the conclusion arrived at here in no way alters the observation made above that biblical thought is not concerned with the philosophical-metaphysical dimension. The basic, central concern of biblical thought remains focused on the religious signification of the monotheistic aspect and not on the philosophical-metaphysical signification of the *creatio ex nihilo* formulation. Indeed, biblical thought remains so unphilosophically and unmetaphysically oriented that this implication of the monotheistic aspect (namely, that the safeguarding of the monotheistic aspect in its specific signification of divinity as absolute being implicates the affirmation of a *creatio ex nihilo* view) is not apparently grasped within biblical thought itself.[22] Biblical thought does not seem to be aware of this implication and consequently not only does it not explicitly affirm a *creatio ex nihilo* view but it seems to tolerate the negation, albeit an implicit negation, of a *creatio ex nihilo* view.

Creation in the Talmud

When one moves now from examining biblical thought to the examining of talmudic literature one can encounter some opening towards the metaphysical domain.[23] One would expect, therefore, to encounter here a more explicit discussion and formulation with regard to the issue of *creatio ex nihilo,* seeing that this issue is a metaphysical issue, an issue that one would expect to arise in the context of metaphysical concern and discussion. This, however, does not seem to be the case. For part of the rabbinic discussions regarding the tenet of creation, in similarity to the biblical narration, revolves around the "how" of creation. The biblical account clearly lends itself to such speculations as it is rather laconic in its description, leaving out many of the details regarding the "how" of creation. Particularly for the rabbis who studied the text so carefully and thoroughly (for whom every word, every letter, its sound, its spelling, its location, had special signification to convey), and who had a penchant for detail and precision, the biblical account provided fertile ground for speculation with regard to the "how" of creation. Thus, for example, we have such speculation reflected in the controversy between the school of Shammai and the school of Hillel as to whether the heaven or the earth was created first (according to Rabbi Shimon Bar Yohai the two were created simultaneously);[24] or, again, we have it reflected in the controversy between the two schools whereby the school of Shammai is saying that the thought was at night and the deed during the day, while the school of Hillel is saying that both thought and deed are during the day (with Shimon Bar Yohai maintaining that thought is both during day time and at night, while the deed is confined merely to sunset).[25] Such reflections, interesting as they may be with regard to some other issues, evidently do not impinge upon our concern here, i.e., upon the issue of *creatio ex nihilo*.

Of course, there is also considerable amount of reflection on the part of the rabbis that impinges more substantively on the metaphysical dimension of the tenet of creation. However, the main concern in these discussions seems to be the issue of dualism. This is understandable inasmuch as gnostic dualism constitutes at this juncture the challenge to Judaism from the surrounding environment. Indeed, it cannot be denied that traces of its infiltration into the thought-world of the rabbis can be detected in the literature. Thus, already in the tannaitic period we have, for example, the story of Rabbi Simeon ben Zoma and Rabbi Joshua ben Hananiah which, although very obscure and difficult to interpret, nonetheless would seem to convey gnostic dualistic speculations on the part of ben Zoma.[26] We can also see the concern with dualistic interpretations of Scripture in the discussion between Rabbi Ishmael and Rabbi Akiva regarding the first verse in Genesis, which the gnostics apparently interpreted to say that heaven and earth were co-creators rather than created beings.[27] Similarly, the fact that the creation of darkness is not mentioned in the Genesis account gave rise apparently to dualistic interpretations with the rather weak response from the rabbis that on this point there is no solution. This mythological dualistic infiltration would seem to have increased with the onset of the amoraic period; it seems to find expression in the literature much more freely and openly. Thus, for example, in a number of stories an independent status prior to creation is given to a "prince of the sea" or to a "prince of darkness"; the existence prior to creation of other elements such as fire, water (or snow), *tohu* and *vohu* is also mentioned.[28] And of course we have the celebrated reference to the pre-existence of the Torah serving as a blueprint which God, on the analogy of an architect, consulted in creating the world.[29]

Still, the burden of the rabbinic view is to reject the gnostic dualistic view. The very presence of references to dualistic views is often due to the fact that they are mentioned in order to be rejected.[30] Thus, the most that can be said is that the dualistic alternative was known to the rabbis and was sufficiently of a challenge at that time so that it could not be ignored; it had to be confronted, and this is precisely what the rabbis do – they bring into the open the dualistic versions in order to reject them (either in an outright manner or through interpreting them so as to remove the dualistic rub). Indeed, in the very instances where such dualistic views may be suspected (in the examples mentioned above as well as in other instances), their unequivocal rejection is also stated. Thus, for example, in the ben Zoma story Rabbi Joshua ben Hananiah rejects vigorously any interpretation that has any inkling to the gnostic view, and Rav (in whose name many stories having a mythological-dualistic flavor are brought) interprets away the gnostic-dualistic reading of the creation account.[31] The mainstream position of the rabbis is opposed to the gnostic-dualistic view. Their position is perhaps best summed up in their comment on Isiah 44:25 explaining the end of the verse "who is with me" to say "who was a partner with me in the work of creation?"[32] The basic idea of the rabbis was always that God alone created everything.

But the question of dualism does not really impinge on the very crux of the subject that is before us, i.e., on the question of *creatio ex nihilo*. For, strictly speaking, the question of dualism refers to the aspect of the creator, i.e., to the divine – did God have partners in the work of creation or did he create all by himself? On the other hand, the formulation of *creatio ex nihilo* refers to the aspect of the created, i.e., to the substance of the world – was the created world merely formed of a pre-existing coeval substance or was the very substance of the created world brought into being by the act of creation? True, both the negation of *creatio ex nihilo* and the dualistic formulation impinge negatively on the monotheistic viewpoint in that both provide a coeval being beside God in the act of creation. As such, both formulations are pernicious to the monotheistic viewpoint, and it is understandable that very often the two formulations will be presented and dealt with interchangeably in the literature.[33] Still, a distinction is present whereby dualism formulates itself in the domain of the creator while the negation of *creatio ex nihilo* formulates itself in the domain of the created (in the sense of being merely formed).[34] But if dualism does not impinge directly and unambiguously on the issue of *creatio ex nihilo,* the question of primordial matter clearly does. Quite evidently, the affirmation of primordial matter necessarily negates the formulation of *creatio ex nihilo* and, vice versa, its negation necessarily implicates the formulation; indeed, the question of primordial matter is the question of *creatio ex nihilo.* Thus, if we want to know the position of the rabbis with regard to the formulation of *creatio ex nihilo,* we must attempt to determine what they have to say specifically about the question of primordial matter.

But talmudic literature is not too helpful in this regard. There are really very few references that impinge on the question of primordial matter. And the treatment of the question in most of these references (with one notable exception) is certainly not explicit and clear-cut. As was the case with regard to biblical thought, one must therefore resort also here to inference. Thus, for example, we find Rav mentioning the creation of time in his enumeration of the ten things created on the first day;[35] since, as we have seen above, the existence of matter would necessarily implicate the existence of time, the statement by Rav necessarily implies that matter was not in existence prior to the first day (for if it were, time too would have been in existence prior to the first day). In other words, it necessarily implies the absence of primordial matter.[36] Or, in a discussion as to whether light or darkness was created first,[37] Rabbi Nehemiah (following Rabbi Ishmael's methodology of interpretation) declares that the whole world was created on the first day,[38] which again may be taken to imply the negation of primordial matter. True, there are also some references which may be taken to imply the affirmation of primordial matter. Thus, for example, the story about ben Zoma mentioned above would seem to indicate that ben Zoma was implying the existence of primordial matter;[39] and the declaration "there is no solution" with regard to the question of the creation of darkness (*Tamid* 32-1) would also seem to allow the alternative of the existence of primordial matter. But such clues indicating possible affirmation of primordial matter would seem to come only from a few peripheral quarters indulging in such esoteric speculations under the influence of the outside environment. The burden of the rabbinic view, however, seems to negate the existence of primordial matter and thus to imply *creatio ex nihilo.*

The position certainly expresses itself explicitly and clearly when the rabbis are challenged by views denying *creatio ex nihilo.* Thus, not only do we have the answer of Rabbi Yehoshua to ben Zoma's intimations regarding the existence of primordial matter (mentioned above), we have the much clearer and more decisive encounter between Rabban Gamaliel and a philosopher. A philosopher told Rabban Gamaliel, "Your God is a great artist but he certainly found good materials that helped him," to which Rannan Gamaliel asked, "What are they?" and the philosopher replied, "*tohu, vohu,* darkness, water, wind and the depths;" to which Rabban Gamaliel responded with a curse saying with regard to all of them "creation" is written.[40] There can be no question that Rabban Gamaliel rejects most forcefully and unequivocally the existence of any primordial matter. And this answer would seem to reflect in the main the position of the rabbis although, as said above, it must be admitted that on their own, when not challenged from the outside, the rabbis do not enter into the philosophical-metaphysical speculations which the creation narrative so clearly suggests. Their speculations stick rather closely to the scriptural text,[41] dwelling on the finer particulars of the "how" of creation and not going beyond the text to its metaphysical implications. Specifically on the matter of *creatio ex nihilo,* they remain by and large silent. It has been suggested that the rabbinic silence on *creatio ex nihilo* is due to the fact that the tenet was so firmly accepted that it was taken for granted and therefore not much discussion ensued.[42] This observation may have some truth in it; it is certainly difficult to argue from silence. In any event, it would seem to us that the important consideration is to be found in the fact that the rabbis on their own have no disposition to enter metaphysical speculation (following in this respect the biblical example). Indeed, we have any number of statements enjoining us not to enter or pursue such speculation. Thus, one is not to inquire into what was prior to the creation of the world, what is above and what is below, what is before and what is after the world; and any one looking into these four things (i.e., the domains of mystical-metaphysical speculation) deserves not to come into the world.[43] One has no business with the mysteries of the world and is not to pursue what is beyond human grasp. The business of man is with the world as already given and available to man. And as to the origin of the world, the burden of the rabbinic view was straightforward scriptural (without entering the labyrinth of the metaphysical problematic); as E. Urbach states, it was always that God alone created the world by his word. "The view of the rabbis regarding the creation of the world found its pithy expression in the attribute 'He who said and the world was.'"[44]

"Creatio Ex Nihilo":   Medieval Period

Explicit, systematized formulation of the view of *creatio ex nihilo* does not really appear till the medieval period. This is understandable as in the medieval period the philosophic examination and articulation of the faith, and thus the interest in the metaphysical dimension, really penetrates Judaism (through the agency of Islam), and we encounter for the first time a full-fledged, sustained, philosophic, i.e., metaphysical, expression in Judaism. In such a context the articulation of a *creatio ex nihilo* view is made feasible. Moreover, such a feasibility becomes actually a necessity inasmuch as the penetration is the penetration of Greek philosophy and metaphysics (i.e., the penetration of the Aristotelian and Platonic views) where the view of *creatio ex nihilo* is clearly repudiated. In the medieval period Judaism under Islam encounters the full force of the challenge of Greek philosophy to its implied view of *creatio ex nihilo* and the need to defend it is clearly present.[45] It is under these circumstances that a fully explicit articulation of a *creatio ex nihilo* formulation finds a clear-cut and forceful expression in medieval Jewish philosophy. All the major figures in medieval Jewish philosophy reject the Aristotelian assertion of the existence of primordial matter[46] and likewise the Platonic view of a hylic substance.[47] For medieval Jewish philosophy it is unequivocal that all is created by God out of nothing. Moreover, medieval Jewish philosophy claims that this assertion of *creatio ex nihilo* is an essential, inextricable tenet of the faith of Judaism[48] and that it has always been, from the earliest expression of the faith of Judaism, i.e., the biblical record, the unequivocal position of Judaism.[49] Thus, medieval Jewish philosophy not only explicitly formulates the tenet of *creatio ex nihilo;* it also claims that it merely articulates a tenet that has characterized Judaism all along and, indeed, characterized it as an essential, inextricable expression of its faith.

A Basic Tenet of Judaism?

Now, as we have already seen, the claim that the *creatio ex nihilo* view characterized Judaism all along from its very beginnings, when taken from a purely historical perspective, is rather dubious. But in any event, as far as our topic here is concerned, this claim is of rather peripheral interest. Much more central and important to our topic is the claim that the *creatio ex nihilo* view is a basic and inextricable tenet in the essential structure of faith of Judaism. And here there are a number of considerations that would indeed support this claim. First and most significantly, as we have already seen, the negation of the *creatio ex nihilo* view impinges negatively, albeit only in a partial but nonetheless important sense, on the monotheistic aspect; and the monotheistic aspect is certainly a basic and inextricable tenet in the essential structure of faith of Judaism. Thus, a case can be made that although in itself the *creatio ex nihilo* view may not be a basic and inextricable tenet in the essential structure of faith of Judaism, it becomes so by virtue of its impingement upon the monotheistic aspect.

Furthermore, a similar case can be made with the argument that the *creatio ex nihilo* view, this time when it is affirmed rather than negated, necessarily implicates the desacralization of nature. For inasmuch as the desacralization of nature is a basic, inextricable element in the essential structure of faith of Judaism (seeing that Judaism by its very essence is not a "nature religion") the *creatio ex nihilo* view, by virtue of the fact that it necessarily implicates the desacralization of nature, becomes likewise a basic, inextricable element in the essential structure of faith of Judaism. Now, that the affirmation of the *creatio ex nihilo* view necessarily implicates the desacralization of nature is indeed shown by the very same consideration which has shown above that the negation of the *creatio ex nihilo* view impinges negatively on the monotheistic aspect – all that one has to do is to draw its implications now with regard to nature rather than with regard to the divine. For the affirmation of the *creatio ex nihilo* clearly implies that the being of nature is not absolute and therefore that it is not divine (divine in the signification of absoluteness of being). But this is to say – inasmuch as the notion of desacralization signifies precisely the removal, i.e., the abrogation, the absence, of the divine – that it clearly implies the desacralization of nature.[50]

It should be clear that the implication of the desacralization of nature by the *creatio ex nihilo* view is feasible only on the presupposition that the *creatio ex nihilo* view is articulated in a theistic and not in a pantheistic context. For clearly, in the pantheistic context, if the tenet of creation is to be maintained at all, creation can only signify emanation, and the notion of emanation necessarily attributes divinity to the being of nature. If the being of nature is seen as merely an extension, an overflow, of the divine being, if the being of nature and the being of God are one and the same, then the being of nature is evidently divine. Indeed, the very logic of the notion of desacralization requires that the *creatio ex nihilo* view and the pantheistic formulation be mutually exclusive – a being cannot be both desacralized and at the same time constituted as part and parcel of the divine being. Only in the theistic context, where the being of nature is distinct, separate and set over-against the being of God, can *creatio ex nihilo* signify the desacralization of nature. Here, *creatio ex nihilo* can signify the desacralization of nature by negating the attributes of eternity and independence, namely, by negating the divinity that may be claimed to inhere in a separate, distinct being of nature. If *creatio ex nihilo* is to signify the desacralization of nature then *creatio ex nihilo* and theism just go hand in hand – *creatio ex nihilo* safeguarding against the constituting of nature as divine by virtue of its being a separate, second divine being parallel to the divine being of God, and theism safeguarding against the constituting of nature as divine by virtue of its being part and parcel of the divine being of God.[51] Thus again, a case can be made here that *creatio ex nihilo* is a fundamental element in the essential structure of Judaism, albeit not by virtue of its own intrinsic signification but by virtue of the fact that in its implication of the desacralization of nature it necessarily presupposes the theistic formulation, a formulation which is fundamental to the essential structure of faith of Judaism.

One can therefore agree with the observation that *creatio ex nihilo* is fundamental to the essential structure of faith of Judaism. It is fundamental, however, not by virtue of its own immediate, inherent signification but by virtue of the fact that it necessarily implies fundamental elements in the essential structure of faith of Judaism, that is, by virtue of the fact that it necessarily implies the monotheistic aspect, the desacralization of nature and the theistic formulation. Still, important as this is, the real significance of the *creatio ex nihilo* formulation for Judaism lies, in the last analysis, not in these implications but rather in the way in which it impinges on man's relation to nature. In other words, for Judaism the real significance of the *creatio ex nihilo* view lies not so much in its impingement upon the metaphysical domain (i.e., for example, in its implication of the desacralization of nature or of the theistic structure) as in its impingement upon the ethical domain (and this is so even though the *creatio ex nihilo* view in its own terms is a view which, as we have seen, is formulated in the metaphysical domain).

Man: Accountable to God for Creation

This impingement upon the ethical domain expresses itself in the fact that the *creatio ex nihilo* view reintroduces the dimension of accountability and responsibility into man's relation towards nature. As we have seen above, in the view of Judaism nature is seen to be constituted as an It-being,[52] and as such nature, by its very constitution, could not exact accountability for the action directed toward itself. But now, by virtue of the *creatio ex nihilo* view, nature is seen as the handiwork of God and therefore as belonging to him as its sole possessor. This in turn means that in relating to nature one necessarily relates also to its creator and owner, i.e., to God – any action directed towards nature necessarily implicates God, the ultimate possessor of nature. For any action directed towards an object is, at the same time, of necessity directed also towards the creator and owner of the object. Unlike nature, however, which because it is constituted as an It-being cannot exact accountability, God being constituted as a Thou-being can and does exact accountability for any action implicating him (and, as we have seen, in the context of *creatio ex nihilo,* action directed towards nature necessarily implicates God as the creator and owner of nature). Thus the *creatio ex nihilo* view reintroduces accountability and responsibility although they are directed, it is true, not to nature but to God. That is, while remaining not accountable and responsible to nature, man is now accountable and responsible to God for nature.[53] Indeed, the very sanctioning of man's right to act at all towards nature is, under these circumstances, contingent on God's permission; and as such, of course, the permission may well circumscribe and condition the action that it allows.

This is precisely the stance with respect to man's relation to nature that the *creatio ex nihilo* view establishes within Judaism. For Judaism, nature is neither ownerless, existing in itself, nor is it possessed by man. Nature is the possession of God, and it is merely entrusted to man with the permission, indeed enjoining, to act upon it (and because nature is constituted as an It-being the action that is feasible is essentially utilization and manipulation).[54] This permission, however, is not given *carte blanche;* the option of circumscribing and constraining the action is exercised. Thus, man is enjoined to utilize and manipulate nature but only inasmuch as this is needed to sustain and benefit his life; he is not permitted to utilize and manipulate nature wantonly and capriciously.[55] Secondly, the cruelty and pain which are inevitably implicated in the utilization and manipulation of nature are to be kept, as much as possible, to a minimum.[56]

This delineation of man's relation to nature is certainly consistent with the essential structure of faith characterizing Judaism, particularly with its view of the ontological constitution of nature as an It-being and with its expression of the *creatio ex nihilo* view, and as such the rationale for this delineation is available. There is, however, one point that needs some further clarification, namely, what is the rationale for the actual imposition of constraints on man's action towards nature and, indeed, for the specific constraints outlined above. Granted that, as we have argued above, such imposition is in principle feasible (given the view of Judaism that nature is ultimately in the possession of God), this does not explain why the imposition is actually carried out and, indeed, why the specific constraints are imposed. In more traditional language, the question arises as to why God actually places limits and directives upon man's action towards nature, and why specifically those limits and directives are articulated in the tradition. Why not leave the utilization and manipulation of nature completely free and unrestrained in the hands of man? Why not let man's action towards nature be arbitrary and capricious? After all, as was noted above, Judaism is not a "nature religion," and indeed in its structure of faith neither the human predicament nor the religious vocation (i.e., the working towards redemption) is constituted in terms of nature (as for example, in terms of the flux and finitude of the beings of nature or in terms of the fertile and destructive forces of nature). Why then should the action upon nature make any difference or be of concern to Judaism?

In answering this one must indeed admit, as we have stated above, that nature does not play a central role in the essential structure of faith of Judaism. Namely, it is true that the central categories of the human predicament and the religious vocation are constituted in terms of society, i.e., in terms of the relations of man to his fellow-man, rather than in terms of nature, and that consequently they are formulated in the context of history and ethics rather than in the context of ontology and metaphysics.[57] Still, nature functions here as the necessary and inescapable stage on which the religious drama in its totality unfolds. For not only the predicament (which is to be expected and is fairly common) but the very realization of redemption is formulated in a this-worldly context – the redeemed just society is a this-worldly society, and this means that it is inescapably moored within nature. Thus, although nature does not constitute the "stuff" of the religious drama (neither the predicament nor the redemption formulate themselves in terms of nature), it does constitute its necessary presupposition. As such, the continued existence of nature is necessary not only for the unfolding but for the very realization of the religious vocation and this, in turn, means that nature cannot be simply entrusted, i.e., entrusted without constraints or directives, to the hands of man since the arbitrary and capricious action of man is all too readily destructive.

Preservation of Nature in View of Man

On the other hand, given the structure of faith operating there, the constraints and directives that are introduced, and whose purpose is to safeguard nature against utilization and manipulation, i.e., against its destruction (for utilization and manipulation necessarily implicate destruction), cannot be such as to safeguard nature against any and all utilization and manipulation. For after all the required preservation of nature here is not for its own sake but for the sake of the social entity which is moored in a this-worldly context (since it is in its terms that the religious vocation, i.e., the vocation of establishing social justice, is formulated); and this, in turn, means that, in the last analysis, it is for the sake of man as he is constituted in a this-worldly context that the preservation of nature is required.[58] But man as a this-worldly entity is constituted as an inextricable union of nature and the divine. As against viewing nature as an It-being and God as a Thou-being, Judaism views man as an inextricable It-Thou being; indeed, as Genesis presents him, man is at one and the same time part and parcel of nature, a creature (by virtue of being an It), and a carrier of the divine image (by virtue of being a Thou).[59] Thus this means that as such for man to exist, the preservation of nature is required. For inasmuch as man, in an inextricable aspect of his being, is part and parcel of nature, i.e., an It-being, his very existence depends upon the preservation of nature, and the destruction of nature inevitably means his own destruction.[60] Yet paradoxically, at the very same time, precisely in being an It-being, a being of nature, man in order to exist, let alone prosper, must inevitably utilize and exploit (and thus partially destroy) nature. The very existence of man and certainly his well-being and prosperity necessarily implicate his utilization and exploitation of nature. Thus, some utilization, i.e., destruction, of nature must be allowed while at the same time the preservation of nature is required.

Evidently, the directives which the tradition articulates in order to delineate man's relation to nature find their rationale in this rather paradoxical situation which man's ontological constitution dictates. Namely, it is man and his needs which determine the stance that the tradition takes with regard to nature. Thus, in forbidding, on the one hand, the wanton destruction of nature, it reflects the need to preserve nature; on the other hand, in sanctioning and indeed commanding the exploitation of nature when this is done for the sake of man, it reflects the realization that man's existence and well-being inevitably involve the exploitation of nature.

Accountability to Fellow-Men

These considerations suggest, by the way, that my fellow-man is yet another being (beside God) that can exact accountability and indeed, as we shall argue presently, exact accountability specifically for the action directed towards nature. For, as we have seen above, to exact accountability a being must be constituted as a Thou; thus, in contradistinction to nature, God being constituted as Thou can exact accountability. By the same token, however, it also follows now that my fellow-man too is a being that can exact accountability, for he too is constituted as a Thou, albeit only in one dimension of his being, but this is all that is required (especially since it is an inextricable dimension of his being).[61] But granted that my fellow-man being constituted as an It-Thou being can exact accountability by virtue of the fact that in one inextricable dimension of his being he is constituted as a Thou, can this capacity impinge upon action directed towards nature? What rationale, what justification, does my fellow-man have for exacting accountability for action directed towards nature? In the case of God, as we have seen, the rationale and justification were derived from the consideration whereby nature is made the possession of God (this being established through the *creatio ex nihilo* view) thereby giving God a stake in what is done to nature. This evidently does not apply to my fellow-man. Are there then other considerations which will give my fellow-man a stake in what is done to nature, thus providing the rationale and justification for his exercising his capacity to exact accountability with regard to the action directed towards nature?

We would submit that there are two such considerations. First, my fellow-man has a stake in what is done to nature by virtue of the fact that he is also constituted in the other inextricable dimension of his being as an It, i.e., as an inextricable part and parcel of nature. As such, what is done to nature impinges very much upon his very being and consequently he has every justification to exact accountability for the action directed towards nature. Secondly, my fellow-man has a stake in what is done to nature by virtue of the fact that he is entrusted with the vocation of realizing redemption, i.e., with the vocation of establishing the righteous community. True, this redemptive task is not constituted in terms of nature but in terms of history (indeed my fellow-man is entrusted with this vocation by virtue of his being a Thou, a being transcending nature, and not by virtue of his being an It, a being which is part and parcel of nature). Still, inasmuch as the pursuit and, indeed, the very realization of this vocation remain in a this-worldly context, nature is inescapably involved – the preservation of nature is a condition *sine qua non* for the pursuit and realization of the redemptive task. As such, keeping in mind that this redemptive task constitutes the *raison d'etre* for man's existence and, indeed, the source providing the meaning to his life, my fellow-man has again every justification to exact accountability for the action directed towards nature.[62] Thus, not only God but my fellow-man too has a claim on what I do to nature. My accountability and responsibility to God for my action towards nature can now be further extended or, so to speak, refracted into accountability and responsibility to my fellowman.

Conclusion

Thus, Judaism succeeds in establishing accountability that is firmly moored both in the divine and in man for the action directed towards nature, even though nature is viewed as being constituted as an It and as such incapable in its own terms of exacting accountability for action directed towards itself. Indeed, though in its own terms nature is not the bearer of value (as an It-being it is neutral to valuation), value is placed on nature by virtue of the role it is assigned in the economy of redemption (which economy unfolds in the sphere of the Thou). In other words, by virtue of being the stage on which the drama of redemption is to unfold itself, by virtue of providing the inescapable context in which both the pursuit and the realization of redemption can take place, it is invested with a positive valuation – "and God saw that it was good" (Gen 1:12, 18, 31). Thus, in Judaism nature is neither negated nor is it romanticized; it is neither neglected nor is it placed on a pedestal. Neither reverence, awe or passive submission, on the one hand, nor callousness, disregard or arbitrariness, on the other hand, constitute the proper relating to nature. Nature is to be utilized but it is to be utilized with responsibility. Nature is an It-being but it is an It-being which is the handiwork and possession of God; it is an It-being which is necessary for the fulfillment of the vocation of the Thou.

It is in this middle, balanced position which Judaism strikes that a distinctive contribution towards a tenable and viable view of nature is made. It realistically sees nature as being constituted as an It-being and draws the inescapable implication from this. Yet, at the same time, it does not abandon nature to whim and caprice by leaving it outside the sphere of ethical concern; it succeeds in incorporating nature into the bounds of the ethical domain, thus imposing accountability and responsibility for our action towards nature.

---

[1]At the very start we should hasten to point out that the stance that Judaism takes with regard to this subject is not monolithic. In its various expressions we can encounter rather radically different conceptions of nature and consequently rather radically different formulations of man's relation to nature. This follows from the fact that Judaism, as indeed any other historical religious tradition, is not monolithic as regards its basic religious *Weltanschauung* (what we would call "the essential structure of faith," i.e., the basic view of man and the world and consequently the conception of what constitutes the ultimate predicament and commensurate to this the formulation of the salvation offered and the view of the divine). Rather, it is a mixture of different religious*Weltanschauungen* held together by the sharing of common symbols, rituals and institutions (the differences manifesting themselves when one comes to ascertain the signification attributed to these common symbols, rituals and institutions). In view of this, it is important to note that the description and analysis that are to follow undertake to represent only one specific trend within the historical religious tradition of Judaism. They undertake to represent what might be designated as the prophetic trend in the biblical context and the non-mystical, halachic trend in the rabbinic context. This certainly leaves out other trends which found expression within the historical religious

tradition of Judaism. In particular, it leaves out the priestly-wisdom trend in the biblical context and the mystical trend in the rabbinic context; and there is no denying that the "picture" which emerges in these trends is quite different from the "picture" which emerges in the trend represented here. Our defense for leaving out of consideration these trends and centering on the non-mystical, socio-ethical trend lies in the following two considerations: a) we would want to argue that unlike the other trends, the trend represented here formulates a religious *Weltanschauung* — and specifically, given our concern in this paper, a view of the relation of man to nature — which is distinctive and, indeed, unique; b) we would want to argue that although granting that the mystical trend was quite pervasive, the main thrust of the phenomenon of Judaism lies nonetheless in the trend represented here. In any event, it should be kept clearly in mind that throughout this paper the Judaism represented is the Judaism expressing itself in the non-mystical halachic trend.

[2]This stance is most clearly delineated already in the story of Adam's and Eve's transgression. Though the earth had in no way taken part in the transgression, it is cursed because of Adam's transgression (Gen 3:17). This is even more poignantly expressed in the story of the flood. The land and all life is destroyed because of the social evil-doing of man (Gen 6:11-13). But perhaps the most explicit expression of the passive role given to nature, making its fortunes dependent on man's conduct, is to be found in Deuteronomy 11:13-17 where the productivity of the land is explicitly made contingent on the obedience of man to God's commandments.

[3]It will be noted, however, that the case of the It-being was formulated somewhat differently from the way the case of the Thou-being was formulated. In the case of the It-being we said that an I-Thou relation would not "make sense" while in the case of the Thou-being we said that an I-It relation would not be "feasible." We would want to argue that this is indeed the case if the matter is to be delineated precisely. Namely, one can address an It-being, but to do that would not make sense; on the other hand, one cannot relate in an I-It fashion to a Thou-being because the very I-It relating excludes the other to which one relates from being a Thou-being. This is so inasmuch as the Thou-being, i.e., the being-of-Consciousness, arises from the I-Thou relation. The Thou-being is by its very ontological constitution relational and can be constituted only by the I-Thou relation. Thus, an I-It relation would not constitute a Thou-being. Here indeed, the relation is ontologically primary and this means that the relation determines the kind of being involved rather than vice versa. (Of course, the presence of a Thou-being would as such necessarily implicate the presence of an I-Thou relation.) The It-being, i.e., the being-of-Power, on the other hand, is not relational in its very ontological constitution; it is not constituted by the relation. The relation is here external and, indeed, secondary. As such, the It-being is not determined by the relation and consequently an I-Thou relation towards it is in principle feasible as far as its constitution is concerned (though in the last analysis it is not really feasible inasmuch as the required mutuality for the I-Thou relation cannot be forthcoming from the side of the It-being and consequently the other, i.e., the "I" in the I-Thou relation which must be constituted as a Thou cannot be so constituted). What can be said for sure, however, is that vis-à-vis an It-being an I-Thou relation would not make sense.

In this connection it may be also noted, however, that Buber does mention an I-Thou relation with a tree. Does this mean that Buber claims the feasibility of an I-Thou relation with an It-being? There is no denying that it is very difficult to understand or accept Buber's claim. It is interesting to note that Buber himself, having made the claim, fails to develop or enlarge upon it; in the large corpus of his writings where the theme of the I-Thou relation is so pervasive, the application of this relation is confined almost exclusively to the domains between man and man and between man and God. Namely, the I-Thou relation is applied to beings-of-Consciousness and not to beings-of-Power. Still the claim that an I-Thou relation with a tree is feasible is made. How is one to explain it? Perhaps we can explain it by suggesting that Buber is reflecting here, albeit in his It-Thou terminology, the ontological view of Lurianic mysticism. According to this view, every being in creation is constituted alike — a *nitsots*, i.e., a divine spark, enveloped by a *kelippah*, i.e., a shell. Thus, there is no qualitative distinction in the ontological constitution of the realm of beings constituting creation. The only distinction available is a quantitative distinction — the thickness of the shell enveloping and concealing the spark. Now, inasmuch as the spark is clearly a Thou-being (while the shell is an It-being), an I-Thou relation with every being in creation is feasible and understandable. it is feasible with a tree or, for that matter, with a stone just as much as it is feasible with a fellow human-being. The only difference is that as compared to man, in a tree or, even more so, in a stone the shell is much thicker and the Thou-being is consequently less clearly manifested, making the establishment of a I-Thou relation that much more difficult. In any event, on the basis of this explanation there is no problem between Buber's assertion of an I-Thou relation with a tree and our contention that an I-Thou relation can be constituted only with a Thou-being, i.e., a being-of-Consciousness. For the I-Thou relation with the tree is constituted by relating to the *nitsots* which is a Thou-being, a being-of-Consciousness.

[4]The presentation of the snake in the story of the Garden of Eden conversing with Eve (Gen 3:1-5) is clearly a relic from pre-biblical pagan mythology; the story in which Balaam's mule is made to talk (Num 22:28-30) would seem to be a folk-tale; the presentation of trees talking in *Mashal Yotam* (Judg 9:8-15) is clearly an allegory. But even so there are very few such instances, and by no stretch of the imagination can they be taken to suggest that the biblical view endows nature with consciousness. Still, it must be granted that the further question of where precisely to draw the dividing line between the domain of the It-being and the domain of the Thou-being is not so clear or easy. That is, it is not clear whether the dividing line is to be drawn through the human realm or through the animal realm; in other words, it is not clear whether animals are to be relegated *in toto* to nature, i.e., to the domain of the It-being, or whether they are to be viewed as transcending nature to some extent, albeit minimally, thus sharing in the domain of the Thou-being. The latter view would seem to be reflected in the attitude of *za'ar ba'alai haim,* i.e., compassion for animals, and, even more significantly, in the commandment of the Noachite covenant according to which the blood of the animal is not to be eaten, for the life or the soul of the animal resides in its blood (Gen 9:4). This suggests the presence of the Thou-dimension in the animal, i.e., its soul or life, which as such, of course, cannot be related to as an It, namely, it cannot be eaten. Still the burden of the attitude towards animals reflects the former view, i.e., they are related to as It-beings inasmuch as they can be utilized and exploited as labor, as human nourishment, or as guinea pigs in experimentation.

[5]In the context of an ontological bifurcation that precipitates exclusively the alternative between a Thou-being and an It-being, the exclusion of the Thou-being necessarily implicates the presence of the It-being.

[6]In this connection it is important to point out that man's relation to nature being an I-It relation does not preclude the relation from being one of enjoying nature. On the contrary, enjoyment is very much an I-It relation; it is nothing else but a refined form of utilization. Enjoyment is contingent on perceiving the object as beautiful and beauty, in turn, is contingent on order, proportion, balance, harmony – all being functions of quantity which is an aspect belonging exclusively to the It-dimension. Likewise, man's relation to nature being an I-It relation would not preclude the relation from being one of awe and wonder before nature. Awe and wonder are expressions of the I-It relation if only because they are elicited by magnitude and complexity, i.e., quanticized categories, and as we have just noted, quantity is an aspect belonging exclusively to the It-dimension. Wonder and awe are contingent on perceiving the object as powerful and intricate – if the Power manifested is sufficiently overwhelming or sufficiently intricate, awe and wonder will be elicited. Both fascination and dread, beauty and awe are linked to the manifestations of Power and can consequently arise only in relation to an It-being. Thus, the various expressions of the enjoyment of nature or of the wonder and awe before nature which we do encounter in biblical and rabbinic literature, far from contradicting and undermining our contention actually fit very neatly and logically with it, namely, they are consistent with, and indeed, derived from the perception of nature as being constituted as an It-being.

Furthermore, the conception of nature as being constituted as an It-being would also not preclude the possibility of man participating in nature and feeling at one with it. For if we keep in mind that man, as we shall see more fully below, is viewed as being constituted as an It-Thou being, as a being constituted by both the It-dimension and the Thou-dimension i.e., as a being sharing both in the dimension of Power and in the dimension of Consciousness, then by virtue of his It-dimension man can indeed participate in nature and feel at one with it.

Thus, expressions to this effect that may be encountered in the tradition are quite consistent with the view of nature as being constituted as an It-being.

[7]See, for example, Is 27:1, 51:9-10, Ps 74:13-14, Job 7:12.

[8]See, for example, Job 38:4-8, Is 40:12, 21-22.

[9]The fact that we have here two different versions stemming from different traditions, and that indeed there are some significant variations and differences between the two versions, does not impinge upon our main thesis in this paper and consequently we need not go into it here.

[10]It is not surprising, therefore, that most treatments of the subject of creation in later Jewish tradition turn to this chapter as the main, indeed almost exclusive, source of the biblical conception of creation.

[11]Indeed, the other biblical references to creation given above, i.e., the references in Job, Isaiah, and Psalms, also deal exclusively with the "how" of creation and as such, aside from the other considerations given above, are not of much use to our purposes here.

[12]For time is contingent on motion which, in turn, is contingent on matter. Thus, the category of time can be available only if matter exists. Creation in time, therefore, necessarily implicates the pre-existence of matter. Only in the formulation of *creatio ex nihilo* is the act of creation not in time; here time is brought into being in the very act of creation. This consideration, by the way, should be kept in mind in interpreting the medieval formulations of *creatio ex nihilo*, particularly the formulation of Maimonides, as regards the *homer kadmon*, i.e., primordial matter. See especially I. Epstein, *The Faith of Judaism*, ch. 9 (pp. 88-92 in the Hebrew translation) and his disagreement with the interpretation given by H.A. Wolfson in his essay "The Platonic, Aristotelian and Stoic Theories of Creation in Hallevi and Maimonides" in *The Herz Jubilee Volume*.

[13]Here perhaps lies the rationale for inferring a *creatio ex nihilo* view from creation by speech alone, i.e., from the formula "And God said let there be ... and it was so." For one would expect that the creation, i.e., fashioning, of matter would implicate concrete, mechanical action inasmuch as only concrete, mechanical action can affect matter. One would not expect speech to impinge on matter; namely, one would not expect that speech can in any way affect matter. Thus, creation by speech alone would lead one to exclude matter as the object of creation. Creation by speech alone would imply the absence of pre-existent matter and therefore creation out of nothing, i.e., *creatio ex nihilo*. But of course what may be the case in the ordinary course of events is not necessarily also the case in events pertaining to the divine. Indeed, the Genesis narrative clearly states that the divine speech does affect matter. Thus, for example, in Genesis 1:9, God commands the water to gather in one place and it is done; or in Genesis 1:11 God commands the earth to bring forth grass and trees and it is done. Clearly, the Genesis narrative, taken in its own terms, does not support the inference that creation by speech alone would preclude pre-existent matter. On the contrary, it clearly implicates creation by speech alone with pre-existent matter. Thus, in the context of the Genesis narrative creation by speech alone does not imply a *creatio ex nihilo* view.

[14]Aside from the model of the artisan suggesting the pre-existence of matter, the very notion of creation here as the establishment of order out of chaos suggests the pre-existence of matter. For chaos and order are evidently but manifestations of matter – they denote states of the being-of-Power. Thus, the pre-existence of chaos would suggest the pre-existence of some matter which is in a state of chaos and which is then transformed to a state of order (the latter comprising the event of creation).

[15]G. Ernest Wright, *The Old Testament and Theology*, New York: Harper and Row, 1969, pp. 74-75. See also Benhard W. Anderson, *Creation or Chaos*, New York: Association Press, 1967, ch. 2.

[16]Is 51:9-11.

[17]See G. von Rad's essay, "The Theological Problem of the Old Testament Doctrine of Creation" in *The Problem of the Hexateuch and Other Essays*, New York: McGraw Hill, 1966.

[18]G. Ernest Wright, *op. cit.*, p. 80. This motif is also clearly stated in the treatment of creation in the Psalms. See, for example, Psalms 104-106.

[19]G. Ernest Wright, *op. cit.*, p. 76.

[20]The imposition of order over chaos and the model of the artisan express, precisely in their metaphysical signification, the fundamental pagan view of creation and are widely reflected in the various creation epics of paganism, though, of course, they receive their classic explicit expression later on in the Platonic myth in the *Timaeus*.

[21]This, however, is a partial signification of the notion of the divine. For a fuller analysis of the notion of the divine as it impinges on our topic here, see below footnote 50 on p 37. It should be noted therefore that we are not claiming here that the *creatio ex nihilo* aspect does in truth impinge negatively on the monotheistic aspect, only that such a view may suggest itself. In truth it impinges negatively on the monotheistic aspect only partially, namely, only when the notion of the divine is taken in its partial signification of absoluteness, i.e., of being the being that is non-dependent and non-contingent.

[22]Only considerably later on, in the medieval philosophic expression, is this implication grasped and is, indeed, taken as the basis for the claim that the affirmation of a *creatio ex nihilo* view is present in biblical thought from the very beginning. Though from a historical perspective such a claim would seem to be wrong, from the perspective of the inner logic of biblical thought it is insightful and valid.

[23]This is perhaps due in part to the fact that in the state of exile-existence (i.e., the state prevailing in talmudic times) the historical dimension is truncated.

[24]*Genesis Rabbah* I.15.

[25]Gen. R. XII. 14.

[26]Gen. R. II. 4.

[27]Gen. R. I. 14.

[28]See, for example, Gen. R. IV. 7 or I. 9.

[29]Gen. R. I. 1.

[30]E. Urbach suggests this with regard to the mythological references, most of which originated at the end of the tannaitic and the beginning of the amoraic period (Rav in particular is credited with a good many of these stories). See*Hazal*, Jerusalem: Magnes Press, 1969, p. 170.

[31]See E. Urbach, *op. cit.*, pp. 172-173.

[32]Also, in this connection one should note the number of amoraic statements rejecting the notion that the angels were partners in the act of creation. See, for example, the speculation in Gen. R. I. 3 regarding on which day the angels were created (the second and fifth day are proposed), but particularly the statement of Rabbi Isaac that all agree that it was not on the first day so that no one could say that they helped God in the work of creation. The significance of these statements becomes even more poignant when one keeps in mind that the notion of the angels being partners in creation is a common, central motif in the gnostic-dualistic view.

[33]Indeed, at times, this interchangeability is justified objectively by the intertwining of the two formulations, namely, when the creator, divine coeval being is identified with the created, substantive coeval being, the two becoming one being; this is possible inasmuch as the creator, divine coeval being here is a "nature god" and as such has its essence in the domain of nature, i.e., in the domain of the created, in the substance of the world. Thus, we get the identification of the "prince of the sea" or the "prince of darkness" with the primordial waters or the primordial darkness respectively.

[34]Thus, it is possible to have a dualistic formulation without necessarily having at the same time a negation of *creatio ex nihilo* as, for example, when the creator co-being is itself a

created being but created prior to the creation of the world. As such, all acts of creation may well be *ex nihilo* while at the same time in the creation of the world God has a partner. Theoretically at least, this should certainly be possible; but the status given to the angels or the "prince of darkness" in some of the rabbinic statements may well implicate such a situation in the literature. Of course, the negation of *creatio ex nihilo* does necessarily implicate dualism, but only in the fundamental sense of there being two ultimate independent beings and not in the more specific sense of there being a partner-creator which, however, is the sense in which dualism is used here.

[35]Hag. 12:1.

[36]In this connection, however, we should mention the view of Rabbi Judah in the name of Rabbi Simon that time existed prior to creation (see Gen. R. III. 7). Given our argument above, this should suggest the existence of primordial matter. This, however, does not seem to be really the case here. For the statement here reported by Rabbi Judah would seem to receive its rationale from the view propounded by Rabbi Abbahu that God created and destroyed any number of worlds prior to creating this world. As such, if anything, the statement clearly links the existence of time to the act of creation and consequently its clear inference is to negate the existence of primordial matter. The statement only pushes the act of creation further into the past prior to the creation of this world. Thus, while with regard to this world time is indeed already in existence, it is not in existence prior to any act of creation, i.e., from eternity. It is, however, this latter consideration which constitutes the crux of the matter and it clearly implicates the absence of primordial matter.

[37]Gen. R. III. 1.

[38]And therefore, as to the specific question under discussion, this excludes any consideration of precedence between the creation of light and the creation of darkness.

[39]The *ayin*, the nothingness, which he mentions would seem to be hypostatized; of course, we should also note that in this very same incident Rabbi Joshua ben Hananiah unequivocally rejects any hint of such affirmation.

[40]Gen. R. I. 9.

[41]See E. Urbach, *op. cit.*, p. 167.

[42]Y. Epstein, *Emunat Hayahadut*, Jerusalem: Mosad HaRav Kuk, 1965, p. 86.

[43]Hag. 2:1. This is also expressed in one interpretation of why the creation account begins with the letter *beth* – to show that "you have no permission to inquire what is above, what is below ..." Gen. R. I. 10.

[44]E. Urbach, *op. cit.*, p. 189. But strictly speaking, this leaves the question of *creatio ex nihilo* somewhat ambiguous. For even though, as was pointed out above, creation by speech alone may suggest a *creatio ex nihilo* view, creation here nonetheless may still be taken to signify the introduction of order into chaos, the mere molding of chaotic primordial matter into an ordered universe on the model of the artisan forming his artifact.

[45]See Yechezkel Epstein, *Emunat HaYahadut* (translation of the *Faith of Judaism*), Jerusalem: Mosad HaRav Kuk, 1965, p. 86.

[46]Thus, for example, see Saadia, *Beliefs and Opinions*, I, pp. 1-15; Maimonides, *Guide to the Perplexed*, II, pp. 13-31; Albo, *Ikkarim*, I, p. 23.

[47]Though here we have the notable exception of Gersonides. See *Milhamot Adonai*, IV.

[48]See, for example, Albo, *op. cit.*, I, p. 23. Maimonides, however, would seem to be a clear and important exception. Maimonides accepts the *creatio ex nihilo* view, but only because, according to him, it is not possible to philosophically prove or disprove the existence of a primordial substance. Namely, since rationally one cannot decide between the two alternatives, one is faced with an arbitrary decision between the Aristotelian position affirming the existence of primordial substance, and what he takes to be the biblical position affirming *creatio ex nihilo*, and in these circumstances (and only because these circumstances prevail) he opts for what he takes to be the biblical position, i.e., the affirmation of *creatio*

ex nihilo. But most significantly he adds that if philosophical arguments could be adduced in favor of the existence of a primordial substance, he would have no problem in adopting Aristotle and rejecting the affirmation of *creatio ex nihilo.* Thus, clearly, for Maimonides the *creatio ex nihilo* view is not an inextricable tenet of the essential structure of faith of Judaism.

[49]There are many attempts to establish this in conjunction with the Hebrew verb *bara* which is used in the biblical account of creation, as, for example, Saadia in his commentary to Isaiah, Maimonides in the *Guide,* III, ch. 10, Ramban and Bahia ben Asher in their respective commentaries to Genesis 1:1.

[50]In this connection it may be instructive to briefly compare the desacralization of nature in Judaism with the desacralization of nature effected by Greek philosophy. It has been claimed that the desacralization of nature is brought about both by Judaism and by Greek philosophy (see, for example, J. Ernest Wright, *op. cit.,* pp. 72-73). Judaism brings about desacralization by constituting the being of nature as a created being, i.e., as a dependent temporally finite being, while Greek philosophy brings about desacralization through demythologizing nature, i.e., by converting the nature gods into symbols. Thus, it is suggested that Judaism and Greek philosophy differ only in the way by which they effect desacralization (Judaism effecting it through its *creatio ex nihilo* view, while Greek philosophy effects it through its assertion of the supremacy of reason over myth), but that the end result attained, i.e., the desacralization of nature, is the same. This, however, is misleading. For clearly, the demythologizing of Greek philosophy desacralizes nature in a different sense than does the *creatio ex nihilo* view of Judaism. The *creatio ex nihilo* view desacralizes nature in the sense of denying it absolute being. As against this, Greek philosophy desacralizes nature in the sense of denying it personal being – it converts the personified being, the apparent Thou-being, which the mythopoetic imagination attributes to nature, into an impersonal being, an It-being. Greek philosophy certainly does not deny the absoluteness of the being of nature. Indeed, its very essence, i.e., the supremacy of reason, dictates its uncompromising negation of the *creatio ex nihilo* view (out of nothing nothing can come), and consequently its affirmation of the absoluteness (i.e., the primordial status) of the being of nature. Clearly, the notion of divinity and correspondingly the notion of desacralization bear here two distinct and different significations – personhood and absoluteness. *Creatio ex nihilo* and philosophic demythologizing each abrogate divinity, i.e., desacralize, in the sense of only one of these significations but not of the other. Still, in the context of Judaism this partial desacralization brought about by *creatio ex nihilo* actually effects the radical, total desacralization of nature. For, as we have seen, nature from the very start is already constituted as an It-being (and not as a Thou-being). In other words, as regards the signification of personhood, nature is never divinized to begin with, or in other words, it is already desacralized (and as such, with the desacralization effected by *creatio ex nihilo,* nature in Judaism is now radically and totally desacralized both in the signification of personhood and in the signification of absoluteness). In the context of Greek philosophy, on the other hand, nature continues to be divinized in the signification of absoluteness, and the only desacralization effected here is in the signification of personhood.

[51]No wonder that creation and theism are so intimately linked in biblical and rabbinic thought. Indeed, perhaps the real significance of the notion of creation by the sole agency of speech alone (a notion originating in the Genesis account and widely expressed in rabbinic thought – see the references to *b'ria bema'amar,* i.e., to creation by speech, as for example, in Avot 5. 1, Mekh. 10 (p. 150), Gen. R. XVII. 1, or to God as "He who spoke and the world was," as, for example, in San. 19 a) lies in the fact that it very much suggests the theistic structure – speech and command suggest over-againstness between the speaker, i.e., the creator, and the recipient or the object of the speech, i.e., the created.

In this connection, however, it is interesting to note that in the Kabbalah the formula of *creatio ex nihilo* is used in a context where creation is understood in terms of emanation, namely in a context that is pantheistic. This is done by identifying the divine with nothingness – God is nothingness. For the literal meaning of the tenet of *creatio ex nihilo,* particularly in its Hebrew formulation of *yesh me-ayin,* states that that which is (i.e., the *yesh*) is brought forth from nothingness (i.e., the *ayin*). But now on the basis of identifying nothingness (i.e., the *ayin*) with the divine, the tenet is made to state that that which is, i.e., the world, is brought forth from the divine – a clear expression of creation understood as divine emanation. Evidently, what we have here is a signification that is totally different from and, indeed incompatible with the signification that the formulation bears in the Judaism presented here. It is a good example of how radically different significations, i.e., essential structures of faith, can be held together under the rubric of the same historical religious tradition by virtue of the adoption of the same verbal expression of the tenet.

[52]Indeed, one is tempted to say that by the same token that God is viewed to be constituted as the "eternal Thou," i.e., as the being which by its very constitution cannot be but a Thou, nature can be viewed to be constituted as the "eternal It," i.e., as the being which by its very constitution cannot be but an It. By the way, it is this qualitative distinction between the being of God as the "eternal Thou" and the being of nature as the "eternal It" that provides the ultimate rationale, i.e., a rationale grounded in the ontological domain, for the non-pantheistic, i.e., theistic, posture of Judaism.

[53]This implicates a further radical difference between Judaism and Greek philosophy as regards the desacralization of nature, the difference here lying in the impingement of the desacralization of nature on the ethical domain. For while in Judaism accountability and responsibility for action directed towards nature are retained in spite of desacralization (or more precisely put, they are retained because of desacralization, the desacralization being effected by *creatio ex nihilo*), in Greek philosophy, precisely because there is no desacralization effected by *creatio ex nihilo,* the desacralization that is effected and which constitutes nature as an It-being leaves nature (*qua* It-being) as an absolute being (i.e., as an independent and coeval being), and consequently without any possibility whatsoever of introducing accountability and responsibility for the action directed towards it. Thus, in Judaism, because of *creatio ex nihilo* accountability and responsibility are reintroduced even though nature is constituted as an It-being; on the other hand, in Greek philosophy there can be no accountability or responsibility with regard to the action directed towards nature.

[54]See our comments above regarding Genesis 1:28 where man is enjoined to subdue and dominate nature.

[55]This constraint finds expression in the various laws coming under the heading of *Bal tashhit* (i.e., you shall not destroy). Thus, for example, felling a tree for the purpose of kindling fire is allowed, but when done for mere fun it is forbidden; or, killing an animal for the purpose of eating is permitted, but killing an animal for the sport of hunting is forbidden. On this latter example see the interesting responsum by Rabbi Yechezkel Landau quoted in S. Freehof, *A Treasury of Responsa,* pp. 216-219.

[56]This is particularly elaborated in rabbinic literature. See, for example, the laws pertaining to *shehita,* i.e., the slaughtering of animals.

[57]In this connection it is interesting to note the claim made by von Rad, that the notion of creation (a notion that is most intimately connected with nature and which, indeed, can arise only when nature is a central concern of the structure of faith) does not find expression in the ancient credo of biblical Israel nor, indeed, in the Yahwist and Elohist accounts. According to von Rad the theme of creation enters the picture considerably later only when it could be theologically linked with the distinctive and primary concern of biblical Israel which lay in the domain of history, i.e., encountering the saving acts of God in history. That is, the theme of creation, which originally and by the very essence of its signification is concerned with the domain of nature, when it is incorporated into the structure of biblical faith is given a signification that refers to the domain of history, i.e., it is the first of the saving acts of God constituting salvific history. Even so the theme of creation is not the central concern, and it is often used (e.g., deutero-Isaiah) merely "in a subordinate clause or in apposition ... intended to reinforce confidence in the power of Jahweh and his readiness to help." Only in wisdom literature does the theme of creation occupy a central position. Here it is "referred to for its own sake" and serves as "an absolute basis for faith" (see G. von Rad, *Old Testament Theology,* Vol I, pp. 136-139). Clearly, the Judaism presented here is not grounded in wisdom literature; it is grounded in prophecy and the historical narrative. Indeed, when in a theological context the alternative is set between Creation and the Exodus as to which is to constitute the foundation stone of the structure of faith, the Judaism presented here clearly opts for the Exodus.

[58] In Judaism, the religious drama and vocation revolve around man as a this-worldly entity (most significantly, the realization of the religious vocation does not transcend man as a this-worldly entity). Thus the preservation of man as a this-worldly entity is a condition *sine qua non* for the structure of Judaism.

[59] By the way, Judaism views this ontological constitution of man as an inextricable It-Thou being as good. Thus, the predicament is not located in the ontological constitution of man; it is not located in the very presence of the It dimension (there is nothing wrong with man being constituted in one aspect of his being as an It, as a creature). Rather, the predicament is located in the improper balance that man in expressing himself strikes between the It and the Thou dimension. The predicament lies in the fact that all too often man yields to the "imperialistic" tendency of the It dimension to dominate the totality of his life; even more specifically, it lies in the It dimension assuming the direction of life rather than submitting itself to the guidance and direction of the Thou dimension. Commensurate to this, redemption here constitutes itself not in extirpating the It dimension (thus constituting redeemed man as a "new being," as a pure Thou), but in restoring the proper balance between the It and the Thou dimension. Clearly, predicament and redemption are formulated here not in the ontological domain (indeed, we encounter here no doctrine of a Fall) but in the ethical domain; they are formulated not in terms of how the being of man is constituted but rather in terms of how man expresses and realizes the being that he has, i.e., in terms of man's behavior, actions and relations. Indeed, as such, i.e., being formulated in the ethical domain, the burden of the predicament centers itself on the imbalance between the It and the Thou dimension as it expresses itself not internally in terms of the individual as such, but rather externally in terms of the relation of the individual to his fellow-man (the imbalance constituting in this context social exploitation, i.e., social injustice); and correspondingly, the burden of redemption directs itself likewise towards the social context rather than towards the individual as such – it directs itself towards establishing the right balance between the It and the Thou dimension as it expresses itself specifically in the relation between man and his fellow-man, namely, it directs itself towards establishing the righteous community.

Furthermore, it is here, in the working towards establishing the righteous community, i.e., in the working towards redemption, that man by virtue of his Thou dimension is capable of being a partner to God, i.e., a co-worker and co-creator with God. Indeed, this is the meaning of the designation of man in the tradition as a partner to God. Man as a Thou is a partner in realizing the goal of creation, i.e., in bringing about redemption, but not in the act of creation itself; he is a co-worker in the making of history, i.e., in establishing the righteous community, but not in the making of nature, i.e., in constituting the physical universe; in short, he is a co-actor in the drama but not a co-worker in setting the stage for the unfolding of the drama. Indeed, in terms of reason and the workings of the inner logic of the Thou dimension, one may see that being a co-worker and co-creator is feasible with regard to history and society but not with regard to nature. The creation of nature (in the sense, of course, of *creatio ex nihilo* and not of the artisan shaping his artifact) is an act surpassing rationality and excluded by the inner logic of the Thou dimension. How a Thou can create i.e., bring into being, an It is a mystery which as such can be, perhaps, attributed to the divine (and even here, as seen, its signification is shifted from being scientific or metaphysical to being ethical and religious) but certainly not to man. Thus, when it comes to the creation of nature the tradition is quite clear that man is not a co-worker. In setting the stage God has no partners or collaborators; he is the sole creator. And man who is to play such a central role in the drama that unfolds on this stage is himself a created being. This is poignantly stated in *Sanhedrin* 4.5. The rabbis asked: "Why was man created last?" and they answered: "so that the heretics would not say: there was a partner with him (i.e., God) in his work (i.e., in the work of creation)." This represents the considered view of the rabbis and it is not undermined, it would seem to us, by one or two references in the Talmud which on the surface may appear to suggest that man is viewed as a partner to God in the work of creation. Thus, we have the statement of Rabbi Hammuna that a person reciting on the eve of the Sabbath "and the heaven and the earth were finished" is considered as though he had become a partner to God in the work of creation (Shab. 119 b); or, we have the statement that a judge who dispenses justice with complete fairness even for one hour is considered as though he were a partner to God in the work of creation (Shab. 10a). But these statements do not really say that man is actually a partner in the work of creation. The qualifier "as though" is crucial here to the proper understanding of these statements. What the statements actually say is that some acts are prized so highly by Scripture that a person who performs them receives the great credit of being considered by Scripture *as though* he were a partner in the work of creation. Furthermore, it is rather interesting to note which acts are so highly prized – the sanctification of the Sabbath and the dispensation of justice. Both symbolize not the work of creation but rather the goal, the end, of creation – that for the sake of which the world is created. (True, the two instances mentioned signify radically opposed notions of the end, the Sabbath signifying the cessation of activity and the transcending of the flux of creation, thus fulfilling creation by its negation, while justice signifies the proper dispensation and use of activity, thus fulfilling creation by its negation, while justice signifies the proper dispensation and use of activity, thus fulfilling creation by its affirmation. Evidently, these two goals have far-reaching ramifications and implicate radically different structures of faith, though we obviously cannot pursue this matter here. Suffice it to say that the Judaism presented here sees the goal of creation as lying in the pursuit of social justice.) We would want to say, therefore, that the statement "man is a partner in the work of creation" is to be understood as elliptical, its full meaning being that man is a partner in the work toward fulfilling the goal of creation. Such elliptical usage may be quite understandable inasmuch as the goal of a thing constitutes the very essence of the thing.

[60]Thus, each man should say "for me was the world created" (Sanh. 4.5). The world was created not only for me to enjoy (as the statement is sometimes interpreted to mean) but in order to make my very existence feasible.

[61]Indeed, this capacity to exact accountability is one of the essential expressions of his being a bearer of the divine image.

[62]Indeed, this accountability goes beyond my contemporaneous fellow-man. In terms of the first consideration it is extended to my fellow-man who is to exist in the future (though not to my fellow-man who existed in the past); for what I do to nature impinges on whether or not he would have the possibility of existing in the future. In terms of the second consideration, however, it is extended not only to my fellow-man in the future but also my fellow-man in the past; for the vocation of realizing the goal of creation, i.e., redemption, belongs to all the generations of man and the dead have a continued stake in the fulfillment of this vocation.

Chapter Three

Some Reflections on the Question of Divine Providence When Viewed in the Context of Mainstream Judaism

There can be no denying that mainstream Judaism, i.e., the prophetic strand within the Biblical period and the non-mystical halachic strand within the subsequent Rabbinic period, has consistently maintained the notion of divine providence as a fundamental tenet of its *Weltanschauung*. Indeed, so fundamental was this tenet that the rabbis defined the atheist, i.e., the person who negates the very root of the faith, not as the person who denies the very existence of God but rather as the person who denies divine providence. True, it has been suggested that this formulation came about only because it was unthinkable for the rabbis to entertain the possibility of denying the very existence of God; excluding this possibility, therefore, the rabbis moved to the next most fundamental tenet which is, indeed, the tenet delineating the involvement of the Divine in the affairs of the world. Alternatively, it has been suggested that the formulation receives this particular format because it happened to be formulated specifically in response to the claim of Epicureanism (where indeed, as is well known, the gods are left intact and are merely denied awareness and involvement with the world).

Now, both suggestions may well be valid. Still, is one to account for the fact that the Rabbis choose to respond to Epicurus, or that they choose Epicurus as the prototype of the unbeliever and, indeed, convert his proper name into a Hebrew common noun which comes to denote an unbeliever, a person who denies the root, merely by the fact that this happened to be the challenge that confronted them at the time? We would suggest that a more profound factor is operating here than the mere happenstance, the mere contingency, of historical encounter. For it is not as if any other philosophical formulation could have elicited the same response from Judaism. Rather, Epicureanism elicits the response that it does because its specific and distinctive formulation, i.e., its formulation whereby the gods are denied awareness of and involvement with the world, impinges upon the most fundamental and sensitive aspect of the structure-of-faith of Judaism. Indeed, we would want to argue that in contradistinction to philosophy, where speculation about God as He is in Himself does indeed constitute the very core of the philosophic enterprise, in the context of the religious enterprise such speculation constitutes idle luxury. For the core of the religious concern is not with God in Himself but rather with God as He relates to man and to the world. In contradistinction to the philosophic concern, the religious concern is never purely theoretical, a detached curiosity, a mere game of the intellect. The religious concern has an inextricable practical dimension to it; it is inextricably concerned with human redemption, with helping man. Yes, religion is concerned with God but it is just as much, if indeed not more so, concerned with man. As such, the concern of religion with God, and for that matter with man, is never really a concern with these entities in themselves but rather always an interest in these entities as they relate to each other. Thus, the object of interest for the religious concern is ultimately neither God in Himself nor man for himself but rather God as He relates to man and man as he relates to God. For religion the ultimate object of interest and concern is not an entity but a relation – the divine-human relation. As such, it should be clear that the Epicurean formulation, while it may not impinge upon the ultimate object of the philosophic concern, does impinge upon the ultimate object of the religious concern. The rabbis were right, therefore, in viewing Epicureanism as signifying the denial and rejection of their faith on the most fundamental level.

That the denial of Epicureanism goes to the very heart of the structure-of-faith of Judaism can be seen from yet another angle. For in denying the involvement and concern of God with the world, Epicureanism clearly implicates a denial of the God who is constituted as a Thou-God. This is so inasmuch as concern for the other, specifically in our case, concern for the world, constitutes the very essence of the Thou dimension. A Thou-God, therefore, must be by His very essence, by His very constitution, a God who is concerned for the other, specifically, a God who is concerned for the world. But if this be the case, then the view of Epicureanism must clearly be seen as rejecting and abrogating the possibility of a Thou-God, offering in its place the exclusive availability of an It-god. And this, in turn, means that Epicureanism hits at the very heart of the structure-of-faith of mainstream Judaism. For we would want to argue that the very heart, the very essence and the most distinctive feature of the structure-of-faith of mainstream Judaism lies precisely in its assertion that God is a Thou-God. This is the most fundamental and inextricable assertion of the structure-of-faith of Judaism from which all else follows. Thus, in denying and rejecting the possibility of a Thou-God Epicureanism does indeed constitute itself as a denial and rejection of the very root of the structure-of-faith of Judaism. As far as mainstream Judaism is concerned, God by virtue of his being a Thou-God must be involved and concerned with the world. Whatever else God may be, on this point of His involvement and concern with the world there can be no compromise.

Now, this involvement with the world, since it is derived from and, indeed, is the expression of a Thou-being, is of necessity to be mediated through the medium of time rather than through the medium of space. For a Thou-being is a being-of-consciousness (and this in contradistinction to an It-being which is a being-of-power) and as such it is perforce a being that cannot have extension, which means that it can under no circumstances be pinpointed or localized within space. Evidently, within the medium of space one can only encounter beings-of-power, i.e., It-beings, but never beings-of-consciousness, i.e., Thou-beings. A being-of-consciousness can be encountered only within the medium of time – it is in the moment rather than in the location that the being-of-consciousness and its primary expression in the act of confirmation can be encountered. This clearly provides the rationale for the observation made by Heschel that Judaism sanctifies time and not space. For at bottom the category of sanctification signifies nothing else but the presence of the divine (or, conversely, a belongingness to the divine), seeing that sanctification is, in the last analysis, a phenomenon that arises directly as a result of the presence of the divine or as a consequence of encountering the divine. Thus, inasmuch as the encounter of the divine here (i.e., encountering the divine when it is constituted as a Thou-being) is relegated exclusively to the medium of time, it is understandable that sanctification here would also be feasible only in the realm of time and not in the realm of space.

By the way, a further interesting implication of the above, i.e., of the fact that involvement and concern with the world are derived from and are an expression of a Thou-being, necessitates that the mode of relating that obtains here, i.e., the mode of relating that is established between the world and the divine constituted as a Thou-being, can only be a theistic mode of relating. The pantheistic mode of relating is clearly excluded here (again, the pantheistic mode of relating being feasible only in terms of It-beings, i.e., beings-of-power). In other words, in terms of a Thou-being the involvement with the world can only express itself in terms of encounter, of address; it cannot express itself in terms of infusion or identity. This latter mode of infusion or identity is feasible only in terms of beings-of-power. For while power does indeed constitute itself as a continuum, consciousness can constitute itself only as an over-againstness.

But be this as it may, the task that is much more immediate and far more important to our concerns here is to determine the nature and content of this involvement with the world. What kind of involvement with the world does the divine manifest? How does He express His concern for the world? We would submit that in the main there are two basic alternative modes in which such concern may express itself. On the one hand, it may express itself in the mere act of acknowledgement and acceptance of the world as it is. It expresses itself by the divine making itself present to the world inasmuch as its mere presence conveys its affirmation of the world. In other words, the concern for the world and thus its affirmation are expressed here through the act of divine forgiveness. The concern is established here by the divine giving and the world receiving – the divine only is the active agent while the world remains passive. On the other hand, the divine concern for the world may express itself in its demand for justice. Namely, the divine acknowledges and affirms the world by placing upon it the demand to establish justice. The presence of the divine connotes here a demand rather than a giving, a challenge rather than an acquiescence. Here is the world that is to be the active agent while the divine is merely to provide the challenge, the impetus for such activity. Clearly, either mode of expression would be feasible with respect to a divine that is constituted as a Thou-being.[1] For both express concern for the world and in that concern convey an affirmation of the world except that one does it by giving while the other does it by challenging.

Now, it would seem to us that in mainstream Judaism it is primarily the latter mode, i.e., the mode centering on the challenge for justice, that is operative. Namely, in mainstream Judaism the divine constituted as a Thou-being expresses its concern for the world essentially by challenging the world to establish justice. This, in turn, would implicate, we would suggest, that the world with which the divine is involved and for which it expresses its concern is essentially the human world and not the inanimate world of nature. For clearly, the challenge to establish justice, the demand to pursue justice, can be meaningfully addressed only to man. Moreover, it would further implicate that the human addressee here, i.e., the human pole in the divine-human encounter, be constituted by a collectivity of men rather than by an individual man. For justice is a category that applies not to entities in themselves but rather to the relations between entities, essentially to the relations between man and his fellow-man. Thus, for the category of justice to operate at least two men are required and this is already a collectivity. Finally, it would implicate that if the whole gamut of possible relations between man and his fellow-man is to be encompassed, the minimal collectivity that is required is the ethnic-national collectivity. Thus, if the demand for justice is to be applied to all the possible relations between man and his fellow-man, i.e., to the social, economic and political relations, then the human pole in the human-divine encounter must be primarily constituted by the ethnic-national collectivity.

Now, the fact that the human world with which the divine here is concerned and involved is constituted by an ethnic-national collectivity of men rather than by an individual man necessarily implicates, in turn, that the medium of time, through which, as we have seen above, the concern and the involvement of the divine with the world are mediated, be concretely constituted as history. For if the notion of the passage of time is not to remain an empty abstraction, the passage of time must be constituted with reference to a specific agent. And, indeed, what we understand by the notion of history is nothing else but the passage of time that is constituted with reference to an ethnic-national collectivity. It follows, therefore, that since in the context of the structure-of-faith of mainstream Judaism the passage of time is constituted with reference to an ethnic-national collectivity rather than to an individual, to say that the divine is encountered through the mediation of the dimension of time rather than through the mediation of the dimension of space (this being due, as we have seen above, to the fact that the divine is constituted here as a Thou-being and not as an It-being) is tantamount to saying that the divine is encountered in history rather than in nature. A god who is concerned and involved with the world is a god who is encountered in history rather than in nature.

Thus far we have attempted to establish 1) that constituting a connection to the divine is a fundamental and necessary feature of religion generally; 2) that the fundamental and distinctive feature of mainstream Judaism lies in the fact that it encounters a god who is constituted as a Thou-being, i.e., a personal being; 3) that in consequence of the preceding observation the god of mainstream Judaism is inescapably a being who is concerned for and involved with the world, specifically, the human world; 4) that this concern and involvement must express itself through the dimension of time rather than through the dimension of space; 5) more concretely and specifically, that this concern and involvement must express itself through history rather than through nature; 6) that mainstream Judaism opts to express the concern and involvement of its god with the world in terms of demand and challenge, i.e., the demand to establish justice, rather than in terms of acceptance and presence; 7) that the primary human pole, i.e., the human entity with which the divine is primarily involved and concerned, is constituted by the ethnic-national collectivity of men rather than by the individual man.

Of course the main point underlying this exercise was the attempt to show the inner-logic which operates within the structure-of-faith of Judaism, the inner-logic which connects and necessitates the expression of these various aspects within the structure-of-faith of Judaism thus providing the rationale for them. That these aspects are in fact present within the structure-of-faith of Judaism (and are, indeed, fundamental to it), both as it operates in the prophetic strand of the biblical period and in the nonmystical halachic strand of the rabbinic period, cannot be seriously doubted. Our sources, both biblical and rabbinic, amply establish this fact beyond any doubt. I don't think that anyone could seriously entertain the possibility of denying that the sources of mainstream Biblical Israel and Rabbinic Judaism clearly establish that their God is essentially constituted as a Thou-being, i.e., a personal being, that they sanctify time rather than space, that they encounter their God in history rather than in nature, that they address themselves primarily to the nation of Israel rather than to the individual Jew, and that their essential message and concern impinges upon the demand for justice. We did not try, therefore, to further buttress the factuality of these claims by reference to the sources. Rather, taking their factuality for granted we have tried to show how they all hang together by the necessity of logical implication – how one aspect necessarily implicates another.

But even more significantly for our concern here, it would seem to me that in the process of delineating the workings of the inner-logic here, we have also clearly established that if by the tenet of "divine providence" we mean nothing more than the divine concern for and involvement with the world, specifically, the human world (or more particularly, if the notion of "providence" signifies nothing more than concern and involvement), and if, further, the parameters of this tenet are clearly kept within limited boundaries so that the tenet is applicable only in the context of history and not in the context of nature, and then only with reference to nations and not to individuals, then such a tenet of divine providence is, indeed, a fundamental and inextricable aspect of the structure-of-faith of mainstream Judaism both in its biblical and in its rabbinic forms of expression. The tenet of divine providence when taken in terms of the above signification and with the limitations on its applicability is necessitated by the very inner-logic of the structure-of-faith of mainstream Judaism and it cannot be abrogated without at the same time tearing out the very heart of this faith.

※※※

We must recognize, however, that historically speaking the tradition did not stop with the delineation of the tenet of divine providence at which we have arrived at the end of the preceding section. Namely, from its very beginning, the tradition, it would seem, took an additional step which goes beyond what our analysis has required; it introduces an additional factor which our analysis above did not require and did not implicate. This additional factor is power. The tradition attributes power to the divine. And, of course, since the divine is ultimate and absolute, the power attributed to the divine must, in turn, be infinite, i.e., omnipotence. Needless to say, this attribution of power to the divine per force transforms the signification which the notion of divine providence carries. The significations of concern and involvement which fundamentally constitute the notion of providence may no longer signify merely a challenge and a demand (or a presence); with power, indeed, with infinite power, attributed to the divine, it is only natural that the significations of concern and involvement would now come to signify the actual governance and determination of events, the actual running of the show, so to speak, and not merely a challenge and a demand (or an acceptance). Thus, within the historical tradition of Judaism the tenet of divine providence comes to signify that God is running the show. It comes now to implicate the absolute lordship of God – YHWH is the universal Lord of history, the absolute Lord of the world.

The introduction of the factor of power, indeed, of infinite power, into the picture seems to instigate an expansion of the boundaries of the tenet of divine providence. It seems to propel the tenet of divine providence towards encompassing more and more territory, indeed, towards encompassing ultimately all available territory. For power is quantifiable and consequently its introduction into the picture here necessarily introduces the element of quantifiability into the delineation of the tenet of divine providence. Since the notion of the divine necessarily implicates the notion of absoluteness, the tenet of divine providence must ultimately come to encompass whatever there is to be encompassed (by the same token that the power attributed to the divine becomes inevitably, in the last analysis, infinite power, i.e., omnipotence).

Thus, it should not be surprising to see the tradition, at one time or another, attempting to expand the parameters of the tenet of divine providence in various directions. Three such instances deserve to be noted: 1) the Lordship of God over history is expanded from applying exclusively to the history of Israel to applying to universal history, i.e., to the history of all nations (of course, in this context the expansion is also propelled by the implications of the monotheistic idea), 2) divine providence is expanded to apply not only to collectivities of men, i.e., to nations, but also to individuals (this expansion would seem to have been first introduced in the Second commonwealth after 587 B.C.E., i.e., after the Babylonian exile, and to have come very much to the fore in the context of rabbinic Judaism, the Judaism of diaspora-existence – evidently, the loss of statehood and sovereignty is an important contributing factor for this shift), 3) divine providence is expanded from impinging exclusively on the historical realm to impinging on the realm of nature as well, indeed, to impinging on the world in its totality. It is expanded from impinging exclusively on the human domain, i.e., on the domain of conscious beings, to impinging upon all domains of being animate and inanimate, conscious and unconscious.[2]

Now, these three expansions in the parameters of the tenet of divine providence, i.e., the expansion to universal history, to the individual and to the world of nature, certainly find widespread expression within the concrete historical tradition of Judaism. There is no denying that they characterize the view of many within the tradition, and not only the view of the uneducated masses but equally the view of the learned rabbis. Still it is important to note that these various expansions in the parameters of the tenet of divine providence were not established (and indeed could not be established) in terms of the inner-logic delineated in the section above. It is introduced and established by attributing the factor of power to the divine.

The introduction of the factor of power, however, not only greatly expands the range of applicability of the tenet of divine providence, it also opens up the possibility for a most serious inner contradiction in the structure-of-faith of Judaism, precipitating a most fundamental problem for the life of faith of Judaism. Namely, it precipitates for all intents and purposes the problem of theodicy. For in adding to the consideration of justice, i.e., to the consideration that God is just, the further consideration that God is omnipotent, i.e., the further consideration that God is actually running the show in every one of its details and having the capacity and possibility to run it as He sees fit, one inevitably precipitates the challenge of theodicy, namely, one inevitably exposes God to the challenge that judged by our experience, life all too often is not run justly – the righteous suffer while the evil prosper.

Indeed, the challenge of theodicy is raised within Judaism right from its very inception when Abraham cries out "Is the judge of all the earth not to do justice?" And this challenge is raised again and again throughout the three millenia of Jewish history when again and again the justice of God's dealings with Israel is thrown into question, be it after the first destruction of the temple in 587 B.C.E. or after the destruction of the second temple in 70 C.E. or after the crusades in the 12th century or after the Chmelnitzky massacres in the 17th century or, finally, in our own day after the Holocaust. One might well say that Judaism is characterized by this challenge – rather than submit and accept, Judaism challenges and questions. Raising the challenge of theodicy is an authentic expression of the ethos of Judaism. Indeed, it is to be noted that in the context of Judaism the raising of the challenge of theodicy is by no means to be viewed as being tantamount to an act of atheism – an act of rejection, of rebellion or defiance against God. On the contrary, the raising of the challenge can be and, indeed, ought to be seen as an expression of faith, an act of witnessing. One might even go so far as to say that it is the primary act of witnessing. For clearly, in the very act of raising the challenge one inevitably introduces the implication that God is a being who is concerned with the world and who is just, and this after all is the bedrock act of witnessing to the divine on the part of Judaism (one is reminded in this connection of the rabbinic definition of an atheist, i.e., of an *epicorus,* which states "who is an *epicorus* – he who states there is no judge and there is no justice").

It may be perhaps precisely because of this consideration that the structure-of-faith of Judaism could go on functioning in spite of the fact that no satisfactory answers to the challenge of theodicy were really forthcoming within the tradition. Namely, Judaism could go on functioning with the challenge, with the question mark but without its resolution in an acceptable answer, precisely because the challenge and the question were in themselves acts of witnessing, acts of faith.

Of course, this is not to say that it is not incumbent upon us within the context of Judaism to try and come up with a satisfactory answer to the challenge. Indeed, in the long history of Judaism many different attempts were made. Thus, for example, we have the "solution" offered by the book of Job whereby the answer is to remain a mystery inasmuch as God's ways are not ours and our ways are not God's. Alternatively, we have what might be described as the "gnostic solution" in which the consideration of justice is cancelled out, inasmuch as the divine or, more precisely, He who is in charge of this principality, this world, is perceived as devoid of justice, as an evil god. If the god running this universe is indeed unjust then clearly the challenge of theodicy is removed.

Neither of these formulations, however, is really acceptable to Judaism. The gnostic formulation is unacceptable because it is, for all intents and purposes, tantamount to committing suicide as far as Judaism is concerned. For it means capitulating that which constitutes the very heart and essence of the structure-of-faith of Judaism, namely, the assertion that God is just. Evidently, Judaism cannot appropriate this solution and remain Judaism. And as regards the Jobian "solution," while it is true, as we have noted, that the structure-of-faith of Judaism can go on functioning without an answer and a resolution to the challenge of theodicy, thus being capable of accepting the claim that the answer to the challenge of theodicy is a mystery, inasmuch, however, as the mystery is offered here on the basis that God's ways are not ours, namely, inasmuch as the resolution here is based on a complete separation between the human and the divine with no common denominator between them (as for example justice), this "solution" is unacceptable. For the implication that necessarily follows from this is not only that there is no answer to the challenge of theodicy but that the very raising of the challenge is inadmissible. But, as we have seen, the raising of the challenge of theodicy constitutes a primary act of witnessing and consequently the exclusion of its possibility would have to be construed as an undermining of the structure-of-faith.

Indeed, the "solution" that is most characteristic and typical of the tradition of Judaism, a "solution" that has been invoked again and again in the face of the various tragedies that befell the community, is to argue that indeed the community has sinned most grievously so as to be commensurate with the suffering that befell it, a suffering which as such can then be construed as a just punishment. Clearly, this "solution," in contradistinction to the "solutions" cited above, attempts to achieve its goal not by adjusting and tampering with the status and attributes of the divine but rather by tampering and tailoring the evidence of our experience. It leaves the divine intact and turns to the human domain for adjustment. It is this, no doubt, that made this "solution" attractive to the tradition. Still, this solution is unacceptable. For one wonders whether it can really be authentically appropriated in the face of the overwhelming evidence of experience to the contrary. In any case, to deduce a conclusion on the basis of certain *a priori* assumptions and considerations of logical consistency, irrespective of what the evidence of experience indicates, must be unacceptable. Indeed, a good case can be made that the tradition of Judaism itself, when its better instincts prevail, would not accept it. Judaism is too much this-worldly oriented to dismiss the evidence of experience; as such, it cannot accept as true statements that go against the evidence of experience. It cannot countenance building its faith on a basis that belies the evidence of experience.[3]

✳✳✳

Obviously, in order to overcome the challenge of theodicy, an adjustment with respect to any one of the three factors which are involved in precipitating the problem of theodicy (namely, the factor of divine justice, that of the evidence of human experience and that of divine omnipotence) should suffice. For inasmuch as the problem of theodicy can be precipitated only if all three factors are present, it follows that it can be overcome or mitigated by neutralizing or adjusting any one of these three factors. So far we have dealt with the strategies that have tried either to remove the consideration of divine justice or to deny the evidence of human experience and we have seen that neither of these two strategies is really acceptable to the structure-of-faith of Judaism, although it must be granted that in both instances the problem of theodicy as such is clearly overcome. This leaves us with the third possibility which is to remove the consideration of omnipotence. Namely, to deny that God is omnipotent. Clearly, this too would overcome the problem of theodicy. For if God is not omnipotent then evidently He is not running all things and therefore not responsible for all things and this would allow one to exonerate Him from responsibility for those events that lead to injustice. What still remains to be seen, however, is whether this adjustment can fare better with the requirements of the structure-of-faith of Judaism.

Now, in attempting to think our way through to an answer, we must first note that the strategy, as it has been formulated thus far, leaves open the further question of whether it proposes to attain the abrogation of divine omnipotence by limiting the power attributed to God or whether it proposes to attain it by the much more radical step of denying the attribution of any and all power to God. Is the abrogation of omnipotence to be attained by merely denying the "omni" or is it to be attained by the much more radical denial of the very "potency" involved? That the formulation of the strategy does not not spell itself clearly with respect to this alternative is, in a way, quite understandable. For when viewed from the vantage point of overcoming the problem of theodicy – and this after all is the very *raison d'être* of the strategy in the first place – the difference between the two alternative approaches disappears. Namely, with respect to exonerating God from responsibility for injustice (i.e., for the unjust infliction of suffering) both approaches attain the goal equally well. Clearly, God can be exonerated from responsibility by denying Him power altogether – if He is deprived of any and all power whatsoever He clearly cannot be the one that brings about the suffering nor the one that has the capacity to remove it if He so chooses, and consequently He cannot be held responsible if the suffering is unjust. But God can be equally well exonerated from responsibility by merely limiting His power without abrogating it altogether; for all one needs to exonerate God from responsibility is some area (and it does not matter how small it may be) in which God's power does not prevail, seeing that we can then always save the exonerated from responsibility. Thus, indeed, for the purpose of overcoming the problematic of theodicy all that is needed is that the divine omnipotence be abrogated and it is not terribly important how exactly this is to be achieved, thus allowing one to remain vague on this point.

But if from the standpoint of overcoming the problem of theodicy there is really no difference between the approach which denies to God any and all power whatsoever and the approach which merely limits the extent or degree of God's power, from the standpoint of evaluating these approaches in terms of their acceptability to the structure-of-faith of Judaism there is most certainly a fundamental and all-important difference between these two approaches. We would want to claim this even though, admittedly, the claim would have to be confined specifically to Judaism (or somewhat more extensively to the family of biblical faiths) and not to the vast preponderance of all the other religions (i.e., the non-biblical, pagan religions) and even with respect to Judaism it would have to be established in clear opposition to the position that, historically speaking, Judaism (and the other biblical faiths) took. Let us attempt to briefly sort things out and make clear what we have in mind.

There is no denying that one of the most pervasive and persistent notions which one encounters in the study of the phenomenon of religion is the notion that the divine cannot be devoid of power. God and power go together inextricably. A divine being must possess power – for God to be God He must have power. This notion can be encountered in practically all religions. Indeed, more specifically to our case, it must be readily admitted that it has come to characterize the religious traditions of biblical faiths and as such, most significantly for us, the religious tradition of Judaism from its earliest beginnings to the present. Even more, seeing that Judaism and the other biblical religious traditions formulate themselves on the basis of the monotheistic principle, the attribution of power to the divine becomes here of necessity the attribution of infinite power. God must possess not only power as such but specifically infinite power – He must be not only potent but omnipotent. There can be no denying that in all its concrete historical expressions Judaism perceived God as possessing infinite power; its God is presented again and again as an omnipotent being.

Indeed, so deeply is this perception of the divine moored within the religious consciousness of Judaism, that in the many and various attempts to alleviate the problem of theodicy made throughout its long history, the option of tampering with divine omnipotence (and thus readily alleviating the problem) was not pursued. This becomes all the more striking when we realize that all the other alternative options (including even the abrogation of the attribute of justice in the divine!) were at one time or another attempted. It is only in recent days that tampering with the attribute of power in the divine has been attempted in some quarters. But, rather interestingly, these attempts have clearly confined themselves only to limiting the power of God, not to abrogating it completely. They do not propose a powerless God; only a God whose power is finite. Namely, what is tampered with is only the *omni;* the *potence,* the power as such, is left intact. Thus, even these attempts clearly reaffirm, in the last analysis, that the divine cannot be devoid of power. For the solution they offer is squarely placed within a context of divine power. That the divine may not possess any power at all does not come into question. The only thing that comes into question is the degree of power.

Indeed, one must grant that this solution is in many ways quite clever. True, it does compromise the dimension of infinity associated with the power that is attributed to the divine – the power that God possesses must be less than infinite. But this impinges merely on the monotheistic aspect (as we have seen, it is the monotheistic aspect that required the dimension of infinity) and not on the more fundamental and pervasive aspect of religiosity. And even this, i.e., the compromise of the monotheistic aspect, can be considerably mitigated (as many of the formulations of a finite God actually do) by rejecting the possibility of there being any other being possessing more power and, even more so, by safeguarding ultimately infinite power for the presently finite divine being so that at a certain point in the future it may well come to possess infinite power. Finitude is ascribed to the divine being only with respect to the present and the past but not necessarily with respect to the future. As such, the monotheistic aspect is not compromised in a substantial, permanent manner; it is merely suspended on a temporal basis. The solution, therefore, seems to achieve a most important victory, i.e., the overcoming of the problem of theodicy at not too high a price, indeed, at what would seem to be the least possible price. It almost seems to have performed the miraculous – eating the cake and having it too. Certainly, in the context where the divine is identified with power it must appear as an attractive solution.

To return, however, to our initial and main concern, it is clear that we have not established thus far the difference in the evaluation of the two approaches when viewed from the standpoint of the structure-of-faith of Judaism. On the contrary, our handling of the matter has shown that the two approaches are essentially the same, differing only with respect to degree. Namely, in both approaches we are in essence dealing with the limitation of power in the divine, the approach in which the divine is denied any and all power being merely the instance where this limitation of power is pushed to its maximal degree.[4] To press with the attempt to clarify and substantiate our claim, we must push beyond the mere description of the data (e.g., the various positions and evaluations taken by different historical expressions of the religious phenomenon) and inquire for the rationale, the inner-logic that operates in these data.

Now, in pursuing this line of inquiry, the first and, in many ways, the most central question that must be raised is the question: why is it so pervasive and basic in the religious consciousness that the notion of the divine is inextricably bound to the notion of power? Why is it that so many of us feel that a god must possess power, that a god devoid of power cannot really be a god? From whence this close association between god and power? The answer to this question lies, we would suggest, in the following observation: the divine constitutes itself in the very terms of the context in which its structure-of-faith (i.e., the structure-of-faith in which it operates) formulates itself. Thus, for example, if a structure-of-faith formulates itself in the context of power, or as we may say in the context of the It-domain (seeing that one may well argue that the It-domain is but the domain whose ontology is constituted by power), its divine being, as indeed every other being in its structure, will by its very essence be constituted in terms of power – it will inescapably be a being-of-power, an It-god. Or, to put it conversely, an It-god, as indeed any other It-being, can under no circumstances be devoid of power because it cannot possibly be devoid of the very dimension of which its being is but an expression and yet at the same time be perceived as in some way existing. Thus, when we feel that a god cannot possibly be devoid of power (i.e., when we have the sort of feeling of "what kind of god is it that does not possess power"), the god involved is necessarily an It-god. Namely, it is not necessarily with respect to any formulation of the divine that an inextricable association with power must be established; it is only with a divine that is constituted specifically as an It-god that such an association with power must be established. For it is the notion of the It and not really the notion of the divine as such that necessarily implicates an inextricable association with power. And if this be the case, then clearly the fact that the association of the divine with power is such a deep-seated feeling within us merely indicates that the notion of the divine as an It-god is a deeply-ingrained notion within us; and the fact that this feeling is so pervasive throughout the overwhelming preponderance of the world's cultures and civilizations merely indicates that the religious phenomenon in most of its concrete expressions does indeed articulate itself in the context of power, in the context of the It-domain – or in other words, it merely indicates that the overwhelming preponderance of the various concrete, historical religions have structures-of-faith that formulate themselves in the context of the It-domain.

Indeed, this can be shown without too much difficulty to be the case. Here is not the place, however, for us to carry out this task. Instead, what is all-important is for us to point out that there are notable exceptions. Namely, while we would want to argue that most concrete expressions of the religious phenomenon formulate themselves in the context of the It-domain, we would also want to argue that there are a very few expressions which do not. Specifically, we have in mind biblical faiths and here in particular mainstream, normative Judaism. Indeed, it is our contention that the very distinction of mainstream, normative Judaism (and of the mainstream expressions of the other biblical faiths) lies in the fact that essentially it does not formulate itself in terms of the It-domain but rather in terms of the Thou-domain – the Thou-domain, in contradistinction to the It-domain signifying power or matter as the constitutive principle, signifies here consciousness or spirit as the constitutive principle.[5] And again, while it would seem to us that this could be argued for without too much difficulty, it is also clear that here is not the place to do it. Suffice it to remind us that, as we have noted above, the distinctiveness of mainstream Judaism (and, of course, also of some other expressions of biblical faith) lies in its thrust to constitute the divine as being by its very essence a personal being, a Thou-God, so that one ought to encounter here the divine as the Absolute-Thou or the Eternal-Thou (Judaism and these other expressions of biblical faith being monotheistic, the divine must be absolutized in its essential aspects).

But if one wants to claim that in mainstream Judaism (and in other biblical faiths) one encounters the divine as the Absolute-Thou (as many of us, no doubt, would want to do), one must be prepared to openly accept the implications that follow. And the most significant implication here is the realization that attributing power to the divine is no virtue; indeed, it is outrightly destructive. Far from inextricably associating the divine with power, the divine here cannot be associated with power, not even with one iota of power. For power inevitably introduces the It-domain into the constitution of the divine, thus undermining the absoluteness of its being a Thou-being, constituting it instead as an It-Thou being. By the same token that a god constituted as an It-god cannot but possess power, a god constituted as a Thou-god cannot but be devoid of power. Thus, while the formulation denying any and all power to the divine is totally untenable with respect to a god constituted as an It-god, it is actually implicated and necessitated with respect to a god constituted as a Thou-god; reversely, while the formulation merely limiting the power attributed to the divine is quite feasible and applicable with respect to a god constituted as an It-god, it is totally untenable with respect to a god constituted as a Thou-god.

Evidently, the evaluation of the two approaches to the issue of power delineated above would differ radically depending on whether the god involved is constituted as an It-god or as a Thou-god. Indeed, it would not really do to judge the evaluation obtained when the God involved is a Thou-god from the vantage point of an It-god and vice-versa. For as seen, what is from the vantage point of the It-god unthinkable and unacceptable is precisely what is required and, indeed, implicated from the vantage point of the Thou-god and vice-versa. One must be very clear, therefore, from which vantage point one undertakes to judge each evaluation. Thus, if in our case, i.e., the case of mainstream Judaism, we deal with a god constituted as a Thou-god, and as such judge and evaluate the various alternative approaches from this vantage point, as indeed we should, then the approach which totally denies any and all power to the divine should be fully acceptable, seeing that it overcomes completely the problem of theodicy while remaining fully consistent with its point of reference, i.e., with God constituted as a Thou-god (indeed, all the problems that may arise with this approach would arise only when we unawares shift its point of reference to a god constituted as an It-god). On the other hand, the approach which merely reduces and limits the power attributed to God cannot be acceptable here, seeing that it undermines and destroys its very point of reference, i.e., a god that is constituted as Thou-god. Needless to say that in these circumstances the other consideration of overcoming or mitigating the problem of theodicy becomes academic (and although admittedly various strengths and advantages may be discovered in this approach, they would all arise only when we shift its point of reference to a god constituted as an It-god). Thus, from the vantage point of the inner-logic operating within the structure-of-faith of mainstream Judaism, where the linchpin notion is the notion of god *qua* Thou-god, the approach which denies any and all power to the divine should clearly be preferred over the approach which merely limits the power attributed to the divine.

But this preference of the approach which totally denies any and all power to the divine over the approach which merely limits the power attributed to the divine can be established not only exclusively with respect to a Thou-God (as we have just done above). We would like to argue that it can also be established with respect to an It-God even though, as we have just seen above, the inner-logic emanating from the notion of an It-God leads precisely to the opposite preference, i.e., the preference of the approach which limits the power attributed to the divine over the approach which totally denies any and all power to the divine. For there is yet another consideration, it seems to us, which completely undermines the validity of the approach which limits the power attributed to the divine and this irrespective of whether the divine here is constituted as a Thou-God or as an It-God. This is so inasmuch as this consideration is derived exclusively from the very signification of the notion of the divine as such and is totally independent of the implications of such further notions as that of the It or of the Thou. Of course, this being the case, this consideration will apply wherever the notion of the divine is involved, irrespective of whether the notion of the divine is further characterized as an It or as a Thou.

But what is this consideration? What is there in the signification of the notion of the divine as such that will give rise to it? Our answer is based on the claim that the notion of the divine, by its very essence, ought to signify the aspect of ultimacy and absoluteness – to be divine ought to necessarily mean being ultimate and absolute. Herein lies, we would submit, the qualitatively distinctive signification which the notion bears. Now, there can be no denying that such signification is clearly borne out in the context of monotheistic religions.[6] But at the same time there can also be no denying that equally clearly this signification is not borne out in the context of polytheistic religions. In the context of polytheistic religions the notion of the divine clearly does not signify ultimacy and absoluteness; there is no gainsaying that the gods of the pantheon signify penultimate entities (indeed, is is precisely because they are penultimate that it is possible to have a multiplicity of them). Thus, we certainly have a counter-example of the usage of the notion of the divine where our claim that the notion by its very essence ought to signify ultimacy and absoluteness is clearly contradicted.

What are we to say to this? Well, we can conveniently set the contradiction aside by limiting our claim to the monotheistic context. Namely, by qualifying our claim above (i.e., the claim that the notion of the divine, by its very essence, implicates the aspect of ultimacy and absoluteness) to say that it applies only to the notion of the divine that one encounters in the context of monotheistic religions, we remove the counter-example and hence the contradiction. For in the context of monotheistic religions the notion of the divine does indeed implicate, by its very essence, the aspect of ultimacy and absoluteness. Now, resorting to this strategy may be justified by more than the merely pragmatic consideration that it works, namely, that it removes the contradiction and thus makes the claim viable. It may be justified by the fact that our concern in this paper is after all confined to the context of monotheistic religions (seeing that it centers on that expression of the religious phenomenon which constitutes biblical faiths, specifically, mainstream Judaism) and that this being the case it is only understandable and, indeed, justifiable that we will be concerned with the characterization of the notion of the divine (as, indeed, of every other notion) only to the extent that it is carried out in this context. Thus, restricting our claim to the context of monotheistic religions is more than merely a clever formal logistic move in the art of argumentation; it has substantive validity in terms of the very subject matter at hand.

Alternatively, we can in a parallel fashion utilize the very argument, except that this time it will be carried out with regard to the question of theodicy rather than with regard to the aspect of monotheism. Namely, we can argue that since our concern here is with the problem of theodicy, the only notion of the divine that can be involved in such a context is the notion of the divine that implicates the aspect of ultimacy and absoluteness. For clearly, the problem of theodicy could not arise with respect to a divine being that is not ultimate and absolute, with respect to a divine being that is merely penultimate, if only because this would always leave open the possibility of shifting the responsibility for the injustice incurred from the divine to some other factor. Thus, regardless of whether the notion of the divine, generally speaking, must implicate the aspect of ultimacy and absoluteness, it certainly must do so when it is involved in the problem of theodicy. In other words, for us here, concerned as we are with the problem of theodicy, the only notion of the divine that is available is the notion in which ultimacy and absoluteness are necessarily implicated. Indeed, it should not be surprising in view of this that historically speaking the problem of theodicy arose in connection with the monotheistic and not the polytheistic traditions, namely, in the context of biblical faiths rather than pagan religions.[7]

Lastly, we can point out that in the context of polytheism the notion of the divine does not carry a qualitatively distinctive signification; indeed, its signification is merely quantitatively distinctive. In kind, the gods of the pantheon are at one with the forces of nature. Even more to the point, they are at one with man except more so – they are but man writ large (both being lodged ultimately within nature). But if this be the case, then polytheism does not really provide a counter-example to our claim. Our claim is made on behalf of a notion of the divine which carries a qualitatively distinctive signification while the notion of the divine provided by polytheism carries a merely quantitatively distinctive signification. The confusion arises because both use the same word, i.e., the same phonetic sound. But the claim is clearly not with respect to the phonetic sound but with respect to the notion which it represents, and here we obviously have two quite different notions. Indeed, the notion of the divine in our sense may be encountered also in the context of polytheism,.except that it does not refer to the gods of the pantheon but rather to the realm that lies beyond them, be it called Moira, Fatum, Ma'at or something else. And with respect to this realm the notion does indeed signify the further aspect of ultimacy and absoluteness so that far from counter-exemplifying our claim that the notion of the divine implicates by very essence the aspect of ultimacy and absoluteness, it actually provides a clear exemplification of it.[8]

But if the notion of the divine does indeed necessarily implicate the aspect of ultimacy and absoluteness (as we have already tried to show above that it does, certainly with regard to the notion of the divine which is involved in the issues under discussion here), then clearly the first of the two approaches delineated above, namely, the approach which proposes the mere limitation of the power arrogated to the divine, is really untenable. For this approach contains within itself an inescapable self-contradiction, seeing that it proposes to limit the power arrogated to the divine, i.e., that it proposes to constitute the divine as a limited, finite being, at the same time that the very signification of the notion of the divine necessarily implicates that a being that is divine be ultimate and absolute, i.e., that it be an unlimited, infinite being. It proposes to effect what is logically impossible, namely, to constitute as limited and finite a being which by its very definition is to be unlimited and infinite. To speak of a limited, finite God is a contradiction in terms – it is to state that something is at one and the same time both limited and unlimited, finite and infinite. Thus, this approach, notwithstanding the fact that in recent times it has found favour in some important theological circles, is really not viable for us.

We should clearly be better off with the alternative approach, namely, the approach which proposes to devoid the divine of any and all power whatsoever. For we would not encounter here the problem of a contradiction in terms as we so clearly did in the formulation of the previous approach, seeing that the infinity of the divine, i.e., its ultimacy and absoluteness, is not undermined here. Indeed, if its signification is properly grasped, this approach introduces no limitation, no finitude, whatsoever with respect to the divine. It introduces no intimation which may suggest that the divine in any of its aspects or characteristics is less than ultimate and absolute. We can see this when we come to grasp that what this approach really signifies when it devoids the divine of any and all power is not that the power possessed by the divine is reduced to a point of disappearance but rather that from the very start the divine in this context is not to constitute itself within the domain of power. Namely, the total absence of power from the divine is not to be seen as the representation of the last and most radical stage in the process of limiting and reducing the power arrogated to the divine. Rather, it is to be seen as the representation of the point of origination of a context that is qualitatively altogether different from the context presented by the other approach.

Clearly, the difference between the two ways of grasping the signification of this approach is very important, particularly as regards the consequences which may ensue. For with the former signification whereby this approach is seen as but a limiting-case of the limitation of power arrogated to the divine, we are clearly back to being saddled with the quandary of having a contradiction in terms on our hands in the same way as was the case with the other approach, seeing that the divine here is also constituted as limited and finite; indeed, it is constituted here as being the most limited and finite being possible, inasmuch as its power is reduced the most (indeed, reduced to the point of disappearance).[9] As against this, however, with the latter signification one overcomes completely any danger of a contradiction in terms, seeing that in terms of this signification the approach in no way undermines the claim that the divine be ultimate – it merely dictates that it be not constituted in terms of the domain of Power but in terms of some other domain. Given our analysis above, it should be clear that this signification, far from undermining, is actually quite congruent with the notion of the divine delineated above. For, as will be recalled, our analysis above yielded two essential points regarding the notion of the divine, first, that the notion of the divine does not necessarily implicate that it be constituted within the domain of Power (i.e., that it is not at all necessary that the divine should possess power) and secondly, however, that it does necessarily implicate its being constituted as ultimate and absolute, and both of these points are clearly met in this signification of the second approach.

Furthermore, the second approach (i.e., the approach which we recommend and which delineates the divine as totally devoid of any and all power) has a decisive advantage over the first approach (i.e., the approach which a number of theologians and philosophers in recent times have put forth and which delineates the divine as merely being finite, limited, in its power) not only, so to speak, in a negative sense, namely, in the sense that its apologetic escapes falling into a self-contradictory situation but also in a positive sense, namely, in the sense that a divine being that is constituted as an eternal Thou requires that it be constituted as devoid of any and all power. Thus, devoiding the divine of any and all power not only safeguards the ultimacy and absoluteness of the divine and in this way greatly strengthens the efficiency of the apologetic by avoiding positing a situation that is self-contradictory; even if this consideration did not apply, devoiding the divine of any and all power would still be called for if the divine were constituted as a pure Thou, as an eternal Thou.

Now, seeing how central and essential for the structure-of-faith of biblical faiths (and in our case here specifically for the structure-of-faith of Judaism) is the grasp of the divine as an eternal Thou, this last consideration, one would have thought, should certainly have clinched the argument in favor of the second approach. But this is clearly not the case. As may be recalled, we have tried to account for this in terms of the strong pull that the It-domain must exert and in consequence of which most people would find it very difficult to accept a notion of a divine that is totally devoid of power. Indeed, as we pointed out, so strong is the pull of the It-domain that the divine itself functions, for all intents and purposes, as if it were constituted not as a pure Thou-being, the eternal Thou, but as an It-Thou being. This bond of the Thou and It dimensions with regard to the divine must surely respond to some very important and deep-seated psychic and emotional needs, seeing how strong and widespread is the tendency toward such a bond in all concrete, historical religious traditions. No wonder that the preponderant tendency in theological circles is to preserve this bond, i.e., preserve the contention that the divine possesses power. It is, however, precisely our claim that whatever the psychological and emotional advantages may be, with respect to the intellect this bond exacts a heavy price, for we would contend that most of our "big" theological problems arise precisely because of this bond. When applied to the divine (as distinct from when it is applied to man) this bond becomes unholy, bringing about insoluable problems. Finally, we would submit that in the last analysis, the only way in which these problems can be overcome is by dissolving the very bond that gave rise to them in the first place.

It is these considerations which lead us to break with the preponderance of theological tradition, indeed, to fly in its face, and recommend that in our theology we consciously and openly affirm that the divine be constituted as utterly powerless – the God delineated in our theological edifice must be utterly powerless. As we have tried to show, such a delineation when judged in a theological context, i.e., in a context of rational thinking, keeps all the advantages on its side. It clearly removes the problem of theodicy and it does that without in any way compromising the ultimacy and absoluteness of the divine. Indeed, it is actually implicated by the notion of the divine as the Eternal-Thou, i.e., it flows authentically from the very workings of the inner-logic characterizing the notion of the Eternal-Thou. Thus, this delineation of the divine as totally devoid of any and all power is not only successful in overcoming the problem of theodicy but, unlike the alternative delineations which would also admittedly overcome this problem, this delineation does not have to pay a price for its success either in terms of undermining the notion of the divine or in terms of compromising the structure-of-faith of biblical faiths, particularly the structure-of-faith of mainstream Judaism. On the contrary, it is required by it and flows directly and organically from it. Lastly, at the risk of repeating ourselves, it is extremely important to emphasize again a point made at the beginning of this paper, namely, that devoiding the divine of any and all power is by no means to be taken as tantamount to devoiding the divine of any and all concern for the world. If it were, then indeed, we would have been compelled, notwithstanding all its other advantages, to renounce this delineation. For the very essence of being a Thou is the concern for an other – take this away and the Thou collapses. Thus, without a concern for an other, i.e., for the world, the divine cannot be constituted as a Thou. But no delineation in the context of biblical faiths could possibly accept it. After all, the identification of the divine with being a Thou constitutes the very heart of biblical faiths and as such it is non-negotiable (the deistic option is evidently not viable for biblical faiths). Indeed, as pointed out above, the tenet of Providence is so central and fundamental to biblical faiths because at bottom it carries this signification, i.e., because it signifies God's concern for the world. It is because of this signification and not because of any further significations which the tenet may carry that the tenet is so central and fundamental to biblical faiths. It is, therefore, very important to make it crystal clear that the tenet of Providence in terms of this fundamental signification is preserved in this delineation. What this delineation changes is only the mode of expressing this concern. God's concern for the world can now no longer be expressed in terms of His ruling and directing the occurrences of nature and history, of His, so to speak, actually running the show; rather, it must be expressed in terms of His continuous challenge and call to man to run the show better. This change clearly does not affect the point at issue here, i.e., God's concern with the world, and therefore is in no way detrimental; indeed, if anything, it is advantageous, seeing that the mode of expressing the divine concern for the world which it introduces is far more congenial to the *Zeitgeist* of Modernity than the traditional one.

All in all, it would be difficult to deny that the advantages of the formulation put forward here are very impressive. The one negative consideration lies in the poor psychological and emotional reactions which most of us would no doubt have towards this formulation. But to a considerable extent, this is due, we suspect, to our not being used to this formulation, indeed, to our being used to precisely the opposite formulation; psychological and emotional reactions of this kind are but manifestations of habit and familiarity. But if this is so, then it can be overcome in the course of time – we would get used to it as we got used to women occupying the pulpit in churches and synagogues. For now, what we have to do is not so much think about the powerless God as about the God who is constituted as the Absolute Thou, the Eternal Thou – and take this thought with utmost seriousness. If we do this, then we will inevitably be led, we submit, to the formulation recommended here.

---

[1]Indeed, these modes are feasible only with respect to a divine that is constituted as a Thou-being – with respect to a divine constituted as an It-being they would not make any sense.

[2]Clearly, attributing power to the divine would propel the divine to become involved in the domain of nature by virtue of the fact that a point of contact is now established between the divine and the domain of nature, seeing that the latter is by its very essence constituted by power.

[3]One should not forget that the friends in *Job* who were trying to do precisely this, namely, construe the evidence of experience to suit their assumptions, were rejected by God while Job, who kept insisting on remaining truthful to the evidence of his experience, is accepted as a "faithful servant."

[4]And as such, this approach is merely expressing the instance where the limitation of divine power is, quantitatively speaking, the worst but an instance nonetheless which is, qualitatively speaking, one and the same with all the other less radical instances of the limitation of divine power.

[5]We should note that this observation applies to the question of which domain serves as the matrix for establishing the constitutive principle and not to the question of how the structure-of-faith, established in one domain, may relate to another domain, which in our case will be the It-domain. By the way, with respect to this latter question there are obviously a number of different approaches available such as, for example, battling, transforming, capitulating to or escaping from the other domain; indeed the choice that is made here may serve as the criterion by which the various concrete expressions of biblical faith may distinguish themselves from one another.

[6]Indeed, the arithmetical oneness characterizing the divine, this being the obvious hallmark of monotheism, is but a necessary expression of the divine being ultimate and absolute, seeing that in any one system there can only be one entity that is ultimate and absolute inasmuch as ultimacy and absoluteness, by their very definition, cannot share dominion nor tolerate competition – one cannot have two kings sit on the same throne at the same time.

[7]In this connection, however, one should further note that while the ultimacy and absoluteness of the divine is a necessary condition for the problem of theodicy to arise, it is not a sufficient condition. Namely, even if the divine is ultimate and absolute the problem of theodicy would not arise unless the divine is further constituted as an It-Thou being or, put conversely, the problem of theodicy cannot arise if the divine is constituted either as a purely It-God or as a purely Thou-God. For in the former instance, where the divine is constituted purely as an It-God, the divine is evidently not a personal being, a being-of-consciousness, and therefore as such it cannot possibly be a bearer of responsibility; being an It, it does not make sense to hold the divine accountable for any of its actions. And in the latter instance, where the divine is constituted purely as a Thou-God, the divine is evidently devoid of any and all capacity to concretely effect things things and therefore as such it cannot possibly be the causal agent of any of the happenings in the concrete, material world; being a Thou, no event whatsoever in the concrete, material world, including any and all events of injustice, can be ascribed to the divine as their author. In the former instance, i.e., in the instance of the It-God, we can assign to the divine efficacy but not responsibility; on the other hand, in the latter case, i.e., in the case of the Thou-God, we can assign to the divine responsibility but not efficacy. Evidently, in order to be able to assign both – clearly both are required (in addition, of course, to the aspect of ultimacy and absoluteness) if the problem of theodicy is to arise – the divine must be constituted as both an It and a Thou, an It-Thou God.

And indeed, if we examine the instances where the problem of theodicy arises we will see that essentially it arises in biblical faiths where although the ideal thrust of the structure-of-faith is to encounter a divine being that is constituted purely as a Thou-God, the preponderant reality nonetheless represents a divine being that all too often is constituted as an It-Thou God. For as we have had occasion to note above, the pull and enticement of the It-domain are very strong. Perhaps, even more fundamentally, what constitutes the real pull is the tendency to perceive the divine in terms of man – to perceive God as but man writ large (and to perceive God as an It-Thou being is certainly to perceive the divine in terms of man). Indeed, viewing matters from this angle, we can see this same fundamental process at work not only in biblical faiths but also in pagan religions, except that in pagan religions it proceeds, of course, in the opposite direction. Namely, instead of introducing the It-dimension into the Thou-domain, it introduces the Thou-dimension into the It-domain. Thus, instead of arrogating power to consciousness, it places the face of consciousness upon power; instead of allowing consciousness to express itself through power, it personifies the manifestations of power. The end-result, however, is the same – the divine is no longer purely an It-being or purely a Thou-being but an It-Thou being.

But if this be the case, if in both biblical faiths and pagan religions as regards their concrete historical manifestations one ends up with an It-Thou God, then one should have had every right to expect that the problem of theodicy would have arisen just as readily in the context of paganism as it did in the context of biblical faith. But this is evidently not the case. The problem does not arise in the context of pagan religions; it arises only in the context of biblical faiths. How is one to account for this? We would suggest that this can be accounted for by the fact that whereas in biblical faiths the It-dimension is introduced into the Thou-domain on the level of ultimacy, in the pagan religions the Thou-dimension is introduced into the It-domain only on the level of the penultimate. Namely, in biblical faiths the It-Thou is established with respect to a divine being that is encountered as an ultimate and absolute being (e.g., in Judaism it is YHWH, the ultimate and absolute being beyond whom there is none, who is given power) while in pagan religions it is established with respect to a divine being that is encountered merely as a penultimate being (i.e., it is only the divinities of the pantheon that are personified but not the realm beyond them which is variously referred to as Moira, Fatum or Ma'at, the realm which constitutes the true ultimate and absolute being). But as we have seen, the problem of theodicy, in order for it to arise, requires not only an It-Thou being but an It-Thou being that is ultimate and absolute. Now, this two-fold condition is quite clearly present in the concrete, historical manifestations of biblical faith but not in the concrete, historical manifestations of pagan religion and consequently it should be quite understandable that the problem of theodicy would arise in the former but not in the latter instance.

[8]By the way, it is interesting to note that this notion signifies also an arithmetical oneness – the realm beyond the gods is one – thus supporting our further claim that the aspect of ultimacy and absoluteness necessarily implicates the aspect of arithmetical oneness and that indeed monotheism in this arithmetical sense is quite universal, seeing that it can be encountered even in so-called polytheistic religions. As such, a notion of the divine that is formulated in terms of arithmetical monotheism – and therefore a notion with respect to which the necessary implication of the aspect of ultimacy and absoluteness can be established – is by no means parochial but, on the contrary, quite universal in its applicability.

[9]No doubt those who prefer the formulation of a finite-divinity to that of a powerless-divinity share in this train of thought. Namely, they see a powerless-divinity as but a limiting-case of the finite-divinity and as such, of course, there is every reason to prefer the finite over the powerless. For inasmuch as we can all agree that in the last analysis, the finitude of the divine carries negative valuation, the less one has of it the better off one is. Now, clearly, there is less finitude in a finite-divinity than in a powerless-divinity, it being only partial in a finite-divinity while it is total in a powerless-divinity. But if this be the case, then a clearly finite-divinity is the lesser of the two evils.

Part Two

THE ANTHROPOLOGICAL POLE

Chapter Four

The Jewish Image of Man
and Its Relevance for Today

What is the image of man in Jewish tradition? What answers does Judaism give to the basic questions which inevitably arise regarding man? Who is man? Is he in essence spirit or body? Where is he coming from, and where is he going? What is he supposed to do with his life? Does his existence have meaning and worth? Is man intrinsically evil, or is he basically good and only corrupted by society? What is his relation to society?

These questions that man has persistently raised about himself constitute the basic concern of every religion. For religion speaks not to God's situation but to the situation of man. And the questions man asks about himself reflect the ultimate situation in which he finds himself. All else is contingent on the answers to these questions. Nothing makes sense unless man has a basic frame of orientation. The paramount task of religion is to provide this frame. And even though Judaism has not expressed itself doctrinally and systematically in theological formulation, and though its tradition reflects many nuances, Judaism offers a basic image of man which is definite and constant.

To examine this basic image is an undertaking that has a particular urgency in the modern world. The crisis which encompasses every facet of contemporary culture and life is at bottom the crisis of man. Who is man? is still the fundamental question, but the answer is not heard with a clear and unambiguous voice. The fierce and fearsome conflict between the various ideologies, religious and pseudo-religious, of our world is fundamentally the conflict between different answers to the question, Who is man? It is here that the battle lines are drawn and that the issue of man's future will be decided.

The Jewish view of man may have been promulgated long ago, but it speaks to man's present situation with the same force with which it was spoken at Mount Sinai. In these matters there is no obsolescence. The basic problem of Who is man? has not changed with time and the accumulation of new knowledge. In technology and science, the twentieth century is worlds apart from the biblical era. Yesterday's avant-garde ideas are today's obsolete fancies. The Bible, however, or, for that matter, the texts of any religious or philosophical tradition, are outside the passage of time. The Upanishads, the Bible, Plato's dialogues, are contemporaneous with every age regardless of the date of their composition. Two thousand years ago, man was confronted by the same mystery and challenge that confront him today. What changes and distinguishes one period from another is whether or not a period can accept an answer as the basic orientation of its existence, and what answer is accepted. An answer that is acceptable to the temper of one period may prove unacceptable to that of another.

This points to a basic difference between answers to scientific questions and answers to our questions about man. Questions about man are not scientific questions. They cannot be answered scientifically. Their truth is not objective and impersonal; it is subjective and existential. The answers cannot be deduced from empirical data, nor can their validity be tested in experiments. They can only be accepted or rejected. And what one person accepts as existentially valid may be rejected by someone else as meaningless.

This is what is meant when we say that these answers must be taken on trust. The risk is always present that the answers may be objectively false; yet we accept them on trust and hope they are true. For the believer, the truth of these answers will be decided only when the Messiah comes and ultimate questions will be settled. In the meantime, the only criterion at man's disposal is his authenticity to himself. Each person must decide for himself whether or not the answers speak to him meaningfully. Thus, it is not possible to "prove" the objective truth of the Jewish portrayal of man or to demonstrate its validity as against other portrayals. What can be done is to outline its basic features and delineate some of its implications.

I

The question Who is man? is short and succinct, yet it contains the most profound searchings and yearnings of the human spirit. And the answer that Judaism gives is equally short and succinct. Man is a creature created in God's image. The rest is commentary and explication.

The first thing to note about the statement that man is a created being who shares in the likeness of God is the paradox that it attributes to the being of man. It describes man as a creature, yet asserts that man partakes of the divine image, whose very essence is never to be a creature. Man belongs both to the natural and to the divine realms; more precisely, he belongs exclusively neither to the natural nor to the divine. Man thus appears to have a being which is suspended between two worlds, sharing in both yet never a full and exclusive citizen of either.

Does this mean, however, that there are ultimately only two distinct categories of being, the natural and the divine, and that the being of man is but a composite of these two elemental categories? Is man merely a derivative or combination which can be dissolved into its two primary constituents? If so, another question inevitably arises. Where, in which category, does the essence of man, his ultimate destiny, lie? Is man essentially divine, a creating spirit, although in his present existence he is fallen and thus limited by the natural and the material? Or does man essentially belong to the natural kingdom, although he possesses the peculiarity of consciousness and with it the ability of self-transcendence?

These age-old questions will become more familiar to us if we turn to the widely used distinctions between body and soul or matter and spirit (distinctions for which, by the way, we often use in most of the other essays of this volume the Buberian bifurcation between the It-dimension and the Thou-dimension as a convenient shorthand formula whereby the It-dimension stands for body, flesh or mater while the Thou-dimension stands for soul, spirit or mind, seeing that the former are but manifestations of power while the latter are but manifestations of consciousness). Thus, granted that man is a composite of body and soul, of the It- and the Thou-dimensions, wherein lies his essence and true self? Is he essentially matter or spirit, an It or a Thou? Plato answered that the true essence of man resides in his soul. But, alas, the soul of man is fallen and thus finds itself imprisoned within a body. The body is a mere prison which confines the soul. Man's true destiny is to escape the body and free the soul. The free, unfettered soul is man's true self.

A whole cluster of traditions – spiritualism, idealism, corporeal asceticism, Manicheism – which crisscross the length and breadth of the history of western culture emerges from Plato's view that man's true essence is his spirit and that his realization, therefore, calls for the negation of matter and all bodily concerns. But we also recall Aristotle's answer: man belongs essentially to the natural, material universe. His soul, or reason, is but a distinct attribute which his body evolved and by which he can be differentiated from the other members of the natural domain. True, man's soul and reason are the highest and noblest achievements of his evolution; nevertheless, they remain but aspects or attributes of his corporeal essence. From this view too, a whole cluster of traditions, such as naturalism, empiricism, materialism, has emerged, pervading the history of western culture.

Judaism – and Christianity as well, to the extent that it follows Judaism in this matter – represents a third position. For Judaism, the being of man is no longer a loose and dissoluble union of two primary categories of being, body and soul, an It and a Thou. Nor does the essence of man inhere either in a spirit imprisoned by matter or in matter evolving spiritual qualities. Through the union of body and soul a new independent and irreducible *sui generis* category of being emerges which encompasses body and soul, It and Thou, as one inextricable unit.

Thus, the being of man forms a qualitatively distinct and irreducible category of being. Soul and body, It and Thou, are inseparable dimensions or predicates of this being. You cannot have one without the other and still have the being of man. Man's essence inheres equally in both. Thus, the moment we speak, for example, of the soul without the body or of the body without the soul, we no longer speak, not even potentially, of the human body and soul as they are understood in Judaism.

This equality, this inextricable unity of body and soul, of the It- and the Thou-dimension, is a fundamental tenet of Judaism. It underlies the whole of Jewish thought and law. The body no less than the spirit is the creation of God. Hence, Judaism requires of the body just as much as it requires of the spirit that it bear witness to the glory of God. At the same time, it invests the body, no less than the spirit, with the sanctity and worth befitting the handiwork of God. The body's needs and functions are not base and despicable. Nothing could be farther from Judaism than the statement attributed to Epictetus that he was ashamed of his body. A Jew is called upon to worship God with every member of his body, each singing the praises of God's marvelous work. By the same token, he not only is forbidden to inflict on his body any form of molestation or deformity, but he is actually required to guard its health by proper nourishment and cleanliness. When the doctrine of resurrection was introduced into rabbinic Judaism and became part of the normative tradition, it was so formulated as to apply equally to soul and body. Although the notion of the resurrection of the body has been a source of severe intellectual difficulties in later generations, the tradition, with an unerring instinct, resisted any change and insisted that the doctrine applied equally to body and soul. Indeed, it had to, since man, according to Judaism, would cease to be man if one of these two aspects was missing. Man's body and soul are inseparable. Hence, man constitutes a third kind of being which is distinct from and irreducible to the other two kinds of being known to us, the being of nature and the being of God.

Consequently, any formulation which attempts to establish a continuum, partial or whole, between nature and man or between man and God must be rejected by Judaism. Judaism opposes pantheism, materialism and idealism precisely because they violate the basic threefold distinction between the being of the world, of man, and of God by asserting, to a greater or lesser extent, a continuum between them. Pantheism eliminates man and the world as distinct beings. There is only one category of being – the being of God. The being of man and the being of the world are ultimately but manifestations of the divine being, the sole reality and being.

Materialism eliminates the threefold distinction in the opposite direction. It declares that the only being is the being of the material world; the being of man and the being of God are reduced to the being of matter. Both pantheism and materialism are monistic views which assert the ultimate reality of only one kind of being, absorbing the other two into the one. They express a total and comprehensive continuum which stands in radical opposition to Judaism.

In contract to these views, idealism, in most though not all of its formulations, expresses a partial continuum. It distinguishes between the being of the world, on the one hand, and the being of man and God, on the other, but eliminates the distinction between the being of man and the being of God. A continuum is established between the being of God and the being of man, which in essence is reason or spirit. The being of man is eliminated, and we get a dualistic view with just two categories of being – the being of the material world and the being of the spiritual divine. Christianity could in many of its classical formulations ally itself with this kind of idealism. For Judaism, however, the distinction between God and man is basic and cannot be bridged under any circumstances. Consequently, Judaism must reject any attempt at man's apotheosis or God's humanization. The road of salvation in Judaism can never lead toward apotheosis.

II

The distinction between man, God and the world does not, however, imply that interaction and communication among them are impossible. For Judaism, the interdependence and interaction of the world, man, and God are just as fundamental a tenet as is their separate reality. The basic Jewish understanding of reality is in terms of *relation* or *dialogue,* not of *isolation.* The essence of man, the world, and God lies not in their isolated and self-sufficient being but in their relation, which is all-pervasive. But what kind of relation is it which, according to Judaism, binds God, man, and the world together?

Let us remember that in the Jewish definition of man the verb "created" occupies a crucial position. God created the world and man. However, the relationship between God and man which is embodied in the act of creation is still impersonal and general. It is impersonal inasmuch as it is based on God's impersonal attributes of glory and dominion. It is general inasmuch as it relates God to the totality of created nature; man participates in this relation only by virtue of the fact that his being is also a created being. This relationship is now concretized and personalized in a special relation which is established between God and man. It is rooted not in creation but in what is really the fulfillment of creation, in historical revelation. Revelation can be defined as "the fulfillment of creation" because the act of creation itself is already an act of revelation. It is the act through which God's power and dominion are ever-presently revealed. Indeed, this is the reason why some Jewish thinkers refer to creation as "continuous revelation." This "continuous revelation" is now fulfilled in historical revelation when God, through his free gift of grace, chooses to reveal Himself to the people of Israel at certain moments in their history in order to communicate specifically to man that He, God, is not only all-powerful and glorious but also compassionate, demanding, concerned, and loving.

In other words, God establishes a relation with man in which both "partners" are conscious, personal beings. In this relationship, certain demands are placed on man, and certain promises are offered in return. Through these demands man knows that God is a personal being who is concerned with man. God's concern originates in His love for man. This fact does not preclude the possibility of God's anger and displeasure with man. God, indeed, may also be an angry and punishing God. But the interplay between a forgiving and an exacting God is secondary to the fact that, in both, God is revealed as a personal being who is concerned with and aware of man.

The act of historical revelation completes the relationship between God and man established by the act of creation. Whereas in creation the relationship neither refers uniquely to man nor involves God explicitly as a personal being, historical revelation establishes a unique relation between man and a living, personal God.

It is only in this relation that man comes to know fully that he is not alone and isolated but that there is an ultimate, supreme consciousness which is always aware of him and continuously concerned with what he does. In the presence of this personal God man can never be alone. As Rosenzweig pointed out, the major achievement of Judaism was that it managed to overcome the isolation and loneliness of pagan man. In paganism – and this applies to the various expressions of modern and contemporary paganism as much as it did in ancient, classical paganism – man, in the last analysis, is alone. Ultimately, there is no other being that is concerned with him. The ultimate for paganism is blind, impersonal fate.

In this sense, modern man certainly lives in the context of paganism, seeing that his pervasive experience is of being alone. The technical advances of modernity have given man immense power but not companionship. To this extent Sartre has capture the authentic situation of modern man – he is alone. Whether man today accepts his situation heroically and stoically or tries frantically to escape it, his basic orientation shackles him to his tragic loneliness. The crowd, the multitude, the hectic involvement in activities, are but feeble reactions to his condition. In the midst of the many he remains alone – a tragic nonentity.

This sorrowful and pitiable image is, however, only one side of the coin of man's aloneness. The other side is the madness and irresponsibility to which aloneness tends to lead. There is no one to whom man is ultimately responsible for his actions. There is no standard, no demand for accountability to limit man's raving appetites and impulses. Brutal and impersonal power is the final judge and standard of man's actions. All is permitted as long as you have the power with which to back it up. Lonely man can be as tragic and pitiable as a driven leaf, but he can also be as terrifying in his cruelty as a ferocious beast.

Yet these psychological and political manifestations do not reveal the full depth of the predicament of aloneness. It is basically an ontological predicament. For the being of man is a being-for-someone and as such it needs continuous confirmation and recognition. The worst suffering man can inflict upon his fellow-man is to ignore him. Indeed, man would rather be hated, maligned, and beaten than ignored. For being hated denotes at least recognition and confirmation of one's being, and any kind of recognition is superior to indifference. Without the confirmation of our being we are nothing.

In the faith of Judaism, God, the ultimate personal being, is the "other" who confirms man's being. The man who lives in the faith of Judaism may suffer and be persecuted, but he is never alone. The believing Jew, therefore, never presents a tragic figure. In the midst of tribulations, his being and the meaning of his life are known and confirmed by God. This is the ultimate significance of the relation established by historical revelation. It confirms man's being and gives it meaning and value.

III

The relationship which creation and historical revelation establish is, however, not yet completely defined. It still is a one-way road leading from God to man, in which God gives and man is merely the recipient. True relationship must be a two-way street, a mutual give-and-take. The relationship, to be complete, requires then that man contribute his share; he must actively respond.

One way of responding is vertical – the confessional prayer which man can address to God. But there is another way. Man can respond through his deeds and acts which are directed horizontally toward the world. In the Jewish scheme of things, man responds primarily in the second way. Man is to respond to God's act of revelation by his deeds toward the world. The world, although created by God, is not yet completed. It still stands in need of redemption. And man is called upon to respond to God's revelation by becoming God's partner in the work of redemption. He responds to God by the way he acts toward the world. Man's relation to God, first established by the act of creation and then specified by the act of revelation, is now fully consummated in the act of redemption.

But it is precisely in the task of redemption – the final stage and pinnacle in the process of man's fulfillment – that man's transgression and evil manifest themselves. Evil exists or arises where man fails to respond to God – where he fails to carry out his task of sharing in the work of redeeming the world. Evil is thus a failure of will and decision. This failure, however, is not the inevitable consequence of the creaturely status of man's being. Man, admittedly, is a creature and consequently a limited being. This, however, is not the cause of his evil. Judaism utterly rejects the ontological view that evil is rooted in man's nature as a finite being, that as a finite being he is imperfect, and that, being imperfect, man cannot help but sin.

Judaism rejects this concept of "original sin." Man's finiteness and creatureliness are not the inescapable source of his transgressions. On the contrary, man is to live in accordance with his status as a creature. It is a constant reminder to him that he is dependent and that nothing is ultimately his by right. Whatever man has, be it his earthly properties, his talents, or even his very life, is ultimately not his own but merely entrusted to him for a given period of time.

Hence, evil arises not when he acts in accordance with his creatureliness but when he attempts to transcend it. It is when man forgets his status as a creature that he commits what to Judaism is the basic transgression and evil – the transgression of pride and rebellion against God. Only the awareness of his creatureliness keeps man within his proper bounds and restrains the Faustian urges that often culminate in inflicting cruelty and disaster upon mankind. It checks man's all too ready inclination toward arrogance and boastful pride, which can lead only to his self-destruction.

But if the creaturely aspect of man's being is not the source of his evil, we must seek its source in the other aspect of his being, the divine aspect. Judaism does, indeed, view the divine aspect of man as the source not only of his goodness but also of its potential downfall. The source of his spirituality and creativity can also be the source of his transgression and debasement.

To understand this seeming paradox, we must clarify what Judaism conceives to be the "divine aspect of man's being." In what way does man reflect the divine image? By possessing divine knowledge, divine power, or divine eternity? Surely not. These are attributes of perfection whose very essence is to transcend all finiteness, whereas man, as a created being, is neither perfect nor infinite. Judaism does not challenge this, yet it asserts that this created and, therefore, finite being is endowed with a will that is free. Man is a created being yet has an ability to choose and decide freely his course of action. And it is precisely in this ability that man reflects the divine image. For the unique aspect of the Jewish conception of God lies not so much in His attributes of perfection, omniscience, and omnipotence, nor in His mathematical unity, but in His supreme will, which is completely free and unconstrained.

Man, as the possessor of free will, is therefore truly the bearer of the very essence of the divine image. It is here that his creativity and distinctiveness from the rest of creation reside. Indeed, it is only by ascribing free will to man that the scheme of relationships which underlies the Jewish view of reality is made possible. For there can be no true two-way relationship between God and man unless man is able to enter it by his own free will. The relationship has meaning and validity only because man is free to enter it.

But man's very freedom involves the danger that he may choose not to enter the relationship. If man is truly granted free will and choice of decision, this possibility will always exist. Man can choose to transgress and do evil by choosing not to respond. Evil is thus the consequence not of his inevitable creaturely being, but of his free will which is the reflection of the divine image in him. It is important to note, however, that Judaism affirms the *possibility* of man's transgression, but not its *necessity*. Man may, but need not, commit evil. The good and righteous act is an equally open and feasible alternative for man. Good and evil are both contingent on his free decision, and one is as real and imminent a possibility as the other.

Because of this view Judaism has often been described as an "optimistic" religion. This designation is frequently used in a derogatory sense, especially at a time when pessimism is a mark of profundity. Judaism is said to be superficial in its optimism which, supposedly, fails to see the depth of human evil and man's utter incapacity to combat it, and which considers redemption an easy matter that is just around the corner. This view is utterly unjustified. Judaism is keenly aware of the frailty of man's good intentions and his great capacity for evil. It knows how difficult it is for man to do what is right and to live by it. It is fully cognizant of the other side of the coin – man's evil impulse. Judaism is anything but superficially optimistic about man's redemption. But neither is it utterly pessimistic and resigned, proclaiming that man is totally helpless and must await his redemption from above. Judaism knows the wickedness of man, but it also knows the good in him.

Thus, Judaism is optimistic, if optimism implies the faith in man's ability to choose the right and do the good. Judaism says not that it is easy, but that it is possible. And it can insist that it is possible because it has never despaired of man and creation. God created man and the world and, as God's creation, they are basically good. The story of the fall does not symbolize for Judaism the utter deprivation of man but the first in a long series of wrong decisions that man has made. It is the archetype of man's decision against God. But the possibility to choose the right was never foreclosed by it. As long as man is endowed with free will he continues to reflect the image of God, and the possibility of making the right decision remains open. Thus, man assumes an active role in the work of redemption. Much depends on what he does or does not do, for his actions leave their imprint on the destiny of the world. Judaism does not allow man to take what, in the last analysis, is the easy way out and say "There is nothing I can do about it."

IV

Three important corollary views emerge from this position. First, in maintaining that man has free will, Judaism places the burden of responsibility squarely on man's shoulders. There can be no responsibility without free will. I cannot be held accountable for something I was constrained to do. Only if I am given the capacity to choose freely and determine my action can I be held responsible.

Second, only with responsibility comes human dignity. Without responsibility man is reduced to being a cog in a machine manipulated by outside forces. The inviolable dignity of every man, regardless of his talents or station in life, precisely because he is the bearer of responsibility and thus of the divine image, is perhaps the most important facet of Judaism's relevance for today. The annihilation of this elemental dignity is the most imminent danger, aside from total nuclear suicide, confronting man today. The drift of our contemporary secularized and technological society is toward inhuman and impersonal totalitarianism in which man is deprived of all dignity.

Third, it is only in this elemental dignity that the equality of all men is found. We know men are not equal when we judge them by any of the naturalistic criteria at our disposal. We are not equal in our talents, health, disposition, appearance. Here inequality reigns supreme. Indeed, it is no wonder that in this context it is only death which can be considered the great equalizer; only in death are we all equal. As against this, however, if we go beyond the naturalistic context, if we allow man to transcend it, we can get another equalizer, indeed, an equalizer that operates in life, namely, we get dignity as the great equalizer. For dignity is invested in every human being by virtue of every man's ability to choose freely and thus to assume responsibility. We are equal because all men – from the bum in the Bowery to the great creative spirits of all ages – are bearers of the divine image. This fundamental equality in life transcends all inequalities that accompany man through life.

These three basic views are contingent on free will and can be maintained only if we assert that man is indeed endowed with free will. But the assertion that a created being has free will vis-à-vis God must lead to logical and theological difficulties. How can the will of a created being that is limited and determined, not itself be limited and determined? And how can one maintain an omnipotent and omniscient God and, at the same time, endow man with free will? Judaism, with a boldness of spirit that defies logical and theological niceties, has held fast to both. Everything is in God's power and knowledge, yet man is free to choose. Evidently, the intent of Judaism is not to offer a neat, objective, logically consistent, abstract and self-enclosed theological package, but to deal with the concrete, existential, human situation. This situation is paradoxical and full of tensions. Judaism is a way of life, not a system of thought. And here man is a created being, but he also mirrors the divine image. Man is determined and contingent, but he is also free to choose. Only by maintaining this tension is Judaism able to present us with its portrayal of man. The physiology of the human body works by maintaining an equilibrium of the tension between two opposites. The physiology of the human spirit may work in a similar way.

The faculty of the will is thus the locus of both man's transgression and his realization. Will expresses itself, however, in decision, and the matrix in which decision can be expressed and concretized is time and history. Consequently, man is view and understood in Judaism principally by means of the categories of time and history, not of nature. The Jewish portrayal of man is dynamic, not static. Man is placed in the movement of time. His life is seen as a drama of action whose center is the will. The will can decide, if only partially, the destiny of man, and the decision is made in time and history. Hence, the essence of man, its corruption and realization, is within history.

But true history is possible in terms of the group only and not in terms of the isolated individual. The primary unit, the carrier of history, is the community. The individual's destiny is immersed in and inextricably linked to the destiny of his community. Consequently, for any further understanding of man one must turn to the community of man. In our case we must turn to Judaism. The Jewish image of man must lead to and culminate in the Jewish image of the Jew, i.e., the image of man in the context of his community.

Chapter Five

Some Reflections on the Question of Jewish Identity

The Questions To Be Posed

If it is true that the essential meaning and significance of different eras in human history can be captured by a word or a phrase (for example, "enlightenment" for the 18th century, "faith and reason" for the 13th century, or "the age of insecurity" for our own time) then the present era in Jewish history is most accurately and insightfully captured by the phrase "the crisis of identity." For what essentially captures the situation of the Jew today is his bafflement regarding his own identity. This bafflement is clearly manifested in the persistent and widespread occurrence within present-day Jewry of two questions – "Who is a Jew?" and "What is a Jew?"

Evidently, both questions raise the issue of Jewish identity (hence the intimate connection between them) but they raise it on different levels. The question "Who is a Jew?" asks for the identification of specific individuals who are to be known as Jews. It raises the issue of Jewish identity, therefore, on a concrete, immediate, empirical level. As such, it is understandable that the issue would come before the public eye, i.e., receive its publicity, drama and notoriety, in the form of this question.[1] The question "What is a Jew," on the other hand, asks for the criteria by which to determine who is a Jew. It raises the issue of Jewish identity, therefore, on an abstract, general, theoretical level. At the same time, however, it raises the issue in a much more fundamental and essential sense. For, quite clearly the answer to the question "Who is a Jew" will be contingent upon the answer to the question "What is a Jew." For, if I know what constitutes being a Jew, namely, if I know the criteria by which a Jew is a Jew, then I should be able to determine which specific individuals do satisfy these criteria and which do not, thus deciding who is a Jew and who is not. There may be *practical* difficulties in determining whether a specific individual actually satisfies the criteria or not but in principle, *theoretically,* the procedure is unproblematic and straightforward.[2] Thus, if I have a satisfactory answer to the question "What is a Jew" there should be no problems with the question "Who is a Jew."

This means that the essence of the problem of Jewish identity lies ultimately in the present-day perplexity of Jewry over the question "What is a

Jew." It is here that the difficulties and problematics of the issue reside. Indeed, any difficulties connected with the question "Who is a Jew" are ultimately grounded in and derived from difficulties connected with the question "What is a Jew"; any specific concrete problem of determining who is a Jew inevitably points to and ultimately leads to the question "What is a Jew." To come to grips in a serious way, therefore, with the present-day problem of Jewish identity one must deal with its expression in the question "What is a Jew." It is this question that poses the fundamental problem and which cries for a satisfactory answer. But it is precisely the absence of a satisfactory, generally accepted answer to this question which essentially characterizes Jewry today.

Criteria for an Authentic Answer

Under these circumstances it is not surprising that we get today a great abundance of "answers" to the question.[3] If the search for and the acceptance of the answer, however, are not to be completely arbitrary, one must first of all be clear of what would constitute a satisfactory answer to this question. Namely, one must be clear about the criteria that a proper answer will have to satisfy. We would suggest that the authentic, proper answer will have to satisfy the following considerations:

(1) The answer must refer to, i.e., cover, the group and not the individual as such. Namely, it will not do for the answer to merely satisfy the individual so that he can say "that is what being Jewish means to me; that is the sense in which *I* am Jewish" and let the thing go at that. It may be very democratic and broadminded (it would certainly be in tune with the decidedly individualistic temper of our time) to allow such a procedure but the fact remains that it will not be tenable. And it will not be tenable for the simple reason that the term "Jew," i.e., the term whose position our answer must provide, is a term which is supposed to define a group and not an individual as such; it defines the individual only *qua* member of the group, only to the extent that it shares in that which characterizes the group. If the term "Jew" were merely to describe individualized characteristics then we could easily have as many different meanings of the term "Jew" as we have individuals who may choose the term by which to refer to certain aspects of their being. But as such the term becomes so relativized as not to tell us anything unless we spell out *in each instance* what it is supposed to stand for. And this, of course, means that the term itself becomes superfluous and meaningless. To the question "What is a Jew" the answer here will have to be "anything anybody fancies." Obviously, this answer is not a real answer but a veiled admission by the propounder of this position that the term "Jew" is empty for him. He does not really know what the term stands for. The answer is but a reiteration of the question, namely, of the ignorance that engendered the question in the first place, but with this distinction, that now the ignorance no longer evokes puzzlement and the search for an answer by which to dispel itself but is confirmed as that which ought to be. The ignorance is legitimized as the

desired, permanent state of affairs. Evidently this will not do if we seriously want to search for a valid, viable answer to the question "What is a Jew." In order to seriously deal with the question we must require that any proposed definition of the term "Jew" must contain the claim that the term apply not to the individual as such but to the group as a whole. Namely, even if the answer is put in the first person it must mean to say "I am a Jew in such and such a sense because this is the sense of the group to which I belong and by virtue of which I am Jewish."

(2) It follows that the definition of the term "Jew," i.e., the answer to the question "What is a Jew," will have to include all the members, and correspondingly exclude all those who are not members, of the group. For as stated in the previous consideration, the term we are attempting to define denotes a group. Hence its definition in order to be valid must enable it to fulfill its function and this is to account both for the inclusion of all members of the group and for the exclusion of all non-members. Any definition which would not cover all members or which would cover more than the members of the group would fail either to delineate the group fully or to set it apart as a distinct entity from other groups and thus fail in either case to denote the group properly. This means that the definition in order to be acceptable must capture that which is the common denominator of all the members and only of the members of the group.

(3) It further follows that in the last analysis it is not the individual but the group as such which must define itself. Namely, no only must there be a claim made for the definition to cover the group as a whole, but the definition in order to be valid must be appropriated by the group as a whole. If the individual cannot accept the group's self-definition it is he and not the group that has a problem. In the case of groups which are voluntarily constituted the individual has the option of either withdrawing from the group or staying in and attempting to convince the rest of the group to accept his definition (his definition, however, ceases to be a mere individual idiosyncrasy and becomes a valid definition only if and when it is accepted by the group as such). Indeed most human groups fall into this category, i.e., they are groups which are constituted voluntarily – see, for example, the various political, philanthropic, social, professional, religious, and other ideological groups all of which are formed through free association. There are, however, certain groups which are not voluntarily constituted but which are constituted by the objective factors of biology and history – see, for example, such groups as the family, the race or the ethnic group. Here the individual cannot withdraw and renounce his belonging no matter how strongly he may disapprove of or dislike the group to which he belongs. Belonging to the group here is not through the individual's consent (which can be withdrawn) but is imposed; and it is imposed not by human convention (which can be changed) but by unchangeable biological determinants and the fait accompli of past history. Thus, belonging here is

determined for the individual and it is determined at birth. The individual does not join the group, he is born into it. And once born into it there is no way in which the individual or, for that matter, anyone else can abrogate this belonging. The individual is stuck with it till his last day regardless of his views, feelings and wishes. The only possible question that can arise here is how the individual appropriates his belonging, how he relates to it, whether he succeeds or not in coming to terms with it. The belonging itself is unchangeable.

(4) This means that while the groups belonging to the first category, i.e., the groups constituted through voluntary adoption and consent, can freely define themselves as they wish, the groups belonging to the second category, i.e., the groups constituted through involuntary, inescapable imposition of belonging, are not free to define themselves as they wish. For while in the former instance the group is formed, so to speak, by its self-definition, in the latter instance it is formed by biological and historical factors. As such, in the latter instance the group exists as an objective reality, as a distinct, identifiable entity, prior to any self-definition. The objective reality of the group precedes its self-definition (it is constituted and exists as a group regardless of whether the group possesses a self-definition or not). Under these circumstances the self-definition of the group, in order to be valid, must conform to the given reality of the group. Otherwise it is mere wishful thinking, out of touch with reality. The self-definition here cannot be formulated arbitrarily in a vacuum and then through its application create the group. Rather the self-definition must be abstracted from the already existing, concrete, identifiable group, the group that is already a given, objective datum established as such by biological and historical factors. Its legitimate task can only be to capture the common denominator of all the members of the already existing group to the exclusion of all the non-members, but not to create or exclude members arbitrarily and wishfully irrespective of the given objective reality of the group. Now, if the Jewish group were to belong to this latter category (and we would want to claim below that indeed it does), then to define "What is a Jew" irrespective of the given objective reality of the group may be of interest in revealing the perplexities or the desires of the definer but it can have no validity as far as clarifying and articulating the reality of what a Jew is. For such a reality is not formed by one's definition (and it is irrelevant here whether the one is an individual or the group itself); rather the valid definition must conform to the given reality. Thus, not only cannot the definition of "What is a Jew" be left to the whim and fancy of the individual (see our first consideration), it also cannot be left (according to this consideration) to the whim and fancy of the group. For here the valid definition can come only to describe, not to create, the group.[4]

(5) Our last consideration extends the requirement of the previous consideration by introducing into it the dimension of history, i.e., the objective reality of the group in the past. Namely, the previous consideration required only that the definition conform to the objective reality of the Jewish group as it

is today. It applied this conformity, so to speak, only horizontally in the present. Now, this consideration requires the extension of the conformity vertically to cover not only the objective reality of the Jewish group as it is today but also as it was in the past. For after all the group here did not come into being just now; we do not start *de novo*. We are dealing with a group that has a history, namely, that constitutes an essentially homogeneous entity in the ever-changing ongoingness of history. Of course, the passage of time inevitably means continuous change and any entity subsisting in history, the Jewish group included, must perforce undergo change. But this is not to say that the change must be so radical as to impinge on the very essence of what constitutes the group. Indeed, if this were so we would have to continuously change the name inasmuch as we would have essentially different entities to deal with. To go on applying the same name to a group which has metamorphosed to an essentially new group is unjustified and misleading. Thus, if the Jewish group today is a new phenomenon essentially different from what the Jewish group of the past was then we should not go on calling it "Jewish" pure and simple.[5] If, however, the present-day group preserves an identity of the essential structure with the group of the past (and this notwithstanding the possible substantial changes in the manifestation of this essential structure, a claim which we would readily grant) thus constituting essentially one group subsisting through the changes of history and therefore justifying the continuation of the reference "Jewish," then we must take the past historical reality of the group into consideration in formulating our answer to the question "What is a Jew." For the term we are attempting to define, i.e., the term "Jew," refers to a dimension which remains constant through the changes of time. The objective reality, therefore, to which according to the previous consideration we are enjoined to conform in our definition is not only the objective reality of the present but of the past as well.

Now, the first three considerations are analytical and *a priori*. Namely, they follow from the very meaning of the term we are attempting to define here. The last two considerations, on the other hand, are embeded in experience and as such are in no way *a priori*. Namely, they follow either from our direct experience of the present reality of the phenomenon (i.e., the fourth consideration) or from our knowledge of its past reality (i.e., the fifth consideration). It is these last two considerations which constitute the crux of our problem. For any formulation which conforms to the objective reality which these considerations require will also satisfy the first three considerations. Indeed, only such a formulation can satisfy the first three considerations.

In view of this we would submit that the objective reality of the Jew is constituted by the inextricable union of the ethnic and the religious, namely, the Jewish group is at one and the same time, and is so inextricably, a community of faith and an ethnic reality, and as such only that formulation which succeeds in capturing this inextricable union can be valid.[6] We would further submit that what characterizes the various formulations of what is a Jew proposed in our day is precisely that they all dissolve this inextricable union, either by negating the religious pole or by negating the ethnic pole or, indeed, by negating both poles of this union. As such however, it is not surprising that in the last analysis they all fail to meet one or another of our considerations and consequently must be judged untenable. Let us exemplify this contention by examining some of the more prominent formulations which have been suggested in recent times.

Some Answers Suggested in Recent Times – Ethnic or Religious Group?

One such formulation current in our day proposes to leave the determination completely up to the individual. This formulation usually expresses itself with regard to the question "Who is a Jew" propounding that anyone is a Jew who so considers himself. But evidently the basis and justification for this formulation is provided by the answer to the other question involved here, i.e., the answer to the question "What is a Jew," an answer which in the circumstances can only be that the determination of what is a Jew is to be left completely to the opinions and wishes of each individual. For clearly one can leave the determination of the answer to the question "Who is a Jew" in the hands of each individual only if the determination of the answer to the prior question "What is a Jew" is left to be determined exclusively by the opinions and wishes of the concerned individual. Only as such could the thorough-going *laissez faire* view of this formulation regarding the question of "Who is a Jew" be propounded. For indeed, in these circumstances, and in these circumstances only, the answer to the question "What is a Jew" does not imply some objective norms by which one could further determine the answer to the question "Who is a Jew" thus perforce leaving this determination to be arbitrarily decided by each individual according to his whim and fancy. But to allow each individual the role of deciding arbitrarily whether or not he belongs to the Jewish group is just as self-defeating and senseless as leaving the determination of the meaning of the term "Jew" to the arbitrary notion of the individual. A group that allows anybody to belong to it on his own arbitrary terms does not stand for anything. As a group it is meaningless. It has no meaning of its own, for if it did it obviously would not have been possible for it to allow the ascription to itself of any meaning whatsoever. To be potentially everything is to be nothing in particular.

The individualistic formulation of the answer to the question "Who is a Jew" given here which manifestly presupposes the parallel individualistic formulation of the answer to the question "What is a Jew" is evidently in direct contradiction to the requirement stated by our first consideration and as such cannot be valid. He who propounds it is in truth but confessing that Jewish reality has become bankrupt and irrelevant for him. The seeming tolerance and broadmindedness shown here are in truth false, stemming from unconcern and irrelevancy. For only he to whom Jewish reality is meaningless and of no concern could propound a view which states in effect "do with it what you want, let it be the possession of whoever wants it with no questions asked."

It is interesting to note that this radical admission finds expression more widely and readily among Israeli Jewry than among diaspora Jewry. This may be explained perhaps by the fact that Israeli Jewry has another form of belonging, i.e., identification, which is emerging and on which it can fall back, an alternative which is not available to diaspora Jewry; this other form is an Israeli, as distinct from a Jewish, belongingness. Having an Israeli belongingness emerging for him, the Israeli Jew can afford to express the problematics of Jewish belongingness in its most radical form, namely, in a form which completely empties it of all objective meaning thus in essence disposing of it completely. The diaspora Jew, on the other hand, to the extent that he remains Jewish and as such not having any other form of belongingness emerging to replace his Jewish belongingness, cannot afford to empty his Jewish belonging of all objective meaning no matter how problematic this belonging has become for him (indeed, we will find that formulations current in diaspora Jewry invest the notion of the Jew with some, no matter how minimal, objective meaning). In this connection, by the way, it is interesting to note that this "tolerance" and "openness" vis-à-vis Jewish belonging, which this formulation current among Israeli Jewry manifests, are *in effect* offered not to the world at large but only to those living in and wishing to be identified with Israel. Namely, it is only with regard to people living in Israel who wish to consider themselves Jewish that this formulation would leave such determination to the subjective whims and wishes of the individual. But what is really interesting to note is the further observation that in this context when it comes to determining Israeli belongingness (as distinct from Jewish belongingness) this "tolerance" and "openness" are completely lacking. Belongingness to Israel is not allowed to be determined by the fancy and whim of the individual whoever and wherever he may be; rather, it is insisted upon that it be determined by such objective criteria as, for example, actual residency in the country, the assumption of citizenship responsibilities, participating in the life and destiny of the community, speaking its language, living its culture, etc. Thus, the *laissez faire* formulation of Jewish belonging encountered among Israeli Jewry, is to be seen as an aspect of the attempt to substitute Israeli belongingness (not only in a political but in an ethnic sense) for Jewish belongingness. Jewish belongingness is recognized at best as having been valid in the past but its validity for the present and future is denied. Not wanting to allow the criteria for Jewish-belonging to interfere with the new criteria of Israeli-belonging, Jewish-belonging is interpreted in such a way that, as we have seen, it cannot possibly function and in this way it is for all intents and purposes abrogated. But what the substitution of Israeli-belongingness for Jewish-belongingness ultimately means is the extirpation of the religious dimension (a dimension which is, in our view, of the very essence of Jewish-belongingness) leaving the ethnic dimension as the sole dimension. Namely, Israeli-belongingness differs from Jewish-belongingness in that it reduces the polarity of the ethnic and the religious, the polarity which constitutes the essence of Jewish-belongingness, to the ethnic dimension exclusively, seeing the ethnic as the sole dimension constituting the essence of the Jew. As such, according to this formulation, the religious dimension, though it may well have characterized the Jew in the past widely and persistently, never constituted part of his essence (the essence having been always constituted exclusively by the ethnic) and as such it can be dispensed with as indeed it is by so many Israelis.

As against this formulation which settles on the ethnic exclusively another wide-spread current formulation – this time among diaspora but not Israeli Jewry – maintains that the term "Jew" denotes a purely religious affiliation. The Jew is but a member of a religious group. It understands the denotation of the term "Jew" as equal to the denotation of the term "Christian," namely, as denoting communities of faith, pure and simple. The crux of this formulation is that the term "Jew" as defined here is, like the term "Christian," deprived of any ethnic denotation. The Jewish group as a purely religious group is conceived as transcending and criss-crossing the various ethnic groupings and in no way impinging upon this dimension of man's belongingness. Thus, the Jew, as here understood, may belong to any ethnic group and indeed this formulation claims that in fact he does belong to a great many and varied ethnic groups. The only common denominator uniting these various ethnically-belonging people, characterized by affixing the adjective "Jew" to them, is their belonging to the same religious group, i.e., the Jewish community of faith.

In order for us to better grasp this formulation, however, we should be clear about how it perceives the notion of religion when it propounds it as the sole meaning of the term "Jew." Now, we would submit that for this formulation religion is essentially a set of universal, eternal, abstract truths and the religious community is that group which carries these truths by confessing and proclaiming its belief in their validity. (Usually this formulation will attribute to Judaism a set of ethical beliefs in contradistinction to the noetic-metaphysical beliefs which it attributes to Christianity.) What is important for us to note in this connection is that this means that the phenomenon of religion is structured here essentially in terms of the individual. For as a set of universal and abstract truths, namely, truths which are not mediated through concrete history, religion bypasses the historical-ethnic group and is made accessible directly to the individual. Conversely, it can be witnessed to, in the last analysis, only by the individual *qua* individual for the witnessing calls for the free, volitional act of belief which only the individual as individual can provide. The religious community here, therefore, is but the grouping, the sum-total, of such professing, believing individuals. It is constituted by these individuals through their free association. Thus, it is the believing, professing individual who is the primary entity here while the religious community is but a secondary, derivative entity. As such, the primary aim of this formulation, indeed the very *raison d'être* for its being propounded, is safeguarded. For when religion is thus understood it can have no ties to the ethnic dimension. For such a religion can in no way claim its members at birth and by virtue of this moment of birth hold on to them irrespective of what they believe or do. It is important to emphasize this point, for evidently if the religion which this formulation ascribes to the Jewish group were such that it could claim its members at birth then it would inevitably be linked to the ethnic dimension and thus present a totally different picture as far as our analysis and evaluation are concerned. Indeed, if this were what this formulation meant by religion then we would have had to conclude that the definition which it presents is quite valid, for clearly by saying that the Jewish group is only a religious group we would be in effect saying also that it is an ethnic group. But this obviously is not the intention of this formulation. On the contrary, the very essence of its intention is precisely to reject any ethnic belonging. When it says that the Jewish group is only a religious group it wants to say that it is religious to the exclusion of any ethnic belonging, namely, that it is a confession of certain beliefs which as such carries no ethnic connotation. It uses the category religion as it is commonly understood in the West as transcending and distinctly separated from any ethnic belonging.

But defining the Jew as exclusively religious in this sense manifestly fails to meet our considerations and as such must be judged by us as untenable. For certainly there are many people today who everyone would take to be Jews (and legitimately so since they do constitute a part of the objective reality of Jewry) but who clearly do not profess the religion of Judaism, or for that matter any other religion, as conceived in this formulation. We are not referring here to the even greater number of people who are universally considered to be Jews and who do not *actively* profess and practice the religion. These could still be viewed perhaps as nominal members of the religious group – poor, minimal members but still members – and as such fall under this purely religious common denominator. We are referring to those people, and their number is by no means small, who consciously and actively reject every profession of the Jewish religion and religion in general being thorough-going, jealously fanatic atheists or agnostics. How can these people be considered Jews if the term "Jew" is to denote exclusively a religious group in the sense of this formulation, i.e., a community of faith pure and simple? But these people are Jews! This means that the formulation fails to account for all the members of the group or, to put the matter differently, that the common denominator which it propose fails to capture adequately the bond given in objective reality which unites all members of the group (as our second and third considerations would require). For example, it fails to capture the bond that unites an atheist Jew from Poland and an observant, believing Jew from Morocco. According to this formulation there is no common bond between the two (except of course, the universal bond of humanity) and the former, strictly speaking, should not indeed be considered a Jew[7]. Or even more poignantly, it must fail in capturing any Jewish common bond between two brothers or a father and a son when one believes and practices the truths of the Jewish religion while the other professes himself an atheist. By this formulation one is a Jew while the other is not. It should be clear without having to go on presenting other examples that this formulation patently fails to conform to, and thus to cover satisfactorily, the reality of the Jewish phenomenon.

But this is not all. This formulation presents us with a further difficulty which is even more manifest and fundamental. For the question must inevitably arise as to the ethnic belonging of these Jews who according to this formulation are by virtue of their Jewishness merely members of a religious community which excludes any ethnic belonging. Given the way the world is, mankind is divided into ethnic groups and every individual perforce must belong to some ethnic group. To be a floating member of mankind in general without some distinct ethnic membership is just not feasible and anyone who puts forth such a claim is merely indulging in wishful daydreaming. Thus, the question remains "What is the ethnic belonging of the members of this Jewish group if this group is purely a community of faith?" The answer which this formulation gives (and which indeed it wants to but also must give) is that the ethnic belonging of the Jews is as varied as the ethnic constitution of the various countries to which they belong. Namely, the proponents of this formulation in Germany claimed to be ethnically German, and those in England English, and in France French, etc. But such a claim is manifestly contrary to what the objective reality is. The French Jew or the German Jew can shout as loud as he wishes that he is ethnically French or German, the fact remains that he is not. Indeed, even if the ethnic group in question was ready to consider him as ethnically belonging to it (a speculation which is purely hypothetical for the sake of making a point and which in reality is as farfetched as anything could be), it would still not be the case. For ethnic membership is not determined by voluntary, human consent. It is not in the hands of man, not even of the group as a whole, to bestow or to withdraw. It is determined objectively by past history and the moment of birth – two factors which are simply not changeable by human volition.

Race and Land?

That such a claim could at all be entertained by some is due to the fact that the ethnic dimension in emancipated Jewry is greatly weakened in its expression, though not in its reality, and as such is being obscured thus allowing itself to be confused with one or another of its expressions. The ethnic entity in its essence is an historical entity. It is created by history; it is created and sustained in being the carrier of a common past and thus of a common destiny. Thus, a common past and a common destiny are the essential characteristics of the ethnic group. This means that a common ancestry becomes, so to speak, the acid test for the ethnic entity and this in turn is safeguarded by inbreeding within the group. As such the biological dimension, i.e., the blood relationship, is introduced into the ethnic entity. It does not constitute, however, its essence, only an important means by which its essence, the historical dimension of a common past and destiny, is safeguarded. The ethnic entity in its essence is not a biological but an historical category. Here lies the fundamental difference between the ethnic and the racial entity. For as against the ethnic being an historical entity, the race is a purely biological entity, i.e., an entity determined by a certain pool of genes thus delineated by certain physiological-biological characteristics. True, the ethnic needs the biological dimension to safeguard it and to this extent the biological determinant is operating here also. But the crucial point is that the ethnic entity does not have to keep itself racially "pure" in order to preserve its ongoing identity. External breeding through inter-marriage, when it occurs within limits and in favor of the group, namely, under circumstances favoring the offsprings inbreeding within the group, can occur without disintegrating the self-identity of the ethnic group. For in these cases it would be the heritage (i.e., the common past, destiny, culture, vocation, etc.) of him who comes from the group, i.e., the insider, that would prevail thus preserving the continuation of the ethnic identity of the group. The outsider, so to speak, dissolves himself ethnically into the group – not, of course, as far as he himself is concerned (this is not feasible for the individual is "stuck" with the ethnic identity into which he is born) but as far as his progeny is concerned. The progeny here may continue as full-fledged carriers of the heritage and thus become ethnically completely absorbed. The genes however remain. They may be diluted but not eradicated. Here lies the discrepancy between the ethnic and racial mixture. For while in terms of the short range, i.e., for the first two or three generations, the mixture persists both ethnically and racially, beyond that in terms of the long range the mixture persists racially but ethnically it disappears completely into the ethnic belonging of the group in whose midst the progeny settled. Thus, it is not tenable to equate the ethnic with the racial. Racially most, if not indeed all, groups are a mixture. Certainly the Jewish group is racially a hopeless mixture and it is simply nonsense to speak of the Jewish race. On the basis of race, pure and simple, there is indeed no such definable group as the Jewish group. But those who assume that Jewish identity bases itself on race and then proceed to refute it (which should not be too difficult) believing, however, that thereby they have also refuted all ethnic identity of the Jewish group (since they indiscriminately take the ethnic group as equivalent to the racial group) are wrong. For in the midst of racial mixture the ethnic can and does exist as a distinct, separate, well delineated (i.e., unmixed) entity. Blood relationship, race, is indeed a dimension connected with the ethnic but it is not its essence and as such it is not equivalent to it. Thus, although granted that the Jewish group cannot be identified as a racial entity it does not follow by any means that it cannot be identified as an ethnic entity.

In order, however, to allow the ethnic entity to prevail, and this in spite of racial mixture, the group requires the help of special propinquity, namely, its concentration in a certain geographic location and thus its possession of this location. In order to preserve a common past (a category of time and history) a common land (a category of space and nature) is called for. As such, the possession of a certain specific land becomes yet another dimension associated with the question of ethnicity. As a matter of fact this dimension was already present in the background of our analysis above regarding the relation subsisting between the ethnic and the racial. For in order for the ethnic entity to be able to maintain the inbreeding necessary for its survival and furthermore be able to absorb ethnically the progeny of external breeding, it has to form a togetherness spatially, i.e., concentrate itself and thus form the prevailing majority in a certain part of the world. Indeed, the overwhelming majority of ethnic groups could maintain their ethnic identity only as long as they remained attached to a specific land. Thus, the ethnic survival here is made contingent upon the ethnic group possessing its own land leading to equating this dimension with the very essence of ethnicity (this is nicely illustrated by the land receiving its name from the ethnic group thus having one and the same name for both the ethnic group and the land it possesses). Such an equation only naturally would lead to the conclusion that the Jewish group ever since its exile no longer constitutes an ethnic group, for in diaspora it no longer possesses its own land (hence also the opening here for viewing it as a mere religious community, and when the majority of the members of the group are no longer religious, as is evidently the case today, one is driven to all sorts of farfetched formulations of sophistry). But such a conclusion, though in a way understandable, is wrong. For the possession of a land does not constitute part of the essence of the ethnic group. Our analysis has shown only that it constitutes a necessary means for the ethnic survival and even as such not as applicable universally but only as applicable to most ethnic groups. Thus, all we can say here, and this would be perfectly justifiable, is that the Jewish ethnic group with respect to the dimension of possessing a land presents an exception to the general rule (and this exception is not even necessarily unique, the gypsies, for example, presenting a similar case in this respect). The Jewish group could survive as an ethnic entity even though it did not possess its own land. And it could thus survive because a) its religion being time-bound and not space-bound could survive without the possession of a specific land, and b) the structure of its religion was such that it could take over the function of preserving the ethnic group which in most other ethnic groups only the possession of the land could fulfill. Thus, the survival of the Jewish group need not be, as some people feel, all that mysterious and unique. What is certainly unique here is the structure of the religion, making the ethnic group contingent upon it and thus in turn weakening the bond between the ethnic group and the land so that it is not of the same status and nature as it is in most other ethnic groups.[8] Thus, although there is no denying that the unifying power which possession of a land can lend the ethnic group is missing here (and for those viewing this reality exclusively on the model of other ethnic groups the weakening must be seen as going all the way to the elimination of the ethnic reality), the fact remains that in this instance, because of the unique structure of the religion of the group, the ethnic reality is preserved even though the group is not concentrated in a specific land and thus in its possession.

The dimension of possessing a land has in modern times expressed itself in a corollary which all too often is confused with the ethnic reality. This is the question of citizenship. The group possessing the land has in modern times organized itself and its possession of the land in the form of the modern political state in which membership is accorded through citizenship. Citizenship is a political-juridical category setting forth a system of obligations and privileges and is, in principle, accorded by convention. As such it can be and is in fact accorded, ethnically speaking, to various people. As part of the process of Emancipation the Jews too were accorded citizenship, mostly in the states where they happened to reside. This allowed them ultimately to partake in the political life of the state, to benefit from its privileges and also to share in the burden of its obligations. But the possession of citizenship is often confused with belonging to the ethnic group which essentially constitutes the citizenry of the state. This is nicely illustrated by the ambiguity which the term nationality has assumed as a result of being applied to both the aspect of citizenship and to that of ethnic belonging (namely, in asking for one's nationality we may be asking either for one's citizenship or for one's ethnic belonging). Through this confusion the citizenship of the Jew in the host country, i.e., his nationality as far as his passport is concerned, serves to befuddle the question of his ethnic identity, i.e., his ethnic-nationality, leading some to consider his passport-nationality as his ethnic-nationality and thus to consider him not only as a citizen of the host country but also as belonging ethnically to the host nation. This however is totally untenable and can be maintained only when one's consideration of the subject is murky and superficial.

In a way it is of course strange that a confusion of these two categories which are so radically different (the one, i.e., the ethnic, being a deterministic, historical category while the other, i.e., the citizen, being a conventional, voluntaristic political-juridical category) should at all be possible. Yet on further reflection it should not appear strange at all. For the state and its citizenship are after all but one more concrete expression, as is the possession of a land, of the ethnic reality though albeit an expression that has come to the fore only in more recent times. As such, there is the inherent tendency of viewing the relationship as a one-to-one relationship and, indeed, in reality it is so by and large. But since citizenship is but the expression and not the very reality of the ethnic dimension, and furthermore it being but a conventional expression, it can be opened to people beyond the ethnic bounds as indeed residence in the land can be opened to outsiders. There is nothing inherent in these expressions which would bar an outsider from either living in a land possessed by another ethnic group or becoming a citizen of its state. But there is also nothing inherent which would necessitate his admittance. Indeed, his admittance is completely up to the attitude which the host-dominant ethnic group chooses to take (and as we saw it is in principle free to admit or reject though, of course, its own past tradition and heritage, its national character, its form of government and many other factors will have an important bearing in determining its attitude). Yet though in principle admittance is feasible and, indeed, is actually extended, there is no denying that at the same time an inherent tendency manifests itself in all ethnic groups to maintain an essential one to one relationship between themselves on the one hand and the land and state (including of course its citizenry) on the other. This is clearly seen in the fact that sooner or later a limitation is placed on admittance; some ethnic groups may be more tolerant, others less tolerant, but eventually all have a limit on their tolerance. And indeed furthermore, in the last analysis all tolerance shown, be it to a lesser or greater extent, is temporary, based on the assumption and expectation that the outsider, being a minority and usually a small minority at that, will be quickly absorbed and disappear in the host ethnic group. Tolerance is not really extended on a permanent basis.[9] This tendency is understandable since in order for land and state to serve the ethnic group respectively as its support and expression an essentially one-to-one relation must be maintained.

Now, within this context it was possible to grant the emancipated Jew citizenship even though ethnically he was an outsider. But it was also possible because of the close relationship between the aspect of citizenship and that of ethnic-belonging to overlook the essential difference between the two and thus all too easily but superficially equate passport-nationality with ethnic-nationality. This was greatly aided in the case of the emancipated Jew by the fact, as we shall soon see, that so many of the other concrete expressions of the ethnic reality, e.g., land, language, culture, were either totally absent or in a state of disintegration and thus greatly weakened. As such, since the distinctive ethnic reality of the Jew was not clearly and concretely manifested, a vacuum, so to speak, was created in which passport-nationality could be taken as also signifying (as, indeed, normally is the case) ethnic-nationality. But although the process leading to this claim may be understandable the fact remains that in the case of the Jew it is a wishful, untenable illusion.

Other Dimensions Connected with the Ethnic Reality

We have thus far considered two dimensions, i.e., race and land, which with respect to the reality of the Jewish group may lead to the erroneous impression that the group is not ethnic. These two dimensions function as means enabling the ethnic group respectively to come into existence and to preserve itself. There are, however, other dimensions connected with the ethnic reality which function not as means to its existence and preservation but as channels through which its essence, i.e., the carrying of a common past and a common heritage, can concretely express and manifest itself. Such dimensions are, for example, a common language, a common culture, a common pattern of living both internally in terms of character, i.e., a basic pattern of thinking and values, and externally in terms of mannerisms and customs.

Now, the interesting thing to note is that these dimensions continued to characterize the Jewish group throughout its diaspora-existence even though it lacked the all-important support of a common land. The amazing thing about Jewish diaspora-existence was precisely the fact that although physically the Jews were widely dispersed in all corners of the world, spiritually they were unified in one world. Their bodies may have walked in the midst of different lands with different cultures, languages, customs and mannerisms but their spirit walked in their own "world" with its own culture, language, pattern of thought and evaluation, a "world" that was essentially one and the same be they in Eastern Europe or in North Africa. As such, the ethnic reality of the group was clearly manifested and expressed in spite of their not possessing a common land. They managed to carry a common past, a common heritage, and go on living in it despite their physical dispersion.

These dimensions, however, have been rapidly disintegrating and disappearing in recent times with the rise of the Emancipation. The emancipated Jew is emancipated precisely in the sense that he no longer adheres to his own culture, language and pattern of life, thought and evaluation, i.e., to his own ethos, but adopts the ethos and pattern of life of the people in whose midst he lives and into which he has been emancipated. Thus, for example, his language now is no longer Hebrew (as his spiritual, creative, i.e., sacred, language) or Yiddish or Ladino (as his everyday, i.e., profane, language) but German, English or Russian; his literary heroes are no longer a Rabbi Akiba but a Goethe, a Shakespeare or a Pushkin, nor are his political-military heroes a King David or a Judah Maccabee but a Lincoln, a Nelson or a Napoleon; his ideal is no longer the brilliant student of Talmudic lore but the secular professional and scientist; his outward appearance, his customs, his modes of entertainment are all indistinguishable from the environment in which he lives. There is no denying that with the disintegration and disappearance of these dimensions the reality of the Jewish group as an ethnic entity is thrown into question. For an ethnic reality cannot be a mere abstraction; it must be concretely expressed, and it is precisely in these dimensions that this concrete expression is articulated. Thus, the disintegration and disappearance of these dimensions with respect to emancipated Jewry means that the main avenues through which the concrete expression of its ethnic reality can manifest itself are being undermined and this, in turn, would certainly obscure its ethnic reality (since it remains unmanifested); but even more seriously, it would throw into question there being such a reality at all (since it is questionable how long such a reality can subsist without being concretely expressed). Viewed from a Jewish viewpoint, this is certainly a serious situation. The situation, however, becomes even more aggravated when we see that emancipated Jewry not only fails to concretely express the reality of its Jewish ethnicity but that it actually adopts the expressive dimensions of other ethnic groups (and this is feasible since these dimensions are not biologically determined and as such are transferable). As a result the concrete ethnic expression of emancipated Jewry becomes split into a manifold of different expressions giving the impression that it is constituted of different ethnic groups. Given this situation it is no wonder that the emancipated Jew is not clearly conscious of his Jewish ethnic identity, that he is profoundly ignorant of what this ethnic reality is and what it signifies, that this reality is consequently meaningless for him, that he has the illusion of his belonging to other ethnic groups or, when he still maintains his sense of reality and knows such a claim to be an illusion, that he would be searching out of profound puzzlement and bafflement for his identity, for that which makes him a Jew, i.e., for the common denominator which still may constitute emancipated Jewry as a distinct group.

As said, there is no denying that this situation constitutes a fundamental crisis in the reality of the Jewish group and moreover that the prognosis which it indicates is anything but bright. Still, this crisis is only in its initial stages and the fact remains that thus far emancipated Jewry still constitutes a distinct group. It is our contention that to the extent that it constitutes itself as a distinct group it does so by virtue of its being an ethnic group. For no matter how weakened or even completely eradicated – something which is really not yet the case with most emancipated Jews – the expressive dimensions of Jewish ethnicity be, this as such cannot cancel the ethnic reality (not only for the present which goes without saying since the ethnic belonging is determined at the moment of birth and can under no circumstances be changed but also for the future in terms of the preservation and continuation of the ethnic belonging of the progeny). The ethnic reality, in the last analysis, can be cancelled, i.e., disappear, only through the wholesale intermarriage out of the group. As long as the group continues to intramarry it preserves the link to the past and as such continues as a carrier of the past thus preserving its own ethnic reality no matter how minimal, sterile and meaningless this reality may have become. Intermarriage out of the group is, so to speak, the "sound barrier" which one has to break in order to cancel the ethnic reality for one's progeny.[10] And this breaking of the "sound barrier" has in most instances not occurred (the pessimist would add not yet).[11] As such, emancipated Jewry is still constituted as a distinct group and it is so constituted by virtue of its continued ethnic reality notwithstanding the serious problematics and precariousness of this reality. To claim therefore, as this formulation does, that the Jew, or even only the emancipated Jew, is a purely religious entity devoid of any distinctive ethnic belonging simply distorts the objective reality of the Jewish phenomenon.[12]

Legitimacy of the Ethnic and Religious Characteristics

We must grant, however, that although we had to reject in the last analysis the two proposed formulations given thus far, they could not be dismissed as totally missing the mark. Some truth and some legitimacy remain in their claim. Even though rejected and found untenable (and this in a decided, final way) they cannot be viewed as the work of pure, idle sophistry built on no true foundation in reality. This is due, no doubt, to the fact that both formulations build their claims on substantial, valid aspects of the authentic reality. They settle on one pole (the former on the ethnic and the latter on the religious pole) of the inextricable union and to this extent they contain truth, capturing an authentic part of the reality of the Jewish phenomenon. Their downfall and bankruptcy lie in their rejecting the other pole, making a part of the truth and of reality the whole truth and reality (and in this process inevitably also corrupting the part they have kept). But a kernel of truth, of substance and of seriousness remains.

The many and various other formulations that one may encounter today lack even this partial degree of substance and seriousness. For they are all distinguished by their negating both poles of the inextricable union, the ethnic and the religious, and basing their definition of what is a Jew on yet other criteria, claiming of course, that they capture the essence of the Jewish phenomenon, and thus serve as the common denominator for all members of the Jewish group. In truth, however, these various proposed criteria are completely off the mark capturing, if anything at all, only superficial and accidental characteristics of the Jew. They certainly do not capture the essence of the reality of the Jewish phenomenon and they certainly fail to serve as the common denominator constituting the Jewish group. This failure should be obvious and it should be fairly easy to see that these proposed criteria manifestly and massively fail to meet our considerations. They simply cannot be taken seriously. Their only value is in revealing the depth of meaninglessness and emptiness to which the Jewish reality of their proponents has sunk.

The variety of the criteria suggested and to which the above remarks would apply is quite sizeable, running the whole gamut of possibilities. Here we can only point briefly to a few illustrations. Thus, we may mention what may be referred to as the "gastronomical criterion" according to which Jewishness is characterized and determined by predilection to certain food dishes. This criterion is obviously so ludicrous in its superficiality and untenability that it really deserves no refutation and yet it is current among many Jews (and only half jokingly so). Another more serious criterion which is fairly commonly proposed is what may be called the "educational criterion." According to this criterion it is the knowledge of the Jewish heritage which ought to determine the Jew.[13] But evidently such a criterion though much more substantial and commendable than the previous criterion is just as untenable.[14] For obviously there are people who everyone would agree are not Jews and yet have great knowledge of Judaism (even indeed great scholars) and vice versa there are people who everyone would agree are Jews and yet are very ignorant of Judaism. Lastly, we must mention the whole array of criteria which are derived from the sociological and psychological domains according to which one's Jewishness is essentially determined by one or another social or psychological trait such as, for example, the Jew's loyalty and devotion to family, his predilection to study and intellectual pursuits, his adaptability and initiative, or his mental capabilities and energy, his insecurity, his anxiety, his restlessness, etc. Now, these social and psychological traits no doubt characterize some, and indeed even many, Jews. But they simply do not, and this after all is what is essential and crucial for our purposes here, characterize all the members of the Jewish group. For certainly there are Jews, i.e., people that we would all agree are Jews, who lack these traits be they the predilection to study and intellectual pursuits, mental capabilities, adaptability or even the insecurity-anxiety-restlessness syndrome. And not only do these traits fail to cover the group, so to speak, horizontally, they fail to cover it vertically, i.e., in its continuation through history. Traits that may have characterized one generation, and even here only partially, would in no way characterize another. These traits, therefore, are variables both as far as their extent and as far as their constancy are concerned and as such cannot possibly capture the essence of the Jewish phenomenon. And still further, these traits by no means characterize the Jewish group exclusively thus excluding all non-Jews. Certainly each one of these traits can, and in fact no doubt does, characterize some non-Jews. As such, these traits cannot and do not delineate clearly the group from the outside world, a function which is essential if they are to be taken as the criteria by which to define the Jewish phenomenon. Actually, the failure of the social and psychological traits to define the Jew should not be surprising for these traits are culturally and biologically determined and we have already seen that here the Jew, certainly the emancipated Jew, does not necessarily present a distinct, homogeneous group. But we have also seen that in spite of this the ethnic can maintain its distinct identity, at least for a while.[15]

Thus, the failure to define the Jew from a sociological or psychological viewpoint does not mean the absence of his ethnic reality or the possibility of satisfactorily defining it from another viewpoint. Indeed, even if a definition from a sociological or psychological viewpoint were possible here, it would be very superficial. For to say that what binds Jews together and accounts for their reality and destiny are some patterns of behavior or certain psychological traits is manifestly superficial. One cannot seriously account for the reality of a group which is a carrier of a past of thousands of years, which is so clearly set apart in so many different lands over such an extended period of time, which has had the inner strength to persevere in such an adverse destiny of persecution and suffering and which has found in recent times enough energy and resources to reestablish itself in the land of its ancestors, on the basis that the sole essential bond constituting the group is one or another social or psychological trait.

Origin of the Difficulties in Finding an Answer

Thus we must conclude that all the various formulations currently proposed in answer to the question "What is a Jew" are untenable and hence also the perplexity of what is a Jew and the ongoing search for an answer to the question.[16] But why should there be this perplexity and the apparent lack of an answer to the question "What is a Jew"? The phenomenon after all has been in existence for quite awhile. The Jew is not a new creature which is only now in the process of coming into being and where therefore a search for identity would have been understandable. Having been in existence for so long, it is not feasible that an identity would not have been by now already crystalized and that, therefore, an answer to the question "What is a Jew" would not be available. This indeed is the case and we have already submitted that the authentic Jewish reality is constituted by the inextricable union of the ethnic and the religious thus dictating that the only valid answer to our question is the answer which captures and conveys this inextricable union. Thus, the problematic of our situation is not that an answer is not available but that the traditionally available answer is not welcomed to a great many Jews.

But how is this possible? If we look at the present situation we shall see that one or the other pole of this inextricable union of the ethnic and the religious, or indeed both, will be unsavory to the emancipated Jew. Thus, for the diaspora emancipated Jew, the ethnic reality is certainly problematic and unsavory. For after all it is, in the last analysis, the real stumbling block to his complete emancipation, i.e., to his complete acceptance by the surrounding host group. It should be therefore perfectly understandable that many an emancipated Jew should want to insist that his Jewish belonging does in no way imply a distinctive Jewish ethnic belonging. On the other hand, the religious pole is equally unsavory to the emancipated Jew. Here the problematic is on two levels. On the one level it arises when the religious in Judaism is equated with Orthodoxy. For here a clash must inevitably ensue between the openness of ongoing profane history, the entry into which is the very meaning of Emancipation, and the closed, all-inclusive and predetermined structure of Orthodox Judaism, a structure which ideally fitted and represented the existence outside profane history of diaspora "ghetto" Jewry. On the other level it arises vis-à-vis the very essence of the religious as such (and not merely vis-à-vis a particular form of its expression). For the tendency to secularism in the emancipated Jew is only too well established; indeed, such a tendency is readily understandable seeing that the emancipated Jew enters and adopts a world which is "modern," which means that he enters and adopts a world which is becoming more and more secular. Indeed, he does not only adopt the secularism of the modern world, he becomes its champion and vanguard. And this too is understandable, for certainly we have at work here the known phenomenon of the zeal of the new convert and, perhaps, even more significantly, the wish of the diaspora Jew to remove religion as a divisive factor, hoping thereby to find complete equality in the no-man's land of secularism; though in the case of the Israeli Jew, where the foregoing may not apply, the reason may well lie in the fact that in the Israeli Jew we encounter anew the ancient Biblical temptation of wanting to be a nation like all the other nations, i.e., a nation divorced from the religious dimension, the dimension which makes the Jewish nation a peculiar entity set-apart.

But while we can understand the predicament that the ethnic and religious poles may present to the emancipated Jew in his striving for emancipation, and consequently his wish to deny them, the fact remains that the subjective feelings and wishes of the emancipated Jew are of no consequence to our analysis. For the question of finding the valid formulation of Jewish identity must be determined exclusively by the objective reality of the Jew and the subjective wishes of the Jew are essentially beside the point.[17] What in the last analysis really lends weight to these subjective wishes is the fact, as we have seen above, that in the objective reality of the emancipated Jew the religious and the ethnic dimension (as far as their concrete expressions are concerned) are indeed greatly weakened. It is this which really threatens the validity of the formulation. But as we have argued, the ethnic dimension among emancipated Jewry in diaspora, although certainly seriously weakened in its concrete expression and as such certainly justifying every concern for the prospects of its survival in the future, is certainly as far as the present is concerned an inescapable reality. And this, in turn, implies that in the context of emancipated Jewry, no matter how weakened and even outrightly rejected the religious dimension may be, it remains viable, though albeit minimally, from the viewpoint of Judaism as long as the reality of the ethnic belonging of the Jew is not severed. For the mere act of ethnic belonging (an act which is imposed at birth and from which the individual himself cannot escape) is in the context of the religion of Judaism the basic act of religious witnessing and as such as long as this act persists the basic, minimal religious reality persists no matter what the individual wishes or thinks. Thus, strange though it no doubt may seem, in the context of the religion of Judaism people who profess atheism, agnosticism and whatnot but who ethnically are Jewish are continuing to carry, albeit minimally, the religious witnessing thus continuing to constitute the religious pole in the Jewish phenomenon.

The Traditional Halachic Answer

Thus for the present the Jewish phenomenon continues to be constituted by the inextricable union of the ethnic and the religious, and as such we submit that the only satisfactory definition, i.e., the definition which captures the inextricable union, is the traditional definition. But here we run into a problem in the way the tradition articulated itself. For we shall find that the tradition in its formal articulation did not at all address itself to the question "What is a Jew." Rather, it addressed itself exclusively to the question "Who is a Jew." But this should not really surprise us all that much. For clearly the question "What is a Jew" would arise and demand the formulation of an answer only when a crisis of identity is precipitated (as we are witnessing today). In the normal flow of existence when a community knows instinctively and immediately its identity, affirming it by its very living, the question of intellectually and theoretically formulating its essence would not arise. Hence, since Jewry till recent times was not plagued by a crisis of identity the challenge of the question "What is a Jew" did not arise and consequently there was no occasion to formulate a speculative theoretical answer to this question and therefore such an answer is not formally available to us today. In the case of Judaism, however, there is another consideration to be taken into account, indeed, a consideration which in contradistinction to the preceding consideration is quite peculiar and distinctive to the religious structure of Judaism. Namely, as it has been observed, the religion of Judaism expresses itself in the main not in the metaphysical but in the ethical domain, and thus Judaism expresses itself in the main not in a body of doctrines but in the Halacha, i.e., in a body of legislation. But as such it is clearly to be expected that in this context, i.e., in the context of the Halacha, the question that would arise would be the question "Who is a Jew" and not "What is a Jew." For it is to the former and not to the latter question that the Halacha must address itself and give a clear and formal answer. Indeed the traditional formulation of the Halacha in this context is clearly in terms of an answer to the question "Who is a Jew."

But as argued above the questions "Who is a Jew" and "What is a Jew" are intimately related to each other constituting in effect two sides of one and the same coin. As such, the traditional halachic answer to "Who is a Jew" clearly reflects, though not openly articulates, an answer to "What is a Jew" and this answer, we submit, captures the inextricable union of the religious and the ethnic. Namely, we would submit that the halachic answer to "Who is a Jew" is determined by the considerations which flow from understanding the Jew as an inextricable union of the ethnic and the religious, thus clearly presupposing this as its answer to the question of "What is a Jew." Let us briefly illustrate this contention.

The halachic answer to "Who is a Jew" is: He who is born of a Jewish mother. This and this alone determines who is a Jew. There can be no question that this formulation is from a legal viewpoint, i.e., from the viewpoint of the task which it is to fulfill, a most satisfactory formulation. It is precise, unambiguous, easily and objectively applicable. But it is often considered by many today as arbitrary and devoid of all spiritual, religious meaning. To define the religious belonging which the term Jew signifies by a brute, neutral, biological fact seems to many people to be parochial. But this formulation is not only legally very convenient, it captures in the most penetrating and valid way the religious meaning of the Jew. For clearly this formulation is determined by the ethnic pole. It is the ethnic which is determined at birth and which consequently determines the halachic formulation to define the Jew by the biological dimension as this is fixed at the moment of birth.[18] Thus, the halachic definition of the Jew safeguards the ethnic dimension. But in so doing it also safeguards the religious dimension on its primary level. For as we said, the primary basic act of religious witnessing in Judaism is the belonging to the Jewish ethnic group. Such belonging is not, religiously speaking, neutral. It is a religious belonging. Thus, the halachic definition is not only satisfactory in being precise, objective and easily applicable, but it is also most penetrating in capturing not only the ethnic dimension but at the same time the most fundamental, primary act of religious witnessing within the context of the religion of Judaism. The halachic definition is not only tenable from the viewpoint of the ethnic pole of Judaism but equally from the viewpoint of the religious pole. As such, the definition fulfills its task admirably well.

Yet, though the ethnic and the religious dimensions meet in Judaism and become one at the most fundamental level (i.e., the act of ethnic belonging is at one and the same time the primary act of religious witnessing), there is no escaping the tension that must develop from the different and indeed contradictory demands that the ethnic and the religious dimensions exact. After all the ethnic and the religious are by no means similar dimensions and as such it is only to be expected that some requirements of the one would clash with some of the other. This indeed is the case and the traditional halachic formulation, as it expresses itself with regard to the question of defining the Jew and with regard to the closely related question of the conversion to and from Judaism, reveals very nicely this tension and its ingenuity in overcoming it in as good a way as possible.

Two Inconsistencies

In the main there are two inconsistencies, the first being an inconsistency of degree while the second is an inconsistency of actual contradiction. The first inconsistency arises in the very question of defining the Jew. We said that the biological act of birth is taken as the determining factor in defining the Jew because of the ethnic consideration (which of course, in turn, is seen in Judaism as a religious category). But from the viewpoint of the ethnic, pure and simple, ethnicity is determined by both parents. From the ethnic viewpoint a gradual transition is possible and one can speak of partial ethnic belonging (e.g., half-English, half-French). Thus, if the definition of the Jew were to be determined exclusively from the ethnic perspective, both parents should have been taken as determining factors and the possibility of a half-Jew admitted. The religious perspective, however, cannot admit a half-belonging. Here, as with the proverbial illustration of pregnancy, there is no halfway; it is a case of either-or. It is because of this consideration of the religious dimension, it would seem to us, that the traditional halachic formulation determines the question of one's Jewishness in terms not of both parents but of one only (and here the mother is chosen rather than the father because of the consideration, perhaps, that with the mother, unlike the father, the question of parenthood cannot arise). As such, there is no possibility of a half-Jew. The child whose mother was Jewish at the moment of birth irrespective of the father's religion, race or ethnicity, is a full Jew.[19] This, of course, sets the Jewish halachic conception of who is a Jew at some variance with the world's consensus. For the world's consensus is determined purely by the ethnic perspective, the ethnic perspective that in no way is refracted by the considerations of the religious perspective. Thus, the case may easily arise where a person in the world's consensus is considered as a half-Jew while in the Jewish Halacha he may be considered either as fully a Jew or not at all a Jew. And this, when given a number of generations, may lead to the discrepancy where the descendants would be viewed by the world's consensus, i.e., from the purely ethnic perspective, as fully Jewish while in the view of the Jewish Halacha they will be strictly speaking fully non-Jewish, or vice versa, they will be taken as fully non-Jews by the world's consensus while in the Jewish Halacha they will be considered fully Jewish.[20]

There is no denying that such a discrepancy violates our above consideration, which requires that the group's self-understanding be in consonance with the world's consensus. The saving feature is that the discrepancy occurs in a very few marginal cases, and thus numerically highly infrequently. As such, the viability and tenability of the halachic formulation is not undermined.

That the discrepancy arises is of course due to the fact that in Judaism the ethnic is not only not the sole criterion for the definition of the Jew (as is the case in the world's consensus) but in the last analysis it is subservient to the religious. This discrepancy illustrates what was said above, namely, that the uniqueness of Judaism lies not in the inextricable union of the ethnic and the religious as such but in that the inextricable union is constituted by the religious and not the ethnic, i.e., the ethnic is a religious category rather than the religious being an expression of the ethnic. This means that when there is a clash between the requirements of the religious and those of the ethnic, the religious will in all likelihood prevail but it will prevail in a way that will attempt to accommodate every requirement of the ethnic that can be accommodated without abrogating the religious requirements.[21]

This is further exemplified in an even more striking measure with regard to the related question of the conversion to and from Judaism. From the ethnic perspective as such the very possibility of conversion is excluded, for the ethnic is determined at birth and it is a determination which is unalterable. As said above, one is inescapably stuck with the ethnic-belonging that is given at birth. Thus indeed, in those other religions where we witness an inextricable bond between the religious and the ethnic dimensions conversion is really not admissible (a good example is classical Hinduism). This is understandable for in these religions, as we have claimed, the inextricable bond between the ethnic and the religious is grounded in the ethnic, i.e., the ethnic, so to speak, is the dominant partner with the religious being its expression and as such the requirements of the ethnic (which, of course, exclude the possibility of conversion) prevail and the requirements of the religious must submit to them. In the case of Judaism, however, the inextricable bond between the ethnic and religious is unique in that the bond is grounded not in the ethnic but in the religious, i.e., it is the religious which is the dominant, determining partner (the inextricable bond comes about here for the sake of the religious and not as a consequence of the ethnic). Now, the religious dimension in Judaism being monotheistic it is ultimately universalistic and as such it must of necessity implicate the possibility of conversion to itself, i.e., it must remain open to one and all who wish authentically to embrace it. But at the same time the religious dimension in Judaism because of its very essence and structure cannot possibly give up the requirement that its adherents must belong to the Jewish ethnic group. But, as we have seen, an ethnic conversion is not feasible. Evidently, we have here a head-on collision between two essential requirements of the religious dimension in Judaism – the requirement to be open stemming from the monotheistic, universalistic aspect and the requirement to remain closed stemming from the ethnic aspect.

Judaism overcomes this problem by satisfying both contradictory requirements, as indeed it must, but at the inescapable price of having to resort to legal fiction. Namely, conversion to Judaism is admitted (interesting to note that the purely religious requirement prevails and is satisfied!). But at the same time through recourse to legal fiction the convert is considered as "a newly born babe." Through this legal fiction the convert is given another moment of biological birth where he is born into the Jewish ethnic group, his new biological parents, so to speak, being Sarah and Abraham.[22] It is important to emphasize that the "new birth" here is quite different from the "new birth" phenomenon commonly encountered in many other religions. It is not a spiritual new birth; it is not that a new being, i.e., a different being, emerges. No transformation in the status of the being takes place. The convert remains the same kind of being as he was before. The "new birth" here is by virtue of the legal fiction an ordinary birth, a birth of the same character and status as his first birth was, only that now he is born to Sarah and Abraham and thus he is born into the Jewish ethnic group. Of course, since the Jewish ethnic group through its inextricable bond with the religion of Judaism is thoroughly infused with the meaning and significance of the religion of Judaism, it being not just an ethnic entity, pure and simple, but equally and essentially a religious entity, the biological new birth into the Jewish ethnic group necessarily also implies an entry into a new religious order with a new spiritual vocation and obligation (but this in Judaism does not signify a transformation into a "new being"). This however follows as a consequence of the peculiar nature of the Jewish ethnic group and not as the primary thrust and meaning of the "new birth." The primary thrust and meaning of the "new birth" here is biological so as to enable entry into the new ethnic entity.[23]

Thus, the Halacha clearly provides for the possibility of conversion to Judaism, though because of the ethnic factor this was not an easy task, exacting every ounce of ingenuity and necessitating the recourse to legal fiction. This however, was necessary for it is essential from the viewpoint of the religious factor that conversion to Judaism be made feasible. At the same time, however, it is by no mans clear that it is equally essential for the religious factor that conversion out of Judaism be made feasible. As such, the ethnic factor with its requirement that conversion out of Judaism be impossible is not as clearly overcome here as it was in the case of conversion to Judaism. Indeed, it would seem that essentially the ethnic factor which states "once a Jew always a Jew" is allowed to determine the situation here. For the Halacha clearly takes the position that "an Israelite even though he sinned is still an Israelite." Excommunication in the sense of reading a person out of the community of faith, i.e., declaring that he is no longer a member of the group, is not available to Judaism precisely since the ethnic factor is allowed to ascertain itself and as such the community is not just a community of faith but an ethnic community and from the latter one cannot be read out. Thus, no matter what the Jew believes or does not believe, what he does or does not do, he remains a Jew.[24] This is understandable since the ethnic-belonging is already in the context of Judaism an act of religious witnessing. Thus, not withstanding the erroneous beliefs of the transgressor or his rejection of the beliefs of Judaism, his belonging to the Jewish group is already an act, albeit a minimal act, of religious witnessing and as such he remains, not only purely ethnically but indeed religiously, a Jew.

The extreme test of the logic of this position is the case where the Jew actually converts to another religion. For what is crucial here is not the adoption of what from the viewpoint of Judaism are erroneous beliefs but the fact that such conversion involves the joining of another group. The question now is whether such joining abrogates the belonging to the Jewish group. Here we would have to say that as far as the Jewish group is an ethnic group the answer would seem to be "no" but as far as the Jewish group is a community of faith the answer is "yes" for the community of faith of Judaism is exclusive and would not tolerate double membership at one and the same time in itself and another community of faith. The question, therefore, is which consideration, the religious or the ethnic, would prevail while the convert is actually a member of another community of faith.[25]

It is interesting that for rabbinic Judaism the ethnic consideration prevails here and the convert though he joins another community of faith nevertheless remains a Jew. "An Israelite even though he sinned is an Israelite" is interpreted to the limit, including the joining of another community of faith. This, of course, is only of a theoretical significance, i.e., the abstract determination of the status of such a person. Practically, however, such a person is excluded, and understandably so, from all aspects of the life of the community. While theoretically he may remain a Jew practically there is no concrete recognition whatsoever of his Jewishness. This shows how strong the ethnic dimension is in Judaism.

Still, it would seem to us that a more logical and consistent formulation, and one in which the theoretical understanding would correspond to the practical application, is to resort to the same strategy used in the question of conversion to Judaism, i.e., the resort to legal fiction, but this time in the reverse direction. A such, the convert out of Judaism would be considered as if he ceased to exist for the duration of his conversion. The convert would be considered, through legal fiction, as a different person, as a "newly born babe" this time born not into but out of the Jewish group. Thus, the convert is not rejected (this indeed is not feasible); he does not cease to be a Jew, but rather, through legal fiction, he (qua Jew) ceases to exist. And when the convert renounces his apostasy and returns to his Jewish faith, his former existence, again through legal fiction, is re-established. In this formulation the religious consideration prevails not by abrogating the ethnic but by getting around it. This, it seems to us, would be the most satisfactory solution in such a situation[26]

Conclusion

Thus, the traditional halachic definition determining the Jew in terms of the Jewishness of the mother is far from simple-minded, crude tribalism; nor is the halachic policy of resorting to legal fiction and postulating a new moment of biological birth (as in the conversion to Judaism) a case of indulging in idle, spurious, fantastic sophistry; nor, indeed, is the halachic insistence on holding tight to the Jew unto the moment of death in all circumstances (even in the conversion from Judaism) merely a case of exhibiting a jealous autocratic narrowmindedness. Rather, it is just a case of being faithful to the objective reality of the Jewish phenomenon. Its formulation, in its straightforward simplicity and in its convoluted twists and turns, is dictated by this objective reality. It, and it alone, has the merit of thus faithfully capturing this peculiar phenomenon of Jewish reality and the value of penetrating so profoundly into its meaning and significance. That it is not readily and universally accepted today reveals the serious malaise, perplexity and upheaval in present-day Jewry. This cannot be denied. Jewry is going through a period of radical crisis and possible profound transformation. It is possible that Jewry in the future will so change as no longer to support this traditional halachic definition. The future is open and we do not indulge in auguries. We will state, however, two things: first, for the present the reality of Jewry has not so radically changed and therefore the traditional halachic formulation remains the sole, tenable formulation, and secondly, if by chance Jewry in the future does undergo this radical break with its constitution (i.e., with its being constituted as an inextricable union of the ethnic and the religious), then the issue confronting us would no longer really be the mere issue of a new definition but rather the much more radical issue of a new reality, namely, we would be confronting a new kind of entity, a new phenomenon, which in terms of its very essence is no longer the same as the one we have known for the past three and a half millennia.

[1]This is particularly so when this question is raised in the context of the state of Israel. Here it becomes a public issue of the first order finding expression in court action and even in governmental crisis (see the Cabinet crisis of 1958). The reason for this is clear. Only in the state of Israel does the Jewish community possess the power to regulate its life, and consequently the issue becomes a practical issue of public policy and legislation and as such an issue which impinges all too concretely on the fortunes and life of the people. Diaspora Jewry, on the other hand, living under the power of non-Jewish states is spared the task of imposing the practical, concrete implementation of the issue; the issue can have practical significance only for those Jews who voluntarily choose to raise it. That the issue is raised in Israel and cannot be ignored there is not so much because orthodoxy is a kind of state-religion (this impinges only on the question of marriage and burial) as because the state of Israel in its very creation and existence is but a part of the wider phenomenon of Jewish peoplehood thus necessarily having an ultimate and inseparable connection to the ethos and problems of this entity. This is nicely exemplified in the area which has caused the most publicized and widespread uproar in connection with this question, that of gaining Israeli citizenship (e.g., the Brother Daniel case). The question of "Who is a Jew" is raised here only because the state has formulated its law of citizenship in such a way as to give a special, preferred position to Jews, i.e., *Hok Ha-shevut*. And the state so legislated only because it sees itself, and rightly so, as part and parcel of the larger phenomenon of Jewish peoplehood. But such legislation inevitably invites the issue of "Who is a Jew?"

[2]There is, however, one possibility where a theoretical difficulty may present itself. This is the case when we have more than one criterion involved and the individual satisfies some but not all of the criteria. This difficulty, however, is avoided in the case of Judaism. For although there are, indeed, two criteria involved in the answer to the question "What is a Jew," the formulation of Judaism, as we shall see below, is such that the authentic satisfaction of the one *ipso facto* necessitates the satisfaction of the other. As such, the two criteria function as one with regard to this question and the possibility of partial fulfillment (thus presenting a theoretical difficulty) cannot arise.

[3]Abundance in this area, however, is tantamount to not having any answer. Having many answers is equal to having no answer at all. For it is precisely the absence of an accepted single answer which allows the multiplicity of the various formulations which are proposed as the answer. This multiplicity is but the other side of the one and the same coin – the crisis of identity in present-day Jewry. The raising of the question and the abundance of the proposed answers reflect one and the same thing – not a richness and fullness but a paucity and perplexity of spirit.

[4]Of course, once the definition is arrived at in this way it not only describes but also prescribes the group by serving as the norm by which to determine who is and who is not a member of the group when the question arises in specific cases, namely, in cases which, as is to be expected, are likely to be questionable, border cases. Thus, when we say that the question "What is a Jew" is more ultimate and precedes the question "Who is a Jew," this is on the reflective, speculative level, the level which comes to the fore when the problem of Jewish identity arises, when the *question* of who is a Jew has to be confronted. This does not contradict, however, our stating that the *reality* of who is a Jew, i.e., the reality that this and that person is a Jew and that this and that person is not a Jew, precedes the formulation of the definition of what is a Jew and indeed controls it (in as much as it is the entity to which the definition must conform). For the one enjoys the precedence in the realm of reflection while the other enjoys it in the realm of reality. True, to a very small extent the definition does actually create the group in that in questionable, border cases it determines the belonging to the group. But in this respect it merely conforms to the common, expected functioning of all definitions, and certainly such determining can in no way be construed as determining, i.e., creating, the group as such.

[5]Indeed, if the group has lost its essential structure completely then we must face the truth that this signifies the demise of the group and in this case we are not justified in continuing to use its name. The name should be reserved exclusively for the phenomenon of the past which is no longer. But even when the change is not that radical, thus allowing the group to go on

preserving its essential identity, when it is substantial enough we characterize it by qualifying the name with an adjective. A good example of this is the use we make of the adjectives "biblical" and "rabbinic" with regard to the name "Judaism." Keeping the same name indicates the preservation and continuation of the essential structure, while the introduction of the adjective indicates that a radical enough change has occurred in the manifestation of this one and the same essential structure. Evidently, in attempting to answer the question "What is a Jew" we are attempting to capture the essential structure of the group which is not changeable.

[6]Admittedly, such an inextricable union of the ethnic and the religious may appear peculiar and unique. It may appear so particularly in the context of Western culture where the dimension of religion, as manifested by Christianity, transcends and is clearly separated from the ethnic dimension. But the inextricable union as such is not really unique and we can meet other such instances in non-Western cultures, the most notable example, perhaps, being provided by Hinduism. Yet this inextricable union in the case of the Jewish phenomenon does have a unique aspect and if we are to understand and appreciate the Jewish phenomenon fully and properly it is important that we be clear about it. The uniqueness does not lie in the union as such nor in its being inextricable but in the way it is constituted. For in all other instances where we meet this inextricable union the union is grounded in the ethnic dimension. Namely, the religious dimension is the expression, i.e., the creation, of the ethnic spirit. As such it belongs to it, being its private, exclusive possession. In the Jewish phenomenon, on the other hand, the relation is reversed. Here the inextricable union is grounded in the religious dimension – it is the ethnic that is grounded in the religious. For it is of the very essence of the religious "make-up" here that it requires an ethnic entity. Thus, here it is the ethnic which is appropriated by the religious. It is, so to speak, created by the religious and as such becomes its private, exclusive property. The ethnic becomes the essential vehicle and means for the expression and realization of the religious. Thus, while in the other instances the religious is but an expression, albeit the highest expression, of the cultural, spiritual creativity of the ethnic entity, here the ethnic entity is thoroughly infused with religious meaning and made into a fundamental, primary religious category. This fact will bear heavily, as we shall see below, on some important questions connected with the Jewish phenomenon.

[7]And if pressed hard because of the evident presence of some bond between the two then the only way by which this formulation can account for it is to point to the fact that the ancestry of the atheist Polish Jew was in all probability observant and believing like the Moroccan Jew and his ancestry; namely, the common bond between the atheist Polish Jew and the believing, observant Moroccan Jew is based here on the fact that the former's ancestry had a purely religious common bond of the same beliefs and practices with the latter, a bond, however, which is no longer in existence. It is thus based on whatever vague, sentimental attachment the memory of ancestry may evoke. But evidently this is an extremely tenuous, weak common denominator which cannot account for the strength and viability of this bond as we experience it and as, indeed, it is in reality. Indeed, if the bond between the respective ancestries was to be the mere sharing of common religious beliefs and practices then it would be very difficult to understand that this bond of the past could continue to provide a common denominator, forming as distinct and closely-knit a group as the Jewish group is, long after it itself ceased to function and is no longer a reality (and especially in terms of this formulation which understands religion purely in terms of the individual thus excluding any religious affiliation by heredity). Furthermore, it must remain an unexplained puzzle that we can still identify as a distinct group the non-believing, non-practicing descendants if the common denominator of the group was to start with only the sharing in common of certain religious beliefs and practices.

[8]This, interestingly enough, is reflected in the fact that the correspondence between the name of the ethnic group and that of the land is not clear-cut. The name of the ethnic group did not impose itself on the land in an unambiguous way to the exclusion of all other names. The name of an ethnic group previously in possession of the land, i.e., Canaan, or the name of an ethnic group which possessed previously only part of the land, i.e., Philistine, kept their hold on the land. Furthermore, the Jewish group itself referred to the land by its previous ethnic name, i.e., the land of Israel, which referred to a much wider ethnic reality than that referred to by its contemporaneous name of Jewry. And even this ethnic name of the past was by no

means its exclusive name for the land. It is significant to note, perhaps, that one of the names in prominent use was a name full of religious but not of ethnic relevance, namely, the Holy Land.

[9] Although we cannot enter into this question here it should be evident that these considerations carry important implications for the proper understanding of the phenomenon of modern anti-semitism.

[10] Even the Nazis with all their fanaticism, made so devilish and cruel because of their confusing the ethnic Jewish phenomenon as a racial phenomenon, did not go beyond a three generation limit. As a matter of fact even the three generation limit was theoretical and, except for a few outstanding cases, inapplicable.

[11] Of course, in those instances where it did occur the Jewish ethnic reality was abrogated as far as the progeny is concerned. An interesting example is provided by Spanish aristocracy where apparently Jewish "blood" streams, so to speak, in the veins of most of its families. Still, no one would dream of claiming them as Jewish. This, by the way, provides also a good illustration for the point we made above whereby the ethnic and the racial are not commensurate.

[12] In this connection it is interesting to note that not only does this formulation distort the Jewish phenomenon as such but that the very religious dimension which is here offered as the sole dimension constituting the Jewish phenomenon is also distorted. For the religion which is here offered as the Jewish religion has very little in common with the religion that is commonly known as the Jewish religion. Indeed, it has very little in common with the religious phenomenon as such being much more a kind of a rationalistic, humanistic philosophy and as such hardly distinguishable from unitarianism or the ethical-cultural movement. This need not surprise us for according to our understanding of the Jewish religion the ethnic dimension is absolutely necessitated by the very essence of the religion and any attempt to extirpate the ethnic from the religious must inevitably distort the religious.

[13] True, this criterion is usually raised in the question of conversion, e.g., in the case of a child of a mixed marriage with a non-Jewish mother who is brought up within the Jewish community. But clearly as such it also states the criterion, so to speak, for the "native Jew." For what is required in order to become a Jew is what determines the Jew as such.

[14] It is important to note here that we are not considering the issue of what makes a *good* or a *full* Jew, namely, we are not considering the question of the criterion by which the *degree* of the realization, the living or the expression of one's Jewishness is to be determined. We are considering the criterion by which the very reality of one's Jewishness is determined and as such, of course, this is a criterion which requires the absolute minimal expression. The two criteria are by no means the same though clearly the kind of criterion by which the former question is to be determined is directly dependent on the criterion which determines the latter question. Thus, while the "educational criterion" may well be a legitimate criterion for the former question, i.e., for the question of the degree of realizing one's Jewishness, we are analyzing its legitimacy vis-à-vis the latter question and here its applicability is evidently illegitimate.

[15] Namely, a group can preserve its ethnic identity even though it has become biologically intermixed with other groups if the process of intermarriage, the process which serves as the vehicle for biological intermixing, proceeds in its favor (i.e., when the progeny of the intermarriage go on to marry within the group). A group can also preserve its ethnic identity even though it has lost its distinctive cultural identity but now only if this loss of cultural identity does not lead to intermarriage with outside groups. The prospects, however, of avoiding intermarriage when the cultural identity has been lost are very dim and in these circumstances intermarriage would clearly pose a most serious threat to the preservation of the ethnic identity of the group. Indeed, in no small measure, Judaism could maintain its ethnic identity throughout its long history because it succeeded in preserving its cultural identity. While biologically there was apparently always intermixing, culturally the pre-emancipated Jew held his own by and large. It is only in recent history, namely, only in the context of the Emancipation, that Judaism has been losing its cultural identity. It is only the emancipated Jew who no longer lives in his own "cultural home" thus no longer preserving a

distinct cultural identity. As such, there is no denying (and we certainly do not wish to deny) the serious and precarious situation which this brings about regarding the ethnic identity of the emancipated Jew and the gloomy prospects it indicates regarding his chances of survival (though, of course, the return to Israel introduces a balancing favorable factor). But here we are not concerned with making predictions of the future but with analyzing the present, and in the present the fact remains that an ethnic identity is still preserved even though the cultural identity has disintegrated.

[16]Of course, we could not cover all the many specific formulations with all the finer points that one may encounter or that conceivably can be proposed. But this is not really required. The ones we dealt with cover the main possible lines of formulation and any additional formulation not covered here would in all probability differ only in the finer points. The main possible themes are stated; the many possible variations cannot, and indeed need not, be exhausted here. We should however, mention one more formulation which may perhaps qualify as a theme and not merely as a variation. This is the formulation or set of formulations which propose to define Jewish identity on the principle of a Jewish consciousness. Namely, the Jew is constituted by having a certain conscious identity with the Jewish heritage (what specifically one ought to be conscious of in order to constitute a Jew may vary, it may be a conscious identification with Jewish destiny, with Jewish history, with its religion, language, culture, etc.). Without going into detailed examination and evaluation we should point out that the flaw in the approach of this formulation lies in that it locates the determination of Jewish identity within the subjective and not the objective sphere, namely, within the sphere of one's consciousness. Our considerations, however, have shown that the Jewish reality and thus the question of its identity are determined objectively and not subjectively. Certainly, ideally there should be complete conformity between the objective, independent reality and the subjective acceptance of this reality in one's consciousness. But it is the objective reality that determines and to which the subjective consciousness must correspond and not vice versa. In the approach under consideration here, however, it is the reverse. It is the subjective consciousness, albeit taken as an objective datum, which is made the determining factor. This subjectivism is untenable.

[17]Of course, there is no denying that when such a discrepancy between the subjective wishes and conceptions of the individual on the one hand and objective reality on the other arises, the individual has a problem. Ideally, one's own conceptions and wishes and the objective reality should be in consonance. If not, one can certainly try to change the objective reality though clearly this may succeed only in cases in which the objective reality lends itself to change but not in cases in which it does not. In any event, it is certainly naive and untenable to substitute one's subjective wishes and conceptions for the objective reality.

[18]This is clearly to be distinguished from infant Baptism. The one factor the two have in common is that membership in the religious community is not through the conscious, voluntary entry of the member himself. In both cases it is given but in the case of Judaism it is given by the act of birth while in Baptism it is given by the automatic efficacy of the sacred inherent in the act. Thus, in the former membership is limited by ancestry while in the latter it is universally open. In this connection one should emphasize that membership into the Jewish community of faith is not determined by the act of circumcision and it is a mistake to equate circumcision with Baptism. Circumcision is one of the 613 commandments enjoined on the Jew to fulfill and failure to fulfill it as failure to fulfill any other of the 613 commandments may well impinge on the question of how good a Jew the person is, i.e., to what extent he expresses and fulfills his membership in the Jewish community of faith, but it in no way impinges upon the question whether or not he is a member of the community of faith. A person born to a mother who at the moment of birth is Jewish is fully a Jew regardless of whether he is circumcised or not and vice versa a person who is born to a mother who at the moment of birth is not Jewish though he be circumcised (but of course without conversion) is not a Jew.

[19]The finer points in the Talmudic discussion on this question raising, for example, the point of the Jewish status of the mother not only at the moment of birth but at the moment of conception (i.e., the Jewish status of a child who is conceived by a non-Jewish mother who

however, prior to birth converts to Judaism) in no way changes the conclusions we have derived.

[20]Thus, if a Jewish woman marries a non-Jew, and the *female* offspring through the generations keep marrying non-Jews, with no conversion of course taking place, then the offspring after a number of generations would be taken by the world's consensus as complete non-Jews (since the world's consensus decides by the weight of the majority and the Jewish fraction being here so small as to be completely cancelled out) while in the Halacha, strictly speaking, they would be considered full Jews (since there is here an unbroken chain of the mother being always Jewish). And the reverse would equally hold true if the same model is kept but with the mother and thus the succession of the female offspring being non-Jewish.

[21]In this connection we may mention one more formulation which comes very close to our understanding yet differs in an essential respect. This is the formulation which might be referred to as the Torah-centered formulation of Judaism, a formulation which defines the Jew in terms of the observance of the commandments, namely, a Jew is he on whom lies the obligation to fulfill the commandments. This formulation does indeed hold tight to the ethnic while at the same time giving primacy to the religious – the religious pole is the essential pole and it is by virtue of the religious pole that the ethnic pole is held. This is from our viewpoint a valid and penetrating insight into the reality of the Jewish phenomenon. Our difference with this formulation (and in spite of the importance of similarity it is an essential difference) lies in that this formulation makes Torah, i.e., the all-inclusive body of Pentateuchal and rabbinic commandments, the very essence of the religious dimension in Judaism, while for us Torah is but one mode of expressing the essence of the religious dimension in Judaism, a mode developed during and suitable to the diaspora existence of the community. As such, a number of divergences must follow suit. Thus, for example, for us the binding force of Torah may be abrogated without necessarily undermining the essence of the religious dimension of Judaism (in the circumstances of non-diaspora existence a different mode of expression may evolve) while for this formulation abrogation of Torah must be taken as tantamount to doing away with the very religious dimension of Judaism. Also, while for us the ethnic belonging is as such the primary act of religious witnessing, for this formulation the primary act of religious witnessing is the fulfillment of the commandments and the ethnic-belonging merely delineates the group on whom this obligation devolves. Lastly, this formulation cannot, in the last analysis, escape the charge of parochialism in as much as it limits the obligation of fulfilling the commandments, i.e., of maximally fulfilling the religious vocation, to a certain ethnic-belonging in a way which is final and permanent. For us, on the other hand, the parochial Jewish ethnic-belonging is but a means, albeit a necessary means, to a religious vocation whose fulfillment is ultimately incumbent on the world as a whole, at which time, indeed, the particular, parochial religious vocation of the Jewish ethnic-belonging will be transcended and cancelled.

[22]Of course, while strictly speaking the life of the person prior to conversion must now be considered as belonging to another person and indeed it is so considered by the Halacha, still for the sake of "the peace of the world" the halachic law recognizes the continuation of responsibility in the civil and criminal domain (e.g., continued responsibility for debts or criminal deeds incurred prior to conversion), thus in this respect admitting by inference the non-fictional reality that we are dealing not with two persons but with one and the same person. This however, is a necessary practical adjustment which in no way should be seen as vitiating the intention of the Halacha whereby the convert, through legal fiction, becomes a totally different person, i.e., "a newly born babe."

[23]We can perhaps find in the situation which this analysis reveals yet another and deeper reason for the known observation that Judaism is not a zealous, missionary religion and that for most of its long history it did not actively seek converts, if not in fact actually discouraging them (one notable exception may perhaps be the period from the Maccabean rule through the second century C.E., but even here certainly the forceful conversions imposed by some of the Maccabean kings were more out of political considerations than religious zeal). Aside from the historical reasons given like, for example, the fact that under Islam and Christianity mission activity were punishable by death, or the fear of the infiltration of a "fifth column," or the need to direct all energy and concern inwardly in order to survive

against the heavy odds of diaspora existence, reasons whose validity we do not deny, our analysis should explain what would appear to be an innate tendency in Judaism against active missionizing (as distinguished from and in addition to the above contingent, historically-determined attitudes). For it shows the considerable force of the ethnic-belonging in Judaism, a force which must be detrimental to missionizing concerns and activities. True, Judaism overcomes it to make conversion, when it is really desired, possible. But this would seem to be the extent of its success in overcoming the negative factor of the ethnic-belonging, namely, it succeeds in removing, so to speak, the impassable block which the ethnic places before conversion. But this is a far cry from disposing Judaism toward initiating and maintaining an active drive of missionizing activity. With the ethnic remaining a central factor in the structure of Judaism just the reverse would seem to be called for. Indeed, if active missionizing were to be undertaken by Judaism, then by the same token that the structure of faith of Judaism requires the centrality of the ethnic in its structure it would also have to require that such missionizing be directed toward ethnic groupings, i.e., other nations, and not toward individuals as such. For the redemptive message of Judaism is addressed not to man in his individuality but to man in his social-ethnic context, i.e., to the nations of men (indeed, the few outstanding missionizing undertakings in Jewish history would seem to lean out of proportion toward the conversion of whole kingdoms). In Judaism redemption will come through the nations being converted and not through the increase in number of the Jewish nation by individual conversions (the quantitative size of the Jewish nation is immaterial as far as the fulfillment of its task in the economy of redemption is concerned). Thus, missionizing in the sense of saving individual souls is ultimately meaningless in the context of Judaism, though, of course, the individual who wishes to share in the peculiar vocation and destiny of Israel is not barred.

[24]This is not to say that he remains a "good" and full Jew but that he remains minimally a Jew. This is also not to say that Judaism, commensurate to a person's transgressions, does not restrict and limit his participation in the life of the community and in the privileges it bestows upon its members. In this sense it certainly resorts to excommunication and to other punishments including the death penalty. But in all this the transgressor remains a Jew (even when he is executed for violating his religion he is executed as a Jew). Judaism because of the ethnic factor cannot do a thing about the Jewishness of the transgressor.

[25]Thus, there is no problem with the convert who changes his mind and renounces his conversion. He is a repenting Jew. No reconversion to Judaism is required. This is understandable since from the ethnic perspective he has been a Jew all along and from the religious perspective the difficulty of a simultaneous membership in another community of faith is now removed.

[26]This theoretical formulation was apparently adopted by the Karaites. It certainly underlies the custom (not a law) practiced by some Jews of mourning a close member of the family who converted in the way of mourning the dead.

Chapter Six

The Dilemma of Identity
for the Emancipated Jew

Judaism today is characterized by a question mark. For what finds expression most often and most authentically within contemporary Jewish consciousness is a question: "What is a Jew?" This question is manifest in all of contemporary Jewish life – in detached philosophical-literary speculation, practical political-juristic formulation, and the ill-articulated but existentially immediate awareness of the ordinary individual. The existence of the Jew of today is marked by pervasive perplexity, which is thus authentically expressed by this recurring, nagging question. In the immediate lived reality of his existence he finds that he is unique. But what constitutes this uniqueness he does not know. He does not know what makes him a Jew.

Thus, Jewish life today can be most accurately characterized as a search for identity. Closely bound up with this search, however, is a search for the vocation that the adjective "Jewish" is supposed to connote. For the Jew's identity is intimately enmeshed in his distinctive calling and task in this world. Indeed, his identity can be determined and articulated only in terms of his vocation. Thus, underlying the question, "What is a Jew?" is the further question, "What is the vocation of the Jew?" In these two questions lie the crisis of present-day Jewry.

I

From a historical perspective we can see quite clearly that it was the phenomenon of Emancipation that posed these two questions for the Jew. Throughout Jewry's long history, from earliest times up to the recent era, the issue of vocation and consequently that of identity did not arise for Jewry. Generally speaking, Jewish consciousness had attained clearly formulated and acceptable answers to these questions. The Jew understood his vocation essentially in religious categories: his was the vocation of faith. He was called to be a witness to the presence, glory, justice and providence of God ("On this day you are my witnesses"). This vocation, however, was assigned not primarily to the individual but to the community, i.e., the nation, which was the primary carrier of the task and was, indeed, conceived to have come into being as a nation only by being assigned this vocation. Such vocation as the individual had was derived from that of the nation, and only by belonging to the nation could he participate in the religious vocation. His religious vocation implied and, indeed, required his ethnic identity as part of the peoplehood of Israel. Accordingly, the Jew understood his vocation and identity in terms of an inextricable union of religious and ethnic categories. This self-understanding characterized the Jew throughout his entire history until recent times, and served as the constant, unshakable foundation of his self-image. Clearly, in these circumstances the question of what constituted his Jewishness could never arise.

However, while this call to witness through ethnic identity remained constant, the concrete form of its expression, i.e., the *mode* of witnessing, could and did change. For the mode of witnessing is, after all, contingent upon the conditions of life, seeing that it is they which provide the witnessing with the material for its expression. Thus, if and when the conditions should change radically, the mode of witnessing, if it is to continue to be viable, i.e., capable of concretely articulating the witnessing, must likewise change and adapt itself to the new conditions.

Indeed, viewed from this vantage point, the radical turn which separated and distinguished rabbinic Judaism from biblical Israel was due to a change, not in the nation's vocation or in its content (these remained constant), but in its expression. Jewry's mode of witnessing changed because of the radical change in conditions: from an existence in its own sovereign state to an existence in diaspora. When it possessed an independent state, biblical Israel had at its disposal the machinery and the reality of exercising power (how limited this power might have been in comparison with the power of other states matters little in this context). The state could make and enforce decisions, and thus actively and concretely fashion the course of its history in all its dimensions: political, economic, and social. Biblical Israel lived in the concrete political world and had the task of charting its destiny within profane, secular history. Consequently, its life was in turn fashioned by that history into an ongoing process that was ever-changing and ever-new. Correspondingly, its mode of witnessing was made into an ever-open, situational kind of witnessing. This mode expressed itself in and through profane, secular history by the very exercise of Israel's power. The witness of Israel could not be predetermined, but had to enter the flux of profane, secular history, there to risk and expose itself ever anew in specific decisions. A succession of such open decisions, the warp and woof of the fabric of history, made its witness by directing and transforming profane, secular history in response to the divine challenge. Thus, the biblical mode of witnessing can be characterized essentially in two aspects: 1) the material of the mode was the power afforded by the concrete world and its profane, secular history; 2) the form of the mode was the open, situational decision-making.

The loss of the state and the exile into diaspora-existence signified a radical change in the conditions of life of the Jewish people. Essentially, it meant that having lost their state, they no longer had at their disposal the possibility of exercising power, for the exercise of power is afforded a nation only through the machinery of the state. Without power the Jewish people as a people could no longer exist in the concrete political world nor could they impinge upon and thus influence its profane, secular history.[1] To exist outside that world meant, however, that the pattern and structure of Jewish existence was no longer submerged in the ongoing, ever-changing process which characterizes the concrete world and its profane history. Hence, Jewish existence assumed a pattern that was closed, unchanging and completed, an existence which let the concrete world and its profane history flow by it.[2]

The rabbinic statement that prophecy had ceased in Israel since the days of Ezra and Nehemiah is not to be read as a mere descriptive statement. It is categorical – it had to be so. While holding fast to the substance of biblical Israel's vocation of faith, diaspora Judaism had to reshape its mode of witnessing to correspond to the new conditions of its existence.

The new mode of witnessing through which diaspora-based rabbinic Judaism expressed the vocation of faith was the Law.[3] We do not imply that this mode of witnessing did not exist prior to rabbinic Judaism; rather, the newness lay in rabbinic Judaism's understanding of the nature and status of the Law.[4] The Law was now conceived as an all-inclusive, eternal and unchanging system of prescriptions. Consequently, the way that followed from its prescriptions was a way that was completed and closed – a way that had already arrived at the end, that was already "there." He who travelled this way was following a precharted, predetermined way, with the navigation of each new turn already known. Indeed, the way was more like a static system that covered and decided in advance every conceivable situation. There was no room for the genuinely new, undetermined and open situation. All-inclusiveness and permanence rather than flux and ongoingness were this way's characteristics. He who witnessed, therefore, through the Law was not called upon to take his ground in open response, risking his decision in the face of ever-new situations. His response was already determined and formulated, at least theoretically, for every conceivable situation. His task was merely to discover the right answer.[5]

Quite clearly, the mode of witnessing through the Law corresponded to the conditions of diaspora-existence. Diaspora-existence and the witnessing through the Law were alike outside the flux and ongoingness of profane history. They were already "there," waiting at the end of profane history, complete, finished, and static. Indeed, the Law could guide and encompass the life of the diaspora community so thoroughly, precisely because it corresponded so intimately to the conditions of diaspora-existence.

II

On the basis of our analysis above regarding the change in the conditions of existence that characterized the transition from biblical Israel to rabbinic Judaism, we should expect that the Emancipation would involve yet another radical change in the mode of witnessing of the Jewish people. This indeed is essentially the case, except that the change in the conditions of existence signaled by the Emancipation presents serious difficulties – difficulties which make the emergence of an appropriate new mode of witnessing highly problematic. Thus is precipitated the crisis of vocation and identity for the present-day emancipated Jew.

The conditions of existence signaled by the Emancipation are the exact reverse of the conditions of existence under which rabbinic Judaism lived. For the Emancipation signals the re-entry of the Jewish people into the concrete world and its profane history.[6] This, quite clearly, has to precipitate a crisis in the mode of witnessing of rabbinic Judaism. For the Law as a permanent, unchanging, and all-inclusive system simply does not fit the conditions of existing in the concrete profane world. We should not be surprised, therefore, that the neglect and even abandonment of the Law follow closely upon Emancipation.[7]

That the Emancipation collides with the mode of witnessing of rabbinic Judaism can be seen not only through the mass exodus of emancipated Jews from under the wings of the Law but indeed in the very religious movements that are representative products of the Emancipation. All of them – Reform, Conservative, and Reconstructionist – center around the question of the Law. For all, the Law is the basic issue of division and all (though in different degrees of radicalness) compromise the *in toto* conception of the Law insisted upon in rabbinic Judaism.[8] Clearly, emancipated Jewry is searching for a new mode of witnessing, struggling to find a more open and flexible expression of the witnessing.

It might seem, therefore, that our analysis ought to come to rest at this point to await the emergence of a new mode of witnessing. Yet in truth the situation of emancipated Jewry is much more problematic and precarious than we have shown thus far. It is not merely that emancipated Jewry is going through a period of transition, though that is a difficult enough problem. The issue goes far deeper than the search for a new, adequate mode of witnessing. *It questions the possibility of there being any mode at all that can authentically express the witness of emancipated Jewry.* In other words, it questions whether an emancipated Jewry is at all possible.

The issue lies in the fact that the re-entry of Jewry into the concrete, profane world takes place in diaspora. This means that it is a re-entry into someone else's world, a world fashioned and governed by, and expressing and manifesting the ethos of, other nations, cultures and religions. It is a world that Judaism and the Jewish people did not create and therefore do not possess or control.[9]

These circumstances imply two important considerations which radically question the possibility of a full Jewish Emancipation in diaspora and introduce a certain element of estrangement and ambivalence into the Emancipation. First, it is difficult to see how Judaism in its vocation as a religion can truly enter into this world and its history. For how, then, will it be able to fulfill its task of guiding and directing the destiny of this world and its history, and, moreover, of sitting in judgment upon the world and the nations? How can a Jewish mode of witnessing authentically express itself in terms of this world and its history when the *sine qua non* for this is the use of power, power that Judaism cannot have because the world and the history which it enters are not its own? Thus, even if we were to suppose that Jewry, as a people, could be emancipated, the truth is that Judaism, as a religion, cannot follow suit and thereby be in a position to formulate and express the vocation of the emancipated Jew. Emancipation, therefore, must be partial – applying to Jewry but not to Judaism, and implying a necessary estrangement between the two. To the extent that Jewry is emancipated, Judaism simply cannot be meaningful to it, for Judaism ceases to be in a position to formulate and express its vocation. But by the same token, Jewry, to the extent that it is emancipated and yet remains Jewish (in the sense at least of not becoming something else), is left without vocation. For from where else can it receive its vocation than from Judaism? We should not be surprised, therefore, that secularism should quickly engulf the majority of emancipated Jews and that simultaneously the crisis of vocation and identity should be precipitated for them.

This predicament is further shown and, indeed, made even more radical by a second consideration: The Emancipation of the Jewish people *as a people* is simply not possible. This truth follows from the fact that the re-entry of emancipated diaspora Jewry into the concrete, profane world is not by right (since the diaspora-world is not its own) or through its own power, but through the grace and permission of the nations who possess and control this world. In the last analysis, it is the host-nations that determine the nature and extent of Jewish Emancipation, and the permission that they extend to Jewish re-entry is far from open and unconditional. Indeed, in this connection the important thing for us to note is that the nations exclude, as indeed they must, the entry of Jewry *qua* nation. For how can they permit another nation to share the power and control of their world?[10] We should not be surprised, therefore, to find that to the extent that the door is opened at all, it is opened not to the Jewish people as a nation, but only to the Jew as an individual.[11]

But what does the term "Jew" signify now, since it can no longer signify either the vocation of faith of Judaism or ethnic membership in the Jewish nation? Clearly, it has become an empty term which at best may signify the past but not the present, not the belongingness or vocation of the emancipated individual. Indeed, it would seem that in the last resort permission to enter upon Emancipation is withheld not only from Jewry as a nation but also from the Jew as an individual. True, there seems to be a distinction with respect to the *offer* of Emancipation; i.e., while the offer cannot even be made to the Jewish nation, it can and is made to the Jewish individual. Yet in the latter's very acceptance of the offer, his Jewishness (to the extent that it can have any specific, distinct meaning for the emancipated individual) must be left behind. The individual may enter the concrete, profane world of the host-nation, but not as a Jew, only as a human being.[12]

Thus, we are forced to conclude that the re-entry of diaspora Jewry into the concrete, profane world, as signaled by the Emancipation, is anything but simple and straightforward. Jewry must pay the highest possible price, a price so high that its very vocation and identity are shattered. Judaism, which formulates and articulates the Jewish vocation of faith, cannot accompany Jewry in its re-entry and must remain outside. In the same way, the Jewish nation, which defines and determines Jewish ethnic identity and belongingness, must also stay outside. Yet, these are the two pillars that from the very inception of Jewry always defined its vocation and identity. Once these are taken away, the term "Jewish" is robbed of all signification. The only "identity" left to the emancipated Jew is to be a member of the human species. But this puts him in an impossible position. To be a human being in general is to be nothing in particular, a mere abstraction.

Theoretically, there are two ways out of this plight of the emancipated diaspora-Jew. One is to carry the process of Emancipation to its logical conclusion and enter not only the concrete, profane world and history of the host-nations but also their ethnic reality and, if need be, their religious vocation[13] (true, the individual cannot enter himself, no matter how much he may want to do so, but he can ensure entrance for his descendents fairly easily through intermarriage and conversion). The other way is to withdraw from Emancipation and thus make possible a complete and authentic return to Judaism, to both its religious vocation and its ethnic-national identity. On either course, the popular understanding of Emancipation as a means by which the Jew can belong simultaneously to two worlds, the Western and the Jewish world, is seen to be untenable, an illusion. The only resolution of the dilemma is to go in one or the other direction. Evidence of both these alternatives is apparent today. On the one hand, intermarriage is very widespread and the prospects are that it will engulf more and more emancipated Jews in the days to come. On the other hand, within some quarters of emancipated Jewry faint but nonetheless real signs are appearing of withdrawal from the world of Western culture. And hand in hand with this withdrawal has come a return to the mode of witnessing of rabbinic Judaism.[14] From the Jewish viewpoint it is this latter trend that will provide the surviving remnant (no matter how small its numbers), a remnant that can alone and without self-contradiction or ambiguity live an authentic Jewish life in the world of diaspora.[15]

III

Thus far our analysis has concentrated upon the predicament which the Emancipation precipitated for Jewry (and Judaism) when the latter finds itself in the context of diaspora-existence. That we have done this is understandable seeing that the Emancipation has been initially introduced in the context of diaspora-existence. Our analysis, however, has clearly shown that the predicament which the Emancipation precipitates for Jewry (and Judaism) results not from the nature of the Emancipation as such, but rather from the fact that it takes place in the context of diaspora-existence and this, in turn, clearly implies that if the factor of diaspora-existence is removed from the picture, namely, if Emancipation is to take place in the context of a Jewish state rather than in diaspora, the predicament disclosed by our analysis above should be removed. For in direct contrast to the situation in diaspora, the emancipated Jew can now enter a concrete world and a profane history that are of his own making. It is a Jewish world that he enters. Consequently, he enters by right and not by sufferance. Every aspect of the world is open to him – political, social, economic, ethical, and cultural. He is given full power and unrestricted opportunity to determine the course and destiny of the concrete world. Most important, no longer does he have to enter as that dubious and ambiguous entity, "man"; he enters as the concrete being he is: a Jew. No one stands in the way to place conditions and qualifications on how he is to enter. Nor is Judaism excluded from entering this concrete world and its profane history. Judaism is there to define and articulate the vocation and identity of the Jew, to give guidance but also to pass judgment. Thus, the re-establishment of a Jewish state in our time can be seen as an answer to the predicament which the Emancipation precipitates for Jewry (and Judaism) in the context of diaspora-existence. The re-establishment of a Jewish state allows the Emancipation, i.e., the re-entry of Jewry into the concrete world and its profane history, to proceed all the way and to do so without compromising in any way the Jewishness of the Jew. Only in the context of his own state can the Jew achieve full emancipation without in any way compromising his Jewishness. If the Jew is to be fully emancipated and at the same time remain fully Jewish, a re-established Jewish state is required. Herein indeed lies the deeper significance of the re-establishment of the state of Israel – it is a response not only to the humanitarian needs of Jewry but also to the theological concerns of Judaism.

And yet, while the dilemma of Jewish re-entry is positively resolved by means of the re-established state of Israel, it does not follow that the other question posed by the Emancipation, the question of the viability of the rabbinic mode of witnessing, is similarly resolved. On the contrary, the crisis of the rabbinic mode of witnessing through the Law is precipitated all the more radically. For while the rabbinic formulation of the Law as all-inclusive, and hence static and unchanging, could serve so admirably as the mode of witnessing of diaspora and unemancipated Jewry, since it corresponded so well to Jewry's trans-historical and trans-worldly mode of existence, the rabbinic formulation fails miserably to serve as the mode of witnessing for emancipated Israeli Jewry. This is because that formulation no longer corresponds to, but is indeed at an opposite end from, its new mode of existence, which is immersed in the open and ongoing character of the concrete world and its profane history. The crisis of the Law as the mode of witnessing, as analyzed above regarding diaspora emancipated Jewry, applies just as much here. If anything, the crisis can be seen more clearly and poignantly, precisely because the entry of the emancipated Israeli Jew into the concrete world is so complete and unambiguous, without any qualifications or half-way accommodations.   Consequently, there are no theological "backdoors" through which the Law can partially re-enter, if only in a mitigated and qualified way, to serve as a vague, half-hearted mode of witnessing. We should not be surprised, therefore, that there should be such a radical crisis of the Law and hence of rabbinic Judaism in the State of Israel today.

However, the contemporary rejection of the Law and of rabbinic Judaism in the State of Israel should not be taken as necessarily a radical secularization of the community in the sense of abandoning the vocation of religious witnessing. This latter alternative is indeed possible, but the collapse of the Law is not necessarily indicative of it.[16] What is clearly indicated is that the mode of witnessing of rabbinic Judaism has been rejected. But we must not identify rabbinic Judaism with the Jewish community of faith or with the phenomenon of Judaism as such. Rabbinic Judaism is but one expression of this community, of this phenomenon, an expression resulting in large part from particular historical conditions. For let us not forget that during the time when Jewry lived in the concrete world and possessed its own state, i.e., during the biblical period, the mode of witnessing was quite different from that of rabbinic Judaism. Indeed, in this connection it is interesting to note that simultaneously with the rejection of rabbinic Judaism in modern Israel we should be witnessing a conscious, enthusiastic turning toward the Bible. Modern Israel feels a strong kinship with the Bible while rabbinic Judaism has become an estranged, alien phenomenon, and this in spite of the fact that the latter is so much closer in time. The mode of existence is evidently the determining factor for the mode of witnessing. Thus, it may not be perhaps too far fetched to look forward to a new mode of witnessing emerging in modern Israel, a mode which will resemble the mode of witnessing of biblical Israel.

The Jewish community of faith is living today in the midst of a period of radical crisis. In the thousands of years of its history there has been only one comparable instance: the change from the biblical to the rabbinic period. We can see only the negative, destructive side of this crisis – the collapse of a structure and pattern of life, or, as formulated in the present essay, the collapse of a mode of witnessing that defined, guided, and regulated the vocation of the community. Accordingly, this exposition had to deal primarily with the negative side. The positive side has not yet emerged. One can only hope for the coming of another mode of witnessing that will implement the vocation of the community. We are not able to project the course of the development. The future remains always open and does not admit of prophecies.

---

[1]Of course, as individual human beings the Jews continued in a sense to exist in the profane world, as there is no place else for individual human beings to exist. But as the Jewish nation they were excluded, and it is in terms of the Jewish nation that this analysis is conducted. Our very understanding of the concepts "concrete world" and "profane history" in terms of power and the machinery of the state applies quite evidently only to an analysis of nations rather than to that of individuals. Furthermore, even as individual human beings the Jews, precisely because of their Jewishness, led a passive existence. They were, by and large, objects receiving the action of the world, not subjects who directed and fashioned that world and its history.

[2]Naturally, in the course of almost two thousand years of diaspora-existence there were also changes. But many of them were accommodations necessitated by the strategy of survival, while others were very often imposed from the outside. In neither case did these changes really affect the essential structure of Jewish diaspora-existence. They were incidental changes – necessary and minimal compromises and accommodations.

Franz Rosenzweig's description of Judaism as "outside the world and history" is thus a perceptive and profound description of rabbinic Judaism as it reflects diaspora-existence, though not of the phenomenon of Judaism as a whole. It does not apply to other modes of witnessing which the community of faith could and, indeed, did assume. Only if we equate rabbinic Judaism with hte total phenomenon of Judaism can Rosenzweig's analysis stand. Such an equation however, is not really justified. Along the same line, Arnold Toynbee's description of Judaism as a "fossil" can be understood only as a judgment upon diaspora Judaism given from the viewpoint of profane history. From that viewpoint, with its essential criterion of power, diaspora-existence is essentially a "fossil" since it cannot participate as an active, living organism in the fashioning and directing of profane history. Thus, Toynbee's description must be taken seriously. But this is not to say that there is no other dimension of living beyond that of profane history. Here lies the basic justification for accusing Toynbee of "intellectual anti-Semitism," particularly since he himself, when he ceases to be a descriptive historian and turns into a religious "apostle," preaches a mode of existence which is akin to that of diaspora Judaism.

[3]The word "Law" stands here for both the *Halacha,* "the way," and the *Torah,* "the Teaching." Although strictly speaking the two terms refer to two distinct entities, the *Torah* referring to the source from which the *Halacha* is formulated, they are related in a very intimate way. The point we are trying to make here applies to the Law as both "the way" and "the Teaching."

[4]Witnessing through the Law was always characteristic of the phenomenon of Judaism and certainly manifested itself already in the biblical period. But in that period (1) the Law was only one among other modes of witnessing and by no means the most basic or distinctive; (2) the Law did not presume to encompass the totality of life in all details; (3) there were a number of codes of law reflecting the legislation of different parts of the country and different segments of the population. Hence, the Law of the biblical community was anything but monolithic, unchanging, and all-encompassing. Rabbinic Judaism, on the other hand, while continuing the mode of witnessing found in the biblical period, radically transformed its nature and status by (1) making the Law the only normative mode of witnessing; (2) extending it to all possible contingencies of life in all their details; (3) hypostatizing the Law, giving it independent existence as a permanent, unchanging, unitary, and all-encompassing code. Thus, it was through these changes in the conception of the nature and status of the Law rather than

through the introduction of a totally new mode of witnessing that rabbinic Judaism signaled a radical turn in the expression of the phenomenon of Judaism.

[5]Thus, the office of the rabbi, the office *par excellence* of rabbinic Judaism, was simply that of interpreter and explicator. The *Torah* revealed once and for all at Sinai was taken to be eternally and absolutely valid, or at least (as taken by some, e.g., Rabbi Yosi, a third century Babylonian Amora) absolutely valid until the coming of the messianic age, which was, by the way, to coincide with the end of diaspora-existence (this latter view is certainly most suggestive and intriguing when seen from the vantage point of our interpretation, though it was certainly not the reasoning behind this rabbinic view). Furthermore, and this is the crux of our point, the *Torah* was taken in principle to cover every conceivable situation. When confronted with a supposedly "new" situation (from the viewpoint of *Torah* there was of course no genuine newness), the rabbi's task was merely to discover, interpret, and apply the appropriate response. Of course, some responses did not fall into this predetermined category but were authentically new and open – evolving from man's decision in face of a concrete situation. These were the *g'zerot,* the rabbinic edicts. They resulted from the fact that, in however limited a way, diaspora Jewry was still inevitably involved in profane history. But even here the rabbis were extremely reluctant to resort to a "new" mode of response. They sought with all their ingenuity to find the appropriate, preformulated response in the *Torah.* When the genuine newness of profane history made this impossible, recourse to the edict was inevitable. However, even then, the rabbis considered such recourse a forced temporary exception (*g'zerat Hashaa,* an edict of the hour) placed in a separate category from response formulated in the *Torah.* Furthermore, the view that in many instances the rabbis were really formulating their own response, which they then read into the *Torah* as the alleged source, does not present a problem to our interpretation. What is important here is not what we maintain or even the reality of the situation, but the claim made by the rabbis. That claim is very clear: The *Torah* given to Moses at Sinai is all-comprehending, unchangeable, and eternally valid. The rabbis did not see themselves as initiators or bearers of new responses but as technicians discovering responses already formulated. How different, then, was the office of rabbi, the symbol of rabbinic Judaism, from that of the prophet, the symbol of biblical Israel.

[6]We must emphasize again that the object of our analysis is – and indeed, as pointed out above, can only be – the Jewish people as a whole and not Jewish individuals. Of course, there were prior to the Emancipation individual Jews who were emancipated. As such they provide a fascinating study of how on an individual basis witnessing in the framework of rabbinic Judaism was combined with participation in the concrete world. The price exacted, however, from such persons was a double life, which an individual person may get away with but which a nation as a whole cannot endure. Thus, the distinctive mark of the Emancipation is precisely that the nation as a whole, and not just a certain number of individuals, enter the profane world.

[7]Emancipation has set in at different times in the various geographic locations where the Jewish people lived (e.g., Western Europe, Eastern Europe, Arabic lands). Thus, the correlation between the onset of Emancipation and the precipitation of the "crisis of the Law" can be observed in a great number of instances. No sooner does the former occur than the latter follows.

[8]The *"in toto"* is all important for our interpretation, since the crisis is precipitated precisely because of the incompatibility between the changing character of the concrete world and the mode of witnessing through an unchanging Law. To do away with the *"in toto"* (no matter how infinitesimally small the compromise) means the surrender of the essence of the Law as conceived in rabbinic Judaism.

Emancipated religious Jewry's need for a new mode of witnessing is seen not only in its institutionalized religious movements but also in the various theological thoughts which, although arising in it, are nevertheless clearly concerned with preserving the law in some fashion. Thus, for example, resort is often made in this thought to the principle of "selectivity," either as (a) existential selectivity, whereby the Law is turned into a "reservoir" from which the individual person is to select as binding only what he can truthfully appropriate as his own authentic expression (e.g., F. Rosenzweig), or (b) ethical selectivity, whereby the Law is divided into (1) a small kernel of supposedly unchanging and eternally binding ethical injunctions and (2) the large remaining body of the law, which is seen as the strategy devised to protect the ethical injunctions and which therefore is time-bound and changeable (e.g., L. Baeck). Although a principle of selectivity of sorts is found in rabbinic thought (e.g., the distinction between Scriptural Law and rabbinic Law, or even that between the Law and the "fence around the Law," a distinction that would seem particularly close to the modern way of ethical selectivity), it is quite different from the two formulations just mentioned. For one thing, it locates the selectivity objectively as a means of classification within the Law itself rather than making it subjectively dependent either upon the individual's authenticity or upon extra-revelatory ethical criteria. Second, and more important, in the rabbinic view the principle of selectivity is not allowed to compromise or mitigate the binding force and obligatory nature of the Law as a whole.

[9]This description applies to diaspora Emancipation in all parts of the world, e.g., the Arabic-Islamic as much as the European-Christian world. Of course, the Emancipation has been manifested most clearly and importantly in the latter world, which therefore primarily guides our analysis. The situation in the United States is somewhat different from that in Europe due to the fact that the ethnic-national character of the American people is relatively new and is, indeed, still in the process of formation, thus lacking a clear and definite structure. Also the presence of the black minority complicates the picture. Nevertheless, it is our provisional contention that the position of Jewry in the United States will finally prove to be basically the same as in the rest of the Western world.

[10]This, of course, means that Judaism *qua* religion, seeing that it is a religion which is inextricably bound to the nation, is excluded as well since its carrier, the Jewish nation, is excluded. But even if Judaism as a religion that witnesses "horizontally" through profane history could somehow enter the world without the Jewish nation as its carrier (which in reality is not possible), it would still not be allowed to enter. For how can the nations of the world as custodians of their religions accept another religion to share with their own the guidance and judgment of their actions and policies? And insofar as the nations are secularized, Judaism *qua* religion certainly does not have a place in their world.

[11]We are thus witnessing a unique phenomenon in Jewish history: it is the individual Jew, not the nation as such, that is emancipated. The term "emancipated Jewry" signifies, therefore, only a collection of individual Jews. This situation is entirely different from the phenomena of the exile into diaspora and of the birth of biblical Israel (i.e., Sinai), phenomena appertaining essentially to the nation and not to the individual. This does not contradict what is said above in note 6. There attention is called to the fact that the Emancipation in our day engulfs the vast majority of Jews in contrast to the emancipation of isolated, individual Jews in the past. In this sense, Emancipation today affects the Jewish nation as a whole. Nevertheless, attention must be called to the primary subject of Emancipation in our day: the individual Jew. In other words, the Jewish nation is "emancipated" only because the vast majority of its members are emancipated.

[12]That this condition could have asserted itself in the first place arises from the fact that the offer of Emancipation did not extend to membership in the peoplehood of the nation but only to membership in the state. Under the influence of the Enlightenment, the state was conceived as a separate, independent, neutral entity which could accept any human being as a member, i.e., as a citizen, as long as he swore allegiance to it and abided by its rules. The fault lay in assigning to the citizenry of the state an independent reality that could furnish full identity for its members. This meant a betrayal of the intimate relationship between individual identity and the ethnic-national entity. For in truth, the state and its citizenry are but conventional political-legal expressions of the ethnic-national entity. Consequently, while outsiders may participate as citizens in the conventional political-legal structure called the state, they do so only through the toleration of the ethnic-national entity. Unfortunately, as has been demonstrated only too clearly in our day, the toleration is not too abundant. The ethnic-national entity seems to possess an innate drive to try to appropriate the state exclusively, tolerating outsiders only when they are few and then only on an individual, temporary basis. Thus, the entry into the citizenry of the state that the Emancipation offered

was in the last analysis a sham. Authentic and full entry could only take place in terms of the ethnic–national entity, and it is here that our dilemma arises.

[13]It would seem that the major stumbling block in the path to full Emancipation is erected by the question of ethnic-national identity rather than religious vocation, since the latter is a changeable factor while the former is not. Thus, for example, it is quite possible that the ethnic-national entity into which the emancipated individual seeks full entry should be essentially secularized, in which case conversion to its religion would not be necessary (and, in any event, even if conversion were required or, more likely, desired, there would be no problem in embracing it since conversion to the religions of the world, unlike conversion to Judaism, does not require simultaneous entry into an ethnic-national entity.) As against this, appropriating the ethnic-national identity of the host-nation is always required and yet is never available to the emancipated individual. Here is the insurmountable stumbling block to full emancipation.

This perennial factor of ethnic-national belongingness operates just as effectively from the Jewish side. In holding fast to the view, "once a Jew, always a Jew," Judaism refuses to surrender its claim on anyone who ever was a Jew. But this is a result not of capriciousness but of the fact that being Jewish implies necessarily belonging to the Jewish ethnic-national entity. One simply cannot give this up. Even conversion out of the faith cannot dissolve the ethnic bond. Thus, both from the side of the world and from the side of Judaism it is the ethnic bond that obstructs the exit of the Jew from Judaism and his entry into the nations of the world.

[14]In this connection it is interesting to note the recent rise of the Jewish day-school movement and the return to Orthodoxy manifested in some quarters of emancipated Jewry.

[15]Only if we understand Jewish identity and vocation in religious categories can Jewish existence in diaspora make sense and in a way be justified. For the essence of Jewry is then formulated in terms that transcend the world of diaspora. If we understand Jewish identity in secular categories, its identity is exclusively ethnic. But what justification does an ethnic-national group have for living outside its own land in the midst of other ethnic-national groups? There was no escape from this abnormal state of affairs when Jewry did not possess its own state. With the restoration of the State of Israel how can one whose understanding of Jewry is exclusively secular, i.e., ethnic-national, in character, justify the continuous existence of Jewry in diaspora?

[16]Our assumption here, as above with respect to emancipated diaspora Jewry, is that while it is possible to interpret what is happening in Jewish life today in terms of a thorough and fundamental secularization of the Jewish community – secularization in the sense of a renunciation of the religious vocation – this is not the only interpretation possible. We contend that the facts may suggest a less radical secularization, in the sense of a collapse of one mode of witnessing and the not-yet emerging reality of a new mode. Such secularization is partial since, in principle, it does not reject the religious vocation and is itself transitory.

Chapter Seven

Some Reflections on Death and Immortality in Mainstream Judaism

The concern with the event of death is almost universal in the phenomenon of religion. There is hardly a manifestation of the religious phenomenon from its earliest and most primary manifestations to its most recent and advanced manifestations which is not concerned with the event of death. Even more significantly, this concern is by no means peripheral or accidental to the religious phenomenon. Rather, it constitutes the very center on which the religious concern is focused; it constitutes the very essence of the religious concern. Indeed, for many an expression of religion, death has come to constitute, to use a Tillichian notion, the ultimate predicament which religion must address and overcome. As such, it should not be surprising that for many people religion has become inseparable from death, indeed, almost unanimous with death in the sense that if it were not for the event of death there would be no need for religion to arise. Religion has come into the world because of death and it will disappear only when death is overcome.

This inextricable centrality which death occupies in so many religions is actually quite understandable. For what is ultimately involved in the event of death as it functions here is nothing else but the finitude of our being, its creatureliness, the fact that we are created beings and as such inescapably limited. Death is the expression of this limitation, this finitude of our being. Indeed it is its most poignant expression precisely because it is its most radical expression – the most fundamental and ultimate expression of the finitude of our being. For all other expressions of our finitude are but partial expressions with respect to this or that characteristic of our being and are ultimately grounded in this underlying, all-pervasive finitude of our being, i.e. the finitude expressed by the event of death. At the same time it is also quite clear that this notion of the finitude of our being is, in turn, a notion which is most eminently qualified to express the notion of the ultimate predicament. For after all it expresses a shortcoming that is inherent in the very constitution of our being, that is all-pervasive, that affects our existence in the most fundamental sense. What better candidate for the notion of the ultimate predicament can one find? No wonder that the preponderance of religions irrespective of where and when they arise should come to perceive the event of death as constituting the ultimate predicament which they must address and overcome, and as such, it is indeed understandable that the event of death is so fundamentally and pervasively associated with the phenomenon of religion.

But if the importance and significance of the perception of death as constituting the ultimate predicament is to be fully appreciated, there are two further observations that must be noted. First, it must be noted that the perception of death as the ultimate predicament clearly presents us with an ultimate predicament which formulates itself in the ontological domain. For the predicament here is inextricably connected with the question of the ontological constitution of man. Indeed, it can arise only because we are ontologically constituted as creatures, as finite beings. Secondly, it must be further noted that inasmuch as the predicament here articulates itself in terms of finitude (namely, that it is finitude which actually constitutes the predicament) the predicament can arise only in a context which lends itself to quantification, i.e., in a context which lends itself to a calculus of more or less. For clearly in having the predicament articulate itself in terms of finitude we are saying that we do not have enough (though evidently having some) of whatever it is that we need to have – in our case, this would be the duration of our being, namely, we are saying that the predicament lies in our not enduring long enough. And clearly, in order to be able to assert this, the endurance of our being must be quantifiable which, in turn, means that the very constitution of our being must be in terms of that which is quantifiable. Now, we would submit that, given the alternatives which are viable, this would clearly point to our being constituted in terms of power. For power is clearly quantifiable. By its very signification it implicates quantification – one can have more and more power ad infinitum (and conversely, less and less power). As such, a being which is constituted in terms of power is readily quantifiable both in terms of itself and in terms of all its characterizations and attitudes. And with respect to such a being it makes perfectly good sense to apply such notions as finitude and correspondingly such activities as those which would constitute the increase or the diminution of finitude. With respect to a being-of-power, therefore, the notion of an ultimate predicament which formulates itself in terms of the finitude of being is perfectly admissible.

We may perhaps better appreciate this connection between the view of the ultimate predicament in terms of finitude and the constitution of our being in terms of power if we direct our attention for a moment to what the situation would be with respect to the other major alternative constitution of our being, namely, if we turn our attention to what the situation would be if we were constituted in terms of consciousness. For in this context, where we would be constituted as beings of consciousness, it would not be possible to perceive the ultimate predicament in terms of the finitude of being for the simple, if all determining, reason that consciousness does not lend itself to quantification. One cannot have more or less of consciousness – it simply does not make sense. With the notion or reality of consciousness, as with the proverbial notion or reality of pregnancy, it is a matter of all or none. The logic here is based on the exclusivist alternative of either/or rather than on the quantifiable continuum of more or less. With respect to a pure being-of-consciousness, therefore, the ultimate predicament cannot be perceived in terms of the finitude of being. The ultimate predicament can no doubt be perceived here in terms of any number of things (we would suggest that the aloneness of being would be the most fundamental and poignant formulation); but it certainly cannot be delineated in terms of the finitude of being.[1]

Thus, the centrality of the event of death in a religious formulation would clearly indicate that this religious formulation operates in the domain of power and that the main thrust of its concern is with respect to the ontological question. And since the event of death occupies a central position in the preponderance of religions one can conclude that the preponderance of religions formulate their *Weltanschauung* in the domain of power and with respect to the ontological issue.

Of course, the religious phenomenon is, in the last analysis, not so much interested in merely identifying a problem for its own sake; indeed, it is interested in identifying a problem only because it is ultimately concerned with providing a solution for it. In other words, religion is not interested in diagnostics for its own sake; rather it is interested in therapy – it is interested in curing and healing which as such, of course, implicate the need for the prior establishment of the diagnostics. Thus, religion does not end with the perception of the predicament but rather with the offering of salvation. Of course, the salvation offered must be commensurate to the predicament perceived, if the proposed cure is to be effective and meaningful. In our case, therefore, the commensurate salvation, the fitting solution, would have to consist in the provision of the possibility for the prolongation of life, seeing that the predicament is perceived to lie in the event of death, i.e., in the finitude of life. This indeed is the case. Corresponding to the widespread tendency by the preponderant majority of world religions to perceive death as constituting the ultimate predicament there is a widespread involvement on their part with the prolongation of life.

Of course, this formulation of the solution in terms of the prolongation of life in response to the predicament of death can express itself in a number of different forms. In the main, we may distinguish three basic alternatives: 1. We may distinguish between a prolongation of life that remains finite (no matter how long the prolongation is) and a prolongation of life that becomes infinite, thus actually introducing the notion of immortality; now, while the former may be encountered in some of the more primary religions, there is no question that the tendency in the more literate religions is towards the latter alternative. 2. Further, with regard to the latter alternative of the first distinction, i.e., with regard to the formulation of immortality, we may distinguish between a formulation of immortality which involves the whole person as he is encountered in this world, to wit, the person in both his conscious and physical aspects is transported to a different stage, different world, where he can continue to live indefinitely as he did in this world, and an immortality which involves only the conscious and not the physical aspect, in other words, an immortality which involves only the soul and not the body of man, thus allowing only the soul and not the body to go on living indefinitely (this formulation would presuppose of course the separation of the soul from the body upon death); by and large, the tendency is for the former alternative to be embraced by the more simple-minded masses while the latter alternative appeals to the more philosophically inclined. 3. Lastly, with regard to the latter alternative of the second distinction, i.e., with regard to immortality in terms of the soul only, we may distinguish between the immortality of the soul in its totality and the immortality of only that part of the soul which constitutes its acquired intellect; the significance of this distinction lies in the fact that in the former an awareness of individuation is preserved while in the latter it is given up seeing that the acquired intellect becomes absorbed in a universal all-encompassing intellect in which no trace of individual awareness is preserved. Here too, the latter alternative would appeal to the more philosophically oriented while the former alternative would appeal to the more religiously inclined.

In all this refined analysis of discrimination, however, resulting as it does in a multiplicity of formulations, there are two important things to note. First, the above distinctions not withstanding, all six of the delineated alternatives (and in all likelihood all other possible delineations) express, in the last analysis, one and the same thing and that is that the problematic aspect of death is overcome by a prolongation of life beyond death. The alternatives differ with respect to details but they are at one with respect to the fundamental underlying thought which indeed constitutes the solution to the predicament, namely, the thought that life is prolonged beyond death. Secondly, while all six alternatives find expression within religious thought, by far the most predominant and pervasive expression is that of the latter alternative of the second distinction, namely of the formulation according to which the soul upon death is released from the body and continues by itself to exist indefinitely, i.e., of the notion of immortality in terms of the soul only. Thus, the notion of the prolongation of life beyond death,i.e., the notion of immortality, is most widely represented by the formulation in which it is the soul by itself which goes on living indefinitely after it separates itself from the body upon death.

Indeed, this formulation of the immortality of the soul only is not only pervasive among all the other alternative formulations, but it is the most satisfactory and logically appealing formulation with which to overcome the problematic aspect of the finitude of being and of life signified by death. Thus, the first alternative of the first distinction, i.e., the alternative which offers a continuation of life beyond death but of a finite duration, is an unsatisfactory formulation in that it merely postpones the confrontation with the event of death in all its radicality. The challenge of the problem of death is not really overcome here with finality; it is merely overcome temporarily by postponing the radical encounter to a later date. But such an overcoming is really, in the last analysis, not an overcoming of the problem at all – it is merely a postponement. Similarly, the first alternative in the second distinction, i.e., the alternative which formulates the continuation of life beyond death in both its conscious and physical aspects, is also unsatisfactory but not because it proposes to overcome the problem by depriving death of any and every measure of its impact. It overcomes the problem by neutralizing death. For if life continues after death in exactly the same way as it was prior to death, what possible significance can the event of death have here? Why have death at all seeing that it does not really effect any difference? Indeed, death is reduced here to a fleeting interruption devoid of all significance in the continuum of life, something like the quick turning of the page in the narration of a story. But in these circumstances one has every right to wonder whether one has encountered the real event of death. Finally, the second alternative in the third distinction, i.e., the alternative which formulates that it is not even the soul as a whole which survives death but only that part of it which constitutes the acquired intellect, is equally unsatisfactory though now because of its going overboard in the opposite direction. Namely, it is lacking not in having death effect insufficient change, but rather in having death effect too radical a change, to wit, in having death eliminate from survival not only the body but also all aspects of the soul except that of the acquired intellect. But what is the point of such radicality particularly when it carries with it no intellectual advantages, i.e., no advantages as far as philosophical considerations are concerned? And this question becomes even more pertinent when it is realized that this radicality actually carries with it existential disadvantages, i.e., disadvantages as regard religious considerations. For after all, it is in no way intellectually less comfortable to claim the survival beyond death of the soul as a whole than to claim the survival of only its acquired intellect, seeing that both claim the survival of the same kind of entity, i.e., the survival of a being-of-consciousness, and are equally devoid of claiming the survival beyond death of any physical entity, i.e., the survival of any being-of-power. Put another way, what possible intellectual advantage can there be to claiming that only one aspect of the conscious entity, i.e., the acquired intellect, can survive death in contrast to claiming that other aspects of the conscious entity may survive as well? It would seem to us that if one can claim that the acquired intellect survives death, then one can claim with equal intellectual respectability that the soul as a whole survives death. And furthermore, not only is there no advantage from the intellectual vantage point in restricting survival to the acquired intellect, there is, it would seem to us, a distinct disadvantage from the existential vantage point, and thus from the vantage point of the religious consideration, to so restrict the survival of the soul exclusively to the acquired intellect. For, as we have seen, the survival of the soul as a whole preserves the ongoing awareness of the individual while the survival merely of the acquired intellect abrogates it, allowing it to be absorbed into an all-encompassing universal consciousness; and clearly from an existential and thus also from a religious vantage point there is a great disadvantage to abrogating the ongoing awareness of the individual.

Thus, the second alternative of the second distinction or the first alternative of the third distinction (the two being one and the same), i.e., the alternative which formulates the survival after death in terms of the soul as a whole (excluding the survival of the body but also excluding the limitation of survival to the acquired intellect only), is by far the most advantageous alternative seeing that it formulates itself in a way that is most acceptable both to the intellectual and to the existential vantage points. It is no wonder, therefore, that it is in terms of this alternative that the preponderance of historical religions formulated their ontological solution to the problem of death. Consequently, we too, disregarding the various other distinctions and alternatives, would take the formulation of the immortality of the soul as a whole to be the main and decisive articulation of the ontological solution to the problem of death.

As said, the motif of the ontological finitude of man as symbolized by the event of death and, commensurate to it, the motif of the immortality of the soul are utilized almost universally in the history of religions to constitute the perception of the ultimate predicament and the offering of salvation respectively. The qualifier "almost" in the claim here is, however, of the utmost importance. For there are instances where these motifs are at best only ambiguously used and other instances from which they are missing altogether. Indeed, in this connection mainstream Judaism may provide a most instructive instance. For it is certainly not just another run-of-the-mill religion exemplifying just another instance of the fairly general and universal perception of the ontological finitude of man as constituting the ultimate predicament and, commensurate to this, offering the immortality of the soul as the salvation. Rather, mainstream Judaism constitutes a clear exception and as such it presents us with a most interesting and intriguing formulation which we ought to examine.

Thus, to start with Judaism's earliest expression and, in a sense, its most fundamental expression, namely, its expression in the biblical period, it is a most striking fact, particularly in view of our observations above, that one does not encounter here any serious and sustained concern with the problem of death or any expression of the solution that may overcome this problem. Throughout the vast biblical literature there is hardly any expression of concern with the problem of death and correspondingly hardly any mention of what is to take place beyond death.

Granted, there are two notable exceptions to this assertion – the book of *Ecclesiastes* and *Daniel* 12:2-3, the former expressing the problem while the latter referring to one of the solutions by which the problem can be overcome. But these two instances are clearly exceptions. They can hardly be taken as representing the mainstream orientation of the Bible. Indeed, these sources are of a very late date relative to the rest of this biblical literature (the book of

Ecclesiastes originating from the latter part of the third century B.C.E. and the book of *Daniel* originating from the middle of the second century B.C.E.) and as such, at the very best, they are situated at the very periphery of the biblical period.   But apart from this, and much more significantly than this consideration, these sources in their general tenor and orientation are quite out of step with, indeed, they are quite antithetical to, the tenor and orientation of the overwhelming bulk of biblical literature. Thus, the book of *Ecclesiastes*, beautiful and moving as it may be (and it is one of the most beautiful and moving books!), is in its overall viewpoint diametrically opposed to the biblical viewpoint.   Given its determinism, its utter pessimism and its complete abdication before the meaninglessness of life, it is much more an expression of the Greek-Stoic viewpoint than of the biblical viewpoint. Indeed, one wonders how it ever got into the canon. And as regards the book of *Daniel*, it clearly is an expression (indeed, an expression par excellence) of the apocalyptic viewpoint, a viewpoint which at the very best is only peripherally represented in the Bible. It really belongs together with such books as *Enoch*, the *Syriac Baruch* and *Fourth Ezra* , all books articulating the apocalyptic viewpoint yet at the same time (and this is most important) all books which are excluded from the biblical canon. By no stretch of the imagination can Daniel be taken to represent the biblical viewpoint.

Indeed, seeing that these works represent the Greek-Stoic viewpoint and the apocalyptic viewpoint respectively, it need not at all be surprising to find that the problem of death or the positing of life at a point beyond death is articulated in them. What is astounding and, indeed, most astounding, is that in the rest of biblical literature (thus, in the overwhelming preponderance of this literature and, even more significantly, in that part of the literature which constitutes the most distinctive expression of the biblical viewpoint as, for example, classical prophecy, the historic narrative and the legal corpora) hardly any concern with the problem of death is raised. It would seem that for Hebrew Scripture death and what it signifies, to wit, the finitude of man's being and life, do not present a problem. The biblical view accepts the fact that man is a created being, a creature. This is the way that God constituted him and therefore it must be good; indeed, God pronounced it to be good (Genesis (1:31). And as a created being man, of course, is inescapably a finite being.

Indeed, it would seem that death was accepted in this view as a normal and natural event which presented no predicament (if there was a negative aspect, i.e., an aspect of a predicament, connected with death it arose only in conjunction with premature death or with the absence of a full and proper burial). Thus, the pervasive view, certainly on the popular level, seems to have been that in the natural order of things man upon living his life on this earth dies and thereupon descends to a nebulous, vague region called *Sheol,* there to rest in a state of sleep and unconsciousness (or perhaps in a state of semiconsciousness) for all time to come. Death is viewed as a weakening of the vital forces operating in man to the point that it leads to sleep and loss of consciousness. Indeed, it is important to note that death is placed here in a continuum with illness, being merely a further weakening of the vital forces operating in man (the difference between death and illness thus being only a difference of degree) and that such weakening affects not just one aspect of man but the totality of man as we know him (i.e., there is no separation of soul and body here). As such, by the way, as the weakening process can be reversed in the case of illness so can it also be reversed, albeit only for awhile, in the case of death. Indeed, the possibility of such a reversal, i.e., the possibility of bringing the dead back to life, to consciousness, for a short while, in order to communicate with the living is acknowledged by the biblical view. The Bible knows charmers and necromancers and by implication clearly acknowledges the efficacy of their art, the most prominent and dramatic illustration being the story of the witch of Endor bringing Samuel back from the dead to confront Saul (Samuel I 28:13-19). But while the Bible acknowledges such a possibility it most vehemently rejects its execution – the dead are to be left in peace in their state of unconsciousness. In other words, death is to be accepted as a natural event, as the way of the generations (thus, a common biblical expression to describe the death of a person is to say that he was gathered to his forefathers). The biblical view rejects in the most decisive manner all possibilities and means of reversing the event of death, of overcoming death and bringing the dead back to consciousness. And clearly it can do so only because it does not perceive death as precipitating a fundamental problem, a fundamental predicament, in human life.

We may conclude this point by reiterating the observation that in essence the biblical view does not indulge in speculation or offer teaching about life after death – fundamentally it remains silent and uncommunicative with respect to this dimension of the religious life. Of course, later on in the post-biblical era when Judaism changes its position on this matter and proceeds to adopt teachings about life after death, the rabbis only naturally tried to establish precedent pronouncements on this question in the Bible itself. Namely, given the very method of Rabbinic Judaism, it was essential to maintain that the teaching was not *de novo* with the rabbis but already given in the embodiment of the original revelation, i.e., in the Bible, requiring from the rabbis merely to provide the explication. It is in this context that the rabbis claimed to find reference to the question of death and life after death in the following biblical passages: Ecclesiastes 12:7, Daniel 12:2-3, Job 19:25-26, Samuel I 28:13-19, Samuel I 25:29, Genesis 47:29-30, Jeremiah 31:14-15, Isaiah 26:19, Psalms 48:15, Leviticus 19:31, and Isaiah 57:1-2. But while the rabbis may have believed that these verses do indeed carry some reference to some form of life after death (though this is by no means certain), it is safe to say that the burden of contemporary opinion would agree that one can not find in these verses, when taken at face value, any anticipation of the rabbis' position regarding the question of life after death.

Thus, after all is said and done, the fact remains that Hebrew Scripture presents a most striking exception to what is otherwise an almost all-pervasive concern of the phenomenon of religion, namely, the concern with the event of death; and in view of what was said above, this, in turn, means that Hebrew Scripture presents a notable exception within the universal phenomenon of religion in that it is not primarily interested in the ontological predicament of man and in that it does not formulate itself in terms of the dimension of power, specifically, in terms of positing the being of man as being essentially a being-of-power.

But while there is hardly any reference in Hebrew Scripture to the problem of death or any formulation of life after death, there are plenty of such references and formulations in Rabbinic Judaism. A dramatic change occurs, therefore, in the orientation of Judaism with respect to the question of life after death between the biblical period and the talmudic period which follows it. Now, many scholars pinpoint the occurrence of this change to the Maccabean Revolt which took place in the first half of the second century B.C.E., when many young men gave their lives in the defense of God's honor, thus bringing to the fore the potency of the problem of death. Indeed, this shift manifests itself very dramatically and incisively if we compare the apocryphal literature which was written before the Maccabean Revolt with the apocryphal literature written after the Maccabean Revolt, the latter being primarily of an apocalyptic nature. Thus, *Tobias, Judith,* and *Ben Sirach,* all apocryphal works originating prior to the Maccabean Revolt, exhibit the same stance with respect to the event of death and the question of life after death that we find in Hebrew Scripture, which is to say that they hardly take notice of it. It is quite a different story when we come to the apocalyptic literature and to such books as *Enoch, Fourth Ezra* and the *Syriac Baruch,* literature which originates after the Maccabean Revolt. Here, the predicament of death and the attempt to respond to it by positing some formulation of a life beyond death come more and more to the fore. A new trend is thus clearly established which then continues to express itself ever more fully and explicitly within Talmudic literature. So, while the question of death and the formulation of a life after death are very vague, peripheral and almost non-existent in Hebrew Scripture, they become quite central and widely articulated in Talmudic literature.

We need not take the space here to exhibit in detail the many places in Talmudic literature where the rabbis evidently maintain a belief in a life after death (see for this George F. Moore, *Judaism,* E.E. Urbach, *Hazal,* and Louis Jacobs, *A Jewish Theology* and *Principles of the Jewish Faith*). Rather, we want to focus our attention on the fact that in Rabbinic Judaism there are actually present two "solutions" to the problem of death and try to explicate the significance and far-reaching implications of this fact. Namely, we are referring to the fact that one can encounter in Talmudic literature a formulation of the notion of a life after death not only in terms of the immortality of the soul but also in terms of a resurrection. The difference in the signification of these two formulations is fairly clear: a formulation of a life after death in terms of the immortality of the soul signifies that upon death the soul separates itself from the body, and whereas the body disintegrates and disappears the soul goes on surviving by itself; as against this, a formulation of a life after death in terms of a resurrection signifies that upon death both body and soul cease to exist and that after a period of time of both body and soul being dead (the length of such a period is really immaterial) both the body and the soul will be brought back to life thus presenting again the very same person that existed prior to death. But what is the significance of this difference and what are its implications?

Clearly, the historical observation that the notion of the immortality of the soul enters Rabbinic Judaism from Greek sources while the notion of the resurrection enters it from Persian sources is of little interest or relevance here. A far more meaningful difference, however, is offered by the observation that while the formulation of a life after death in terms of the immortality of the soul implicates the individual the formulation of a life after death in terms of resurrection implicates a collectivity. The rationale for this observation is actually readily available. According to it, the immortality of the soul is clearly carried out in terms of the individual, for as each individual dies the soul separates from the body and continues to survive in itself. As such, effecting the immortality of the soul is an act which repeats itself innumerable times – each time a person dies the act repeats itself. As against this, although in principle the notion of resurrection too can be made to implicate the individual rather than the collectivity (in the sense that each individual in his own particular time has his own resurrection), given the way the formulation is actually formulated, i.e., given the facts that it is actually formulated as a one-time event rather than as a great multiplicity of events, the formulation clearly implicates the collectivity. Namely, for the notion of resurrection to implicate the individual one must have innumerable events of resurrection – an event for each individual. Seeing, however, that within the tradition of Rabbinic Judaism the notion of resurrection is formulated in terms of a one-time event and not in terms of a multiplicity of events, the notion as it functions here clearly implicates that all those that are to be resurrected will be resurrected at one and the same time which clearly means that it implicates a resurrection of the collectivity and not of the individual. Thus regardless whether the formulation involves the whole of mankind or only the people of Israel (or, for that matter, any subgroups of these entities as, for example, only the righteous of mankind and Israel or only the righteous of Israel alone or conversely only the wicked of Israel), the notion of resurrection involved here clearly implicates a collectivity. Thus, in terms of their actual formulation within Rabbinic Judaism, we do have the important difference whereby the notion of immortality implicates the individual while the notion of resurrection implicates the collectivity.

Finally, an even more meaningful difference is ascertained by the further observation that while the notion of the immortality of the soul implicates other-worldliness, the notion of resurrection remains within a this-worldly context. Now, the rationale for this observation is just as readily available (if not more so!) and it runs as follows: clearly, in the notion of the immortality of the soul the body remains permanently disintegrated and is thus cancelled out of the equation; as against this, the notion of resurrection, certainly in the context of Judaism, clearly asserts that it is not only the soul but the body as well that is brought back to life. Now, inasmuch as the body is, so to speak, the umbilical cord that holds the self anchored to a this-worldly context, the continued existence of the body is a condition *sine qua non* for preserving a this-worldly context. And from this, of course, it follows that a continuation of existence in terms not only of the soul but also of the body (as is the case in the formulation of resurrection) would necessarily implicate a continuation of existence in a this-worldly context, while a continuation of existence exclusively in terms of the soul alone (as is the case in the formulation of the immortality of the soul) would necessarily implicate a continuation of existence in an other-worldly context.

But while, as we shall presently see, the last two mentioned differences are indeed very significant and relevant to the point we are trying to make, they do not quite put their finger on the very pulse of the issue or, to change the metaphor, they do not quite go to the very heart of the difference which obtains between the notion of the immortality of the soul and that of resurrection. The above mentioned differences fail to articulate explicitly this fundamental difference – they only articulate important ramifications and corollaries of this difference. Thus, we would submit that the very heart of the difference between the two notions lies in the observation that, in the last analysis, the notion of the immortality of the soul really fits, i.e., corresponds to, the ontological predicament which is precipitated by the event of death while the notion of the resurrection really fits, i.e., corresponds to, the ethical predicament which may likewise be precipitated by the event of death; in other words, the notion of the immortality of the soul really responds, i.e., formulates a solution, to an ontological predicament while the notion of resurrection really responds, i.e., formulates a solution, to an ethical predicament.

How is this so? Well, surely there can be no doubt that the event of death would precipitate an ontological predicament; after all it signifies the end of life. But, and this is not so readily or generally perceived, the event of death can also precipitate an ethical predicament by virtue of the fact that it signifies, so to speak, the closing of the books. And how is this so? Well, given the nature of the ethical, one can rightly claim that in an ethical context it would of necessity always be required that, so to speak, at the end of the story a commensurate balance be attained between the acts and the retributions, namely, between merit and reward on the one hand and between sin and punishment on the other hand.

For after all, the very essence of the ethical lies in the demand for such a balance. True, the demand does not have to insist that this balance be obtained in every individual act – reward or punishment may be deferred. But it must insist that at the end, i.e., when the story finishes, the books must be perfectly balanced. But now, this being the case, it can be readily seen how the event of death, precisely in signifying the end of the story, can precipitate the ethical predicament. For it is more than likely that in most cases, if not indeed in all, experience would unshakably testify to the fact that the books are not balanced and in this case we quite clearly have on our hands a fundamental ethical predicament. Now, this ethical problem can readily express itself in terms of the problem of theodicy, i.e., in terms of the problem of justifying God's action. For in a religio-ethical context, God must be in His very essence a just being (this being the requirement of the ethical dimension) while at the same time He must be constituted as all-powerful and providential (this traditionally would seem to have been the requirement of the religious dimension). But in this context, if a commensurate balance between acts and retributions is not obtained at the time that the books are closed, the ethical problem clearly becomes the problem of theodicy – the problem of accounting for God's actions. For now, seeing that God is just, all-powerful and providential, the fact that the final statement is left unbalanced, thus allowing injustice to prevail, must of necessity raise serious questions regarding the ethical God. Thus, the event of death can indeed precipitate the ethical problem which in the religious context would readily tend to translate itself into the problem of theodicy.

Now, with the above observation in mind, namely, with the observation that the event of death can signify not only the ontological problem but also the ethical problem (or the problem of theodicy), a good case can be made that the formulation of the prolongation of life beyond death in terms of the immortality of the soul is a formulation that, strictly speaking, fits the ontological predicament, while the formulation of the prolongation of life beyond death in terms of resurrection is best fitted to the ethical predicament. Namely, we can see that it is not that resurrection and the immortality of the soul are in their content one and the same, that they effect the same results, only that they effect them in somewhat different ways; we can see that the difference between them is not merely a difference in outward form but rather a difference in substance.

True, there is a sense in which an identification in terms of the very substance of the two formulations is possible and, indeed, it would seem that such an identification was actually perpetrated within the tradition. For after all, there is an identity between the two formulations in that both overcome death as signifying finality, the end. And as such, it would seem that either formulation could be used to overcome both predicaments, the ontological and the ethical predicament. Thus, the formulation of the immortality of the soul would not only overcome the ontological predicament of the finitude of being by providing a being and life beyond death, but it would also overcome the ethical predicament of the imbalance of the books between deeds and retributions by providing the occasion beyond death where the balancing of the books can be achieved – the additional reward or punishment which was lacking at the moment of death can now be meted out to the surviving soul. Likewise, the formulation in terms of the resurrection would not only overcome the ethical predicament signified by death by providing a future point beyond death where the books can be balanced, but it would also overcome the ontological problem by offering a continuation of being and life at that same future point beyond death. And as noted above, such parallelism between the two formulations was not only possible in theory but was actually offered within the tradition at various points. Indeed, because of this tendency to accept the basic identity in substance between the two formulations it was possible to formulate stances within the tradition which combined the two formulations. Thus, for example, we can have a stance in which the formulation in terms of an immorality of the soul is applied first to be succeeded, however, by the formulation in terms of a resurrection; in other words, we can have a stance in which the interim period between death and resurrection is covered by the formulation of the immortality of the soul.

We would submit, however, that such an identity between the two formulations is superficial and that upon more careful reflection this parallelist view, whereby each formulation can address equally well either problem, the ontological or the ethical problem, will be seen to be invalid. Indeed, a good case can be made that we really have here an exclusivist, one-to-one relation between the formulation and the problem, specifically, that the formulation in terms of the immortality of the soul fits perfectly only in the context of the ontological problem but not in the context of the ethical problem and, conversely, that the formulation in terms of the resurrection fits perfectly well only in the context of the ethical problem but not in the context of the ontological problem. For while the formulation in terms of the immortality of the soul is certainly satisfactory vis-à-vis the ontological problem inasmuch as it clearly provides the continuation of being and of life beyond the point of death, one can argue with considerable merit that it is not really satisfactory vis-à-vis the ethical problem, seeing that in this context, where the goal is no longer the prolongation of being and of life, but rather the balancing of the books, only an agent constituted as the whole man, i.e., constituted as both body and soul, will do; man constituted as soul only will not do as an agent. For the validity and feasibility of an ethical balancing of the books in terms of an agent that is constituted exclusively as soul only is very questionable. Certainly, a good case can be made that the ethical act (in the sense of being the act that can be submitted not only to ethical evaluation as regards the goal but submitted to ethical judgment as regards the agent) cannot arise except in the context where the agent is constituted as both body and soul; that either in the context of an entity which is constituted exclusively as body or in the context of an entity which is constituted exclusively as soul, the authentic ethical act cannot really arise. By the same token, the case can also be made that any act of balancing the books, if it is to carry ethical significance, would correspondingly need to implicate an entity that is constituted as both body and soul. Thus, ethics in every one of its aspects and features can validly operate only if it is applied with respect to an entity that is constituted as both body and soul. The Talmudic rabbis, by the way, were fully aware of this and consequently they, indeed, insisted that the full man, i.e., man constituted as both body and soul, be involved in all aspects, bar none, of the ethical process. This is most poignantly and tellingly expressed in the known rabbinic parable of the king who places two watchmen, a lame one and a blind one, to guard his vineyard (Bab. Talmud, Sanhedrin 91: a-b).

Anyway, what sort of reward or punishment could possibly be applied if the recipient is an entity that is constituted exclusively as soul? Certainly, no reward or punishment in terms of this concrete world, i.e., in terms of sensuous experience, would be feasible here. For clearly, one would require for this a body. Indeed, if reward and punishment are to be dispensed in any meaningful way, if the books are to be balanced in any sense that is ethically meaningful (i.e., if one is to satisfy the principle of measure for measure, of attaining a commensurate correspondence between the act and its retribution), then the this-worldly dimension must be present (if only because the original act, be it meritorious or sinful, was of necessity performed in a this-worldly context) and this dimension is evidently missing if the recipient entity is devoid of body, i.e., if it is constituted exclusively as soul only. Thus, if the tenet of the immortality of the soul was indeed formulated for the sake of overcoming the ethical problem then one would have to conclude that it is not a very apt or telling formulation.

Similarly with the tenet of resurrection, it can hardly be said to be a very suitable formulation if its function is to address and overcome the ontological problem, i.e., the problem of the finitude of being and life. For if this is indeed its primary intention, then what is the point of allowing the person upon death to lose his being and exit life (i.e., to actually die) and, indeed, most significantly, to remain in this state of death for a protracted period of time before being restored at some distant future point to his original being and life? Indeed, if anything, this formulation clearly appears to be tailored to the requirements of the ethical problem seeing that all that one would need here is the possibility of deferring matters to a point in the future. Consequently the cessation of being and of life (i.e., the introduction of a state of death for the time being) would present no problem as long as at some point in the future a return to being and life is posited (and this is, indeed, provided by the formulation of resurrection). But for the ontological problem the crucial point is not the possibility of deferring matters to a point in the future but rather the availability of ongoing, continued being and life beyond the point of death. And in this context the formulation of the tenet of resurrection is not really satisfactory, for here one cannot really escape the force of the question: Why keep a person deprived of being and of life even for one hour? Thus, while the formulation of the tenet of resurrection may be quite acceptable if one assumes that its primary intention is to respond to the ethical problem, one cannot but wonder about its fitness and suitability if one assumes that its primary intention is to respond to the ontological problem.

Indeed, the preceding abstract speculations are buttressed by the way the tradition of Judaism actually utilizes the tenet of the resurrection. For given the way the tradition utilizes the tenet there can be no question but that it wishes to link it to the ethical problem. Thus, it is most telling that in the tradition of Rabbinic Judaism the tenet of resurrection is intimately linked to the notion of the Day of Judgment – resurrection takes place specifically and exclusively for the sake of the Day of Judgment, namely, people are to be resurrected so that they can stand and be judged on the Day of Judgment. This, we would submit, clearly shows that the tenet of resurrection is to be linked with the ethical problem. Indeed, this is clearly buttressed by the further observation that the tradition shows absolutely no interest in pursuing any of the implications which the tenet may hold with respect to the ontological problem. Thus, the tradition allows itself to remain quite vague and, indeed, inconsistent with respect to what actually happens after the Day of Judgment has taken place; even more poignantly, in the various formulations that one can encounter in this connection there are not a few which, while projecting a continuation of life beyond the Day of Judgment, project it only as finite (and at that only of a short duration) and not as infinite. Surely, such usage of the tenet of resurrection would hardly be satisfactory if the concern was really with the ontological problem.

Thus, while the tenet of resurrection, as we have seen, can be used in connection with the ontological problem (although, admittedly, it does not lend itself most "naturally" to such usage), the tradition in point of fact does not so use it. On the other hand, in marked contrast to this, the tradition does use the tenet of the immortality of the soul in connection with the ethical problem even though, again as we have seen, this tenet is really geared to deal with the ontological rather than with the ethical problem. Namely, it is interesting to note that with respect to the ethical problem the tradition will put to use all possible tenets, even those which are not primarily formulated for this purpose and, therefore, are not perfectly suited for it but that this is not true in reverse with respect to the ontological problem.

Of course, now that we have established that the tenet of resurrection is connected with the ethical problem rather than with the ontological problem we can more fully appreciate the two further characterizations of the tenet given above. Thus, it is indeed very consistent with the signification of the tenet that it be presented in conjunction with the collectivity rather than the individual (i.e., that it be a one-time event involving the collectivity rather than a multiplicity of events involving the individual). For unlike ontology, which impinges on the substance and the constitution of things and thus grounds itself in the individual, ethics impinges upon the action and relation *between* persons and thus grounds itself in the collectivity (specifically in the collectivity of persons) seeing that action and relation implicate at least a twosome and a twosome is already a collectivity. Thus, while ontology tends towards the individual, ethics will tend towards the collectivity. Likewise we can now better appreciate the insistence of the tradition on so formulating its tenet of resurrection that it comes to signify the bringing back to life not only of the soul but inextricably also of the body. For the bringing back to life of the body provides the necessary linkage to a this-worldly context and, as we have seen, ethics can operate only in a this-worldly context. This is the real significance of insisting on the resurrection of the body – it makes sure that we remain in a this-worldly context and that we continue to deal with men rather than with angels.[2]

In view of the above considerations it now becomes of particular importance to note that while it is true that both the tenet of the immortality of the soul and that of the resurrection find expression within Rabbinic Judaism, it is only the latter and not the former, i.e., it is only the tenet of the resurrection and not the tenet of the immortality of the soul, that receives "official" status within Rabbinic Judaism. Of course, Rabbinic Judaism does not have a list of official tenets thus constituting an official teaching. Still, the tradition makes it abundantly clear that it views the tenet of the resurrection of body and soul as one of the most fundamental and essential tenets of its faith (in other words, if it did have a list of "official" tenets this tenet would be one of the most important ones). Thus, Sanhedrin 10:1 considers it as one of the three most fundamental principles of the faith; even more significantly, it is included in "the eighteen benedictions" which form the very core of the prayer-worship structure of Rabbinic Judaism seeing that its content constitutes the very substance of the second benediction. As against this, there is no "official" status accorded to the tenet of the immortality of the soul. The notion may well be reflected in the thoughts of many rabbis; it was certainly maintained and propagated by the philosophers and the mystics and in all likelihood was very widespread on the popular level – but "official" status it did not have. In clear contradistinction to the tenet of the resurrection it is completely devoid of "official" sanctioning.

This fact becomes especially significant in view of our observations above. For in terms of our observations above it states that the tradition considers "official" only the tenet which is offered in answer to the ethical problem and not the tenet which may be offered as an answer to the ontological problem. In other words, it shows that it is really the ethical problem and not the ontological problem which bothers Rabbinic Judaism. But if this is so, then Rabbinic Judaism does not differ all that much, certainly not in essentials, from the position of Hebrew Scripture. For as we have seen, Hebrew Scripture is also not concerned with the ontological problem. We can now see that as far as mainstream Rabbinic Judaism is concerned this continues to be the case even though the concern with the ontological problem is certainly much more widespread on the "unofficial" and popular level. Still, as far as the fundamental structure of faith is concerned Rabbinic Judaism is an organic and integral continuation of Hebrew Scripture – both formulate their basic *Weltanschauung* in the ethical rather than in the ontological context.

One last word. Granted that both Hebrew Scripture and Rabbinic Judaism formulate their basic *Weltanschauung* not in an ontological but rather in an ethical context (and in view of biblical prophecy and the rabbinic halacha one must admit that the claim is quite persuasive), how is one to account for the fact that an explicit formulation of the tenet of resurrection appears only in Rabbinic Judaism and not in Hebrew Scripture?[3] A quick survey of the history of the ethical problem as it develops within biblical consciousness may give us the answer.

Thus, briefly stated, it would seem that in early biblical consciousness the ethical problem is overcome by the fact that one could transfer, so to speak, the ethical accounts from father to son to son's son. Namely, if the merit or demerit of a person's act can be devolved on that person's son and his son's son to the third and fourth generation, as the biblical verse has it, then evidently one can remove the sting of the ethical problem (certainly, the force of its impact is greatly mitigated). For in such a transfer we have the means of postponing into the future the final settling of the accounts and this should certainly help remove the sting of the ethical problem. This, of course, is the logical side of the solution which in principle is quite valid. But moreover, not only in principle but in terms of concrete reality, this solution may provide a useful advantage. For by allowing a transfer of ethical accounts one extends the potential pool of responsible agents thus increasing the feasibility of identifying an agent (or several agents) to whom responsibility may be allocated for the retribution and in this way making possible, so to speak, the balancing of the books. Still, even so, the real force and efficacy of the solution lie, in the last analysis, not in its logical but in its psychological aspect. Namely, by being able to postpone the resolution of the challenge into the future one greatly mitigates the psychological impact of the challenge, first, by removing from the scene the direct challengers, i.e., the persons who experience the apparent injustice first hand, and secondly, by allowing the intervention of time to cool and moderate the heat of the challenge. Thus, in providing the possibility of transferring ethical accounts early biblical consciousness could mitigate, if not, indeed, suppress, the impact of the ethical problem.

But early biblical consciousness had also its Achilles heel. It lay in the fact that a transfer of ethical accounts could function successfully only in a context where ethical sensitivity was not too highly developed. For a transfer of ethical accounts from father to son must prove an offense to a more highly developed ethical sensitivity. Indeed, such a higher stage in the development of its ethical sensitivity was reached by the community of Israel in the days of Jeremiah and Ezekiel, just around the time of the destruction of the first Temple. For we find these two prophets (first Jeremiah but then even more forcefully Ezekiel) challenging what must have been a popular adage stating that while the fathers eat sour grapes the teeth of the sons are set on edge. The prophets reject the validity of this adage, i.e., the validity of transferring ethical accounts. They articulate this new level of ethical sensitivity which cannot tolerate the transfer of ethical accounts and insists on the principle of individuation in settling the accounts. Thus, to quote Jeremiah verbatim: "In those days they shall no longer say 'the fathers have eaten sour grapes and the children's teeth are set on edge'; but every one shall die for his own sin; each man who eats sour grapes his teeth shall be set on edge" (Jer. 31:29-30, see also Ezekiel 18:2-4).

With the establishment, however, of the principle of individuation in ethical accounting the ethical problem presents itself anew in full force. For clearly the means of deferment to the future is taken away from us now and in terms of the life of the single individual it is more than likely that the irrefutable burden of experience would all too often force upon us the observation that "the rightous man suffers while the evil man prospers." In other words, the upholding of the principle of individuation in ethical accounting would almost inevitably lead to the challenge of Job – there is no escape from Job after Jeremiah and Ezekiel.

As such, this clearly precipitates a new task for the tradition, namely, the task of overcoming Job's challenge; for clearly this challenge cannot be left unanswered. But how is it to be overcome? Well (at least in theory), there is always the possibility of giving up the principle of individuation and going back to the formulation which allowed the transfer of ethical accounts. This, as we have seen, should provide a solution to the problem (certainly psychological but also logical). But while this may well be so, this option is, historically speaking, totally unviable. For once the level of ethical sensitivity manifested in the principle of individuation has been reached, there is really no way back to the more primitive view which would allow the transfer of ethical accounts. Clearly, the principle of individuation was here to stay and in that context the only way to provide a future to which the final settling of the books could be deferred (the deferment to the future being the only viable way of overcoming the ethical problematic) was through the formulation of resurrection. In terms of the one and the same individual, the future can be safeguarded only by the formulation of resurrection. We would suggest that this is precisely what happened within the tradition of Judaism though by the time it actually happened one already finds oneself at the end of the intertestamental period and at the beginning of the Pharisaic-Rabbinic period.

Thus, to conclude this paper let us briefly sum up its thesis. We have tried to show that mainstream Judaism both in its Biblical and in its Rabbinic expression is a religion that formulates itself in the context of the ethical domain rather than in the context of the ontological domain; that consequently it views the event of death as precipitating not the ontological problem, i.e., the problem of the finitude of being and of life, but rather the ethical problem, i.e., the problem of the imbalance between act and retribution. Finally, that commensurate to this, the solution which the tradition offers focuses not so much on the extension of life beyond death as on the deferment of the final judgment to a point in the future, in other words, it focuses not so much on the tenet of the immortality of the soul as on the tenet of resurrection. Now, if this thesis is in the main valid, as we believe it is, then we do indeed have in mainstream Judaism a distinctive and rather interesting expression of the phenomenon of religion.

---

[1]When we do talk in terms of a partial or not-so-clearly-focused consciousness or in terms of some other such qualification of consciousness we are not referring to a pure being-of-consciousness but rather to what we would call a refracted being-of-consciousness, namely, a being-of-consciousness that is linked with and mediated through a being-of-power, as, for example, man is (where consciousness is indeed inextricably linked with and mediated through power), and in this context such qualifications as partiality or greater and lesser clarity of focusing are due to the dimension of power rather than to the dimension of consciousness; it is by virtue of the refraction and only because of it that we can apply these quantifying qualifications.

[2]By the way, the philosophical tendency in Judaism, particularly as it expressed itself in medieval and modern times, completely fails to appreciate this point in its evaluation of the tenet of the resurrection. And it fails to appreciate this point because it really views the tenet of the resurrection predominantly in the context of the ontological problem and not in the context of the ethical problem. Now, while the anchorage in a this-worldly context is a condition *sine qua non* for the ethical context, it is not at all essential for the ontological context. Given in addition the inherent tendency of the philosophic orientation to move away as far as possible from the concrete and the particular towards the abstract and the general, it is understandable that the philosophic tendency would not only fail to appreciate the true significance of resurrecting the body but actually be embarrassed by it. For in these circumstances the resurrection of the body can only signify for the philosophic tendency the complete concretization and particularization of the expression, thus a signification which is diametrically opposed to its own tendency towards abstraction and generalization. No wonder that the philosophic tendency should, therefore, see in the resurrection of the body a remnant of the primitive thought, a vulgarization of the spirit, from which it would want to distance itself as far as possible.

[3]Of course, as said, once the formulation is explicitly articulated, the rabbis claimed to find intimations and references to it in any number of biblical passages.

Chapter Eight

The Distinctive Expression of the Category of Worship in Judaism

Worship is a central category in the structure of faith of all religions. The purpose of this essay is to attempt to explicate the basic signification of this category; moreover, it is to show that in the case of Judaism, specifically in its mainstream expression, the category expresses itself in a special and distinct way.

I

We take the category of worship to signify the relating of man to that which is taken to constitute the ultimate being. Thus, worship in its basic and most inclusive signification signifies an act of relating – not, however, just any act of relating but that act of relating which is specifically directed to the ultimate being, and then only when it signifies the relating as it emanates from the side of man and not vice-versa as it emanates from the side of the ultimate being. It is this relating of man to that which he takes to be ultimate, irrespective of the shape, form, manner or content of the relating, which constitutes the very essence of the category of worship, all other characterizations being in the last analysis implicated by it.[1]

But as such the category of worship necessarily implicates the further category of transcendence inasmuch as we take the category of transcendence to signify the act of surpassing, the act of going beyond oneself (or commensurately, that entity which surpasses, which exists beyond oneself). For clearly, in signifying the relating of man to an ultimate the category of worship necessarily implicates the act of surpassing, of going beyond oneself on the part of man, i.e., it necessarily implicates an act of transcendence on the part of man. Indeed, any act of relating necessarily implicates an act of transcendence; the category of worship being constituted as an act of relating is thus constrained by its very constitution to implicate the category of transcendence.[2]

This assertion, however, requires further clarification. For, in the light of our delineation of the category of transcendence the category may implicate two different kinds of acts. On the one hand, it may implicate an act whose surpassing remains within the confines of the space-time continuum, within the totality of the world of our experience. On the other hand, however, it may also implicate an act whose surpassing goes beyond the very confines of the space-time continuum.[3] Using graphic imagery as a convenient short-hand, we may denote the latter act as a "vertical" act of transcendence and the former act as a "horizontal" act of transcendence. Thus, an act of transcendence can be either a vertical act or a horizontal act, seeing that by definition any act of surpassing is an act of transcendence and that the act of surpassing need not be exclusively a vertical act but can also be a horizontal act.

But surely, we would not want to say that in the context of biblical faith, specifically in the context of Judaism, the act of worship implicates an act of transcendence that is merely horizontal. Surely we would have to say that the act of transcendence which the act of worship implicates here must be specifically vertical. This is so because in the context of biblical faith the ultimate to which one relates in the act of worship is clearly vertical, i.e., it exists outside the space-time continuum. Thus, with respect to biblical faith, i.e., to Judaism, the act of worship must indeed implicate an act of transcendence that is exclusively vertical. It is not sufficient, therefore, to say here that the act of worship necessarily implicates the act of transcendence and let it go at that – one must specify that the act of transcendence implicated here is exclusively vertical.

We should note, however, that the specific, exclusive implication of the vertical act of transcendence is not universally valid with respect to all acts of worship. For although the act of worship signifies by definition a relating to an entity that is taken as ultimate, an entity need not be vertical in order to be taken as ultimate. One can relate to a horizontal entity as the ultimate thus characterizing the relating as an act of worship and in this case one would have, of course, an act of worship that implicates an act of transcendence that is horizontal and not vertical. Thus, for example, one can relate to a nation, to a party, to a cause, to art, to money or to power as one's ultimate and we do, indeed, often characterize the relating in such circumstances as an act of worship, i.e., we say "he worships money" or "he worships power," etc. But these entities are clearly horizontal, i.e., they exist within the space-time continuum, and the relating to them is, therefore, clearly an act of transcendence that is horizontal. Thus, generally speaking, the act of worship can implicate an act of transcendence that is not only vertical but also horizontal. Still, one may argue that in allowing the notion of worship to implicate an act of transcendence that is horizontal one is really vitiating the authentic signification of the notion. For one would want to say that, strictly speaking, the notion of worship belongs to the religious domain and that in the religious domain an entity that is horizontal cannot be taken as the ultimate – in the religious domain the ultimate can be constituted only by an entity that is vertical. Thus, although in principle one can take as ultimate an entity that is horizontal, and as such make the implication of a horizontal act of transcendence by the act of worship come within the purview of the definition of worship, still, it would not be valid to suppose that the act of worship can implicate an act of transcendence that is horizontal since, strictly speaking, the category of worship belongs to the religious domain and in the religious domain an entity that is horizontal would not be taken as ultiamte. The notion of worship can be taken to implicate an act of transcendence that is horizontal only when the notion is used in a derived and imprecise signification, when it is a pseudo notion of worship – when the notion signifies a relating to what is taken to be ultimate (hence its linkage with the authentic signification of the notion) but which from the religious viewpoint – which after all is the authentic, primary context where the signification of the notion is formulated – is not really an ultimate (hence its being pseudo).

But is this argument really valid? For although we may readily grant that the authentic signification of the notion of worship must be formulated in the context of the religious domain, is it further really valid to maintain that in the religious domain the only acceptable ultimate is the ultimate constituted by a vertical entity? But clearly, this can not be the case if one accepts the pantheistic orientation as a legitimate orientation within the domain of religion (as many religionists would no doubt insist on doing). For pantheism in identifying God, i.e., the ultimate, with the world of the space-time continuum, must inescapably implicate an ultimate that is horizontal. Indeed, pantheism by definition, i.e., by its very essence, cannot implicate an ultimate that is vertical. Thus, to the extent that pantheism is a legitimate orientation within the domain of religion, one cannot make the sweeping claim that for the domain of religion as such an authentic ultimate can only be an ultimate that is vertical. But while one cannot validly make this claim with respect to the domain of religion *as a whole* one can certainly make this claim with full validity with respect to the *theistic* orientation within the domain of religion. For evidently, the theistic orientation in placing God, i.e., the ultimate, over-against the world of the space-time continuum necessarily implicates that the ultimate here must be an entity that is vertical and that consequently the relating to it can only be an act of transcendence that is specifically and exclusively vertical. Thus, it is only when the religious domain is identified exclusively with the theistic orientation that one can argue that inasmuch as the category of worship belongs authentically to the domain of religion it implicates exclusively and specifically an act of transcendence that is vertical and not horizontal.

Now, such identification with the theistic orientation, while by no means characterizing the religious domain universally, does characterize biblical faiths. Indeed, in biblical faiths this identification is not peripheral or accidental but constitutes the very essence of the structure of faith – biblical faiths are by their very essence theistic in orientation. As such, it is specifically in biblical faiths (and consequently, as regards our case, specifically in Judaism) that the act of worship necessarily implicates not only an act of transcendence but also verticality, i.e., that it necessarily implicates an act of transcendence that is specifically and exclusively vertical and not horizontal. Indeed, since the theistic orientation constitutes an essential and inextricable aspect of biblical faiths it follows that the implication of verticality by the act of worship is likewise an essential and inextricable aspect of biblical faiths.[4]

Indeed, as such, the implication of verticality can serve as the criterion by which, from the perspective of biblical faiths, the distinction between the authentic religious orientation and the merely pseudo-religious orientation can be established. For one cannot really establish the distinction on the basis that only the authentic religious orientation can provide an all-encompassing *Weltanschauung*, an all-encompassing structure of meaning, a "home" for man to dwell in. Nor can one establish the distinction on the basis that only the authentic religious orientation can implicate ultimacy and the self-transcendence of man. Pseudo-religious ideologies can do the same. Indeed, as has been pointed out, pseudo-religious ideologies (see, for example, Communism) exhibit remarkable similarity to authentic religious formulations on practically every point in the structure (hence the reference to them as "religious"). The only point where a fundamental distinction can nonetheless be validly established is with respect to the implication of verticality – pseudo-religious ideologies do not implicate verticality while the authentic religious orientation ("authentic", of course, in the sense of reflecting the theistic-biblical vantage point) must by its very essence implicate verticality (hence their qualification as *pseudo*-religious).

But even more fundamentally, the implication of verticality can serve as the criterion by which the essential distinction between the authentic religious orientation (again, when viewed from the theistic-biblical vantage point) and the orientation of secularism can be established. For as in the case of the pseudo-religious ideologies, so also here, the aspect of an all-encompassing *Weltanschauung*, of self-transcendence or of ultimacy cannot apply as the criterion of distinction. Secularism can provide these aspects just as well as the authentic religious orientation. But what secularism, in contradistinction to the authentic religious orientation, cannot provide is verticality – the ultimate which exists vertically over-against the world or the act of transcendence which is vertical rather than horizontal. Indeed, we would suggest that the very essence of the notion of secularism lies in its signifying the abrogation of any and all verticality. In the last analysis, this is what the notion really signifies. Namely, it does not signify the absence of ultimacy or the abrogation of transcendence as such (clearly, these are feasible when they are horizontal) but rather the absence of ultimacy which is specifically vertical and the abrogation of transcendence when it is, again, specifically vertical rather than horizontal.

Finally, it should be clear that this implication of verticality by the authentic religious orientation (when taken in the theistic-biblical context) must qualify the argument that inasmuch as man is by his very essence constituted as a self-transcending being he is by his very essence also constituted as a *homo religiosus*. For although there is no denying that man is by his very essence constituted as a self-transcending being (seeing that by his very essence he is constituted as a conscious being and that consciousness necessarily implicates self-transcendence, inasmuch as every act of consciousness is an act of going beyond, of surpassing oneself, towards something else), this does not in any way require that the transcendence must be vertical. Indeed, the consciousness of man can express itself fully in the horizontal act of transcendence – man's inherent aspect of self-transcendence can be fully met by horizontal transcendence and does not require recourse to vertical transcendence. On the other hand, however, what constitutes (in the theistic-biblical context) *homo religiosus* is not just any act of transcendence but the act of transcendence that is specifically vertical. Horizontal transcendence would not constitute here a *homo religiosus*. Thus, it does not follow from the fact that man is by his very essence constituted as a self-transcending being that he is also by his very essence constituted (in the theistic-biblical context) as a *homo religiosus*. All that one can say (seeing that man is constituted as a self-transcending being) is that the vertical transcendence constituting homo religiosus here is an authentic and viable option for man, thus allowing other considerations to make the case that man ought to express his self-transcending in vertical transcendence.

We must repeat and emphasize the point, however, that delineating worship as implicating not just any act of transcendence but specifically only that act of transcendence that is vertical and the considerations that follow from this (i.e., the distinction between the authentic religious orientation, on the one hand, and the pseudo-religious and secularist orientations on the other, and the implications for the question of *homo religiosus*) are applicable only when religion is viewed from a theistic-biblical vantage point. They are not applicable when religion is viewed from a pantheistic vantage point and thus from the vantage point of most, if not all, non-biblical religions. Indeed, from the theistic-biblical vantage point the very formulation of pantheism itself (and thus of all non-biblical religions manifesting this vantage point) must be rejected as a viable expression of the authentic religious orientation; rather it must be viewed as an expression of the pseudo-religious orientation, an expression that, if not actually belonging in the last analysis to the secularist orientation, is nonetheless close and congenial to it.[5]

Of course, if what constitutes the authentic religious orientation is to be defined not from the exclusive theistic-biblical vantage point but rather from some other broader vantage point, then not only pantheism but also the various pseudo-religious orientations and, indeed, even secularism itself may become valid expressions of the authentic religious orientation (namely, the distinction between the authentically religious, the pseudo-religious and the secularist orientation in the fundamental sense proposed here falls away). We should be clear, however, that any such alternative broader vantage point would have the marked disadvantage that in its terms the delineation of the authentic religious orientation would become vague and that, indeed, it would become questionable if one can really use such a delineation in any meaningful and useful way. To paraphrase a rabbinic saying, "If you catch a lot you don't really catch anything." In any event, since our task here is to explicate the signification of the category of worship in the religious context of Judaism, a religion which is certainly a theistic-biblical religion, the theistic-biblical vantage point would clearly apply here and consequently the distinction delineated above between the authentic religious orientation on the one hand, and the pseudo-religious and secularist orientation on the other, should also apply here. But even more to our point, the signification of the category of worship, as a category operating in the authentic religious domain, should implicate here not just the act of transcendence as such but the act of transcendence that is specifically and exclusively vertical.

Saying, however, that worship necessarily signifies a relating that is vertically transcendent does not necessarily implicate the further saying that the *mode* of the relating must be exclusively *direct,* i.e., a relating initiated at a specific point in the horizontal flux of space and time moving away from such a point *perpendicularly* towards the vertically transcendent being. In other words, the mode of the relating must not be exclusively away from this concrete world – the concrete world merely serving at a certain point in its space-time continuum as a jumping-board from which one launches towards the vertically transcendent being. Of course, such a direct mode of relating is possible, and indeed manifests itself quite extensively within the religious phenomenon.[6] But it is also possible that the mode of the relating be *indirect.* Namely, while the relating is horizontal, i.e., between two points in the horizontal flux, this horizontal relating will at the same time implicate a relating to the vertically transcendent being. One relates here to the vertically transcendent being through a relating to the world, i.e., to that which is horizontally transcendent.[7] The relating here would thus proceed through the world; it would be mediated by the world. It would be, so to speak, refracted through the horizontal dimension. Still, such an indirect mode of relating would constitute authentic worship just as much as the direct mode of relating, for *ultimately* the relating here is also directed towards the vertically transcendent being and this after all is what counts. The way by which this relating is carried out, namely, whether it is direct or refracted, exclusive or involving a relating to other intermediary entities, is a secondary consideration which, inasmuch as it does not change the fact that the relating here is *ultimately* directed towards the vertically transcendent being, does not in any way undermine the relating being an authentic act of worship. Thus, the act of worship as delineated here allows either the direct or the indirect mode of relating.

We would suggest, however, that this alternative between the direct and indirect mode of relating is actually linked to the alternative between the ontological and ethical perspective in terms of which an essential structure of faith may formulate itself. (By an "essential structure of faith" we mean the formulation which impinges on 1) the perception of what is taken to constitute the ultimate predicament of man and 2) the salvation that is anticipated commensurately with the perceived predicament – these two considerations determining, in turn, all the other considerations constituting the overall structure of faith as, for example, the kind of divinity implicated, its role, the vocation of man, the cosmological setting etc.) Namely, a case can be made that the direct mode of relating is linked to the ontological perspective while the indirect mode of relating is linked to the ethical perspective. The rationale for this is as follows: given the content and orientation of the ontological perspective (for example, that the ultimate predicament lies in the finitude of being), there is really nothing in its inner-logic that would require that the mode of relating be refracted through the horizontal dimension. The horizontal dimension, i.e., the world, has no role to play if what is at stake is the transformation of man's ontological constitution. Indeed, if anything, it would seem that such an ontological transformation can be effected only by a source transcending the horizontal dimension and consequently the inner-logic of the situation here should implicate a relating that is exclusively in the direct mode. As against this, the inner-logic of the ethical perspective clearly implicates the requirement that the relating be refracted through the horizontal dimension. For the ethical consideration can really arise only in the context of the horizontal dimension, i.e., in the context of the concrete world, seeing that it impinges upon conduct and relations which are embedded specifically within the horizontal dimension; ethics, strictly speaking, does not impinge upon conduct and relations which transcend the world. Thus, if a structure of faith is to formulate itself from the ethical perspective, namely, if the religious relation, i.e., the relation to the vertically transcendent being, is to be infused with ethical meaning, then the religious relation must be refracted through the horizontal dimension, in other words, the structure of faith must resort to the indirect mode of relating.

Indeed, the alternative between the ethical and ontological perspectives is a fundamental alternative which, in turn, implicates any number of rather significant alternatives impinging upon the category of worship. Thus, in addition to showing that it implicates the alternative between the direct and indirect relating, it can also be shown to implicate the further alternative between the individual and the collectivity when these impinge on the human role in the context of worship. Namely, it can be shown to implicate whether the human bearer of the relating expressing worship, i.e., the human pole in the man-god relation, is to be constituted by the individual person or by a collectivity of persons, whether worship is primarily an affair of the individual or of the collectivity. For clearly the ontological perspective would implicate the individual and not the collectivity, seeing that the relating here is ultimately for the sake of an ontological transformation and that such a transformation can be effected only in terms of the individual and not of the collectivity (the notion of collectivity can enter the picture here only secondarily as that which signifies the sum total of individuals seeking or being granted such an ontological transformation).[8]

As against this, the ethical perspective implicates the collectivity rather than the individual. For the ethical impinges not on the aspect of man's constitution but rather on the aspect of his conduct and action. It thus implicates man in relation to an other rather than man in his monadic individuality and the context of man in relation to an other constitutes already a collectivity, albeit not necessarily an exclusively human collectivity (for the "other" need not be here exclusively man – it can be any entity of nature). Still, we would argue that in the case before us the collectivity that is implicated must indeed be a human collectivity, i.e., that the "other" in the relating must be specifically one's fellow-man. For we are not dealing here with the ethical perspective as an independent philosophical perspective grounded in its own terms but rather we are dealing with the ethical perspective as it is grounded in the biblical religious domain. This means, however, that we cannot be dealing here with an ethical perspective that bases itself on egocentric criteria, thus expressing itself, for example, in such formulations as the utilitarian or eudemonistic formulation; we must be dealing with an ethical perspective that bases itself on the criteria of accountability and responsibility to an other. But as such this, in turn, means that it must be an ethical perspective in which the 'other' in the relating is specifically also man, i.e., an ethical perspective in which the ethical concern impinges specifically on the relating of man to his fellow-man. For only a conscious, personal being can exact accountability and responsibility for the action directed towards it and among all the beings of nature only man is a conscious, personal being. Thus, the ethical perspective that is before us here implicates a relating that is specifically a relating between man and his fellow-man, thus implicating a human collectivity (the individual enters the picture here only secondarily and then only by virtue of his membership in the collectivity). Needless to say, this collectivity being a collectivity of men (of men who are not only conscious spirits but also flesh and blood), it is inescapably a this-worldly collectivity. Furthermore, if the ethical perspective is to express itself fully, i.e., if it is to impinge upon the whole gamut of relations that can arise between man and his fellow-man – impinge upon relations belonging to the social, the economic and the political domains of life – the collectivity which it implicates must be the ethnic-national collectivity. For only in the ethnic-national collectivity can all these relationships between man and his fellow-man be encompassed. In any other collectivity, be it sub-national or extra-national (as, for example, the family, the clan, or any professional, ideological, spiritual or political association), only some of these relations, but never all of them, can be encompassed. The ethnic-national collectivity thus becomes a central and primary category in the structure of faith that formulates itself from the ethical perspective. It is transformed by the ethical perspective from being essentially a category of history into being a fundamental religious category – the category which provides the matrix through which the indirect relating to the divine can express itself.

Even more significantly, perhaps, the alternative between the ethical and the ontological perspectives implicates the further alternative impinging on whether the vertically transcendent being, i.e., the category of the divine, involved in the structure of faith is to be constituted as a Thou or as an It. Namely, we would suggest that the ethical perspective (being here specifically an ethical perspective that bases itself on the criteria of accountability and responsibility) would necessarily implicate that the vertically transcendent being involved in the structure of faith be constituted as a Thou (i.e., a conscious, personal being) and not as an It (i.e., an impersonal being of Power devoid of consciousness). For inasmuch as the relating here is subject to accountability, and seeing that although it be refracted through the horizontal dimension it is nonetheless directed ultimately towards the vertically transcendent being, the relating must implicate that the vertically transcendent being be constituted as a Thou. For as we have argued above, only a being constituted as a Thou can exact accountability and responsibility for the action, i.e., the relating, directed towards it. A being constituted as an It cannot do it and consequently a relating subject to accountability cannot arise with respect to it. But that the relating be subject to accountability is the very mainstay of the ethical perspective. Thus, an ethical perspective and a vertically transcendent being that is constituted as an It are mutually exclusive; an ethical perspective must implicate that the vertically transcendent being be constituted as a Thou.

As against this, the ontological perspective need by no means implicate the exclusion of a vertically transcendent being that is constituted as an It. Indeed, a case can be made that while, strictly speaking, the inner logic of the ontological formulation can encompass a vertically transcendent being that is constituted either as a Thou or as an It, its tendency would be to implicate, in the last analysis, a vertically transcendent being that is constituted as an It. For the tendency here would be to place the category of being, the category in terms of which the predicament is perceived, in the sphere of Power (i.e., perceiving being as the manifestation or expression of Power). Thus, for example, if the predicament in the ontological formulation is ultimately perceived in terms of the *finitude* of being (as we would want to argue is generally the case), then the category of being is indeed taken here in terms of the sphere of Power as can readily be seen by the mere fact of its quantification. But if the predicament is perceived in the context of the sphere of power, then commensurate to it the envisioned salvation will be formulated likewise in the context of the sphere of Power and consequently the vertically transcendent being will be constituted as an It.[9] Thus, in the context of the ontological perspective (and in clear contra-distinction to that of the ethical perspective) not only can the implicated vertically transcendent being be constituted as an It but it is very likely to be so constituted.

Now, this alternative between the Thouness and Itness of the vertically transcendent being impinges, in turn, on a most significant aspect in the delineation of the category of worship. Namely, it impinges upon the *kind* of worship, i.e., the *kind* of relating, that is made feasible. For clearly, the only authentic relation that is feasible with respect to a Thou is the relation of address – the affirmation of the other in its otherness. As against this, with respect to an It the only feasible relation is the relation of utilization – either a theoretical utilization which is then tantamount to orientation (i.e., to the "capturing" or the "fixing" of the other in description), or a practical utilization which is then tantamount to manipulation (i.e., to the handling of the other for one's interests). But this, in turn, would clearly implicate the following: 1) that with respect to a vertically transcendent being constituted as a Thou the relating, if it is to be authentic, must be circumscribed to expressing itself either as prayer (when the relating is directly vertical) or as ethical conduct (when the relating is indirect, i.e., refracted through the horizontal dimension), seeing that the only viable authentic expressions for a relating that is constituted as an address are prayer and ethical conduct; 2) that conversely, neither prayer nor ethical conduct could be feasible expressions for a relating directed towards a vertically transcendent being that is constituted as an It, seeing that both prayer and ethical conduct are inextricably expressions of address and that it would simply not make sense to address an It; 3) that, on the other hand, with respect to a vertically transcendent being constituted as an It, the relating, if it is to be feasible, will have to be circumscribed to expressing itself either as divination (when the relating is theoretical) or as magic (when the relating is practical) inasmuch as it is these expressions which constitute respectively orientation (albeit with respect to the future) and manipulation; 4) that these expressions of divination and magic are, in turn, not feasible with respect to a vertically transcendent being constituted as a Thou. Thus, whether the vertically transcendent being is constituted as an It or as a Thou would clearly determine the *kind* of worship that is feasible – magic and divination in the case of the former, prayer and ethical conduct in the case of the latter.

Finally, there are two further sets of alternative characterizations involved in this context and they require some clarification. First, we have the alternative between the relating constituting worship being carried out verbally and it being carried out in action. Now, in terms of the most obvious signification of this alternative, i.e., in terms of the literal signification of its notions (when "verbal" is to signify the mere emitting of sounds and "action" is to signify soundless bodily movements), the alternative is clearly peripheral and not very significant. For, as such, it is an alternative that impinges merely on the outward means of expressing the relating rather than on its very content and signification. Furthermore, it is not really relevant to the further elucidation of the options impinging upon the category of worship in connection with the basic alternative characterizing it, i.e., the alternative between the Itness and Thouness of the vertically transcendent being. For one cannot establish here any exclusive correspondence between the action or verbal expression of the relating, on the one hand, and the Itness or Thouness of the vertically transcendent being, on the other hand. Thus, a verbal relating can clearly be linked with a vertically transcendent being that is a Thou; but it can also be linked with a vertically transcendent being that is an It as, for example, in the case of verbal magic. Conversely, a relating expressing itself in action can certainly be linked with a vertically transcendent being that is an It; but it can also be linked with a vertically transcendent being that is a Thou as, for example, in the case of ethical conduct.

This alternative can become, however, much more significant if we expand its signification, namely, if we take "verbal" to signify not merely the emitting of sound but actual speech and "action" to signify not just bodily movements but the impingement of brute force devoid of intention on an other. For clearly, in terms of these expanded significations the alternative would now impinge on the very content of the relating. Furthermore, one would now be able to establish an exclusive correspondence between a relating that is verbal and the vertically transcendent being that is a Thou, on the one hand, and between a relating that is action and the vertically transcendent being that is an It, on the other, seeing that actual, authentic speech can be directed only to a being that is a Thou and that brute force devoid of intention can impinge only upon a being that is an It. As such, it would appear that with this expanded signification we do have here, after all, a *bona fide* additional alternative impinging on the category of worship in conjunction with the basic alternative between the Itness and Thouness of the vertically transcendent being. A moment's reflection will show, however, that in terms of this expanded signification the alternative here is really reduced, for all intents and purposes, to an alternative which was already delineated above, i.e., to the alternative between address and manipulation. For in saying that "verbal" signifies speech we are really saying that in essence it signifies address, and likewise in saying that "action" signifies the impingement of force we are really saying that in essence it signifies manipulation (by the way, in terms of these significations verbal magic would, of course, have to be taken as a relating that is action while ethical conduct would have to be taken as a relating that is verbal). Thus, there is nothing new here except for the terminology. We must conclude, therefore, that the alternative between verbal and action is not too significant – it is either peripheral or it is a restatement, in a different terminology, of another more essential alternative, the alternative between address and manipulation.

Secondly, and lastly, we have the alternative between intention and precision. This alternative is actually implicated by the foregoing alternative, i.e., the alternative between verbal and action, in its expanded signification, thus, when it actually signifies the alternative between address and manipulation. For clearly, a relating that is an address would implicate that the efficacy of the relating be determined exclusively by its intention while a relating that is manipulation would implicate that the efficacy of the relating be determined exclusively by its precision. The very constitution of an address, it being an act of affirmation (the affirmation of an other), lies in its intention. There can be no affirmation without the intention to affirm – the act of affirmation is an act of intention. On the other hand, in manipulation intention counts for naught. The results here depend exclusively on how the action is executed – to secure the desired results the commensurate action must be executed with perfect precision. This, and this alone, provides its success. This rationale is further buttressed by the consideration that an address is a relating that is linked exclusively to a Thou while manipulation is a relating that is linked exclusively to an It and clearly with respect to a Thou it is intention which exclusively determines the efficacy of the relating while with respect to an It it is exclusively precision. Thus, this alternative fits very neatly into the array of alternatives delineated above. Indeed, whether a relating is "verbal" or "action" (in the expanded signification of the terms) and consequently whether it is a relating to a Thou or to an It can be established by whether its efficacy is determined by intention or by precision. Thus again, for example, verbal magic can now be determined as a relating that is action, i.e., manipulation, by the additional consideration that the efficacy of its relating lies in its precision, and conversely ethical conduct can now be determined as a relating that is verbal, i.e., address, by the additional consideration that the efficacy of its relating lies in its intention.[10] Furthermore, this alternative, unlike the former alternative between verbal and action, is a legitimately new alternative which cannot be reduced to any of the alternatives delineated above. For it impinges on the category of worship from a new angle – it does not impinge on the content, the mode or the object of the relating but rather on the criterion that determines the efficacy of the relating. Still, as we have seen, it is very consistent with these other alternatives even though they impinge on quite different aspects of the relating.

In view of the analysis presented here, therefore, one would have to conclude that the signification of the category of worship (once its basic signification as a relating to a vertically transcendent being is established) is clearly bifurcated – the array of alternatives delineated above could arise only on the basis of such a bifurcation. Thus, we actually have two distinct and quite different expressions of the category of worship depending on whether the category constitutes itself in the context of a structure of faith that formulates itself from the ethical perspective or in the context of a structure of faith that formulates itself from the ontological perspective or, to put the matter more conclusively, depending on whether the category constitutes itself in the Thou-sphere or in the It-sphere.

II

With the help of the above analysis we can now proceed to examine how the category of worship functions in the context of Judaism. The first thing to note is that in the context of Judaism, when it is taken in its all-inclusive entirety, one may encounter both alternative expressions of the category of worship. This should not really be surprising. For Judaism in its concrete, historical manifestation (as, indeed, the other biblical faiths when taken in their concrete, historical manifestations) is by no means monolithic with respect to its structure of faith. Actually, in its concrete, historical manifestation one can encounter a mixture of structures of faith; specifically, one can encounter both the structure of faith which is grounded in the Thou-sphere and the structure of faith which is grounded in the It-sphere. In view of this and in view of the fact, as we have seen above, that the category of worship is determined by the structure of faith, it should not be surprising to find that corresponding to the manifestation of the two basic structures of faith (the one grounded in the Thou-sphere and the other in the It-sphere) the two alternative expressions of the category of worship are also manifested.

Thus, for example, the expression of the category of worship which formulates itself in the It-sphere can clearly be encountered in the sacrificial cult as presented in Hebrew Scriptures. For in the sacrificial cult, irrespective of which of the various interpretations may be given to it (be it that it signifies the "feeding" of the divine on a *quid pro quo* basis or be it the reverse, that it signifies the "eating" of the divine which is present in the sacrificial animal), one inescapably encounters a relating that is directly vertical, a relating that is constituted as manipulation (specifically, the utilization of the divine) and whose efficacy lies in its precision rather than in its intention. In the last analysis, the relating here is by its very essence constituted as a transaction of power and as such it inevitably implicates a vertically transcendent being that is an It and a signification that is ontological rather than ethical – its intention is to increase the power, and thus to strengthen and fortify the being of the sacrificer. Similarly, this expression, i.e., the expression formulating itself in the It-sphere, can also be encountered in the act of prayer and the observance of the commandments when these are taken in terms of the signification accorded to them in the context of Jewish mysticism. For in this context these acts are constituted as means for the mystic's ascent towards union with the divine or, alternatively, they are constituted as means for the mystic's endeavor to unify anew the being of the divine. In either case these acts are constituted here as a "technique" and thus as signifying manipulation rather than address. Indeed, they clearly implicate for the structure of faith in which they operate an ontological rather than an ethical perspective – they clearly impinge on ontological transformations in the constitution of the mystic or of the divine rather than on their ethical conduct – and as such they implicate a vertically transcendent being which is, in the last analysis, an It rather than a Thou. Thus, although the act of prayer and the observance of the commandments would generally be taken (and rightly so) as articulating the category of worship that formulates itself in the Thou-sphere, when these acts are taken now in the context of mysticism, i.e., when the signification of these acts is provided by the context of mysticism, the acts clearly articulate the category of worship that formulates itself in the It-domain.

But while we can encounter in Judaism the manifestation of the category of worship that formulates itself in the It-domain, it must be admitted that we can encounter this formulation of the category of worship only in these strands of the phenomenon which do not constitute the mainstream expression or, even more significantly, the distinctive expression of Judaism. For the category of worship that formulates itself in the It-domain can be encountered in the main only in the "priestly" strand of Hebrew Scriptures and in the mystical strand of Rabbinic Judaism and while these strands are certainly part and parcel of the all-encompassing phenomenon of Judaism they certainly do not constitute the distinctive or, for that matter, the mainstream expressions of the phenomenon.

Indeed the structure of faith that formulates itself in the It-domain, i.e., the structure of faith that formulates itself from the ontological perspective and which implicates a vertically transcendent being that is constituted as an It, is quite universal and consequently expressions similar to the "priestly" and mystical strands in the phenomenon of Judaism can be encountered in most other religions. To locate the distinctive expression of Judaism one must turn to the "prophetic" strand in Hebrew Scriptures and to the non-mystical *halachic* strand in Rabbinic Judaism. For the underlying structure of faith in these strands is one that formulates itself in the Thou-domain, i.e., it is a structure of faith which formulates itself from the ethical perspective and which implicates a vertically transcendent being that is constituted as a Thou, and such a structure of faith is, indeed, distinctive to Judaism (or, more precisely, to biblical faiths) seeing that it is not generally encountered in other religions. But as such, we should, of course, expect to encounter here the category of worship that formulates itself in the Thou-domain, namely, the category of worship which implicates a relating to a vertically transcendent being that is constituted as a Thou rather than as an It, which delineates the relating as address rather than as manipulation, and where the signification of the relating is ethical rather than ontological. This, indeed, is the case. To fully appreciate this, however, we must keep in mind what our analysis above has established, namely, that while the direct mode of relating will, of course, be present here (and given the nature of the relating it will have to be delineated *qua* address), the burden of the relating, in view of its signification being ethical, will tend towards the indirect mode. Only as such, can we come to understand how the category of worship really functions in these distinctive strands of Judaism. Failing to keep this in mind and, therefore, looking only for the direct mode of relating is bound to leave us with an unsatisfactory and, indeed, warped picture of the way the category functions in these strands. For while the direct mode in the form of prayer *qua* address is certainly present in these strands, its presence is not as central and important as one should expect nor is its structure (specifically in the *halachic* strand) quite commensurate with its signification as address. Indeed, if the category of worship in these strands were to consist only of prayer *qua* address, one would be left with a rather perplexing situation – the category which constitutes the very heart and essence of the religious phenomenon functioning in a rather peripheral way and in a manner which does not quite correspond to its signification.

Let us attempt to briefly explicate this contention. To start with the "prophetic" strand, there is no denying that prayer *qua* address can be encountered in this strand – the prophets, though not all of them, certainly pray and some of the most striking and powerful instances of prayer are to be found in this literature.[11] Still, the fact remains that the amount of prayer found in the prophets is quite meager. Moreover, it is quite clear that, strictly speaking, prayer is not part of the prophetic vocation; if anything, it is a clear interruption of it. Indeed, most pertinently, if prayer were to be completely extirpated from prophetic literature, that literature would hardly be affected. Thus, prayer can hardly be taken as the central expression of prophecy. While prayer when it occurs in prophecy is indeed authentic prayer, i.e., it is prayer *qua* address, it actually occurs only to a small extent and rather peripherally.

Moving to the non-mystical *halachic* strand, one must likewise readily admit that prayer can be encountered also here. Indeed, prayer manifests itself here to a considerably larger extent and in a way that is much more central and significant than is the case in prophecy. Even more telling, it is accorded an established status as an expression for the human-divine relating. Still, even so, the status and role of prayer here are by no means what we should expect if prayer *qua* authentic address were indeed *the* central expression of the category of worship, i.e., *the* central expression of the relating of man to the divine. For first, it must be noted that this established status is, strictly speaking, accorded to prayer only on a provisional basis. Namely, prayer is accorded this established status only because it comes to take the place of the sacrificial cult when the sacrificial cult becomes inoperative upon the destruction of the Temple and it is to retain this established status only for the duration, i.e., only as long as the sacrificial cult cannot be reinstituted. Thus, "officially" speaking, prayer is not the permanent, let alone the inherent expression for the relating – the sacrificial cult is. Prayer is merely a substitute and, in principle, a provisional substitute at that. This is hardly an impressive status. Now, to accord prayer this status, i.e., the status of being merely a provisional substitute, must clearly indicate that it is not viewed as a fundamental expression – it is hardly the status one would expect for the central expression of the category of worship.

Of course, one can argue that this unsatisfactory state of affairs as regards the status accorded to prayer is brought about only because of the legalistic mode of thought characterizing the *halachic* strand, but that from the phenomenological vantage point, i.e., from the vantage point of the structure of faith characterizing the strand, the expression of prayer is really permanent and inherent to the *halachic* strand and that, therefore, its status is in reality also much more substantial and significant to the strand. Namely, legalistically speaking the *halachic* strand cannot indeed accord prayer any other status than that of provisional substitute, seeing that in the legalistic context of the *halacha* the Pentateuchal Law is taken as the sole all-encompassing record of revelation, thus as the only authoritative and binding source of its prescriptions, and that the Pentateuchal Law nowhere prescribes prayer. Specifically, its prescription for the direct mode of relating to the divine (the relating which prayer could appropriately express) is that it be expressed exclusively through the sacrificial cult. The expression of prayer is in no way grounded in revelation and consequently, given the legalistic orientation of the *halacha,* it can in principle have no status in its own right. Indeed, its very institution was made feasible only through a rabbinic decree and then only when, upon the destruction of the Temple, the sacrificial cult became inoperative, thus creating a lacuna in the expression of the direct mode of relating which required that it be filled in. This being the case, it is clear that from the legalistic vantage point the status of prayer could not be otherwise than that of provisional substitute, i.e., a substitute only for the duration in which the sacrificial cult remains inoperative.

However, when one proceeds to view the matter not from the legalistic vantage point but from the phenomenological vantage point, i.e., from the vantage point of the requirements of the structure of faith characterizing the strand, a quite different assessment of the status of prayer and of the sacrificial cult emerges. For from this vantage point it becomes quite clear that the only authentic mode of expression in the *halachic* strand for the direct mode of relating is prayer and that the sacrificial cult, its prescription in the Pentateuchal Law notwithstanding, is quite untenable as a mode of expression. After all, as we have seen, the *halachic* strand formulates itself from the perspective of the Thou-dimension and as such it requires that all its expressions be similarly articulated in terms of the Thou-dimension, seeing that it is simply not tenable for an expression articulating itself in terms of the It-dimension to operate authentically and validly in the context of a structure of faith that formulates itself from the perspective of the Thou-dimension (and vice-versa). This being the case, it is clear that prayer, inasmuch as it articulates itself in terms of the Thou-dimension, constitutes an authentic expression for the *halachic* strand; the sacrificial cult, on the other hand, being clearly an expression that articulates itself in terms of the It-dimension, is fundamentally an incommensurate expression for the *halachic* strand. Indeed, the legalistic orientation in attributing the expression of the sacrificial cult to the *halachic* strand was in effect placing an untenable strain upon the *halachic* that could not have been maintained for any appreciable duration. By the way, one may well surmise that with respect to this issue (though not, of course, with respect to other issues), the destruction of the Temple causing the sacrificial cult to become inoperative was rather fortuitous as it provided a ready and convenient way out of the dilemma and that had the Temple not been destroyed the *halachic* strand would have found or devised another rationale to make the sacrificial cult inoperative; by the same token one may well conjure that the *halachic* strand would see to it that the conditions prerequisite for the reinstitution of the sacrificial cult would never be satisfied. Thus, when viewed from a phenomenological rather than from a legalistic vantage point prayer in the *halachic* tradition is far from being a substitute and it is hardly provisional. Its status as a provisional substitute is merely a formal matter necessitated by legalistic considerations; in reality it is inherent within the strand as one of its authentic expressions and is indeed instituted, for all intents and purposes, as a permanent expression.

Still, even so, granting the validity of these observations, the fact remains that the *halachic* strand could acquiesce in the fact that it attributed to prayer, albeit merely in a formal way, the status of being a mere provisional substitute, indeed, that it accommodated itself to such an evaluation and did not feel compelled to change it. This certainly indicates that the *role* which prayer plays within the *halachic* strand is not essential or central. For if prayer were not only an authentic expression for the *halachic* strand but actually constituted its essential and central expression, one would have had every right to expect that the strand would not have acquiesced in attributing to it the status of being a mere provisional substitute and a way would have been found to change it, the legalistic considerations notwithstanding. Surely, an essential and central expression cannot be characterized by the status of being a mere provisional substitute. Furthermore, it is significant to note that the Pentateuchal Law does not prescribe any other expression for the direct mode of relating aside from the sacrificial cult. For this means, of course, that it is only the "priestly" strand in the Law, i.e., the strand formulating itself from the perspective of the It-dimension, that addresses itself to the question of the direct mode of relating and that the "prophetic" strand in the Law, i.e., the strand formulating itself from the perspective of the Thou-dimension, is unconcerned with the question of the direct mode of relating. Now, this observation is most telling, for it clearly suggests that the direct mode of relating is not an essential and central mode of relating for the "prophetic" strand. Indeed, had it been an essential and central mode, the "prophetic" strand would have surely been constrained to address itself to it. Thus, it would seem to us that the fact that the "prophetic" strand in the Pentateuchal Law can ignore prescribing an expression for the direct mode of relating and that the *halachic* strand can acquiesce, albeit merely on the formal-legal level, in the status of prayer being merely that of a provisional substitute, clearly indicates that in these strands prayer does not constitute the essential and central expression of the relating to the divine.

But even more problematic than the fact that the *halachic* strand accords prayer the status of a mere provisional substitute are some of the features which the *halachic* strand imposes on prayer. Thus, the *halachic* strand fixes set times for the recitation of prayer. Furthermore, it fixes the content of prayer, i.e., it predetermines from the outside what is to be recited on what occasion. Lastly, it formulates the content of prayer in terms of the collectivity rather than of the individual, i.e., it is in terms of the "we," the people Israel, rather than in terms of the "I," the individual person, that the content of prayer is formulated. Clearly, these features are very problematic for authentic prayer, i.e., if prayer is to be taken as an act of address. For prayer *qua* address must be spontaneous, an affair of the heart, seeing that it is constituted by its intention and not by the form of its outward expression. It must be the articulation, in whatever outward form, of the intention of a specific, particular moment. As such, it cannot be the act of a collectivity but only of the individual person (the very notion of collectivity can enter the picture here only secondarily and in the abstract as a designation for a summation of praying individuals). Nor can appointed times or content be determined for it in advance or from the outside, i.e., by others. Indeed, the very notion of its prescription or recitation is already a corruption of its authenticity *qua* address. Thus, the fact that in the *halachic* strand prayer is delineated in terms of these features must raise serious questions as to its authenticity, namely, whether prayer is really constituted here as an address.

No doubt the imposition by the *halachic* strand of these features upon prayer is in part due to the fact that, as we have seen, prayer is introduced here as a substitute for the sacrificial cult. For after all it would be quite understandable if one were to transfer to the substitute features which characterized the entity that it has supplanted. This means, of course, that in our case it should be quite understandable if prayer, having been instituted as a substitute for the sacrificial cult, were also to be characterized, as a result of this substitution, by features which really belong legitimately to the sacrificial cult. Indeed, we can readily see that with respect to the sacrificial cult such features as collectivity, predetermined content, appointed times (and, indeed, also appointed places) are quite feasible and legitimate, seeing that the sacrificial cult expresses itself in terms of the It-dimension and that in this context the relating is constituted as a transaction in Power and not as an address. Certainly, with respect to the imposition of appointed times upon prayer, we know that the rabbis consciously and explicitly imposed them to parallel the schedule of appointed times set for the sacrificial cult in the Temple (e.g., the morning and afternoon sacrifice on weekdays and the twofold morning sacrifice on the Sabbath and holidays). But even more fundamentally, perhaps, the imposition of these features is also due to the fact that prayer is institutionalized in the *halachic* strand (as, indeed, it would be in any other concrete expression of religion). For institutionalization certainly implicates uniformity and consequently specification as regards the contents and time of prayer. Namely, in an institutionalized context one would clearly need to have determined when one ought to pray and what one ought to pray.[12] But be this as it may, there is no escaping the fact that the imposition of these features does compromise the authenticity of prayer, i.e., it does compromise prayer *qua* address.

Indeed, it would seem that the rabbis who fashioned the *halachic* strand were aware of this contradiction which arises between the imposition of these features and the requirements of prayer *qua* address and that they tried as best they could to mitigate it. For while arrogating prayer to the collectivity, i.e., formulating it in terms of the "we" rather than the "I", they nonetheless provide an occasion within the set structure of the prayer for the individual, if he is so moved, to express himself spontaneously (they provide a place for a "prayer of the heart"); similarly, while determining in advance and from the outside the contents of prayer they nonetheless keep emphasizing the importance of injecting *Kavanah,* i.e., proper intention, into the set words of prayer.

This clearly shows that the rabbis were aware of the requirements of authentic prayer and that, indeed, they tried to satisfy them. Still, these attempts do not really change, in the last analysis, the situation. For the provision of an opportunity for spontaneous prayer by the individual does not change the fact that the overwhelming bulk of prayer is determined in advance from the outside and is arrogated to the collectivity (and, indeed, this provision is rarely availed of in the ethos of the *halachic* strand). And even more significantly, the emphasis on *Kavanah* does not change the fact that *Kavanah* does not really influence the criterion which determines the efficacy and validity of prayer. Indeed, the signification of the emphasis on *Kavanah* is to be located only in the context of idealism and perfection. Namely, it expresses an ideal desideratum – ideally speaking, prayer should be infused with *Kavanah.* Thus, it is not that *Kavanah* must be an inextricable factor in the very constitution of prayer as such; only that, ideally speaking, prayer, being as such already constituted, be in addition infused with *Kavanah.* It is precisely in this qualification of "ideally speaking" that the rub lies. Indeed, the fact is that even if *Kavanah* is not forthcoming it is still incumbent upon the Jew to recite the set prayers at their appointed times; it is incumbent upon him, so to speak, to go through the motions and perform that which has been prescribed. Moreover, in the last analysis it is precisely this performance which counts. What counts is the execution of the prescription as it is prescribed. Namely, what counts is conformity in action rather than *Kavanah.* Here lies the real crux of the problem. For as such, from the viewpoint of authentic prayer, i.e., from the viewpoint of prayer as address, the act of prayer is inevitably compromised.[13]

It would appear, therefore, that although authentic prayer, i.e., prayer *qua* address, certainly manifests itself both in the "prophetic" and in the *halachic* strands (the strands which constitute the distinctive and main expression of the phenomenon of Judaism), its manifestation is far from adequate if it is to be the main expression by which the relating to the divine in these strands is delineated. For the category of the relating to the divine is the essential and crucial category in the constitution of any structure of faith and consequently its authentic expression must be prominent, central and unambiguous. But while prayer *qua* address is, indeed, an authentic expression for delineating the relating to the divine in the "prophetic" and *halachic* strands (seeing that these strands formulate themselves in the Thou-domain), it is far from occupying in these strands the central, unambiguous and prominent position that is called for. For as we have seen, it is decidedly peripheral in the "prophetic" strand while in the *halachic* strand its constitution *qua* address is rather ambiguous and its position is far from being central or prominent. Thus, if the relating to the divine in these strands were to be delineated exclusively or even primarily by prayer, a most unsatisfactory situation would exist. For it would mean that in the distinctive strands of Judaism the most essential category in the structure of faith, i.e., the category of relating to the divine, would be inadequately expressed. If this were really so, it would be a most puzzling and, indeed, a most untenable state of affairs.

It is at this point, however, that our analysis of the category of worship presented above can come to the rescue and prove most helpful. For this analysis has shown that in structures of faith which formulate themselves from the ethical (rather than the ontological) perspective the relating to the divine need not be exclusively a *direct* vertical mode of relating; it can also be an *indirect* vertical mode of relating, i.e., a relating that passes through the horizontal. Indeed, as we have seen, this latter mode of relating is not only possible here but it actually constitutes the main and essential mode of the relating. It follows from this, therefore, that in structures of faith which formulate themselves from the ethical perspective prayer as a delineation of the direct vertical mode of relating need not be the only expression of the relating to the divine – the relating to the divine can find its expression (indeed, it can find its main expression) in a delineation of the indirect vertical mode of relating. Thus, in the "prophetic" and *halachic* strands, seeing that these strands manifest structures of faith which formulate themselves from the ethical perspective, the relating to the divine needs by no means be exclusively expressed by the direct vertical mode of relating. It can be expressed (and, indeed, it is most likely to be expressed) by the indirect vertical mode of relating. Consequently, the fact that prayer *qua* address (it being the direct vertical mode of relating) is peripheral or compromised in these strands is not so serious in its implications as suggested above. For it does not necessarily mean that the relating to the divine, i.e., that the category of worship as such, is devoid of proper expression here (this would have been indeed untenable). It only means that we have to look for it here in the indirect vertical mode of relating which expresses itself, as we have seen above, in the ethical act and concern. In short, our analysis of the category of worship presented above allows us to realize that in the "prophetic" and *halachic* strands we must not look at prayer as the exclusive delineation for the relating to the divine; rather we must see that ethical concern and the ethical act can just as well delineate the relating to the divine and, therefore, constitute the expression for the category of worship in these strands.

But if this be the case, namely, if in the "prophetic" and *halachic* strands (they being strands that formulate themselves from the ethical perspective) the relating to the divine can express itself in the indirect vertical mode of relating, i.e., in ethical concern and the ethical act, then it can be shown that the relating to the divine, i.e., the category of worship, is afterall properly and adequately expressed in these strands. For there is no denying that the burden of biblical prophecy lies in its critique of the social, economic and political policies pursued by the community, thus manifesting a deep and all-pervasive ethical concern. Indeed, this ethical concern constitutes the very essence of biblical prophecy – take it away and biblical prophecy remains an empty shell. Similarly, there is no denying that the burden of the *halachic* strand lies in its legal formulation, i.e., in the *halacha*. The *halacha* is its central and all-encompassing expression and the *halacha* in its essential and distinctive thrust clearly manifests ethical concern. Of course, the *halacha* covers every aspect of life including the ritualistic aspect and one would certainly not want to claim ethical concern for the ritual legislation. But then a good case can be made that the ritual legislation does not constitute the essential and distinctive thrust of the *halacha;* rather it is the civil, political and criminal legislation which constitutes it.[14] Thus, inasmuch as we are talking here of the essential and distinctive thrust of the *halacha,* we are perforce dealing with its civil, political and criminal legislation (and not with its ritual legislation) and this legislation clearly constitutes itself as an organon which impinges upon the relations between man and fellow-man, which means that it clearly carries ethical signification. Indeed, in the last analysis, it is but the formal, concrete expression of the ethical concern. It is but the crystallization of the ethical concern, i.e., the concern to establish righteous relations between man and man, in universal and objective legal maxims. It is but the concretization of the ethical concern in ethical acts that are delineated *a priori* and universally in prescriptive laws.[15] Thus in both the biblical "prophetic" strand and in the rabbinic *halachic* strand the category of worship is in fact fully and centrally operative (as, indeed, it should be with respect to such an essential category) if we only look for its expression not in the direct vertical mode but in the indirect vertical mode of the relating.[16] In the biblical "prophetic" strand it expresses itself essentially in the social, economic and political critique raised by prophecy while in the rabbinic *halachic* strand it expresses itself essentially in the civil, political and criminal legislation of the *halacha.*

Indeed, so pervasive and all-encompassing is the thrust of the indirect vertical mode of relating in the *halachic* strand that it actually encompasses even the act of prayer. Namely, we would suggest that prayer is not to be viewed here primarily as an expression of the *direct* vertical mode of relating, an independent expression paralleling and supplementing the expression of the indirect vertical mode of relating represented by the *halacha*. Rather, it is to be viewed as part and parcel of the *halacha* and thus as an expression of the *indirect* vertical mode of relating. For the *halachic* strand reduces prayer into the structure of the *halacha* – it constitutes prayer as one of the prescriptions of the *halacha*. As such, prayer becomes one of the ways in which the *halacha* expresses itself and since the *halacha* constitutes itself essentially as an institutionalized expression of the indirect vertical mode of relating, this means that prayer becomes here one of the ways in which the indirect vertical mode of relating expresses itself when operating in an institutionalized context. Of course, if this be the case, then clearly the validity and efficacy of the act of prayer are not to be judged by the criterion of the direct vertical mode of relating, namely, by whether or not the act of prayer actually constitutes an inward act of direct vertical address. Rather, they must be judged now by the criterion of the *halacha,* namely, by the criterion of the indirect vertical mode of relating that is institutionalized. Thus, the determining criterion becomes now (as it does indeed, with respect to all other *mitzvot,* i.e., to all other commandments prescribed by the *halacha*) whether or not the act is executed precisely in conformity with the prescription of the *halacha.* Its validity and efficacy lie in the fact that one is fulfilling a *mitzvah,* a commandment, rather than in the fact that one is directly addressing the divine.[17]

Indeed, in view of this consideration there should be now no problems with the way the act of prayer is delineated in the *halachic* strand; namely, the problems encountered above in connection with the *a priori* and universal determination of the content and timing of prayer, with its collective characterization, with the fact that it lacks a distinctively fundamental status within the ethos of the community, with the fact that its outward performance rather than inward intention constitutes the determining criterion for its efficacy and validity – all these problems can now be set aside. For these problems arose only because we have applied to prayer the criterion of the *direct* vertical mode of relating. But if prayer is constituted as a precept of the *halacha* and if, therefore, the criterion that must be applied is not the criterion of the direct vertical mode but the criterion of the *indirect* vertical mode of relating, then the delineation of the act of prayer in the *halachic* strand would no longer be problematic. Indeed, far from being problematic such delineation is actually called for if prayer is constituted as a precept of the *halacha.*

Thus clearly, an *a priori* and universal determination of the content and timing of prayer is made feasible by the fact that now as a *halachic* precept prayer is constituted as an expression of the indirect vertical mode of relating. For while such an *a priori* and universal determination in the context of a direct vertical mode of relating certainly throws into question the authenticity of an expression that formulates itself in terms of the Thou-dimension (as we have seen with respect to prayer when constituted as a direct vertical address), in the context of an indirect vertical mode of relating the authenticity of the expression can be preserved, albeit not in its most ideal form (as was also the case with respect to ethical action). Furthermore we can see that such an *a priori* and universal delineation is actually called for by the fact that the *halacha* implicates institutionalization and that institutionalization must delineate its expressions in an *a priori* and universal way. Prayer, therefore, when constituted as a precept of the *halacha,* would indeed require that it be delineated in an *a priori* and universal way. Only as such can it be fulfilled as a precept, i.e., executed in accordance with the *halacha*. For clearly, in order for the community to act in conformity with the *halacha* its dictates must be spelled out in advance in the greatest detail and made equally incumbent upon any and every member of the community. Indeed, the very thrust of the *halacha* is precisely to provide in advance such detailed determination that is universally applicable for all its precepts, and prayer as one of these precepts cannot be an exception. Certainly, at the very least, it would have to be determined in advance as to what and when one is to pray, making such determination applicable to any and every person, in other words, at the very least its content and timing would have to be determined in an *a priori* and universal way.

By the same token, it should be clear that the constitution of prayer as an act of the collectivity rather than of the individual i.e., that it is the collective "we" rather than the individual "I" that is the entity that prays, is similarly made feasible by the fact that as a *halachic* precept prayer is constituted as an expression of the indirect vertical mode of relating.[18] Indeed, while in the context of the direct vertical mode of relating such a constitution would simply not make sense (the praying entity, i.e., the primary category, in this context must be the individual, the collectivity being here only a secondary, abstracted category signifying the sum total of all individuals sharing the common denominator of being praying individuals), in the context of the indirect vertical mode of relating such a constitution is not only feasible but is actually called for. This is so by virtue of the fact that the indirect mode of relating expresses itself, as we have seen, in ethical action and concern and that this implicates the collectivity and not the individual as the primary category. For ethical action and concern can be constituted only in terms of the collectivity and not in terms of the individual in himself. In relating to the divine, therefore, through ethical action and concern the human pole in the divine-human axis must be a collectivity of men rather than an individual person. Thus, inasmuch as prayer is constituted as a precept of the *halacha,* i.e., as a precept of a structure whose very essence lies in expressing ethical action and concern, its subject should indeed be the collectivity and not the individual.

And as for the lack of a distinctively fundamental status for the act of prayer in the ethos of the community, this can be accounted for by the mere fact that prayer here is constituted as a precept of the *halacha* (and without even having to resort to the further implication that as such it is constituted as an expression of the indirect vertical mode of relating). For the act of praying in being constituted as a *halachic* precept is after all but one of 613 precepts constituting the *halacha,* its binding-force and status being equal to that of any other precept – no less but also no more. Thus, while as an expression of the direct vertical mode of relating the status of prayer may have well been distinctively central, and, indeed, *sui generis* (seeing that the *halachic* strand formulates itself essentially from the Thou-perspective and that in this perspective prayer *qua* address is the *only* authentic expression of the direct vertical mode of relating), when prayer is incorporated into the structure of the *halacha* as one of its precepts its status is per force equalized to that of all the other precepts.

Lastly, the same consideration involved in the preceding characterization, i.e., the mere fact that prayer is constituted here as a precept of the *halacha,* should also account for the observation that in the *halachic* strand the approach to prayer centers by and large on its proper outward execution, i.e., on its execution in precise conformity with the prescription of the *halacha,* rather than on its inward intentional quality, i.e., on whether or not it constitutes authentic address. For a case can be made that inasmuch as the *halacha* is an expression of ethical concern, its attention must indeed be centered on the outward execution of the precepts. After all, ethical concern, one would want to argue, cannot fully express itself merely in inward intentions; in the last analysis it must impinge on overt, outward acts. But even if this is not granted, certainly the fact that the *halacha* is an objectified and legislated expression of the ethical concern must dictate that it centers its attention on the outward execution of the act. For clearly, objectification and legislation cannot be applied to inward intentions – they are applicable only to outward acts. Hence, it is understandable that for the *halacha* the validity and efficacy of its precepts (and this would, of course, include the act of prayer when it is constituted as a *halachic* precept) must ultimately lie in their outward performance. The proper inward intention accompanying the outward deed may well be an ideal desideratum; still, what really counts, in the last analysis, is the doing, the outward deed.

Thus, the fact that in the *halachic* strand prayer is constituted as a *halachic* precept can satisfactorily account for the various characterizations which, with respect to prayer as an act of direct vertical address, proved to be so problematic. But we must realize that in constituting prayer as a *halachic* precept the *halachic* strand radically transforms the nature and intent of the act of prayer. For now the act of prayer is no longer grounded in man but in the divine. It is no longer a communication to God originating in man but rather a communication to man originating in God. It is an act of divine revelation to man rather than an act of man's address to God. Rather than being an act of human spontaneity it is an act of divine command. For it is now God who wishes man to pray and commands him to do so. Clearly, in this context, man's role in prayer is not so much to address God as to conform to His will. As such, of course, the criterion for the validity and efficacy of the act of prayer must change radically. For now it clearly can no longer be the authenticity of address; rather, it must be the precision of execution in conformity with the dictates of revelation. What counts now is that the divine will be fulfilled. And this, in turn, would of course mean that the inward orientation accompanying the act can no longer be spontaneity, openness and immediacy but must rather be obedience. For in the face of divine revelation the only feasible inward orientation on the part of man is to obey. In this context, therefore, the act of prayer, i.e., the religious act, is no longer an act of address but an act of obedience.[19]

Clearly, the implications of transforming the act of prayer to a *halachic* precept and thus to an expression of divine revelation are far reaching. Indeed, not only the delineation but the very signification of the act undergo a fundamental change. One has certainly come a long way away from the signification and delineation of prayer not only when it is constituted as a direct mode of address but even when it is constituted as an indirect mode of address. How this has come about in the *halachic* strand is, however, a different story into which we need not enter here.

Thus, we may sum up the main thrust of this essay in the thesis that in the context of the mainstream and distinctive strands of Judaism, i.e., in the context of the "prophetic" and *halachic* strands, the category of worship is to be understood on the model worked out in our analysis above of the way the category is constituted in a structure of faith that formulates itself in terms of the ethical rather than the ontological perspective. This means that in the "prophetic" and *halachic* strands the expression of the category of worship is by no means to be confined exclusively to the direct vertical mode of relating; its expression, indeed, the main thrust of its expression, can just as well take place in the indirect vertical mode of relating. Indeed, in the *halachic* strand the tendency for the category to express itself in the indirect vertical mode of relating is so strong that even the act of prayer (which by its essence is an expression *par excellence* of the direct vertical mode of relating) can be constituted as an expression of the indirect vertical mode of relating. If such an exposition appears nonetheless somewhat forced and strange it is because the structures of faith of most religions tend to formulate themselves in terms of the ontological rather than the ethical perspective and consequently we have come to assume that the category of worship must express itself exclusively in the direct vertical mode of relating. It was precisely the purpose of this essay to disabuse us of this assumption and show that there is an alternative expression, namely, that in a structure of faith which formulates itself in terms of the ethical perspective – as is the case in the "prophetic" and *halachic* strands of Judaism – the category of worship can and does express itself in the indirect vertical mode of relating.

---

[1] Thus, for example, the various characterizations commonly assigned to worship, such as its inspiration of awe and reverence or its manifestation of the dimension of the wholly other, of the mysterious, originate and receive their rationale from the fact that the relating here is to the ultimate.

[2] The signification of transcendence as distance in contradistinction to proximity, i.e., its signification in the polarity of transcendence versus immanence, or its signification in the context of the polarity of the *deus absconditus* versus the revealing God, or, still further, in the polarity of the sovereign God versus the God of grace, is evidently a derived signification. Although these various significations are of great importance in the hermeneutics of theology and in the history of religions they are not of immediate concern to us here. For further background discussion of this subject see, for example, the contribution of K. Lehmann in *Encyclopedia of Theology*, edited by K. Rahner, Seabury Press, New York, 1975, pp. 1734-1742, and the contribution of J.A. Hutchinson of *Handbook of Christian Theology*, Meridian Books, New York, 1958, pp. 363-366.

[3]Although we very often may tend to associate the notion of transcendence with the latter act, it is clear that the former act is just as legitimate an expression of transcendence. Indeed, we continuously surpass, i.e., transcend, ourselves in acts that remain within the space-time continuum as, for example, in relating to a fellow-man, to an object, to an idea or to the future. Actually, every act of our consciousness is an act of transcendence and most of these acts remain within the space-time continuum. That we often tend to connect transcendence with the act that specifically surpasses the space-time continuum is due to our association of the category with its use in the context of biblical faith. For in this context, as we shall presently see, the distinctive connotation of the category is indeed linked to the act that surpasses the space-time continuum.

[4]Thus, from the vantage point of biblical faiths it is untenable to take a horizontal entity as the ultimate and commensurately to have the act of worship implicate an act of transcendence that is merely horizontal. Such an act is guilty of substituting that which is not truly ultimate for the ultimate and thus of misdirecting the act of worship. It is precisely what constitutes for biblical faiths the phenomenon of idolatry.

[5]This assertion may appear strange as pantheism is commonly associated with the religious domain. But if we examine the issue carefully we will see that its association with the religious domain is, indeed, centered mainly in non-biblical religions. And although pantheism has certainly penetrated to a considerable extent also the historical manifestations of biblical religions, there can be no denying that all biblical religions deemed it a pernicious and an heretical formulation which they, true to their essence, felt compelled to reject. Thus, the association of pantheism with the religious domain is established only by virtue of its association with non-biblical religions. We, however, are judging it from the view-point of biblical religion and from this viewpoint such an association is, indeed, untenable. Indeed, this diametrically opposed view of pantheism reflects the fundamental and qualitative cleavage between biblical and nonbiblical religions (a cleavage which, by the way, dialectical theology rightly reflects in its distinction between "faith" and "religion"). And as to the further claim that pantheism is actually congenial to the secularist orientation, this can be seen in the fact that cultural awareness whenever secularized (as for example in the case of modernity) finds the pantheistic formulation much less of an anathema than the theistic formulation. This should not really be all that puzzling seeing that pantheism by its very essence abrogates any and all verticality and that, as we have suggested, the abrogation of the vertical dimension is precisely what constitutes the secularist orientation.

[6]See the many religious structures where one's relating to the divine, i.e., to the vertically transcendent being, is confined to specific places or to specific appointed times to the exclusion of all other places and times, thus constituting such places and times as sacred in contradistinction to all other places and times which are constituted as profane. Clearly, such points in space or time serve as jumping-boards from which man launches perpendicularly towards the vertically transcendent being, this status being precisely the factor that constitutes them as sacred in contradistinction to all other points which as such remain profane.

[7]Of course, the feasibility of such a mode of indirect relating would depend on the vertically transcendent being in some way implicated within the horizontal dimension. Such an implication would be clearly available in the pantheistic structure, for here the divine is identified ontologically with the world and consequently relating to the world is tantamount to relating to the divine. But as we have seen above the pantheistic structure is not viable with respect to the category of worship as delineated here. It is only within a theistic structure that the category as delineated here can find full and unambiguous expression. But the implication of the divine, i.e., of the vertically transcendent being, within the horizontal dimension, i.e., within the world, is certainly not self-evident in this structure. In its own terms the theistic structure provides no such implication – on the contrary, its very thrust is to separate the divine from the world. As such, any implication here of the divine within the world certainly cannot be ontological and will have to be provided extraneously. Such implication is provided in biblical religions by the tenet of creation which establishes the world as the possession of the divine and as such makes any act towards the world necessarily impinge upon the divine. In this context, relating to the world, i.e., to the horizontal dimension, is

relating to something which belongs to the divine and consequently relating to the divine itself, i.e., to the vertically transcendent being.

[8]True, such an ontological transformation can be effected in terms of the relating only when the relating proceeds from God to man and not when it proceeds from man to God. Namely, it can be effected only when the relating constitutes providence and not when it constitutes worship. Still, it is clear that the relating when it proceeds from man to God (i.e., when it constitutes worship and when it cannot effect an ontological transformation) will have to be commensurate in its implications with the relating when it proceeds from God to man (i.e., when it constitutes providence and when it can effect an ontological transformation).

[9]True, the ontological formulation does not have necessarily to place the category of being in the sphere of Power; namely, it does not have to implicate the predicament exclusively in terms of the *finitude* of being, thus quantifying being and placing it within the sphere of Power. It can deal with the predicament of being in qualitative terms and consequently implicate a vertically transcendent being that is a Thou. Thus, for example, one may encounter within the ontological formulation a formulation which perceives the predicament to lie in the very presence of the It dimension in the It-Thou constitution of man (or even more generally in the It constitution of nature), and commensurate to this, envisioning salvation in terms of a qualitative ontological transformation of man from an It-Thou constitution (or of nature from an exclusively It constitution) to a pure Thou constitution – salvation thus being the constituting of man as a "new being" (or of nature as a "new creation"). In such a context the vertically transcendent being, by virtue of its representing the ultimate goal of salvation, will essentially be constituted as a pure Thou. Still, even here the vertically transcendent being is inescapably implicated in the sphere of the It and is thus constituted, if only provisionally, also as an It. For the effecting, as distinct from the representation, of such a salvation, i.e., of such a qualitative ontological transformation, must implicate the vertically transcendent being within the domain of Power, i.e., within the sphere of the It – incarnation, i.e., entering the sphere of the It, must precede and is a necessary step for effecting apotheosis, i.e., entering the sphere of the pure Thou. Thus, the ontological formulation even in the most optimal circumstances for constituting the vertically transcendent being as a pure Thou cannot really escape completely the constituting of the vertically transcendent being also as an It.

[10]It would also follow from this consideration that cult and ritual, inasmuch as their efficacy lies in precision, constitute a relating that is manipulation and consequently a relating that can be validly directed only to a vertically transcendent being that is an It; on the other hand, prayer, inasmuch as its efficacy lies in intention, constitutes a relating that is address and consequently a relating that can be validly directed only to a vertically transcendent being that is a Thou.

[11]Thus, see, for example, Jeremiah 15:15-18, 20:7-10, Amos 7:2. Indeed, it would have been strange not to have prayer in this strand as a means of relating, seeing that the underlying structure of faith formulates itself here in the Thou-sphere. By the same token it is not surprising that in this context (i.e., the context of classical prophecy) we do not find the prophet relating to the vertically transcendent being through the cult; we may encounter the prophet praying but not performing cult (of course, this does not encompass the instances of cultic-prophets that may be encountered in Hebrew Scriptures, but then cultic-prophets, the name not withstanding, really express the "priestly" strand and not the "prophetic" strand). Indeed, no matter how much one may mitigate the prophetic critique of the sacrificial cult (for example, Isaiah 1:11-12, Jeremiah 6:20, 7:22-23 or Amos 5:5, 21-25) the fact remains that the prophet's own expression of the direct relating is not through the cult and that he accepts the cult only as a necessary *modus vivendi* and then only after devoiding it of its own signification and infusing it with a signification derived from his own perspective. Namely, the prophet appears willing to acquiesce in the sacrificial cult only if the cult were to be linked to moral conduct (one wonders, however, what justification and rationale the cult can have in such a context). No, the sacrificial cult can operate and have its rationale only in the "priestly" strand, but then in this strand there can be no authentic prayer. We may recall in this connection the interesting observation made by Yehezkel Kaufmann that in Hebrew Scriptures the sacrificial cult was conducted in utter silence – we do not find priests praying.

[12]This, of course, raises the question in a more general way whether authentic prayer, i.e., prayer *qua* address, can find expression in any religious context that is institutionalized. Our considerations above would seem to indicate that the answer is no; it would seem that the contradiction between the dictates of institutionalized religion and the requirements of authentic prayer are too sharp to be overcome. The closest that one can come to preserving authentic prayer in the context of institutionalized religion is most probably the Quaker prayer-meeting and clearly this too does not overcome the problem completely. But even more fundamentally, the question arises whether the very structure of faith which formulates itself in the Thou-domain (and not just its manifestation of prayer *qua* address) can authentically function in an institutionalized context. All our deliberations thus far should lead us to conclude that here too the answer must be no; an institutionalized context is of necessity a context constituted in the It-domain and as such, an institutionalized context can, at best, be viewed from the perspective of the Thou-domain only as a "necessary evil." Still, we would want to suggest below that there is a way in which a structure of faith formulating itself in the Thou-domain can authentically express itself in an institutionalized context. Clearly, if our case proves tenable it will greatly help us to better understand how a structure of faith formulating itself in the Thou-domain can function in the concrete world, i.e., in the world of It.

[13]This may explain, perhaps, why in the *halachic* strand prayer does not command as prominent and central a status as one would have expected. See for example, the *halachic* ruling giving study precedence over prayer. It may also explain the marked tendency in the ethos of the strand to view prayer as an act which one is, indeed, obliged to perform but which one wants to get over with as expeditiously as possible so as to be free to attend to more important business. For clearly the prominence and centrality that one anticipates for the act of prayer is derived from the expectation that it would be the act which delineates the relating to the divine, seeing that such an act does, indeed, command the most prominent and central status in the structure of faith. But in the *halachic* strand, inasmuch as it formulates itself in the Thou-domain, the relating to the divine can be delineated only by prayer that is constituted as address. Thus, the fact that, as we have seen, the structure of prayer as address is compromised here may well explain the lessening of its status – it would certainly allow such a lessening in status.

[14]Indeed, we would suggest that the ritual legislation is encompassed within the *halacha* only because of the *halacha's* legalistic orientation. For the legalistic orientation dictates that in accepting the Pentateuchal Law in its entirety as revelatory the *halacha* is bound to encompass *all* the expressions of its legislation, and this, of course, would include its ritual legislation even though this legislation formulates itself in terms of the It-domain and is, indeed, introduced into the Pentateuchal law by the "priestly" strand. Still, it should be clear that as such the ritual legislation cannot be an essential and distinctive expression of the *halachic* strand. For the *halachic* strand formulates itself in terms of the Thou-domain and not of the It-domain and as such, indeed, is the continuation of the "prophetic" rather than of the "priestly" strand. This being the case, the essential and distinctive thrust of the *halachic* strand can find its authentic expression in the civil, political and criminal legislation but not in the ritual legislation. It would seem to us, therefore, that we are justified in seeing the *halacha* in this context as being constituted essentially by its civil, political and criminal legislation and neglecting its ritual legislation.

[15]Of course such a priori and universalized delineation of the manifestation and concretization of the ethical concern might well compromise its full ethical authenticity. For there is no denying that such universalization and a priorization of the ethical concern must compromise the situational aspect and a case can be made that the situational aspect must be implicated for the ethical concern to be fully authentic. Still, this is not to say that in the absence of the situational aspect the ethical concern is completely undermined. No, the ethical concern can still express itself though admittedly it cannot express itself at its most authentic level. Thus, even though the *halacha* is characterized by a priorization and universalization, it can still express the ethical concern.

Now, this conclusion carries a further implication that is most significant. Namely, it implies that even structures of faith which formulate themselves in terms of the Thou-perspective can after all lend themselves to being institutionalized. For the *halacha* in being *a priorized,* objectified and universalized is clearly an instrument of institutionalization and this, in turn, means that any structure of faith which appropriates the *halacha* as its expression is thereby institutionalized. Thus, while it is, indeed, highly problematic, as we have seen, for structures of faith formulating themselves in the Thou-perspective (but let us note, not for structures of faith formulating themselves in the It-perspective) to lend themselves to institutionalization in terms of their direct vertical mode of relating, i.e., in terms of prayer as the mode of relating, this is not to say that these structures of faith cannot under any circumstances lend themselves to institutionalization. For, as we can see now, these structures of faith can lend themselves to institutionalization in terms of their indirect vertical mode of relating, namely, they lend themselves to institutionalization in terms of the ethical concern as the mode of relating. Seeing that religion – if it is to be an outward affair of the collectivity rather than merely an inward affair of the individual and if it is to maintain itself in the flux of history – must lend itself to institutionalization, this implication does indeed establish a most significant point with respect to structures of faith that belong to the Thou-perspective.

[16]Indeed, it is rather indicative that the Hebrew term used to signify the notion of worship is *"Avoda"* (e.g., *Avodat Elohim* or *Avodat Habore* meaning the worship of God or of the creator), a term altogether different from that which signifies prayer, i.e., the direct vertical mode of relating, that term being *"T'fila."* Namely, it is significant that the term designating the direct vertical mode of relating is not used to signify the notion of worship. This significance is further buttressed by the meaning of these terms. Thus, *T'fila* comes from a root that signifies the moving of one's lips. As such it is, indeed, an appropriate term to designate the direct vertical mode of relating, seeing that it connotes that the relating here is verbal (certainly, in terms of our analysis above, "verbal" in its first signification of being an articulation of sound but also in its second signification of being an address to a Thou). *Avoda,* on the other hand, signifies work or labor. This means, of course, that the notion of worship is designated here, in contradistinction to the designation of the notion of prayers by the signification of work or labor which, in turn, connotes that the relating is constituted here as action (certainly, in terms of its first signification according to our analysis above, i.e., in terms of its signification as bodily movement). Why is this so and how does it come about? The answer lies in the fact that the designation of the term for the category of worship originates with its reference to the category when the category was constituted by the sacrificial cult and, of course, in this context its signification of work is quite *a propos,* seeing that the sacrificial cult does indeed implicate work (indeed, the constitution of the relating here as action is not only in terms of its first signification of bodily movement but also in terms of its second signification, i.e., in terms of its signifying the manipulation or utilization of Power). The problem arises when the usage of the term is continued even though the category is no longer constituted by the sacrificial cult, when indeed its signification would not seem to allow its being designated by a term which signifies work and which, therefore, connotes that the relating involved is constituted as action. Namely, when the category of worship is constituted by a relating that is an address (as is the case in the *halachic* strand), its designation by a term which signifies work and which connotes that the relating is constituted as action must appear questionable and contradictory. For how can the notions of work and action properly designate and describe a relating that is an address? Is it not a fact that a relating that is address implicates intention and not work and that it constitutes itself as verbal and not as action? Thus, it would appear that in using the term *Avoda* to designate the category of worship the strand is guilty of mismatching the term with the phenomenon it is supposed to designate. Of course, one can account for this by the operation of inertia. Namely, once the term has been applied (and originally when applied to the sacrificial cult the application has been quite valid) its usage will tend to continue by the force of inertia even though the nature of the activity it designates has chanted. Still, such a mismatched designation cannot be sustained by the force of inertia forever – sooner or later it must lapse. If the designation holds indefinitely, as is the case in the *halachic* strand, it indicates that it must have some validity after all. Indeed, if we examine the matter more closely this will prove to be the case. Namely, upon closer examination it should be clear that the problems with the designation pointed to above really arise when the category of worship (which is, as we have seen, constituted here as a relating that is an address) expresses

itself in the direct vertical mode. When the category expresses itself, however, in the indirect vertical mode, i.e., when the relating is refracted through the horizontal dimension and expresses itself as ethical action, the problem is greatly mitigated. For refraction through the horizontal dimension, specifically, ethical action, clearly implicates the notion of work and the connotation of action in its first signification, i.e., action in the sense of bodily movement. The only aspect that remains problematic is the connotation of action in its second signification, i.e., action in the sense of utilizing or manipulating Power – this clearly cannot apply here. But the term *Avoda* while necessarily having to implicate the notion of work and the connotation of action in its first signification (i.e., bodily movement) does not necessarily have to implicate the connotation of action in its second signification (i.e., action as the utilization or manipulation of Power). It is quite feasible, therefore, for the term *Avoda* to designate ethical action. Thus, we would suggest that the continued designation within the *halachic* strand of the category of worship by the term *Avoda* is due not only to the force of inertia but to the fact that in this strand the burden of expression of the category of worship lies in the indirect vertical mode, i.e., in ethical action as concretized in the *halacha*, and not in the direct vertical mode, i.e., in prayer as address. Only as such could one account for the fact that the *halachic* strand not only continued this designation but that it actually was quite comfortable with its adoption.

[17]Of course, since prayer signifies an address to the divine, it is very desirable that the act should also constitute an authentic address. Thus, indeed, the full delineation of the act of prayer in the rabbis' view implicates not only *keva'* (i.e., consistency or, in other words, the execution of the act precisely in accordance with its prescription) but also *kavanah* (i.e., intention). But as we have seen, this is a delineation of the *ideal* situation. Ideally, both criteria should characterize the act of prayer. Still, even though *kavanah* may be lacking *keva'* is nonetheless incumbent. In the last analysis, it is *keva'* which counts.

[18]The subject which prays in each one of the prayers is without exception the "we." The individual prays here only by virtue of being a member of the community, only through the "we" of the community. It is the community, i.e., the collectivity, which constitutes here, therefore, the primary category, the individual constituting merely a derived, secondary category.

[19]The fact that prayer is grounded in the divine will, i.e., in revelation, should allow us now, by the way, to understand why, as observed above, study and knowledge are invested with such great importance (indeed, taking precedence over prayer) in the *halachic* strand. For clearly, in order to be able to execute the precepts in conformity with the divine will one must first know as precisely and as fully as possible what the divine will is and this, in turn, means that one must first study and know the sources in which the communication of the divine will to man has been incorporated. It is important to note, however, that this precedence and importance accorded to the pursuit of study and knowledge is accorded specifically and exclusively to the pursuit of study and knowledge of that which incorporates the divine revelation, and for the *halachic* strand this means the study and knowledge of scriptures as interpreted and understood by the Talmud and the subsequent rabbinic commentaries. It is not accorded to the pursuit of study and knowledge in general, i.e., to the study and knowledge of secular disciplines such as the natural or social sciences.

But what is even more significant, it is important to note that this pursuit of the study and knowledge of scriptures, the Talmud and the rabbinic commentaries is not done for its own sake. It is not an end-in-itself but only a means. Namely, the act of study, the possession of knowledge, does not constitute the religious act *per se*. What constitutes the religious act *per se* is the *execution* of the deed. The religious significance and validity of the pursuit of study and knowledge are thus not inherent in the act itself but are derived. They are derived from the fact they they constitute the necessary means for the fulfillment of the religious act. As such, even though the pursuit of study and knowledge is clearly invested with essential value and significance, indeed, with logical and temporal precedence over the concrete execution of the deed, its value and significance are derived and secondary. Thus, for all the prominence and precedence accorded here to the pursuit of study and knowledge, the *halachic* strand does not constitute itself in gnosis.

Part Three

THE SOCIAL POLE

Chapter Nine

Hebrew Scripture and Social Action

To understand theologically the basis in Hebrew Scripture for social involvement one must start by attempting to understand the fundamental structure and orientation of the biblical *Weltanschauung*. Namely, one must understand how Hebrew Scripture views man, where it locates his fundamental predicament and, commensurate to this, what kind of redemption it expects. Only in the light of the answers to these questions can we theologically ground the stance of Hebrew Scripture toward the task of social action and come to see this stance as an integral, organic and necessary component of the biblical *Weltanschauung*.

Hebrew Scripture views man as a unique being. His uniqueness lies in that in a way he is a being of nature, a creature, yet, at the same time, he transcends nature, standing over against it, a being of the spirit, a creator. He is an animal yet the bearer of the divine image. He comes from the earth and returns to the earth and yet he is but a little lower than the angels. His uniqueness lies in that he is neither of nature, pure and simple, nor exclusively of the divine but a being suspended between these two realms, participating in both. To use Buberian terminology, his uniqueness lies in that he is an It-Thou being, a composite being belonging inextricably to both the It and the Thou dimensions, a physical entity, a collection of molecules yet a consciousness, a spirit; he is both a body and a soul. He is thus both a being-in-itself, a being *per se,* an expression of blind force subject to inexorable laws, a determined, passive being, in short, an *It* and at the same time a being-toward-another, a being *pro se,* a consciousness ever transcending itself toward another, an active, free and spontaneous being, in short, a *Thou.*

As such the inescapable destiny of man is to live his life in the continuous tension between the It and the Thou dimensions of his being. However (and this is crucial for understanding the view of Hebrew Scripture presented here), this constitution of man, this tension between the It and the Thou dimensions, is not viewed as his predicament. Indeed it is not only realistically accepted as inescapable but it is seen as the glory of man, as that which lends the dramatic dimension to his existence. The predicament of man, therefore, is seen to be constituted not by the very tension itself but rather in terms of the tension, namely, in the improper balance between the It and the Thou dimensions. Thus the predicament is seen to lie in man's continuous "backsliding" to the It dimension, giving it disproportionate preponderance and rule over his life. It lies in man conceiving of himself and acting as if he were but a being of power, living exclusively in this context, thus on the one hand being subject to its deterministic, blind processes while on the other hand being the manipulator and exploiter of its energy (these two seemingly contradictory attitudes are in truth but the two sides of one and the same coin). It lies in man placing his ego as the sole, determining center of his life thus enslaving himself to its desires, inclinations and schemes. In short, the predicament lies in man forgetting and thus failing to realize his Thou dimension – his transcendence to the other as an equally determining center of his life (thus expressing his concern for and confirmation of the other), his being not only a being of power, a thing, a machine, albeit a most sophisticated one, but also a being of spirit, a free, spontaneous creator, a person.

The view of redemption in Hebrew Scripture being commensurate to the view of the predicament (inasmuch as redemption is to be the answer to the predicament) envisions, therefore, the restoration of the proper balance between the It and the Thou dimensions in man. It requires, therefore, not a qualitative transformation of the being of man but a quantitative change in the realization of his potentialities (to underline this point we should perhaps refer to this transformation as redemption rather than salvation, saving the notion of salvation to signify a transformation that is qualitative, a transformation in the very ontological constitution of man.) Man in the view of Hebrew Scripture never loses his Thou dimension, he only fails to realize it adequately. As such, the realization of the Thou dimension is left in the hands of man. Indeed, it *must* be left to man. It cannot be wrought by another agency and then bestowed from the outside on man, for this would obviously turn man into a passive recipient depriving him of the spontaneity, freedom and initiative which are the essential hallmarks of the Thou dimension, thus undermining and destroying the very gift that is supposed to be given to him. The realization of the Thou dimension in man is constituted by man's *free* response and this only man himself can do, thus prescribing that only he can realize his redemption (what can be bestowed from the outside is the *ability* to respond, the ability to realize the Thou dimension, but as we have noted above, in the view of Hebrew Scripture man is constitutionally endowed with this ability and has never lost it).

However, what man does need from the outside in order to realize his redemption is a challenge, a call, an address from another Thou over against him. This is so since the very ontological constitution of the Thou is relational, interpersonal. A self-enclosed, isolated, single Thou is an impossibility. A Thou comes into being only when called into being by another Thou. Thus, in order for man to be able to realize his Thou he must first be addressed by another Thou.

This is precisely what the faith of Hebrew Scripture affords man. For it knows of an ever-present Thou, an Eternal Thou, YHWH, who confronts man with the continuous presence and challenge of the Thou over-against, continuously pursuing him, calling for him "where art Thou," pestering him to respond, to become a Thou. The necessary conditions for the realization of man's redemption are thus provided by biblical faith. And although biblical faith knows only too well how man has continuously failed to respond, thus failing to actualize the conditions and realize redemption, it nevertheless does not despair and lives in the ever-renewed trust and hope of its ultimate success.

A difficult problem arises, however, in this scheme, a problem whose solution leads us directly to the heart of our theme showing the essential and profound religious significance of social involvement in the context of biblical faith. The problem is: how is communication possible between the Eternal Thou and man? Namely, how can, on the one hand, the Eternal Thou address and challenge man while, on the other hand, how can man respond to the Eternal Thou?

For the Eternal Thou by his very essence is a pure Thou which means that he is a being outside space and time, the correlates of the It dimension. Vis-à-vis man, however, all communication must be mediated through space and time, namely, through the It dimension (though the *meaning* of the communication may very well indeed belong to the Thou dimension). This means that communication between the Eternal Thou and man – both the presence of the Eternal Thou and the response to him – must be mediated through the It dimension. We might choose to leave this problem as the ultimate, unfathomable mystery of religious discourse, a theological procedure which is certainly legitimate. However, if we were to attempt to tackle this problem, then it seems to us that any such attempt must perforce lead us to the relationship that may obtain between man and his fellow-man. For it is precisely in the uniqueness of man's being, namely, in its inextricable union of the Thou and It dimensions, that the possibility of mediating the Thou dimension through the It dimension presents itself. Of course, as such we are confronted here with yet another ultimate, radical mystery, i.e., that of the union of the Thou and the It dimensions in one indivisible being (but though its grasp remains as radically unfathomable as the above mystery, the truth of its reality is available to our experience in a way which the above is not.) At the same time we must realize that it is only because of this mysterious union that we can encounter the Thou dimension in our fellow-man, seeing that our fellow-man can communicate and be present to us only through the mediation of the It dimension. True, this Thou confronted in our fellow-man presents itself to us as contingent and limited inasmuch as it is bound to the It dimension. Still, such a presence of the Thou, notwithstanding its being contingent and limited, allows us to glimpse the presence of the unlimited, non-contingent Thou, the Thou who is not bound to the It, thus addressing us in the fullness of the pure Thou.

In short, in the Thou of our fellow-man we can encounter the Eternal Thou. In this way we can perhaps grasp the possibility of communication between the Eternal Thou and man both in terms of the address, i.e., challenge, of the Eternal Thou to man (though this aspect may further present considerable problems into which we cannot enter here) and, impinging on our theme more directly, in terms of man's response to the Eternal Thou.

What is of fundamental importance for us to note is that according to this scheme the fundamental religious reality, i.e., the vertical relation between man and God, is mediated through the social dimension, i.e., the horizontal relation between man and his fellow-man. As such, the relation between man and his fellow-man, i.e., the social dimension, is invested in a most fundamental sense with profound religious significance. It is the primary means for articulating the primary religious reality. By his acts towards his fellow-man, man responds to the address of the Eternal Thou.

But since, as said above, in the response man realizes his Thou dimension and this in turn constitutes the realization of his redemption, it follows that social action is here invested with the fundamental religious significance of being the road to man's redemption – the working of redemption is the working of social action.

In view of this it is not surprising to find that the burden of biblical concern centers on the horizontal dimension of the interpersonal relationship between man and his fellow-man in all its manifold aspects – social, economic and political (both internal and international). Thus, it expresses itself in the biblical legal corpora in its extensive legislation of the civil, criminal and political domains, domains which clearly impinge on the relationship between man and his fellow-man. Similarly it expresses itself in the theology of history which the biblical historical narrative articulates and where the thrust of history is understood in the light of the horizontal interpersonal norm as it impinges both on the internal inter-human relations within the nation and the external international relations between nations; namely, the goal and task of history and thus also the criterion by which it receives both meaning and judgment are taken to be the establishment of the righteous community both internally in terms of the single nation and externally in terms of the universal community of nations. Lastly, it expresses itself in biblical prophecy where it no doubt receives its most striking articulation. For the very essence of the prophetic message, in its challenge, judgment and consolation, is the concern for the establishment of the properly balanced It-Thou relation on the individual basis between man and his fellow-man, on the collective basis between nation and nation, and as a direct result of these two on the cosmological basis between creation and creator.

This fundamental, all-encompassing, horizontal social concern does not signify, however, the secularization of faith by Hebrew Scripture; rather, it signifies the sanctification of all concrete, this-worldly interpersonal relations. Man's response to his fellow-man, i.e., the horizontal relation, becomes the fundamental act of religious witnessing, the primary act of testifying to God, i.e., the vertical relation. Indeed, inasmuch as Hebrew Scripture exemplifies a religious structure which confirms this concrete world in an ultimate, final sense and has no intention of qualitatively transcending it, it cannot but deal with and confirm the It dimension. Consequently, it can have no *de jure,* watertight division between the sacred and the profane, the vertical and the horizontal.

This grounding of social action in the structure of biblical faith lends it, however, not only a fundamental religious significance but it also prescribes and delineates, in turn, its status and content. Let us briefly mention here three of the implicated aspects.

First, the pursuit of social action in this context is not the expression of charity; it is perforce the expression of righteousness. This is to say that the demand for man's involvement with and concern for his fellow-man need not appeal here to man's generosity, good heart or his going, so to speak, beyond the call of duty. The demand is grounded in the very essence of man's authentic nature, thus making it an essential right (or, in religious language, a God-given right), a demand of that which is only due him.

Secondly, the social concern which is grounded in biblical faith is in no way dependent for its justification on any utilitarian calculus. Its justification is grounded ontologically in the very being of man regardless of whether or not it benefits him economically, psychologically or socially.

Thirdly (and this is by far the most significant aspect seeing that it impinges upon the very content of biblical social concern), social concern is to be directed here to man in the fulness of his concrete being, which means that it is to be directed to both the Thou and the It dimensions of his being (and this is so inasmuch as in the context of the biblical *Weltanschauung* man is and always remains a Thou-It being). True, social concern is grounded in the structure of biblical faith by virtue of the Thou dimension, it being the necessary means for the realization of this dimension. But, as was seen above, this realization necessarily further implicates, in turn, the It dimension inasmuch as the It dimension constitutes the *sine qua non* for making the communication of the response feasible. Thus, the function of social concern in the biblical context as the necessary means for the realization of the Thou dimension demands of it also that it confirm the It dimension. The authentic realization of man through social concern in no way compromises his being a Thou-It being, thus requiring that concern to be directed to both his Thou and It dimensions.

As such the biblical understanding of social concern provides an important corrective to two other formulations which have been and are widely prevalent. Both of these formulations split the inextricable union of the Thou and It dimensions characterizing man, thus resolving the tension and polarity and in consequence allowing them to conceive of man vis-à-vis the question of social concern in terms of one or the other pole.

Thus, one widely prevalent view in our day, present in both the communistic and the capitalistic world-views, perceives man exclusively as an It and in this fashion, by the way, it establishes in the last analysis a fundamental similarity between these two opposing world-views, making them in reality but two sides of one and the same coin, while at the same time it also accounts for the radical antagonism existing between them. Even more significantly, this view of man as exclusively an It is very prevalent in the social sciences and as such it impinges most forcefully on the spirit of our age. Of course, given the context of this view one should not really be surprised to find that the orientation of the social concern here is directed almost exclusively to man's material needs, for example, to man's needs in such areas as nutrition, health, and housing. Now, from the biblical perspective meeting these needs is not only legitimate but absolutely required. Where the evil of this formulation lies is in making these needs the end withal of man's concern, in dulling man's sensitivity to yet other needs which may arise in another dimension, to wit, in the spiritual Thou dimension. But even more seriously, this formulation may become positively vicious when in the process of attempting to alleviate man's material needs it may actually lead, through its methods of approach, to a further tightening around man of the bonds of the It dimension by further reducing man to a cypher of statistics, to a cog in a machine, to an anonymous "thing" devoid of any unique individuality. It is here that the biblical perspective may assume great significance in helping us restore the proper balance. For, more than the ability to exercise power, to enjoy material comfort and to satisfy bodily needs and desires, man needs to be confirmed by his fellow-man as a Thou, as the unique irreplaceable person that he is. In the last analysis, the Thou dimension and the meaningfulness it bestows are more fundamental to man than the It dimension and the benefits it extends.

This alternative view (albeit not as prevalent today as the former view) is nevertheless qualitatively most significant; it goes to the other extreme, to the other pole, in viewing man as essentially a Thou and consequently in apprehending the question of social concern exclusively in the context of the Thou dimension. Thus in this view man's concern for his fellow-man excludes the concern for his material, bodily welfare and the physical benefits of this world. The hardships, injustices and oppressions arising within the It dimension of this world are to be endured for the duration – they are viewed as unessential, transitory, as something ultimately to be transcended. Rather, the concern manifested in this view is purely spiritual. The community for which one is to strive is the community of the saints, the fellowship of pure Thous. As such, in short, the concern is directed to an other-worldly sphere. But clearly here too one needs the biblical perspective very badly in order to provide a necessary corrective and restore a proper balance. The biblical perspective is needed to affirm our authentic and inescapable reality as creatures of this world, a world which manifests not only the Thou dimension but also the It dimension and where consequently man's concern must be directed not only to the Thou dimension but also to the It dimension.

Only the perspective of Hebrew Scripture can provide us with the chart by which to navigate the desired course between these two alternatives, thus allowing us to do justice to the dual dimensions of man's authentic nature. Only the kind of social concern which is based on the viewpoint of Hebrew Scripture can lend itself fully to meeting the requirements of the It dimension without sacrificing the requirements of the Thou dimension and vice versa. Here, in this capacity, lies the profound relevance of Hebrew Scripture for man's destiny and vocation.

Chapter Ten

The Link Between People, Land and Religion in the Structure-of-Faith of Judaism

Our purpose in this essay is to determine the status and role which are assigned respectively to the category of peoplehood and the category of land in the structure-of-faith of Judaism. To help us carry out this task we propose to turn first to modern Jewish thought to see how various figures in this domain perceived and understood these categories in the context of Judaism. The rationale and justification for first undertaking such a review lie in the simple fact that in modernity these two categories have come to occupy an especially central and prominent place in Jewish consciousness and as a result (not surprisingly) modern Jewish thought has come to greatly occupy itself with these themes which, in turn, resulted in the fact that most of the possible formulations (and sometimes even the not-so-possible formulations) regarding these categories have at one time or another found expression in it. As such, a review of this literature (albeit somewhat cursory and haphazard as this review is) should prove most helpful as it will present us with the central options, the main alternatives, that are available with regard to these categories on the basis of which we can then attempt to persue our own analysis and draw from it some conclusions and observations of our own. Thus, this essay divides itself in the main into two parts – the first part being a brief review of some of the formulations propounded in modern Jewish thought regarding the category of peoplehood and that of land, while the second part is a summary of our conclusions regarding these categories.

FORMULATIONS OF PEOPLEHOOD AND LAND IN MODERN JEWISH THOUGHT

We would suggest that in attempting to encompass the distinctive and central expressions of modern Jewish thought one encounters in the main five major trends. These trends are: 1) The philosophical-theological trend, by which we mean those writings which are systematically philosophic-theological in nature rather than publicistic or ideological. This trend expresses itself primarily within German Jewry (e.g., Lazarus, Hirsch, Steinheim, Formstecher, Cohen, Rosenzweig). 2) The Zionist ideological trend. The literature in this trend actually divides itself into two subdivisions: a) the writings of political Zionism (e.g., Herzl, Nordau, Zangwill) and b) the writings of cultural Zionism (e.g., Ahad Ha-Am). This is the main fork in the road within Zionist literature and the distinction between the two subdivisions is usually characterized by the observation that the question for political Zionism is the problem of the Jews while for cultural Zionism it is the problem of Judaism. This is a catchy formulation and up to a point valid but it may not be the most fundamental. For the problem of Judaism and the problem of the Jews are ultimately linked, the problem of one being ultimately the problem of the other. A more basic distinction may lie, as we would try to suggest below, in the scope of ethnicity accorded to the Jewish people in these two alternatives. 3) The culturalist-autonomist trend (e.g., Dubnow). This trend is, in a way, but the other side of the coin of the cultural Zionist trend. The two trends grasp the phenomenon of Judaism in essentially the same way. The fundamental difference between them is that the former affirms exclusive diaspora-existence while the latter sees a need for a settlement in the land of Israel. 4) The socialist trend, namely, the literature concerned with the socialist question, where the Jewish question enters the picture within this underlying context. This trend divides itself, in turn, between those socialist formulations that are Zionist (e.g., M. Hess) and those which are virulently anti-Zionist and diaspora-affirming (e.g., the Bund). 5) Lastly, we have the mystical trend. Namely, we would like to examine some expressions in modern Jewish thought that may be legitimately characterized as mystical formulations of Judaism. Here again, a further subdivision may be introduced between religious and non-religious expressions. Of course, a case can be made that in a certain sense all mystical formulations are religious. But if one is to take specifically rabbinic Judaism, i.e., Orthodoxy, as the criterion for religiousness, a subdivision may be introduced between those formulations that adhere to Orthodoxy (e.g., Rav Kook) and those formulations which vis-à-vis Orthodoxy must be characterized as non-religious (e.g., A.D. Gordon, M. Buber).[1]

Now, it would seem to us that all authentic expressions of Judaism will incorporate the category of Jewish peoplehood, at least in the minimal sense of being a distinct collectivity. This, of course, is not to say that there were no formulations by Jews that denied the category of Jewish peoplehood altogether; but in doing this, such formulations denied equally the general category of peoplehood as such, affirming only one indivisible unitary category, i.e., the category of mankind. Such formulations were entertained, for example, by certain Jews in the Communist camp. But such formulations cannot, by any stretch of the imagination, be taken as authentic expressions of Judaism. At best, they can be taken as the expressions of the pathology of modern Judaism. Formulations that can be taken as authentic expressions of Judaism must, no matter how minimally, affirm the reality of the phenomenon of Judaism. And such affirmation necessitates, in turn, the affirmation of the category of Jewish peoplehood, at least in the minimal sense that it constitutes a distinct collectivity. For without a collective human carrier the phenomenon of Judaism could not manifest itself in reality, indeed, could not have a reality. Judaism as a body of tenets or a body of beliefs or a pattern of behavior or whatever else one may want to describe it as, cannot have reality unless it is carried by a human collectivity. Thus, for any affirmation of Judaism, and therefore for any expression of Judaism, the category of Jewish peoplehood must in some sense be affirmed also.

Indeed, the problem before us is not whether or not the category of Jewish peoplehood is affirmed in the various formulations of modern Judaism; rather, it is to determine how the category of Jewish peoplehood is conceived and understood. Here, three possible formulations suggest themselves. First, Jewish peoplehood can be conceived as a purely religious community, a "church," completely devoid of any national character. Secondly, Jewish peoplehood can be understood as an ethnic entity, namely, as a national entity, in the full sense of the term, thus including not only the cultural and spiritual but also the social, economic and political dimensions. Third and lastly, Jewish peoplehood can be understood as an ethnic entity in a restricted sense of being limited only to the cultural and spiritual dimension.

With regard to the second and third possibilities it should be noted further that they can be formulated either within a religious context or within a secularized context. Namely, the category of Jewish peoplehood either in the full or in the restricted sense of ethnicity can be seen as an instrument within the religious scheme of things, i.e., as an agent in the workings of redemption; as such, the nation is seen integrally and by its very essence, as a holy nation. Or the category of Jewish peoplehood can be seen in purely naturalistic, humanistic terms as a nation like all the other nations without a religious vocation that constitutes its very essence. Although the battle between the religious and the secularized view was severe and is of great significance, we cannot enter it here in detail. Indeed, for our immediate concern it carries no importance since both the religious and secularist views agree as regards the centrality of the category of Jewish peoplehood in the phenomenon of Judaism (and this is the question that concerns us here). Where they disagree is with regard to the question of the status of this category within the whole scheme of things (whether ethnicity is to be taken in a full or in a restricted sense). Suffice it here perhaps to say that for the religious view the category of peoplehood is taken as a means, as an instrument in the realization of the religious vocation and therefore the category receives its meaning and significance, its rationale, from the religious end which it serves, whereas in the secularized view the category of peoplehood is taken as the end in itself, as the primary datum, and therefore the justification and rationale for the category are derived from the primary biological urge and right of every nation's desire to go on perpetuating itself. We may add that while in the last analysis either formulation may be theoretically acceptable as a vantage point from which to understand the phenomenon of Judaism, accepting the secularist formulation may raise for many of us a serious existential problem in justifying Jewish history; namely, it may be very difficult for many of us to justify the perseverance of the people in the past in maintaining their Jewish identity, seeing what a high cost in suffering this entailed, if such perseverance was merely for the sake of maintaining yet another secularized ethnic entity, or merely the result of satisfying the biological urge for self-perpetuation. And even more poignantly, such a secularized formulation could not provide us with the rationale and justification for our on-going determination of our progeny to remain within Jewish ethnicity.

Likewise with regard to the category of the land, there are in principle three possible stances that can be taken vis-à-vis this question. One stance would maintain that the category of the land is not required for the survival or functioning of Judaism. Judaism is a purely spiritual entity, a religious or a cultural phenomenon that can function and survive without attachment to the land, any land. A second stance would maintain that Judaism does indeed require the category of the land but that there is no specific geographical location that is required. Any land, any geographic location, will satisfy the requirements of the phenomenon of Judaism. The third and last stance would maintain that the phenomenon of Judaism requires a specific land, a specific geographic location, namely the land of Israel. The full, optimal functioning of the phenomenon of Judaism requires the specific geographic location known as the land of Israel.

All of these possible formulations (the three, or, rather, five relating to Jewish peoplehood and the three relating to the land) find expression within modern Jewish thought. Let us proceed, then, according to the formulations relating to the category of Jewish peoplehood and corresponding to this deal with the formualtions relating to the category of the land.

Peoplehood as a Religious Community

The first formulation, i.e., the formulation perceiving Jewish peoplehood as purely a religious community, is reflected in the maximal assimilationist trend within Judaism and although it might well have been quite widespread and popular among emancipated, assimilated Western Jewry, it is not really a serious option either in terms of the structure of Judaism or in terms of its reality in the world. Indeed, it does not find significant expression within the more serious, thoughtful literature. We shall, therefore, not dwell upon it here. Of course, with such an understanding of Jewish peoplehood it is clear that the only formulation regarding the category of the land that is feasible here is a formulation that radically negates the need of Judaism for land. Jewish peoplehood as a pure, spiritualized religious community (often the religion here is nothing else than idealized, utopian but commonplace individualistic ethics) clearly needs no land. It should be clear that such formulations serve nicely the desire for full assimilation by removing all factors that may be obstacles to such full assimilation.

But if we were afterall to present this formulation in some greater length, we would be well advised to do it with regard to an expression that while preserving the essential view of this formulation nonetheless argues passionately for the reality and preservation of Jewish nationhood. What we have in mind, for example, is the position of the early Smolensky (prior to his conversion to *Hibbat Zion*). The early Smolensky is the father of the notion that the Jewish people is a "spiritual nation." Jewish peoplehood is seen as carrying a special spiritual teaching, we might even say a religious teaching, and its vocation is to spread this teaching among the nations of the world. It is by virtue of this special religious, spiritual teaching that the distinctiveness of the Jewish nation is constituted and maintained. This distinctiveness is seen as long-lasting, indeed, for all intents and purposes, as a permanent distinctiveness. For the distinctiveness of the Jewish people will be maintained as long as the world at large has not appropriated this teaching, and the occurrence of this event, if it takes place at all, is placed in the remote future. Conceived in this way, i.e., as a completely spiritual, religious entity, the Jewish people have no need for a land or a state or even a national language. As such, of course, Smolensky wants to argue that the distinctiveness of the Jewish people should not constitute an obstacle for their full emancipation, i.e., participation in the social, political, and economic life of the host nation. Since the distinctiveness is constituted exclusively by a spiritual factor and the concrete factors of distinction like land, language, and state are not applicable, there is no reason for the Jews not to adopt the concrete dimensions of national life like language, land, etc., of their host nation. The Jews are a nation but a spiritual nation, a nation not of this world. Thus, in terms of this world the factor of nationhood does not enter the picture. In terms of a this-worldly emancipation, the Jews can be fully emancipated. Yet this emancipation would not obliterate their distinctiveness which comes about by virtue of their being a distinct spiritual entity. Whether this formulation is valid is a different question. What is interesting and most important, however, is that although the formulation here conceives of the Jewish people as a religious, spiritual community, and therefore it should really be understood as a collectivity of individuals sharing the same vocation, Smolensky insists on the ethnic, national nature of the entity. Namely, it is a biological group that is entrusted with this vocation, in turn imparting this vocation to its individual members. Smolensky attacks viciously the Jewish enlightenment precisely on the point that it abrogated and canceled out the dimension of peoplehood in its understanding of Judaism. The giving up of the category of nationhood by the Jewish enlightenment (Mendelssohn) signaled the death-knell for Jewish survival. And quite evidently, as it is clearly implicated by his view of the nature of Jewish peoplehood, for the early Smolensky Judaism has no need or requirement for land.

Peoplehood as an Ethnic Entity

In contra-disctinction to the previous formulation, this formulation, i.e., the formulation perceiving Jewish peoplehood as an ethnic entity in the full sense of the term, is a most significant and important expression. Still, its expression is primarily limited to certain quarters of the Zionist ideological trend, specifically, to the trend of political Zionism. But, although numerically this formulation may not find a wide expression, it is an extremely important formulation in terms of the practical destiny of the Jewish people in our time and, indeed, in terms of the very structure of the phenomenon of Judaism, because it captures and represents (as we shall try to show below) an essential aspect of this structure. So, clearly, the importance of such formulations cannot be decided on a quantitative basis.

A good example of this formulation can be encountered in the view of Leon Pinsker as he expressed it in his *Autoemancipation* (a view which, though by no means identical, is very similar in many respects to the view put forth by Herzl in his *Judenstaat*). True to the orientation of political Zionism, the concern of Pinsker is with the problem of the Jewish people rather than of Judaism. The problem is the problem of anti-Semitism, which for him, in contradistinction to Herzl, is not a modern problem but a problem as old as Jewish diaspora-existence. In his analysis, such factors as economic competition and social incompatibility do not constitute the essence of the problem of anti-Semitism. They are secondary factors aggravating the problem, but not its source. The primary, essential factor which brings about anti-Semitism is the fact that the Jewish nation is perceived as a "ghost-nation." In its diaspora-existence it is perceived as a separate distinct entity, as a nation, and yet it is unlike any other nation known to mankind. It is not concretely a nation, merely a ghost of a nation. And deeply seated within the soul of man there is a primal fear of ghosts, of anything that is ghost-like. Such fear easily links itself with feelings of hatred and mockery, and the constellation of such emotions constitutes the phenomenon of anti-Semitism. Now, the Jewish nation in its diaspora-existence is ghost-like because it does not have its own homeland. Many other people dwell as strangers in other lands, but their condition is not the same as that of the Jews because they have a homeland some place. The Jew, therefore, is not merely a stranger in other lands, but a ghost creature roaming the world. Emancipation, therefore, will not work; it is bound to fail. The only solution is for the Jews to regain a homeland for themselves. Auto-emancipation in the sense of regaining national sovereignty is the solution.

Clearly, the understanding of Jewish peoplehood reflected in this analysis is that of an ethnic group in the full sense of the term. The Jews are ghost-like because their ethnicity is not expressed in this-worldly terms. They are strange and unlike any other nation because they do not possess their own land and as such allow their ethnicity to express itself in the political dimension.

Given this understanding of Jewish peoplehood as an ethnic entity in the full sense of the term, it is clear that the formulation which rejects the need for land will be inapplicable here. Such a formulation of Jewish peoplehood can be consistently combined only with a formulation that requires the appropriation of land for that people. If the Jewish people is to express itself in the political dimension, it must have political sovereignty. The expression of political sovereignty, however, is the possession of statehood. And statehood can be established only with reference to a specific geographic location. Thus the realization of the political dimension requires of necessity the possession of some land. The inner logic of the formulation which perceives Jewish peoplehood as an ethnic entity in the full sense of the term requires the formulation that argues for the need of the Jewish people to have a land of their own. But the inner logic of this formulation does not require that this land be specifically the land of Israel. What is needed is some land so that statehood can be established and it is the establishment of statehood that is vitally needed by the Jewish people. In principle, in theory, any land can serve that purpose. As such, the "Territorialists" or the "Ugandists" were indeed consistent. In real life, however, their position could not be maintained, and most of them veered towards the requirement that the land be specifically the land of Israel. That is, not just any geographic location would do but only, specifically, the geographic location that is the land of Israel. However, the reasons for this requirement did not follow from the inner logic of the formulation but rather from extraneous considerations such as the historical connection or the emotional attachment of the people to the land of Israel and from various other pragmatic considerations. Because of these considerations (and these considerations, though extraneous in terms of the inner logic, are of utmost importance in terms of the realities of life), the preponderance of the formulations that perceived Jewish peoplehood as an ethnic entity in the full sense of the term linked themselves to the requirement for a specific geographic location, i.e., the requirement for the land of Israel.

The above understanding of Jewish peoplehood in its full ethnicity, and commensurate to it, therefore, the need for a land, clearly arose out of the problematic of Jewish existence. A similar understanding of Jewish peoplehood and the need for a land can also arise, however, in the context of socialism. That is, the fulfillment of the socialist program, seen in connection with the question of Judaism and the Jewish people, leads to an understanding of Jewish peoplehood in its full ethnicity and to the need for a land. Thus, within the Zionist trend there was an important expression that derived its stance from considerations emanating from the socialist orientation. But the most interesting illustration of this position may be found perhaps in a thinker who is really a precursor of the Zionist movement. This is Moses Hess. In Hess we find a most intriguing philosophic expression for this stance.

Moses Hess in his *Rome and Jerusalem* clearly grasped the significance of the category of Jewish peoplehood within the context of socialist thought. He had the genius to perceive that the category of peoplehood is the necessary and inescapable matrix for the expression of social relations; and even more penetrating was his insight that the maximal expression of social relations requires the category of peoplehood in the sense of full ethnicity, i.e., the category of peoplehood that implies not only the cultural and spiritual dimensions, but equally the economic and political dimensions. Seeing the Jewish people as being charged by its very vocation to fulfill the socialist ideal, he grasped that the Jewish people had to be taken as a full, all-encompassing ethnic group. And being taken as an ethnic group in the full sense of the term, the Jewish people in order to fulfill its vocation, i.e., to fulfill the socialist ideal, requires sovereignty, i.e., it requires the machinery of a state. And this, in turn, requires that the Jewish people be concentrated in a certain geographic location. The inner logic of his stance should have been satisfied with any particular geographic location, for a geographic location is required solely for the establishment of a state, i.e., for the establishment of sovereignty, so that the ethnic group should be able to express itself in the economic and political dimensions. And any geographic location would lend itself for this purpose. But it is at this point that the romantic side of Hess enters the picture and historical memory and emotional attachment exercise their influence leading Hess to require the restoration of the Jewish people to its ancient homeland in the land of Israel. Thus, he requires specifically the return of the Jewish people to the land of Israel rather than requiring that they establish a state in whatever geographic location is available.

Ethnic Entity in a Restricted Sense

The third formulation, namely, the formulation that views Judaism within a limited ethnic context, i.e., a context which excludes the political dimension, is the most widespread formulation. This is understandable on extraneous grounds. That is, this formulation is the formulation that would be the most congenial to emancipated Jewry in diaspora. For, on the one hand, the formulation does not run head-on against the reality of the Jewish phenomenon in the past, a reality whereby the Jewish people always understood itself and was understood by others as a distinct, separate group of an ethnic nature. Nor does it fly in the face of the present reality where the Jewish entity continues to be distinct not only as a religious community but as an ethnic entity (although in the present many Jews might not want to accept this reality). This formulation, therefore (in contradistinction to the formulation which sees the Jewish people as merely a "church"), precludes the necessity of making the preposterous claim that ethnically the Jewish people are one and the same as the host-nation. This formulation does grasp the distinction as being of an ethnic nature and as such it grasps the distinction authentically, i.e., in accordance with reality. At the same time, however, it does not radicalize this distinction by including the political dimension within the ethnic formulation. Indeed, by leaving out the political dimension it allows an ethnically distinct Jewish people to go on living within a political context which belongs to another ethnic group. Thus, it can serve very conveniently as a rationale for the half-way existence of emancipated diaspora

Jewry, an existence which wants to be both separate and distinct from the host-nation and at the same time included within its social, economic, and political life (but whether such a situation as envisioned by this formulation is feasible is, of course, another question.)

But to return to the main line of our discourse, this formulation, as said, finds wide expression in modern Jewish thought. Indeed, this wide expression reflects itself in the fact that this formulation articulates itself both in the religious and in the secular context. Namely, it articulates itself in terms of a Jewish peoplehood which is defined both in a religious and in a secular context.

a)   Jewish Peoplehood as Defined in a Religious Context

In this form the formulation mainly finds its expression in the philosphical-theological literature created by German Jewry in the last two centuries (of course the religious understanding involved here is by no means the same as the rabbinic, halachic understanding, but then we surely would not want to limit the religious understanding of Judaism and Jewish peoplehood in so restrictive a manner that only the rabbinic, halachic understanding would qualify as religious). Jewish peoplehood is grasped here as the carrier of the religious vocation and in this capacity it is grasped as being of limited ethnicity. And it can be so grasped, i.e., grasped as being of limited ethnicity, because the religious vocation of which it is the carrier is, in turn, formulated here in one of two contexts neither of which is understood as implicating the political dimension.

Thus, the first of these contexts is the ethical context,(a context which was shaped under the marked influence of Kant's philosophy). The vocation of the religion of Judaism is essentially constituted here by the realization of the ethical. This ethical refers, of course, to the relations between man and man and, as such, it is understandable that Jewish peoplehood be the carrier of a vocation so understood, in as much as it is precisely the category of peoplehood which provides the matrix for the relations between man and man. But it is important to note that the ethical here is essentially confined to the relations between individuals and is not extended to cover the political dimension, i.e., to cover the relations between collectivities of individuals; political ethics is not available here. As such, the category of Jewish peoplehood which is the carrier of this non-political ethical vocation need not be ethnic in the full sense of the term, but can be ethnic in a limited sense (of course, whether with such a vocation of individualized ethics the category of peoplehood rather than a mere association of individuals is, in the last analysis, really required, is a different question). Hermann Cohen and Leo Baeck may serve as good examples of this kind of formulation.

The second context is the metaphysical context. Here, the religious vocation is perceived in terms of the realization of another realm of existence, and the category of Jewish peoplehood is seen as an instrument in the realization of this vocation. A good example may be Franz Rosenzweig. For in Rosenzweig's formulation the religious vocation consists, in the last analysis, in realizing an existence which is outside the flux of time and history – an existence in eternity. The vocation of the Jewish people is to carry the presentiment of such an existence while still existing within the flux of history.

Now, clearly for such a task the category of Jewish peoplehood does not have to be taken as ethnic in the full sense of the term. Indeed, Jewish peoplehood in the full sense of the term would not do. For the political dimension is part and parcel of the flux of time and history. Possessing the political dimension thus means being involved, in a positive and affirmative sense, in the flux of history. And this, in turn, means that being ethnic in the full sense would necessarily imply an affirmation and a furthering of the flux. But the vocation here is precisely to ultimately negate the flux. True, one exists passively for the time being within the flux, but the pointing, the vocation, is to that which negates it. The category of ethnicity which implicates the political dimension must, therefore, be rejected. It is only the category of ethnicity in the limited sense that can be used in such a scheme of things (though here too it is questionable whether even ethnicity in the limited sense is really required in terms of the inner logic of the formulation, whether such a scheme of things is not really, in the last analysis, individualistic, requiring at best an association of individuals, a "church," rather than the category of ethnic peoplehood).

In view of this it should not be surprising that most of the formulations within this trend, both in the ethical context and in the metaphysical context, consciously reject the political dimension in their formulation of Jewish ethnicity. Thus, most of them are strongly opposed to political Zionism. They see in the inclusion of the political dimension a secularization of the vocation of Jewish peoplehood. By including the political dimension, so the logic runs, the Jewish people would become like all the other nations and the purity and uniqueness of its religious vocation would be undermined. Now, while it is true that such a danger exists, it is by no means true, as these formulations nevertheless imply, that such a danger will of necessity be actualized.

Commensurate with this understanding of the category of Jewish peoplehood, the various formulations of the philosophical-theological trend do not express any appreciation for the requirement of the category of land; indeed, they expressly reject it. Most of the representative figures in this trend, people such as Steinheim, Formstecher, Hirsch, Lazarus, Cohen, Rosenzweig, and others, reject the category of land. Within their respective representations of the structure of Judaism the category of land is for all intents and purposes not present. And this is in clear contradistinction to the central place given to the category of history. Actually this is quite understandable, seeing that this trend grasps the essence of Judaism as lying either in the ethical (though let us hasten to note in the non-political ethical) or in the metaphysical domain. In either case the category of land would not be significant in such a scheme of things. The domain of ethics does not require space but time. Ethical relations are realized in time and not in space. Thus, if the essential vocation of Judaism is the realization of the ethical, the working towards the bringing about of this realization would require history but not land. And since we are deaing here with non-political ethics, a requirement for statehood is not implied and, therefore, there is also no possibility here of getting a requirement for land through, so to speak, a once-removed process, i.e., through the agency of statehood (for clearly a requirment for statehood would have, in turn, implied a requirement for land). In any event, even political ethics does not imply a requirement for any *specific* land.The domain of the ethical is by its very essence universal and cannot recognize nor appreciate any particularity. And similarly with the metaphysical domain, it too can in no way imply a requirement for land. If anything, just the opposite is the case. For clearly, formulations that articulate themselves in the metaphysical domain will perceive the essential vocation of Judaism in terms of the metaphysical domain and this, in turn, means that for them the essential vocation of Judaism lies in transcending the spacial-temporal flux of this world. Judaism deals with the realm of the beyond but this means that it deals with a realm in which the category of land has no role to play.

b)   Jewish Peoplehood as Defined in a Secular Context

The restricted ethnic formulation can also be found formulated in a non-religious context, i.e., in a secularized context. Here, Jewish peoplehood is seen as the carrier of a national cultural heritage like any other nation. This cultural heritage may, of course, have its special contribution to make, but the existence of the Jewish people, its special contribution, its *raison d'être* are conceived with no reference to a divine cosmic working of salvation. The religious grounding is removed. It is conceived purely in horizontal terms with no vertical reference. Now, this formulation can be encountered in the context of socialism. Here, the vocation of the Jewish people and the significance of its heritage are seen to lie in the bringing about of secularized social justice. The Jewish people becomes the instrument in the realization of secularized socialism.

But the Jewish people is taken here (and this in contradistinction to the instance above exemplified by Hess) in a restricted ethnic sense which means that it does not possess its own political dimension. Rather, it contributes its ideals of social justice to the political dimension of the host-nation. It participates in the political dimension of the host-nation. As such, it is a view of Jewish peoplehood in a socialist context which affirms diaspora existence. We find it expressed, for example, in the Bundist formulation. Thus, within the context of socialism we get not only a formulation that grasps Jewish peoplehood in its full ethnicity, and that correspondingly requires the category of land, but also a formulation that grasps Jewish peoplehood in a limited ethnic sense and which correspondingly denies the category of land.

Another secularized formulation within this context of restricted ethnicity is known by the name of Autonomism and is associated with the name of the famous Jewish historian Dubnow. It has links with the socialist context though it is not essentially formulated within this context. Rather, it can be seen as an outgrowth of Smolensky's formulation given above. What we have here is a reduction of the extremely spiritualized conception of Judaism encountered in the early Smolensky. The extreme abstractness of Judaism is concretized. The religious is secularized. While in Smolensky Judaism is essentially but a system of abstract tenets and teaching, Judaism here is a system of concrete cultural patterns and values; it is much less of an other-wordly entity. Indeed, it is very much within the horizontal, this-worldly context.

As such, it is not possible for this formulation to take the position that Smolensky takes regarding the possibility, and indeed the desirability, of the complete assimilation of the Jew in his host-nation. Smolensky could take this position inasmuch as for him Judaism was completely spiritualized and other-worldly and consequently could not constitute an obstacle to an assimilation that is completely within a this-worldly context; nor was there any objection to such an assimilation since it could not impinge upon, i.e., weaken, the allegiance to Judaism. But in the Autonomist formulation, Judaism being grasped here in a this-worldly context, such an assimilation would not only be deterred by the interests of Judaism but would also impinge in a detrimental way upon these interests. Consequently, the Autonomist formulation envisions Jewish existence in diaspora in the form of ethnic islands with internal autonomy lodged within the host-nations. Not grasping the category of Jewish peoplehood in its full ethnicity, i.e., as including the political dimension, it does not require a specific national homeland and the full sovereignty of the state for the Jewish nation. Instead, it affirms diaspora-existence. But to protect the cultural distinctiveness of the Jewish people it wants to introduce not a political, territorial division but a cultural, spiritual division. The result of this is that it proposes an internal cultural autonomy for the Jewish people which, however, is to be exercised on the land, and within the political framework, of other nations.

It is also to this context of viewing Jewish peoplehood as a restricted ethnic entity that the formulation of a most important and influential thinker, namely, the forumlation of Ahad Ha-Am, belongs. For to Ahad Ha-Am Judaism is a cultural rather than a political entity. It is a system of values and patterns of living, essentially a system of ethical values and teachings. As such, the entity that is its human carrier, i.e., the category of Jewish peoplehood, is commensurately perceived as an ethnic group that is ethnic in the limited sense of being cultural. Perceiving the category of Jewish peoplehood in this restricted ethnic sense, Ahad Ha-Am can and indeed does affirm, in the last analysis, diaspora existence. Granted, such an existence is problematic in our time, given the circumstances of emancipation affecting the Jewish people. The problem for Ahad Ha-Am, however, is not the possibility of the survival of the Jews *qua* human beings, but rather the possibility of the survival of Judaism under these circumstances. And in this connection it is important to note that his diagnosis and solution do not negate the possibility and desirability of the ongoing existence of the Jewish people and of Judaism in diaspora. Indeed, diaspora-existence is for him an inescapable fact of Jewish reality. For the possibility of redeeming the entirety or even the majority of the Jewish people from diaspora existence and constituting them in their own homeland does not seem realistic to him. If the Jewish people, thereore, and thus Judaism, are to survive, a solution for their ongoing, continued existence in diaspora must be found. Thus, in the last analysis Ahad Ha-Am too remains an affirmer of diaspora-existence. He differs, however, from the formulation of Autonomism in that he does not believe that under the circumstances envisioned by the formulation of Autonomism Judaism could have enough strength and vitality to withstand the influence of the foreign culture of the host-nations and thus succeed in preserving the Jewish people in their distinctiveness. His formulation calls, therefore, for a concentration of part of the Jewish people in their own homeland where they would constitute a majority and where, therefore, danger of foreign influence would be greatly reduced. In such a homeland the strength and vitality of Judaism can be revived and then "exported," so to speak, to the bulk of the Jewish people living in diaspora, thus strengthening their Judaism and insuring their survival and even prosperity in the circumstances of diaspora existence.

The geographic location for constituting such a center, such a national home, for a part of the Jewish people is for Ahad Ha-Am the land of Israel. In this sense he is a Zionist. Now, there is no denying that the inner logic of his formulation does, indeed, require a specific geographic location, a land, for the survival of Judaism and the Jewish people in the circumstances of the Emancipation. For Judaism and the Jewish people to survive in these circumstances, part of the people must be concentrated as a majority in a national home. And such a concentration in a national home requires a specific geographic location. But why specifically the land of Israel as the geographic location? Why should one geographic location have any advantage over antother? Afterall, is it not the case that in terms of the inner logic of Ahad Ha-Am's formulation what is essential is that the Jewish people constitute a majority in a certain geographic location rather than which geographic location it is to be? It would see, therefore, that choosing specifically the land of Israel is determined here not by the inner logic of the formulation but rather by extraneous considerations such as historical memory and emotional attachment. In terms of the inner logic of the formulation, the concentration of a part of the Jewish people as a majority in some place like Argentina, Africa or any place else in the world should be as satisfactory and efficacious as its concentration in the land of Israel.

The Mystical Trend

So far we did not include the mystical trend. The reason is that the mystical trend is really separate from the other trends. All the other trends are formulations of Judaism in a mainly this-worldly context. They are essentially horizontally oriented (the one exception is the metaphysical formulation in the philosophical-theological trend, e.g., Rosenzweig, which indeed is in many respects similar to the mystical trend). Not so the mystical trend; it is other-worldly and vertically oriented. As such, we thought that it might be more convenient to consider it by itself. This we propose to do covering both the mystical trend's religious and non-religious orientation, the former being expressed most prominently by Rav Kook while the latter finds a most impressive expression in A.D. Gordon.

It is most interesting, however, for us to note that, notwithstanding the various differences between them, both orientations, the religious and non-religious, affirm the category of Jewish peoplehood and the category of land, specifically, the land of Israel. Even more interesting is the further observation that this affirmation follows from the inner logic operating in these orientations. It is interesting because one would not have expected it, seeing that within the mystical formulation there is really no room for the particularity of peoplehood or of land. Rather, one expects the mystical formulation to operate in terms of the individual (and thus in the context of the universalism which this implies). For afterall, the very essence of mysticism lies in its striving to overcome the flux of this world and to transcend all division and separation into an all-encompassing unity. And these are clearly acts which implicate the individual and not the collectivity, certainly not ethnic collectivity. Yet we have mystical formulations both in the religious and non-religious orientation which do precisely this, namely, implicate the category of Jewish peoplehood and that of the land of Israel (thus implicating collectivity and particularism). But how is this possible? What is the possible rationale that these formulations resort to?

a) The Implication of Peoplehood and Land in the Religious Orientation

There is one possibility where the ethnic entity may be required by the inner logic of the mystical formulation. This is when the mechanism of bringing about the mystical salvation, i.e., the union with the One, devolves on some special powers or attributes which are determined genetically and which as such inhere in the redemptive agent. That is, some people may be endowed with special "mystical talent" while other people are not (on the analogy of some people being endowed with musical talent or with certain physical characteristics). On this basis a case can be made that the mystical vocation may devolve on a certain people by virtue of blood kinship, i.e., by virtue of the genetic common pool which characterizes the ethnic entity. This, of course, introduces the biological-racial dimension into the category of ethnicity, thus transforming the nature of the category from its origianl constitution within mainstream Judaism where it is constituted as a historical and not as a racial category. Still, such a transformation is possible and we do encounter it in the tradition, as, for example, in Yehuda Halevi, Maharal and perhaps Rav Kook. In this connection it is interesting to note that in Rav Kook's thought the status of Jewish peoplehood is determined not solely or even mainly by election *(behira)* but by an inherent special quality *(segula)*. The Jewish people are endowed with a quality whereby the yearning for God and thus the power of transforming the profane into the sacred is more clearly expressed.

Thus, the Jewish people by virtue of an innate quality is the redemptive agent in a universal, cosmic redemption. And since the redemption is envisaged here not as the separation of the holy from the profane, but rather as the transformation of the profane in its entirety into the holy, thus inclusive of the profane political dimension, the category of Jewish peoplehood is grasped here in its full ethnicity (we thus have here an instance of a full political Zionist stance derived from a rabbinic, albeit mystical, orientation.)

Likewise with the category of the land, because the redemptive agency is determined by an innate quality *(segula)*, the rationale is provided for particularity. The category of land in general is introduced because redemption includes the domain of nature. Redemption is not merely an event on the human social level, it is an event on the cosmic level. And the specific portion of land that is the land of Israel is endowed with special redemptive power, or rather, the redemptive power flows through it in a concentrated form, thus making it a redemptive agent in contradistinction to other lands.

b)   The Implication of Peoplehood and Land in the Non-Religious Orientation

In A.D. Gordon too the category of the land plays a central role, seeing that it is the shaper of nationhood (in contradistinction to society), and that nationhood, in turn, is the agency that mediates between man and nature, between man's soul and the cosmic soul. The spirit of a nation, however, is created through contact with the cosmic spirit in a specific place, and the spirit of a nation, in turn, determines the spirit of the individual by virtue of his membership within the nation. Indeed, the link between a nation and its land is permanent and essential. Thus, not only is the category of land and the category of peoplehood essential and inextricable in this scheme of things, but also the particularization of land and people is provided for. For the individual Jew, redemption, in the sense of establishing full communion with the cosmic spirit, necessitates the Jewish people which, in turn, necessitates the land of Israel.

One could not ask for a tighter inner logic establishing the category of peoplehood and the category of land than is given in the thought of Rav Kook and Gordon. But it is established on certain premises which are taken as facts, as given data, and for which no rationale is provided. Thus for Rav Kook the particularity of Jewish peoplehood and of the land of Israel is established on the fact that a special *segula* is inherent in them. For Gordon it is established on the one-to-one relationship between land and nation, and the role of the nation as mediator of the cosmic spirit to the individual. If a critique is to be lodged against these formulations, then it must be lodged at this point, i.e., questioning the validity of these premises. And these premises can be questioned seriously, both as to whether they are really required by their respective scheme of things and whether they authentically reflect the distinctive phenomenon of Judaism.

OVERVIEW AND CONCLUSIONS

The Inner Logic of the Various Formulations

Let us briefly recapitulate the picture that emerges from our short and selective description of the various formulations in modern Jewish thought regarding the categories of peoplehood and land. We have seen that all formulations affirmed the category of peoplehood. The preponderance of formulations, however, understood the category of peoplehood in terms of limited ethnicity, i.e., ethnicity exclusively in terms of ethos and culture; only some formulations understood the category of peoplehood in terms of full ethnicity, i.e., ethnicity that encompasses the social, economic and political dimensions. With regard to the category of land the consensus is not so clear. There were some formulations (and they are significant formulations that cannot be dismissed out of hand as idiosyncratic) that did not affirm the category of land. Still, the preponderance of formulations did affirm the category of land. However, with regard to the affirmation of the specific geographic location that is known as the land of Israel there was no unanimity. Many formulations did indeed affirm the specific geographic location that was the land of Israel . But there were also formulations for which the specific geographic location where the category of land was to be affirmed was of no consequence; any geographic location would do.

A much more intriguing but difficult task was to ascertain the consistency of the particular affirmations of peoplehood and land with the inner logic of the respective formulations. Still, we believe that we have shown that the category of peoplehood is not only necessary in terms of the inner logic of the various formulations but that it is established as a primary category; the only exception was the case of the formulations in the mystical context where some question could be raised as to the legitimacy and necessity of affirming the category of peoplehood (at least as a historical category rather than a biological-racial category). With regard to the affirmation of the category of land the situation was much more complicated and difficult. Our conclusion was, nevertheless, that when the category of land is affirmed, it can be affirmed in terms of the inner logic only as a secondary category, i.e., a category whose affirmation is required by virtue of the needs of the category of peoplehood, the primary category, and not on its own terms. Furthermore, the affirmation of the category of land led in terms of the inner logic only as far as requiring some geographic location but not the specific geographic location that is known as the land of Israel (the need for the affirmation of the land of Israel came from historical, emotional and pragmatic considerations but not from considerations of the pure inner logic of the formulations concerned). Here again, however, formulations in the mystical context presented an exception. In terms of their inner logic the category of land and specifically the land of Israel was required, and indeed required as a primary category. For these formulations it is a holy land not just in name but in reality, not derivatively but directly.

Thus, if the formulations in the mystical context are left out, we can say that the inner logic operative in the remaining formulations clearly places the category of peoplehood as a primary, essential and necessary category within the structure of the phenomenon of Judaism; that, on the other hand, it allows the entry of the category of land within this structure only as a secondary, derivative category; and that, strictly in terms of the requirements of the inner logic as such (thus excluding such considerations as historical association, emotional attachment, and pragmatic feasibility, considerations which are very significant and not to be dismissed lightly but which, nonetheless, are extraneous as far as the inner logic as such is concerned), there can be no specification of the category of land, namely, preference cannot be given to any one particular geographic location, e.g., the land of Israel, over another.

Now, we would want to maintain that this inner logic in its delineation of the status of the categories of peoplehood and land authentically reflects the inner logic that characterizes the distinctive religious structure that constitutes the mainstream expression of the phenomenon of Judaism. Of course, as an historical phenomenon Judaism is not monolithic; it encompasses a number of different expressions implicating different structures of faith and consequently different kinds of inner logic. Still, we would want to maintain that among these various structures there is a structure which establishes, in contradistinction to the rest, the distinctiveness of Judaism within the general phenomenology of religion, that can explain its history and characteristics most adequately, that indeed, historically speaking, found widespread expression within Judaism and that, therefore, can be seen as constituting the mainstream expression of the phenomenon of Judaism. At any event, the crux of the point made here is that the inner logic of this structure delineates the same status respectively for the category of peoplehood and for the category of land that we have encountered in the non-mystical formulations of modern Jewish thought. Namely, in the structure of faith characterizing the distinctive, mainstream expression of Judaism the category of peoplehood is a primary category – essential and inextricable as far as the very existence of the phenomenon is concerned; on the other hand, the category of land can enter the structure only as a secondary, derivative category – a category which certainly carries significance for the optimal, full realization of the phenomenon but which, nevertheless, is not essential and inextricable for its very existence (indeed, the fact that Judaism could survive in diaspora is clear proof for this assertion).

a) Primacy of Peoplehood but not of Land

It is evidently not feasible for us to fully argue and demonstrate this claim here. But if it be granted that the substance of the redemptive vocation as constituted in the distinctive, mainstream expression of Judaism is the establishment in a this-worldly context of the righteous community, then we can attempt to trace quickly the workings of the inner logic operative here as it impinges upon the categories of peoplehood and land, showing that it delineates them in the way suggested above. Thus, with regard to the category of peoplehood, it can indeed be shown that it is of necessity delineated here as a primary category that is essential and irremovable. For quite clearly vis-à-vis a redemptive vocation that is constituted in terms of the establishment of the righteous community, the category which can function both as the principal agent in the working towards its realization and as the sole matrix in which such realization can take place must be the category of peoplehood. The righteous community cannot be established except in the context of the category of peoplehood, and likewise the striving towards its realization can be carried out only in those terms. The establishment of the righteous community cannot be carried out in terms of the individual *qua* individual, nor in terms of a collectivity that is but an association, a sum total, of individuals with a common denominator; it necessarily requires a collectivity that ontologically, if not chronologically, precedes the individual. Namely, it requries the ethnic-national collectivity, the collectivity that in its very constitution provides the social, economic and political dimensions, the dimensions in whose terms only the righteous community can be established; in short, it necessarily requires the category of peoplehood.

But as such, the category of peoplehood is a category of history and not of nature, and its workings towards redemption, as indeed the consummation of such redemption, is in the dimension of time and not of space. The category of land, on the other hand, is a category of space, of nature. As such, it is understandable that the category of land, unlike the category of peoplehood, would not be implicated by the inner logic that is operative here, i.e., an inner logic that flows from the requirements of a redemptive vocation whose substance is the establishment of the righteous community. For the workings of the inner logic here, as traced so far, are exclusively in the temporal-historical dimension, while the category of land subsists in the spacio-natural dimension. Thus, the redemptive vocation implicates directly the category of peoplehood but not the category of land.

The category of land enters the structure of faith of Judaism secondarily and derivatively, through the category of peoplehood implicating it. That is, the category of peoplehood in order to be able to strive for the realization of the redemptive vocation and, indeed, to consummate this striving in a fulfilled realization of the redemptive vocation, needs sovereignty – it needs power to regulate its life both internally and externally. Without the possession of sovereignty, the freedom to decide and direct the life of the community, the category of peoplehood cannot possibly carry out the redemptive task assigned to it. But sovereignty, in turn, implicates the category of land. For sovereignty can be attained only by a people that possesses a land. The possession of a land is the condition *sine qua non* for the exercise of sovereignty (although in itself it may not be a sufficient condition, it is certainly a necessary one). Thus, the thrust of the inner logic operative here is as follows: the redemptive vocation being the establishment of the righteous community, it of necessity implicates the category of peoplehood; the category of peoplehood, in turn, in order to carry out and realize the redemptive task assigned to it, of necessity requires sovereignty; and sovereignty, in turn, of necessity implicates the category of land.

b)   Land Secondary but Essential

Now, we must be clear and precise as to what this presentation actually says with regard to the categories of peoplehood and land. First, although the category of land is secondary and derived (and will always be so in the distinctive structure of faith of Judaism), it should be clear that as far as the redemptive vocation, i.e., the specific task of realizing redemption, is concerned the category of land is no less essential than the category of peoplehood. Without a land to allow the exercise of sovereignty, the fulfillment (and even the very workings) of the redemptive vocation is simply not possible. Where the category of land, in contradistinction to the category of peoplehood, is not essential is with regard to the question of the capacity of the religious phenomenon of Judaism to maintain itself, i.e., to go on enduring in existence. While without the category of peoplehood the phenomenon of Judaism collapses and cannot possibly go on existing, without the category of land it can persevere and go on existing though albeit in a limping and crippled fashion. Thus, the phenomenon of Judaism did endure and survive diaspora-existence. True, it was (and indeed was perceived as such by Judaism itself) a truncated form of existence. In diaspora-existence Judaism could only mark time; it could only, so to speak, hold the fort but it could not actively pursue its redemptive vocation. For the resumption of the active pursuit of its redemptive vocation it had to await and hope for its restoration to the land.

Special Circumstances of the Modern World

We must add, however, that the situation has radically changed in modern times and that the assertions made above must, therefore, be qualified accordingly if they are to apply to Judaism in the modern world. Because of radical changes in the social structure of the host-nations and the rise of nationalism in its modern form which, in turn, lead to a radical change in the conditions of existence of Judaism in diaspora, i.e., leading to a transformation from ghetto-existence to what is commonly called Emancipation, the very possibility of the survival of Judaism in diaspora-existence is thrown into question. Evidently, we cannot analyze and expound in detail on this thesis here (we have done it, in a way, in our essay "The Dilemma of Identity for the Emancipated Jew," which appears in this volume as chapter six). We shall instead state dogmatically that in the conditions of existence afforded by the modern world, the phenomenon of Judaism, if it is to survive, must extricate itself from diaspora-existence. This means that it must regain its sovereignty, and since sovereignty is afforded only by the possession of land this means that Judaism must regain a land of its own. Thus, in the conditions of existence of the modern world or, to put the matter differently, vis-à-vis emancipated Judaism, the category of land is needed not only for the resumption of the active pursuit and the ultimate realization of the redemptive vocation but for the very existence of the phenomenon of Judaism. And of course the question of existence takes precedence over the question of pursuing the redemptive vocation, and therefore it is understandable that in the formulations we have surveyed, formulations dealing with and expressing the situation of Judaism in the modern world, the category of land is considered primarily with regard to the question of existence and not the redemptive vocation (though, of course, by regaining the land for the sake of existence the possibility to resume and ultimately realize the redemptive vocation is also given). Emancipated Judaism cannot survive in diaspora; for it the category of land is on an equal footing with the category of peoplehood – it is essential for the very existence of the phenomenon. But even so, even with regard to Judaism in the modern world, the category of land is not essential in the same sense as the category of peoplehood. For at least theoretically (though realistically it is very unlikely) Judaism can retreat from Emancipation and in this eventuality the impossibility of survival in diaspora-existence is not so definite. This, in turn, means that the need for the category of land for the sake of survival is once again removed. The category of peoplehood, on the other hand, is not affected by such contingent circumstances. The need for it for the very existence of the phenomenon is permanent, determined by the very structure of the phenomenon itself and independent of all conditions of existence; the need for it will persist in all conceivable situations.

a) Requirement of the Category of Land in General

It should be clear, however, that when the inner logic operative here requires the category of land, it requires the category of land in general. It does not require any specific land to the exclusion of others. Any geographic location would satisfy the requirements of the inner logic here. This applies equally to the requirement of land for the sake of pursuing and realizing the redemptive vocation and to the requirement of land in modern times for the sake of the survival of emancipated Judaism. For the need for a land arises in both instances from the need for sovereignty. And sovereignty can be provided by the possession of any land; it is common to all lands. Affording sovereignty is not an attribute possessed by certain lands to the exclusion of others. Of course, again, this is purely on the theoretical level; in reality there are other considerations which bear heavily and significantly on this question and which do indeed particularize and focus on a specific geographic location, i.e., the specific land of Israel, to the exclusion of all other geographic locations.

b) Peoplehood in the Full Sense of Ethnicity

Lastly, it should be also clear that the category of peoplehood indicated by the inner logic operative here is of a peoplehood in the sense of full ethnicity. Clearly, since the redemptive vocation is the establishment of the righteous community, the category of peoplehood that is required is the category of peoplehood that carries the social, economic and political dimensions. The category of peoplehood in the sense of restricted ethnicity would not be capable of providing the matrix for the realization of the redemptive vocation nor, indeed, for the striving for its realization. Of course, in diaspora-existence, since the social, economic, and political dimensions were not available anyway (indeed, the absence of these dimensions constitutes in essence diaspora-existence and characterizes it as a truncated existence), the formulation of the category of peoplehood in the sense of restricted ethnicity would readily suggest itself – it corresponds to, and indeed reflects, the reality of the category of peoplehood existing in these circumstances, i.e., in the conditions of diaspora-existence. Most of the formulations we have surveyed did indeed arise in the circumstances of diaspora-existence so that it is understandable that the formulation of the category of peoplehood in the sense of restricted ethnicity was so wide-spread. Also, formulating the category of peoplehood in the sense of restricted ethnicity would remove, or at least mitigate, some issues on which a potential head-on collision between the claims of the host-nation and the claims of Jewish peoplehood in the sense of full ethnicity could potentially arise; as such, formulating the category of peoplehood in the sense of restricted ethnicity would be more congenial to emancipated Judaism in diaspora-existence, and it is to be expected that formulations arising in the circumstances of diaspora-existence would be disposed, even if unconsciously, towards it. Still, in terms of the phenomenon of Judaism itself, and irrespective of the contingent considerations arising from circumstances of diaspora-existence, the category of peoplehood that is required is the category of peoplehood in the sense of full ethnicity. Only as such can the category of peoplehood fulfill its task in the redemptive vocation and be the primary category that is essential and irremovable. The category of peoplehood in the sense of restricted ethnicity could maintain this status only in diaspora-existence when the active pursuance of the redemptive vocation of Judaism was suspended anyway (it thus maintains this status, in a way, by default due to diaspora-existence). It can maintain this status because the function of Judaism in diaspora-existence was, as we said, merely to mark time and hold the fort. This task the category of peoplehood in the sense of restricted ethnicity could fulfill – it could keep the ethnic identity (i.e., thus holding the fort) and it could endure through the flux of time (thus marking time). But in modern times, with respect to emancipated Judaism and with the need to be extricated from diaspora-existence and regain sovereignty, the need for full ethnicity is clearly reasserted, for sovereignty implicates full ethnicity. Only for the Judaism that retreats from Emancipation is restricted ethnicity still viable.

Concluding Evaluation

In view of this tracing of the inner logic and the structure of what constitutes the distinctive, mainstream expression of the religious phenomenon that is Judaism how are we to evaluate the formulations of modern Judaism surveyed above? Interestingly enough, the formulations belonging to the political-Zionist trend reflect most authentically this distinctive religious phenomenon of Judaism in its present emancipated situation in the modern world. In a way it is ironic, because these formulations professed all too often to be secular and not religious (and indeed were taken as such). But apparently their non-religious stance is in truth only a stance against the rabbinic expression of Judaism, i.e., a stance against the authentic, viable expression of Judaism when it found itself in the circumstances of diaspora-existence. Taking rabbinic Judaism as the criterion of religiousness, they may well appear secular; but vis-à-vis emancipated Judaism finding itself in the circumstances of the modern world they are, in a profound sense, authentic religious expressions of Judaism. Their great advantage is that they perceive the category of peoplehood in the sense of full ethnicity. On the other hand, the many formulations which perceived the category of peoplehood in the sense of restricted ethnicity, though in many ways reflecting authentically the distinctive religious phenomenon of Judaism, fall short of doing justice to the needs of emancipated Judaism in the modern world. They are still expressing the Judaism of diaspora-existence. In a way, they represent an inner, deep-seated contradiction – wanting to express emancipated Judaism while at the same time affirming diaspora-existence. Coupling emancipated Judaism with diaspora-existence is not really possible. Yet in expressing this impossible contradiction these formulations reflect authentically the state of mind and desire of emancipated Jewry. While falling short of reflecting authentically emancipated Judaism they nonetheless reflect authentically emancipated Jewry. Lastly, as regards the formulations in the mystical trend, they evidently express a Judaism that has a different religious structure and consequently a different inner logic than the religious structure and inner logic that we presented above as constituting what we claimed to be the distinctive religious phenomenon of Judaism. We are here, so to speak, in a different ball-park altogether. The two structures differ in their very foundations, i.e., in what they conceive to be the ultimate predicament of man and, commensurate with this, the redemptive vocation for man. Naturally, the inner logic that would operate in the mystical trend would lead to a different understanding of the status of the category of peoplehood and the category of land in the phenomenon of Judaism. The crucial question here, of course, is which trend expresses the phenomenon of Judaism more authentically. We would want to claim that intriguing and attractive as the mystical trend is, it nonetheless does not reflect the phenomenon of Judaism in its distinctiveness; and although there is no denying (not after Scholem's work) that the mystical trend found widespread expression within Jewry, it was not the mainstream expression. But the case that must be made to support this contention must be left to another occasion.

---

[1]We did not include, in a separate heading, the non-mystical, halachic-rabbinic literature because essentially it reflects in its substance the pre-modern, traditional understanding of mainstream Judaism. The halachic-rabbinic literature of the modern period is a continued expression of rabbinic diaspora Judaism, not of the emancipated Judaism of the modern world. The interesting aspect of halachic-rabbinic Judaism in the modern era revolves around the question of how to relate to the Zionist program. But this is a question of strategy and policy, not of substance. To jump ahead of our story, it can be said that the halachic-rabbinic trend clearly affirmed the centrality of the category of peoplehood and of the category of the land, indeed specifically of the land of Israel. The question before this trend was whether Jewry should take action (and in this case, what action should be taken) to secure the return of Jewry to its homeland, or whether such action must be left in the hands of God so that Jewry must remain passive in its diaspora-existence awaiting patiently for the time when God will act. Both sides to this question found expression within the halachic-rabbinic trend. Clearly, the latter view affirmed diaspora-existence and indeed it is the most viable expression among all other formulations affirming diaspora-existence in as much as it also, in essence, resisted the process of Emancipation (S.R. Hirsch may be an exception but his advocacy of emancipation coupled with loyalty to halachic-rabbinic Judaism is, in our judgment, not viable; the emancipation recommended was surface-Emancipation, thus not at all reflecting the process of Emancipation that was actually taking place). The former view which negated diaspora-existence was riddled with hedging and ambiguity regarding the Zionist program. This in a way is understandable, for it meant the readjustment of a religious stance, i.e., the halachic-rabbinic stance, that was geared to diaspora-existence, to existence outside profane history, to a program, i.e., the Zionist program, that negated diaspora-existence and involved the re-entry of Jewry and Judaism into profane history – a readjustment that is, to say the least, very problematic.

Chapter Eleven

Towards Reformulating Zionist Ideology

There is no denying that since the re-establishment of the state of Israel in 1948 the Zionist movement has been floundering regarding its ideology. It appears to have lost a clear and distinct notion of its goal and program or, alternatively, it appears to present a goal and a program that misses the mark, in as much as it fails to address the reality and needs of Jewry in the post-establishment era. As such, it is not surprising that the movement appears to have lost its *élan vital,* its distinctiveness, its centrality and relevancy to Jewish life today. It goes on maintaining its organizational apparatus by the sheer force of inertia, but it is devoid of an ideological thrust which alone could make it a meaningful and vital force in Jewish life today. It coasts along merely as one more "organization" in the myriad of "organizations" characterizing Jewish life on the momentum generated in the past, in the period prior to 1948, but deprived of the capacity to generate its own momentum in the present. This situation is in marked contrast to the situation which characterized the Zionist movement in the period prior to the re-establishment of the state. Prior to 1948 the movement possessed a distinct ideology articulating a concrete goal for which to strive and a well-defined task to be pursued as such; the movement possessed a clear *raison d'être* for its existence. Moreover, and this is the crux of the matter, the goal and task espoused by the movement addressed the paramount and pressing need of the Jewish people at the particular juncture in its history and consequently the movement in its commitment to this goal and task came to express the very ethos of the people and thus to hold the center of the stage in its life.

Thus, it is quite understandable that sooner or later the re-establishment of the state should inevitably precipitate the question as to the relevancy and meaningfulness of an ongoing Zionist movement in the post-establishment era. Having realized its goal should not the movement fold its tent and pass away from from the scene? Does not the very success of the movement in having fulfilled its task signify its demise? Anyway, what can it possibly signify to be a Zionist in the post-establishment era? Is it the striving towards the re-establishment of the state – it is an accomplished reality? Is it the yearning to immigrate and live in the re-established state? Anyone who wishes can instantaneously transform this yearning into a reality. Should not therefore the vocation of being an Israeli supplant the vocation of being a Zionist? Is it not really the proper and honest thing to say that in the post establishment era there can be no more justification for or meaning to the term "Zionist" except perhaps in so far as it conveys the rather tenuous and provisional reference to him who is on the way to become an Israeli? (of course, in this sense the term would have a less provisional use when applied to those Jews who desire to immigrate to the state of Israel but are prevented from doing so by the regimes under whose rule they happen to live; by the same token, however, the use of the term would be equally justifiable and equally less provisional when applied to criminal Jews who wish to become Israelis in order to escape justice in their lands of residency and are prevented from doing so by Israeli law).

This argument for the dissolution of Zionism in the post-establishment era is by no means hypothetical. It is actually held by an appreciable number of Jews, particularly Israeli Jews; it counts among its adherents many who were ardent Zionists and, indeed, some who were illustrious leaders of the movement in the days before the state was re-established. As against this, those who continue in their adherence to Zionism have thus far failed, by and large, to join the issue on the ideological level. Not that they would, or indeed could, deny the fact that the movement has lost much of its vitality and centrality in Jewish life today (though it is an interesting fact that many diaspora Jews remain attached to the movement on an emotional and existential level regardless of any intellectual inconsistency that this may involve). Their response to this predicament, however, has been in the main on a pragmatic level – arguments for organizational realignment and exhortations for more vigorous and efficient work in the field – and not on the ideological level. On the ideological level all that has been proposed thus far is more of the same – more of the ideology that characterized Zionism prior to the re-establishment of the state. Alas, such a response cannot meet satisfactorily the problem of Zionism in a post-establishment era. In the last analysis, there is no escape from confronting the issue on the ideological level. If Zionism is to become once again a viable and central force in Jewish life, one will have to wrestle with the problem on the ideological level and come up with a reformulation of the Zionist ideology that will effectively dispose of the claim that the *raison d'être* of Zionism has come to an end with the re-establishment of the Jewish state.

This is not an easy task. It cannot be denied that the position arguing for the demise of Zionism in the post-establishment era is forceful. Still, we would want to argue that, in the last analysis, this position short-changes the potentialities and resources of Zionism. It fails to grasp the full depth and extent of the Zionist expression of Judaism because it fails to perceive the true structure and essence of the phenomenon of Judaism. For if we look carefully at this position we would see that ultimately it bases itself on a secularist perception of the phenomenon of Judaism, namely, that ultimately it presupposes the perception of Judaism as but an ethnic-national entity and nothing else (and it is understandable that given such a secularist perception of Judaism, the tendency would be to perceive Zionism exclusively in terms of its modern manifestation, i.e., in the context of the rise of modern nationalism, failing to take fully into account, except for occasional lip service for the purposes of edification, the preceding age-old Zionist expression that was in its very essence suffused with the religious dimension). Indeed, the very forcefulness and cohesiveness of this position is, in the last analysis, contingent upon such a secularist perception of Judaism as but an ethnic-national phenomenon, and it should not be surprising, therefore, that most adherents of this position do indeed maintain such a secularist perception of Judaism.

That this is so, by the way, can be seen from the following consideration: if Judaism is but an ordinary, secularist ethnic-national entity, like all the other nations of the world, then the normalization of its existence does indeed become the end withal of the Zionist vocation and, correspondingly, the ultimate task of Zionism is but to bring about the circumstances that would make such normalization possible, which is to say that the ultimate task of Zionism is but to bring about the circumstances which will make possible the transformation of the diaspora-Jew into an Israeli-Jew. Clearly, for such a transformation to be possible the existence of a Jewish state is required and consequently the re-establishment of a Jewish state becomes a necessary goal for the Zionist's vocation. But moreover (and this is really the important point to be made) the re-establishment of a Jewish state becomes here for the Zionist vocation not only a necessary goal but the end withal commensurate with the end withal constituted by the normalization of life of the Jewish nation. For, inasmuch as it is required merely for the sake of normalization and inasmuch as such normalization is attained by mere existence in the re-established state, the very act of re-establishing the Jewish state provides the circumstances that make normalization feasible; and inasmuch as normalization is the end withal, the re-establishment of the Jewish state, being commensurate with normalization, is likewise the end withal for the vocation of Zionism. The crux of the matter is that this position, in perceiving Judaism secularly as but an ethnic-national entity, can offer no other and higher end for the Zionist vocation except normalization and normalization is, as we have seen, commensurate with the re-establishment of a Jewish state. As such, the re-establishment of the Jewish state cannot be taken here as a means, even as an essential and necessary means, to a higher end; it can only be taken as the ultimate end itself. Thus, the re-establishment of the Jewish state cannot be seen by this position as the realization of a step, albeit a most important step, on the way to the ultimate goal; it must be seen as the realization of the ultimate goal itself. Given this inner logic which is derived from a secularist perception of Judaism, the re-establishment of the Jewish state must indeed signify conclusion of the Zionist task and the fulfillment of its vocation and consequently also the demise of the *raison d'être* for its continued existence.

But precisely this point which provides, in the last analysis, the forcefulness and cohesiveness of this position, namely, the secularist understanding of the phenomenon of Judaism, is the very point which is also responsible for the ultimate weakness and untenability of this position; the point which supports the inner logic and rationale of this position is also the very point which betrays its Achilles heel. For a *secularist* perception and understanding of the phenomenon of Judaism is inauthentic to the reality of the phenomenon of Judaism as it expressed and manifested itself throughout its long history and as indeed it was perceived and understood by its adherents and by the world at large. Not that one could deny the fact that the ethnic-national is a fundamental and inescapable category in the structure of Judaism. This must be readily granted. But the distinction of the secularist perception does not lie in this affirmation; it lies in the further assertion that the ethnic-national is the primary and ultimate category in the structure of Judaism, and it is precisely at this point that the issue must be joined. Namely, we would want to argue that in the authentic structure of Judaism it is not the ethnic-national entity but rather the religious dimension that is the primary and ultimate category. The phenomenon of Judaism is in its essence a religious phenomenon. Indeed, the ethnic-national category enters the structure of Judaism because it is necessarily implicated by the religious category. The essential religious category is so constituted in the phenomenon of Judaism that it necessarily binds the ethnic-national category to itself. In this way the ethnic-national is indeed a fundamental and inextricable category in the structure of Judaism but it is so, let us emphasize, by virtue of the special constitution of the religious category in the phenomenon of Judaism. Precisely as such, the ethnic-national category, for all its importance, is not the ultimate category in the structure of Judaism; it is penultimate. It is a means, a necessary and inextricable means but a means nevertheless, for the expression of the religious category. To reverse this relationship between the ethnic-national and the religious, making the ethnic-national the ultimate category and the religious its mere expression, i.e., a part of its cultural creativity, is to stand Judaism on its head. The authentic relationship is the relationship whereby the religious is the ultimate category and the ethnic-national is but a means, albeit a necessary and inextricable means, for its expression.

But if this be the case, then the thrust and forcefulness of the position arguing for the demise of Zionism in the post-establishment era is perforce greatly mitigated. For indeed, if Judaism is perceived to be entrusted with a religious vocation, which vocation constitutes its very essence and *raison d'être,* and if Zionism is seen to be an expression of the essence of Judaism and not merely a strategy for coping with certain historical contingencies, then the re-establishment of the Jewish state as such, in so far as it does not signify the fulfillment of the vocation allotted to Judaism, does not also signify the demise of the Zionist task. Still, although the re-establishment of the state does not signify the fulfillment of the vocation, it most certainly does signify a radical turn in the road towards that fulfillment and such a turn must inevitably precipitate a serious challenge to the meaning of Zionism in the new circumstances created by the re-establishment of the state. Can there be a distinct Zionist stance and perspective that will authentically address the Jewish situation and vocation in the post-establishment era? Can Zionism remain a distinct and relevant movement within the Jewish polity once a Jewish state has been established? To meet this challenge Zionism must clearly reformulate its ideology. Indeed, in recent days one can detect in certain quarters, both in Israel and in diaspora, an awakening to the need of reformulating Zionist ideology in terms of a deeper understanding, i.e., a more spiritual and religious understanding, of the phenomenon of Judaism and the new situation which confronts it in the post-establishment era. The following reflections are a feeble contribution to this all-important enterprise.

I

Before plunging, however, into this difficult and challenging task, we should perhaps note that in a certain way the task of re-establishing the state is not yet really finished; we do not as yet fully exist in a post-establishment era. True, in one very important way the task was brought to a successful conclusion in 1948. 1948 is a watershed. Yet, as reality, particularly the reality that has developed in the past few years, clearly shows, a state is not re-established over night. Particularly in our case, in re-establishing the Jewish state, where the undertaking has been so problematic and the achievement literally bordering on the miraculous, things are a thousandfold more difficult and complicated. Beside the fact that it takes years upon years for a state to establish its structure and organization firmly so that it can stand on its own two feet, there is the all-important question of its universal acceptance and it is here that we are encountering an especially difficult and exasperating problem. The task of establishing a state is not really finished until its existence is universally taken for granted and cannot be questioned. Obviously, we have not arrived at this juncture. It would be a serious mistake, therefore, for us to think that the task of re-establishing the state has been concluded. The state has been continuously struggling for its life ever since its re-establishment and we must be involved in this struggle just as much as we were involved in the struggle leading to its re-establishment in 1948. One must not forget the short life of the second commonwealth.

Thus, in a sense the classical Zionist commitment to the task of the re-establishment of the state has not as yet exhausted itself. But even in this continuation of the task to re-establish the state a re-thinking and a reformulation are required, for the role and strategy pursued by the Zionist movement prior to 1948 are obsolete today. The issues and challenges today are different from what they were prior to 1948 and the *Zeitgeist* to which we are to address ourselves is no longer that of early 20th century Western Europe, but rather the emerging *Zeitgeist* of the 21st century Third World. The need for reformulation in this context, however, impinges only upon the question of strategy, of how best to execute the Zionist commitment, rather than upon the very content and orientation of that commitment. But one day, and hopefully one day soon, this task will be finally concluded – the re-established state will be universally accepted and firmly established. Then, the real challenge, i.e., the need for a reformulation impinging on the very content and orientation of the Zionist ideology, would press hard on us. Can we reformulate and re-articulate the Zionist commitment so as to make it a viable and distinctive force in Jewish life once the state is firmly and conclusively re-established?

II

The undertaking of such a reformulation requires that we view modern Zionism in the context of the totality of Jewish history and, indeed, in terms of the religious structure that constitutes the very essence of the phenomenon of Judaism. Namely, we must realize that the basic orientation of modern Zionism, the Zionism which arose in the latter part of the 19th century, did not start *de novo;* in an important sense, it is a continuation, albeit in a new form of expression, of an orientation that characterized Judaism almost throughout its entire history, an orientation that emerges from the very essence of the structure of faith of Judaism, i.e., the messianic orientation. Thus, the basic orientation of modern Zionism, i.e., the notion of Zionism as distinct from the movement as such, does not first emerge in the second half of the 19th century. It emerges with the Davidic covenant and in this context it comes subsequently to express the messianic hope of Judaism. This is important for us to note. We cannot separate Zionism from the messianic dimension and, vice versa, the messianic dimension in Judaism cannot be separated from Zionism. And inasmuch as the messianic dimension is an essential and inextricable element in the structure of Judaism, Zionism, taken in this its essential signification, is an equally and inextricable, essential expression of Judaism.

In this connection, it is important to keep in mind that prophetic-halachic mainstream Judaism formulates its messianic hope and expectation in this-worldly terms; the messianic hope is projected here towards the concrete world. Such a this-worldly orientation furthermore is not accidental but part and parcel of the very essence of mainstream Jewish messianism. It flows of necessity from the very content that comprises this messianism, for the hope and yearning of this messianism is directed towards the perfection of society, the setting aright of the relations between man and man, the realization of justice and righteousness, in short, it is directed towards the establishment of the true, authentic earthly community in all its dimensions – the social, the economic and the political. As such, indeed, this messianism necessarily requires the sovereignty of statehood, for only the framework of sovereign statehood can provide the power and conditions to effectuate its realization; and this, in turn, necessarily implicates a link between this messianism and a specific geographic location, a specific lot of land, where statehood can be established, i.e., where the builders of redemption, the *bonaich,* and the redeemed community, the *banaich,* can be located. Messianism here is necessarily linked to a specific location in space just as much as it necessarily refers to a specific point in time; and this specific location happens to be Zion, the land of Israel. The messianic vocation in Judaism expresses itself in terms of the earthly rather than the heavenly Jerusalem. Given this inner logic of the structure of faith of Judaism, it is clear that mainstream Judaism had to view diaspora-existence as an interruption, a suspension, of its actual redemptive task and work. In terms of its religious vocation, and aside from all other considerations, diaspora-existence is a truncated existence. It is a calamity not only from the viewpoint of the well-being of the nation, from the viewpoint of the suffering and pain that it necessarily inflicts, it is a calamity from the viewpoint of the religious vocation of Judaism. In diaspora-existence the religious redemptive vocation is suspended or, at best, greatly reduced. Thus, it is perfectly understandable that in the circumstances of diaspora-existence Zionism, precisely as the expression of the messianic hope of Judaism, came to signify first and foremost the yearning and hope for the return of the people to its homeland, to the land of Israel. The return to the homeland being a condition *sine qua non* for the resumption of the work of redemption, the absence of the homeland required that the messianic hope express itself first and foremost in the yearning to return to the land of the fathers. Zionism as the articulation of this yearning to be returned to the homeland was thus an expression of the messianic vocation (and as such an expression of the very essence of Judaism), indeed, the only expression feasible in the circumstances of diaspora-existence. And inasmuch as this yearning was a continuous, uninterrupted expression of diaspora Judaism, diaspora Judaism has always been Zionistic. Indeed, at times the wish and the need to return to the homeland became so strong that the yearning was transformed into action engulfing individuals and even substantial segments of the community (diaspora Jewish history knows of too many false messiahs). Still, for about fifteen hundred years circumstances were such that action involving the nation as a whole was not feasible and the Zionist commitment had to remain only a yearning and hope.

It is against this background that the phenomenon of modern Zionism, the phenomenon of the Zionist movement that had its inception in the latter part of the 19th century, must be understood. Thus, we must first and foremost realize that modern Zionism remains, in the last analysis, an expression of the messianic hope of Judaism (this must be stressed particularly in view of the fact that, as we shall presently see, some other factors played a crucial role in the emergence of modern Zionism and they are likely to overshadow and obscure the messianic dimension). Indeed, one can see the messianic dimension operative not only in the religious-orthodox segment of the Zionist movement but in the movement as a whole, including the ostensibly secularized, atheistic, socialist segment. As Franz Rosenzweig once noted, just another ordinary state like all other states was not good enough; for Zionists of all colors the aspiration was for a special, perfected state, in which the highest social and ethical values will be embodied. But this is tantamount to saying that the modern Zionist movement as a whole, in practically all its segments and variations, is ultimately linked to the messianic yearning of Judaism and receives, in the last analysis, its depth and its elan from this source. Thus, it is the messianic dimension that provides the bond which organically links modern Zionism to the Zionism of the long diaspora-period and, indeed, to the Zionism which, from its inception in the Davidic covenant, came to characterize the very essence of Judaism.

III

But linked as it is to the Zionism of the past, modern Zionism, in an important sense, is nonetheless a distinct and new phenomenon. It is distinct and new, not as regards the content of the Zionist commitment, but as regards the form of its expression; namely, modern Zionism is active in expressing its Zionist commitment. While the Zionism of the long diaspora-period expressed itself in passive yearning, the distinctiveness of modern Zionism lies in transforming this yearning into action. Indeed, conditions in the modern world have not only made it possible but actually prompted this change from passive yearning to active pursuit of the hope of returning to the homeland. Modern technology made the migration of masses over large distances feasible if not, indeed, easy. Modern technology, furthermore, has made the settling of a land that has lain arid and neglected for centuries upon centuries a possibility; true, it was still a high-risk gamble and a difficult challenge but at least now the possibility of success was not completely foreclosed.. At the same time, the rise of modern nationalism in Europe brought to the fore both in Jewish consciousness and in the consciousness of the host-nation the reality of the Jewish people as a nation. And with every national entity in the European continent actively seeking and working for its liberation and self-assertion, the Jewish nation too was swept to actively seek and work for its liberation and self-assertion. Thus, the modern movement of Zionism summoned the energy to carry out in action and in reality the passive hope, yearning and wishes of the previous generations. Instead of passively waiting for God to act, it called upon man to act.

IV

But beside the above mentioned factors, i.e., the rise of nationalism and the advances in technology, there is an additional all-important factor that prompts the activism of modern Zionism and in a special and essential way lends it distinctiveness. This factor is the radical change brought about in the modern world in the conditions of existence of diaspora-Jewry. Indeed, modern Zionism must been as arising specifically in response to this new situation that Judaism and Jewry encounter in the modern world – a situation that precipitates a grave predicament and a serious threat to Judaism and Jewry in diaspora. Namely, the special distinctiveness of modern Zionism is not fully and properly grasped unless it is seen in the context of the problem that the phenomenon of the Emancipation (i.e., Jewish Emancipation) precipitates. This does not divert, however, modern Zionism from ultimately expressing the messianic dimension. For the *response* of modern Zionism to the problem of the Emancipation is such that at one and the same time it is also a program for the renewal of the working towards the realization of the messianic dimension. Still, it must be admitted that while the messianic dimension is definitely present in modern Zionism, its presence is in the background as the ultimate goal and justification of the program. It is not in the foreground as the immediate, direct and explicit objective of the program (but then, the messianic dimension by its very nature can come into the foreground only when one relates to things in terms of their ultimate goal and justification). The immediate, direct and explicit objective of modern Zionism is the solution of the problem precipitated by the Emancipation and it is to this that we must now briefly turn our attention.

There is no denying that the conditions of existence of the Jewish people in diaspora underwent a radical transformation in modern times. The ghetto-existence of Jewry was crumbling and Jews were entering the culture and society of their host-nations. Emancipation was engulfing diaspora Jewry. It soon became clear, however, that despite all the glitter and hope that the Emancipation seemed to hold for the well-being of the Jews, it was by no means an unmixed blessing. With the glitter of material improvement came a two-pronged deadly threat – a threat to the very existence of the Jew, (i.e., to the physical well-being of the Jew *qua* human being) and a threat to the very survival of Judaism (i.e., to the survival of the Jew *qua* Jew). Modern antisemitism, no longer primarily religious but rather ethnic-national in its origin and impetus, reared its head. It was the antisemitism emanating from modern nationalism which could not tolerate the Jew in its midst, not so much because of his belonging to a different community of faith but principally because of his belonging to a different ethnic entity. The Jew was a "foreign element" that had to be removed. The Holocaust was but the carrying out of this position to its "logical" conclusion irrespective of the cruel, inhuman and barbaric suffering that it implied. But one did not have to wait for the Holocaust to occur in order to see the threat to the very existence of the Jew lurking in modern Europe. Assimilation, as long as it was not consummated in complete disappearance (and even then!), would not ameliorate the position of the Jew; on the contrary, it aggravated it. The Dreyfus trial clearly showed this to those who had eyes to see. At the same time, the Emancipation brought into serious question the survival of Judaism. The emancipated Jew paid a high price in entering the host-society in search of material improvement – his ties to the Jewish heritage were of necessity gravely weakened. Ghetto-existence had the all-important advantage that it fostered the viability of the Jewish heritage and safeguarded its transmission. Now that the

Jew entered the host-society he was to live and be educated in the context of the culture of his host-nation. Emancipation means the adoption of the language, the literature, the heroes, the moral values, and the *Weltanschauung* of the host-culture, and forsaking those of the Jewish culture. How could Judaism survive, let alone flourish, in such circumstances?

Thus, the Emancipation precipitated a twofold threat – a threat to the survival of the Jew and a threat to the survival of Judaism. It was this twofold threat that provided the immediate impetus for the rise of modern Zionism which, indeed, divided itself correspondingly into two main camps – on the one hand, the camp of political Zionism (e.g. Herzl) which saw the predicament of the *Jew* as constituting the central problem and, on the other hand, the camp of cultural Zionism (e.g., Achad Ha-Am) which saw the predicament of *Judaism* as constituting the central problem. We need not go here into a detailed analysis of the differences that separated the two camps. What is important to note, however, is that both camps were at one in seeing the solution to the predicament (respectively the predicament of the Jew and the predicament of Judaism) to lie in a return to the homeland. Although the position of political Zionism necessitated the return of the totality of Jewry, while the position of cultural Zionism could be satisfied with the return of only a part of Jewry, the important point is that for both the predicament could be solved only by a return to the homeland.

Thus, in the context of the problem of the Emancipation, i.e., in the circumstances of modern antisemitism threatening the very existence of the Jew and assimilation threatening the very survival of the Jewish heritage, the requirement to return to the homeland no longer constitutes merely the necessary condition for the resumption of the working towards the realization of the messianic hope; it constitutes now the necessary condition for the very survival of the Jewish people and of Judaism. As such, the need to return to the homeland receives an urgency and immediacy which the messianic hope normally cannot command. By and large, one can wait and bide his time if what is at stake is the suspension of the working towards redemption (and this is particularly applicable to Judaism where the religious structure succeeded in adapting itself to an indefinite period of waiting). But waiting and biding one's time is not possible if one's very existence is at stake. Thus, the return to the homeland for the sake of survival (and, as we shall see below, for the sake of "normalcy" which played an important role in conjunction with the question of survival in the Zionism centered on the predicament of the Jew *qua* human being) rather than for the sake of the messianic hope, is the unique and peculiar dimension of the modern Zionist movement. It is within this context that what appears as a secularist concern may find expression within the phenomenon of Zionism. Concern for survival and for "normalcy" is not a peculiarly religious concern; it can just as well be a secularist concern. Still, as we have noted above, even in what appears as a secularist expression of Zionism, the reference to the messianic dimension is by no means missing. Even so-called secularist Zionists did not think of the return to the homeland merely in terms of survival and "normalcy" (and this, after all, is as far as the inner logic of secular Zionism would require its adherents to go). But inevitably the so-called secularist Zionists were motivated to return to the homeland by something more than the mere consideration of rescue and "normalcy." They wanted to build and establish the ideal community. A state like all other states was not good enough for them. It had to be a *special* state where the authentic community was to be realized. What else but a messianic hope is reflected in this deep-seated dream that characterizes so-called secularist Zionists? Thus, the messianic dimension is inextricably present even when the main issue is the issue of survival and "normalcy."

Still, given the fact that the issue of survival and "normalcy" is the main and central impetus to the rise of the modern Zionist movement, it is understandable that the modern Zionist movement would be preoccupied with one and one question only, namely, the return to the land and the re-establishment of a national homeland in the land of the forefathers. It is understandable that the modern Zionist movement would become identified with the re-establishment of the state and that the re-establishment of the state would appear as the end withal rather than as a means, a necessary all-important means, but a means nonetheless, towards a further, higher goal. And in this context it is understandable that once the re-establishment of the state appeared to have been realized in 1948, the task and commitment of Zionism would have been seen as fulfilled, thus signaling the end of the movement.

V

But it is clear that such a conclusion is possible only when one ignores the messianic dimension of Zionism and misperceives its basic commitment as being a commitment to the state as such rather than to the nation. It is not possible in the context of the authentic vocation and in terms of the true commitment of Zionism – a commitment that is not to the state as such but to the viability and well-being of the Jewish people and a vocation that is inextricably bound, in the last analysis, to the messianic vocation of Judaism.

True, the distinctive characteristic of Zionism, in contradistinction to the other ideologies that were put forward in response to the Jewish problem in the modern world, is that it sees the survival of the Jewish people and the viability of its vocation, particularly in the circumstances of the modern world, to be unconditionally dependent upon the re-establishment of the state. The existence of the state, the existence of a homeland, is indeed the cornerstone of the Zionist ideology. (Indeed, one can say that as for rabbinic Judaism the Torah is the cornerstone, so for Zionism the state is the cornerstone and while the two are not mutually exclusive they are certainly distinct). But we must be clear that it is the cornerstone in terms of the *strategy* of Zionism, not in terms of its final goal and fundamental concern. The fundamental concern is the survival, the well-being and the viability of the Jewish people; and, linked to this, the final goal is the active resumption of the messianic vocation of Judaism. The re-establishment of the state is but the distinctive strategy for securing these ends. In the last analysis, therefore, Zionist ideology is not for the sake of the state but for the sake of the Jewish people and its final goal is not the establishment of just another state, albeit a Jewish state, but the resumption of the messianic vocation of Judaism. Indeed, any attempt at the reformulation of Zionist ideology for the post-establishment era will have to be guided by this twofold criterion.

VI

Thus, to the extent that the vocation of Zionism is linked to the messianic dimension of Judaism, the mere re-establishment of the state is far from signifying the consummation of the Zionist vocation. Indeed, just the opposite is the case – the re-establishment of the state signifies not the end but the beginning of carrying out in earnest the messianic task. It signifies not the realization but only the opportunity, the possibility, of realizing the messianic task. For the re-establishment of the state is not *ipso facto* tantamount to the realization of the messianic task; it is only the affording of the possibility of pursuing it inasmuch as the concrete pursuance of the messianic task is necessarily contingent on the availability of a re-established state. Thus, the re-establishment of the state allows the renewal of the messianic task, a task that had to be suspended in diaspora-existence. In the context of the messianic task, working towards the re-establishment of the state was a necessary prologue, not the final act.

This means that for Zionism, when seen in its linkage to the messianic vocation of Judaism, the re-establishment of the state cannot be the end withal. It can only be a means, an all-important and necessary means, but a means nonetheless, toward the realization of the true end, which is the messianic consummation. This, in turn, further implies that for Zionism the re-established Jewish state cannot be an ordinary state, a state like all other states. It must be a state entrusted with a messianic vocation, thus placing upon it special demands and expectations and subjecting its actions and policies to a different, more exacting criterion of judgment than that applied to other states. It is in these terms that the distinctive mark of a Zionist, in contradistinction to a non-Zionist, could be formulated once the state has been firmly re-established. It is the working towards the realization of the messianic vocation in the context of the re-established state that would constitute the distinctive task of the Zionist in the post-establishment era.

This understanding of the Zionist vocation in the post-establishment era would seem to imply the necessity of *aliya,* i.e., the immigration and settling of the Jew in his re-established state. For, clearly, the working towards redemption can be carried out fully and maximally only by the Jew living in the re-established state. Does it mean then that in the post-establishment era there can be a meaningful Zionist task for the Jew living in the re-established state, but not for the Jew living in diaspora? From the viewpoint of the messianic criterion it would appear that the answer would have to be the affirmative, namely, that we would have to say that a full and maximal participation in the Zionist-messianic task can be carried out only by him who lives in the re-established state.

We should note, however, that this conclusion, strictly speaking, applies only to a participation that is qualified by the adverbs "fully" and "maximally." Namely, living in the re-established state is made necessary for the Jew who wants to participate in the messianic work *fully* and *maximally*. This leaves open the question, however, whether a partial or less direct (so to speak, a once-removed) participation in the working towards the messianic fulfillment may nonetheless be still possible for the Jew who opts to go on living in diaspora. Indeed, we would want to argue that such a possibility is in principle feasible. To be sure, we have argued before that the religious vocation of the diaspora-Jew was truncated inasmuch as he could not pursue an essential aspect of his religious vocation, i.e., working towards the messianic fulfillment; namely, we have argued that the possibility of working towards the messianic fulfillment was not open to diaspora-Jewry. But this was in a context where the *totality* of Jewry existed in diaspora and a re-established state was not available. It is a different matter now when a re-established state is in existence and part of Jewry lives in it. Now it is no longer a question of initiating and pursuing the working towards the messianic fulfillment exclusively in the context of diaspora-existence; this indeed is not feasible. Rather it is only a question of participating (and at that, a participation that is only partial and indirect) in a working towards the messianic fulfillment which is already in progress in that segment of the nation living in the re-established state where, indeed, such working could be initiated and pursued because re-established statehood is available.

Whether or not, however, such participation can be materialized would depend on whether the re-established state can see itself in the proper perspective and whether one can constitute the proper structures in which such participation can express itself. Namely, it would depend on whether the state can really resist the temptation to pattern itself on the model of all other states, i.e., viewing itself as the ultimate reality and object of allegiance, and instead accept itself as a special kind of state recognizing its *penultimate* place relative to the entity of Jewish peoplehood; whether it can see itself as a means to the well-being of the Jewish people rather than the end withal; whether it can subject its inherent prerogatives to the needs of the nation as a whole and not only to the needs of that segment of the nation that lives within its borders, i.e., whether or not it can recognize that it has a constituency beyond its geographic borders; in short, whether it can continue to see itself as a Zionist state and not merely just another ordinary, run-of-the-mill state. But beyond such necessary reorientation it would further depend on whether or not one can succeed in devising the structures and institutions that would allow diaspora-Jewry to concretely express its participation in fashioning the destiny of the state, and thus partake in its working towards the messianic fulfillment. Here, one comes to the question of concrete projects and policies. Such projects and policies would have little, if any, precedence to guide one and they would, in all probability, be delicate and intricate undertakings whose delineation would have to be carefully and painstakingly worked out. Evidently, this cannot be done here. But it would seem to us that one would want to think in terms of projects that would encourage partial residency and of structures whereby such partial residency would bestow some of the privileges of citizenship. Perhaps even – seeing that it is becoming more and more an acceptable status to many states – one should think in terms of dual citizenship for diaspora-Jewry. In any case, it is in this direction, in the direction of finding ways and means by which to incorporate diaspora-Jewry in the work and destiny of the re-established state, that the reformulation of Zionist ideology should move.

VII

This discussion of the issue of *Aliya* in conjunction with the messianic criterion of Zionism brings us to consider the reformulation of Zionist ideology for the post-establishment era in conjunction with the second criterion, namely, with the criterion which states that the commitment of Zionism is, in the last analysis, not to the state as such but to the well-being and viability of the Jewish people and its vocation. For here, the all-important issue that needs reformulation is the position of Zionism regarding the question of ongoing diaspora-existence.

As we have noted above, although the fundamental commitment of Zionist ideology is to the well-being and viability of the Jewish people its distinctive feature is its insistence on the need for a re-established Jewish state. As such, it is understandable that prior to 1948 the central and all-absorbing task of the Zionist movement was the striving for the re-establishment of the Jewish state. This meant that prior to 1948 the thrust of the Zionist movement was expressed in the trend of the political Zionism. There is no denying that political Zionism, the Zionism of Herzl, was the authentic expression of the Zionist task and orientation at that particular juncture in Jewish history. This is a fact of history and one that is quite understandable.

Political Zionism, however, by its very inner logic presents a radical negation of Judaism diaspora-existence: diaspora-existence will inevitably elicit antisemitism; it will inevitably deform and cripple the life and person of the Jew; diaspora-existence is an abnormal state of affairs which ought to be "normalized" and it can be "normalized" only by living in a Jewish state. The positive expression of this essential thrust of the inner logic of political Zionism is *aliya*. Vis-à-vis Jewish existence in diaspora political Zionism has only one thing to say – *aliya*. In the circumstances of the period preceding the re-establishment of the state this radical position of political Zionism vis-à-vis Jewish existence in diaspora was necessary. From the perspective of history it is doubtful whether political Zionism could have mastered the required energy for re-establishing the state had it not assumed such a radical position vis-à-vis Jewish existence in diaspora. And with poetic justice it was specifically the issue of *aliya* that precipitated the re-establishment of the state. It was the issue of *aliya* that drove the British to give up the mandate and bring the question before the United Nations where the re-establishment of the state received the sanction of the world community.

But now that the state has been re-established we may have to rethink the radical negation by political Zionism of diaspora-existence and, indeed, rethink the exclusive identification of Zionism with the expression of political Zionism. In doing this we must keep in mind that the negative evaluation and ultimate rejection of diaspora-existence emerge from two different considerations. As we have seen, one consideration is constituted by the messianic dimension and impinges upon the question of the vocation of Judaism and the working towards its realization. Diaspora-existence is negated here because, given the structure of Judaism, the fulfillment of its vocation and, indeed, the working towards its realization, can take place only within a re-established state. As against this, the other consideration is constituted by the modern circumstances of diaspora-existence (i.e., by the rise of modern nationalism and the Emancipation) and impinges upon the question of the well-being and indeed of the very survival of both Jewry and Judaism. Here, diaspora-existence is negated because it imposes upon the Jew abnormal conditions of existence or, even more radically, because it threatens his very survival – either his survival *qua* human being (through the threat of modern antisemitism) or his survival *qua* Jew (through the threat of assimilation).

Now, it seems to us that a Zionist stance cannot possibly give up the negation of diaspora-existence (or, to put the matter in positive language, the commitment to *aliya*) which emerges from the first consideration, i.e., the consideration linked to the messianic dimension. If the Zionist movement of today and tomorrow is to remain organically attached to the Zionist expression that characterized Judaism throughout the ages and, even more significantly, if it is to remain faithful to the source which it expresses, i.e., to the vocation of Judaism, then it cannot give up its intimate link to the messianic dimension of Judaism; and, as we have seen above, the inner logic of the messianic dimension in Judaism necessitates the negation of diaspora-existence. This means that in principle Zionism cannot give up the idea of *aliya*. By the very essence of its orientation it must maintain that for the Jew to express his vocation fully, to be able to participate directly and maximally in the realization of this vocation, necessarily implies *aliya*. This much Zionism must maintain.

But the impetus for placing the commitment to *aliya* in the very center of modern Zionist thinking, for making *aliya* a most pressing tenet of modern Zionist ideology (and indeed not only in the theoretical but in practical terms), emanates not from the messianic consideration but from the consideration of the problem of emancipated Jewish diaspora-existence in the modern world. For although the messianic consideration certainly implicates a commitment to *aliya,* the drive and urgency to concretely implement this commitment in action can by and large not be derived from this consideration; by and large the messianic fervor is not strong enough to bring this about. The impetus for the concrete implementation of the commitment to *aliya* is more likely to come from the need of the people to extricate itself from a pressing predicament than from the fervor of the messianic ideal. Indeed, through its long diaspora-existence Judaism has learned to mitigate, if not indeed neutralize, the impetus of the messianic dimension. It has learned to hold fast to the messianic dimension and its necessary implication of the negation of diaspora-existence and yet at the same time come to terms with diaspora-existence; it managed to do this by relegating the messianic dimension from the realm of action to the realm of hope (to which, by the way, the messianic consideration readily lends itself by virtue of the fact that by its very structure it is future-oriented). And whenever the messianic hope was precipitated into action, thus implicating an active pursuance of the desire to return to the homeland (not in terms of individuals but in terms of the community), a good case can be made that the impetus for such precipitation came primarily not from the desire to fulfill the messianic vocation but rather from the predicament of the conditions of existence at the time. The Zionist expression in modern times is no exception – the impetus for its active pursuance of *aliya,* i.e., for precipitating hope into action, is likewise derived, by and large, from its perception of the conditions of existence, i.e., from its view of the predicament of emancipated Jewish existence in the modern world, rather than from the overt desire to bring about the messianic fulfillment.

To the extent, therefore, that the commitment to *aliya* is linked to the messianic consideration, Zionism can hold fast to it, as indeed it must, without at the same time having to force the issue of the negation of diaspora-existence to the forefront as a most pressing, all-absorbing and central issue of its *raison d'être;* the commitment to *aliya* can be held in principle as the optimal, desirable and ultimate goal without, at the same time, precipitating a radical, uncompromising and active negation of diaspora-existence. It is only when the commitment to *aliya* is linked to the consideration of the problem of emancipated Jewish existence in the modern world that it becomes pressing and radical. Thus, inasmuch as it is, as we shall presently see, precisely the aspects of radicality and immediacy rather than the very notion of *aliya* as such that may require reassessment and reformulation today, any undertaking of a reassessment must be directed not to the perception emanating from the messianic dimension, but to the perception emanating from the problem of emancipated Jewish diaspora-existence in the modern world.

What needs re-examination and reassessment today in the perception of Zionism, in particular the perception of political Zionism, is not so much the basic delineation of its "diagnosis" as the radicality which characterizes it and, corresponding to this, the radicality of the "treatment" which it offers. There is no escaping Zionism's basic perception of the predicament of emancipated Jewish diaspora-existence in the modern world. In its essential thrust it was and remains valid. It is a different matter, however, with the radicality of both the analysis and the solution that it has proposed and which has come to be identified, by and large, with the position of modern Zionism as such. This position is unquestionably radical – under no circumstances can there be a solution within diaspora-existence for the Jewish predicament. The only solution is for Jewry to exit diaspora-existence, i.e., to dissolve diaspora-existence through total *aliya;* the only viable solution is for Jewry to exist in its own state (for only a re-established Jewish state can provide Jewry with the conditions of existence that are no longer those of diaspora-existence). Thus, in this context, the role of the re-established state is exclusively implicated with the liquidation of diaspora-existence.

It is precisely at this point rethinking may be needed. The "diagnosis" of political Zionism was established on the basis of the totality of Jewry existing in diaspora and there being no state in existence. Now, under these circumstances the "diagnosis" of political Zionism may well be valid in all its radicality. The question arises, however, whether the "diagnosis" of political Zionism in all its radicality would still remain valid if a re-established Jewish state were also in existence. Namely, would the predicament of diaspora-existence remain as radical, as it is taken to be in the "diagnosis" of political Zionism, if the reality of Jewish existence were not comprised exclusively by diaspora-existence but rather by a diaspora-existence that is coupled with the existence of a re-established Jewish state? Would the presence of a re-established Jewish state affect the analysis and evaluation of the predicament of diaspora-existence as perceived by political Zionism? In short, can we say that Jewish existence in diaspora, when diaspora-existence is the exclusive and all-encompassing form of its existence, is indeed "deformed," "abnormal" and subject to the predicament of anti-semitism and assimilation but that the existence of a state would significantly mitigate, if not indeed cancel out, this predicament? In the thinking of political Zionism the "diagnosis" of the predicament of diaspora-existence is in no way affected by the existence of a re-established Jewish state. A re-established Jewish state can affect only the "treatment," i.e., the solution, of the predicament but not the "diagnosis."

As against this, we would suggest that the very radicality of the "diagnosis" of the predicament of diaspora-existence is affected by the existence of a re-established Jewish state. The predicament which is so radical in the absence of the state should be considerably mitigated in its presence. Note, however, that in the context of such a re-evaluation the need for and, therefore, the commitment to a re-established Jewish state is as central and essential as it is in the context of political Zionism. The difference lies in the perception of its role – now it is no longer implicated solely in connection with the liquidation of diaspora-existence but rather in making its continued existence viable.

VIII

Evidently, we cannot undertake here a detailed analysis of the impact that the existence of a re-established Jewish state would have on the specific predicaments of "abnormality," "deformity," antisemitism and assimilation that affect Jewish diaspora-existence. Speaking in general terms, however, we would want to argue that in pursuing the analysis in the very terms of political Zionism, the presence of a re-established Jewish state should make an important difference. Thus, we would suggest that a Jewry existing in diaspora (even when it involves the bulk of Jewry), but existing with the simultaneous presence of a re-established Jewish state, is no longer that unusual and strange a phenomenon nor is its existence as precarious and exposed to the vagaries of other nations. Consequently, the "deformation" of life and the reaction of antisemitism which in no small measure were brought about by the oddity and precariousness of total diaspora-existence should be mitigated. The Jew would no longer present the image of a "wandering ghost" among the nations, a disembodied spirit severed from the land and the concreteness of life (thus bringing about an "abnormal" and "deformed" state of existence). Nor would he be any longer an "orphan" with no home, no "parents," of his own to come to his defense, thus making him a readily available scapegoat on which the nations of the world can take out their various frustrations and hatreds (i.e., the perennial victim of antisemitism). Thus, the presence of a re-established Jewish state should make a difference in the circumstances associated with diaspora-existence and consequently the radical negation by political Zionism of diaspora-existence would certainly have to be mitigated.

In any event, all indications point to an ongoing existence of diaspora Jewry. Realistically speaking, one must accept the fact that a considerable part of Jewry opts to go on living in diaspora. If Zionism, therefore, is to remain true to its essential vocation, i.e., a vocation whose ultimate concern is not the establishment of a Jewish state for its own sake but rather the survival and well-being of the Jewish people, it cannot overlook or dismiss this reality. For Zionism, under these circumstances, to go on seeing its task as being *exclusively* that of advocating *aliya* would be tantamount to abdicating all relevancy. Thus, if Zionism does not have the courage to reformulate its ideology along the lines suggested above, it will indeed become an ideology which once had its glorious days in Jewish history but which is now passé and moribund, an ideology, lacking in vitality and relevance, which continues to exist solely by the force of institutional inertia. But if Zionism, true to its essential vocation, does reformulate itself in accordance with the changed conditions brought about by the re-establishment of the Jewish state, it can continue to impinge poignantly and authentically upon the deepest needs and aspirations of the Jewish people. Thus, with respect to the re-established state it will have the task of pointing out ever anew that the state is not to be just another state but rather the matrix in which working towards the messianic realization is to be continued, thus safeguarding the re-established state from the temptation of "canaanization" and preserving its authentic Jewish character. And with respect to diaspora-existence it will have the all-important vocation of counteracting the strong forces of assimilation by fostering Jewish self-awareness and sense of belongingness on the part of diaspora Jewry. Indeed Zionism by virtue of its linkage to the re-established state is better equipped than any other present available strategy to address this serious threat of assimilation facing emancipated diaspora Jewry and as such render invaluable service to its preservation.

In summation, we may conclude that with respect to non-orthodox, emancipated Jewry living both in the re-established state and in diaspora such a reformulated Zionism – a Zionism articulating the vocation of messianic realization in the re-established state and building bridges between it and diaspora – can indeed continue to express and safeguard the authenticity and viability of the Jewish people. Indeed, such a reformulated Zionism may well take over for the era of the Emancipation the role that the *Halacha* performed in the pre-Emancipation era – the role of uniting and preserving the community in its Jewish identity while at the same time expressing most authentically its vocation and *raison d'être*.

Chapter Twelve

The Separation of State and Church and the Rise of Civil Religion Viewed From the Vantage Point of Jewry and Judaism

The purpose of this paper is to delineate the position which Jewry and Judaism take (or ought to take) with regard to the issue of the separation of state and church and to that of civil religion. We should keep in mind, however, that what these issues denote is a complex of different possible situations rather than a clear-cut single situation – their notions convey an array of different significations and not a univocal single signification. It may be helpful, therefore, by way of introduction, to briefly sort out the main possible significations implicated in these notions.

To start with the separation of state and church, there is no escaping the fact that the notion is ambivalent, seeing that within its obvious signification, derived from the straightforward literal meaning of its terms, the notion actually carries a number of different significations. Thus, in its most minimal signification, the notion may merely signify the disestablishment of religion; namely, it may merely signify that religion is not at the service of the state, an office or an arm of the state, being privileged and supported by it, nor that the state is under the control of religion, i.e., a hierocracy. As such, this signification impinges exclusively on the institutional aspect of the relation between state and religion, on the status of the institution of religion within the state, negating any special recognition or support that the state may accord to it or, conversely, any power that it may exercise over the state. It does not impinge, let it be noted, on the involvement of religion within such domains of the public-national life as the social, economic or political domains, i.e., within what we may term the "horizontal dimension" of life.

It is, however, precisely with respect to this aspect, i.e., to the involvement of religion within the "horizontal dimension," that the other possible significations may arise. For the notion may well signify not only the disestablishment of religion but furthermore the exclusion of religion from the "horizontal dimension." And with respect to this latter aspect, the notion may actually implicate two alternative significations. On the one hand, it may signify the total exclusion of religion from the "horizontal dimension," leaving the "horizontal dimension" exclusively at the disposal of the state. It would thus erect a "wall of separation" between religion and the "horizontal dimension," between church and state. Clearly, this presents the most radical signification of the notion – it presents its maximal signification. On the other hand, however, the notion may signify only a partial exclusion of religion from the "horizontal dimension" – religion would be excluded from some but not necessarily from all aspects of the "horizontal dimension." As such, this signification would merely draw a "line of division" within the "horizontal dimension" between those domains upon which religion may impinge (thus sharing involvement with the state) and the other domains from which it is excluded (thus relegating them to the sole concern of the state). This signification is clearly much less radical. It occupies, so to speak a middle ground between the minimal signification of the "disestablishment" formulation and the maximal signification of the "wall of separation" formulation. Furthermore, in contradistinction to these alternative significations, it is rather elastic – it allows a great variety of formulations, seeing that the line of division can be drawn at different points throughout the spectrum of possibilities from the point where religion is excluded from almost all domains to the point where it is hardly excluded from any domain of the "horizontal dimension." Thus, in the main the notion of the separation of state and church implicates three distinct and different significations and we would have to bear this in mind in our analysis below.[1]

Proceeding to the notion of civil religion, one would have to say that it is not so much ambivalent as it is amorphous. Indeed, it can be more readily delineated by what it is not than by what it is – it is not any of the traditional religions. And yet, it carries features and fulfills roles that are commonly associated with traditional religions (hence the reference to it as a "religion"). Thus, it may well implicate an ideological stance or display a structure of rituals. But most significantly, it acts as a cohesive force within the community giving it orientation, meaning and justification. Indeed, it would seem that the most apt delineation of the notion should be in terms of this last characterization. For with respect to the characterizations of content or form the delineation of the notion may well be hopeless, seeing that it may vary in its signification all the way from watered-down versions of traditional religions to neo-pagan versions of nationalist cults to some current secular ideological *Weltanschauungen* (as, for example, Democracy or Communism). Still, although in the context of this paper the notion will indeed be grasped in terms of its social function (namely, we would take the notion of civil religion to signify that body of ideas, goals, customs and ceremonies which takes the place and fulfills the functions of traditional religion within the "horizontal dimension" of life), it will be important to keep in mind the various possible significations of the notion as regards its content and form, for it is precisely these significations that will prove most pertinent to our analysis below.

Furthermore, we may observe that although, according to our delineation here, the notion of the separation of state and church and that of the rise of civil religion are clearly separate and distinct notions, they are nonetheless, precisely in terms of this delineation, notions which are intimately interlinked. For the rise of civil religion necessarily presupposes the separation of state and church, seeing that in order for a civil religion to arise, a religious "vacuum" must be present in the "horizontal dimension" (otherwise, the traditional religion, being present and operative with the "horizontal dimension," will itself function as the civil religion, thus pre-empting the need or the possibility for what was delineated above as civil religion to arise) and the presence of such a religious "vacuum" can, in turn, be effected only through the separation of state and church. Thus, outside the context of the separation of state and church the rise of a civil religion would not be possible.

The link between the two notions, however, is even more intimate. For not only does the rise of civil religion necessarily presuppose the separation of state and church but the *kind of civil* religion that is likely to arise will depend, we would submit, on the *degree* of separation taking place between state and church; namely, it will depend on the extent to which the traditional religion is excluded from the "horizontal dimension," on whether the "wall of separation" alternative or the "line of division" alternative prevails (and in the case of the latter on where the line is actually drawn). Thus, we would suggest that the less radical the exclusion of the traditional religion from the "horizontal dimension" is, the more likely it is that the civil religion, which may nonetheless arise in these circumstances, will fashion itself according to the traditional religion and become a watered-down version of it. On the other hand, the more radical the exclusion is, the more likely it is that the civil religion arising in these circumstances will turn to the secular and profane dimensions of the national ethos in terms of which to fashion itself.

Because of this linkage between the two notions any analysis of one of these notions would necessarily implicate the other notion also. For, as we have seen, civil religion is, in an important sense, a consequence of the separation of state and church and is, indeed, determined by it. Thus, one cannot really deal with the notion of the separation of state and church without weighing its consequences, i.e., dealing with the notion of civil religion without implicating that which brings it about, i.e., without dealing with the notion of the separation of state and church. Indeed, the analysis of one of the notions should clearly indicate the thrust of the analysis regarding the other notion.

Finally, we should take note of the fact that the analysis we are about to undertake is predicated on the issues before us arising in the context of a homogenous rather than a pluralistic nation. As such, we must indeed grant that the results of our analysis cannot be applied without considerable further modifications to the situation prevailing when the context implicates a pluralistic nation. For evidently, the inner logic which would operate in the context of a pluralistic nation would be quite different from the inner logic operating in the context of a homogenous nation, i.e., from the inner logic pursued in this paper.

This being the case, many will, no doubt, object that our analysis has no relevancy to the situation prevailing in the United States. For many would claim that in this situation one must inevitably deal with a nation which by its very makeup is pluralistic. Of course, if this claim is valid then the point of our analysis would be greatly diminished. For there is no denying that the issues before us, i.e., the issues of the separation of state and church and of civil religion, arise most poignantly in the context of the United States.

We must confess, however, that we are not really persuaded of the validity of the claim that the American nation is by its very makeup pluralistic. True, at the present moment (and, no doubt, for yet a number of years to come) one does, indeed, encounter on the American scene a pluralistic society. After all, the American nation is still a nation in the making, a nation of immigrants, and as such it is inescapably pluralistic. But this is not to say that the American nation is by its very makeup and thus permanently constituted as a pluralistic nation. It would be a bad mistake, in our judgment, to take the present situation as reflecting a permanent state of affairs. The present situation is transitional; it is but a stage in the process of the formation of a new ethnic-national entity. When this process, however, finally crystallizes itself into a completed, finished product, i.e., into a formed, established ethnic-national entity, the American nation, we would submit, like all other ethnic-national entities would not be pluralistic. The analysis we are about to undertake here should, therefore, remain relevant also for the situation in the United States, even though it deals with a homogenous rather than a pluralistic nation. For clearly as regards the projected final state of affairs it should remain relevant and indeed, explicitly so. But even as regards the present, transitory state of affairs it should remain relevant though it is implicitly rather than explicitly so. For, in the last analysis, it is only in the light of the final state of affairs that an enlightened and valid policy can be formulated for the transitory stage.

In any event, if one wishes to examine – as, indeed, we do – the problem presented by the issues before us at its deepest and most challenging level, i.e., in terms of its theological implications, one must examine it in the context of a homogenous nation. For in the context of a pluralistic nation the theological implications are inevitably suppressed and obscured by purely pragmatic considerations. Indeed, in the light of these pragmatic considerations operating in the context of a pluralistic nation the case for the separation of state and church and for civil religion is practically made before one starts. Still, from the perspective of religion the issues do present serious theological problems, and this can be seen precisely when examining the issues in the context of a homogenous nation.

I

With these few introductory observations we can now proceed to the substance of our undertaking. Now, there can be little hesitation in stating that the preponderant majority of Jewry today (specifically of American Jewry) are among the staunchest and most dedicated supporters of the principle that state and church should be kept completely separated.[2] Indeed, one can almost say that to oppose this principle or even merely to raise questions or qualifications with respect to its validity would be deemed in many a Jewish quarter as tantamount to being un-Jewish (let alone being un-American) – to committing an act of outright betrayal of the position of Judaism or, at the very least, an act grievously detrimental to its interests.[3] And as regards the issue of civil religion, it may not be too grossly inaccurate to surmise that a considerable number of Jews would prefer not to have it emerge at all and that, certainly, a preponderant majority of Jewry would prefer that it reflect as little as possible of the particularity and specificity of the traditional religion of the host-nation – the less the traditional religion injects its specific doctrinal and symbolic paraphernalia into the civil religion the more accepting will the attitude of Jewry be.

That a preponderant majority of Jewry should take this position is actually quite understandable. It is understandable in the light of what the Jewish experience has been in the past two millenia of diaspora-existence when state and church were intimately united. Thus, given the persecution and discrimination that Jews have suffered during this period at the hands of the religion of the host-nation, when that religion (be it Christianity or Islam) did impinge on the "horizontal dimension" of life and had the power of the state at its disposal, it is readily understandable that Jews would wish almost instinctively and as a gut reaction to separate the religion of the host-nation from the "horizontal dimension" and from the power of the state. Given the heavy price in suffering that Jews had to pay in these circumstances, it is only natural that they would instinctively feel more secure when state and church are separated; indeed, their long history of suffering at the hands of host-religions has psychologically conditioned the Jews to favor the separation of state and church. But it is not just a matter of psychological conditioning; the position of the Jew in favor of separating state and church has also sound logic on its side. Namely, being realistic, i.e., realizing that we live in premessianic times and in a not-yet-redeemed world, one should not expect the disappearance of all rivalry and denigration among competing religions; the existence of friction – sometimes more, sometimes less, but always some friction – between different institutionalized religions is inescapable. This being the case, however, it is clear that by removing the host-religion from the "horizontal dimension" and depriving it of the power which is at the disposal of the state one can at least minimize the threat that this friction would express itself in concrete physical action.[4] Thus, given the conditions of diaspora-existence, it is historically, psychologically and logically understandable that the Jew would favor the separation of state and church.

But aside from these pervasive though somewhat diffused considerations, there is yet another consideration much more immediate and specific which must be taken into account if the rationale for the preponderant support by Jewry for the separation of state and church is to be fully grasped. This consideration is derived from the dynamics operating in the process of the Emancipation, a process which has radically transformed the conditions of Jewish existence in modern times.

Thus, the Emancipation, by essentially signifying the entry of the Jew into the life-stream of the host-nation, necessarily implicates the assimilation of the Jew into the host-nation – the more emancipated the Jew desired to be, the more assimilated he had to become. Indeed, the early protagonists of the Emancipation (who, interestingly enough, came from the host-nation) made the point only too clear.[5] Emancipation was offered to the Jew only *qua* human being, as a member of the human species, but not to the Jew *qua* Jew, as a member of a religious-national community. The Jew was to be allowed to enter and share in the life of the host-nation only on the clear condition that he leave his Jewishness behind – to the Jew as man everything, to the Jew as Jew nothing.[6] Thus, the Jew was to be emancipated only at the price of being "neutralized" of his Jewishness and fully assimilated into the ethos of the host-nation.[7]

But this requirement for full assimilation would clearly necessitate, in the last analysis, the embrace of the religion of the host-nation. For, without embracing also the religion of the host-nation, assimilation would not be complete. Namely, the Jew could fully assimilate himself as regards the language, the culture, the mannerisms, the customs and the professions of the host-nation and yet, inasmuch as he has not also embraced the religion of the host-nation, his assimilation would not be complete. An element, and indeed an important element, remains in the life-stream of the host-nation into which the emancipated Jew is not integrated and this element, i.e., the religion of the host-nation, would inevitably mark the emancipated Jew as still an outsider. Thus, it is quite understandable that many an emancipated Jew would come to see in the religion of the host-nation a barrier to his full emancipation.[8]

Given the fervent desire and need of the modern Jew to be fully emancipated, there are really only two alternatives by which the barrier presented by the religion of the host-nation can be removed. On the one hand, the emancipated Jew can pursue his assimilation all the way and embrace the religion of the host-nation and, indeed, many an emancipated Jew did take this path (clearly converting for the sake of convenience rather than out of conviction) in the belief that this would now allow him full admission into the life-stream of the host-nation. As Heine said, "The baptismal certificate is the ticket of admission to European culture."[9] But at the same time there are also many emancipated Jews who, while desiring and needing full emancipation just as much, cannot and will not take up the alternative of conversion. After all, there can be no denying what such an act signifies – a most fundamental betrayal of one's deepest identity, a most radical severance of the ties to one's past and immediate environment. These emancipated Jews (and for all intents and purposes they only constitute emancipated Jewry, seeing that the other emancipated Jews have opted out of Judaism in the act of conversion, even though *halachically* they may still be considered Jews) grasp the second alternative, namely, the exclusion of the host-religion from the public life-stream of the host-nation. For in such exclusion the barrier constituted by the host-religion is clearly removed. Indeed, the public life-stream of the host-nation would now become "neutralized" of any and all religious considerations, it would become, so to speak, a "no man's land" as far as the religious dimension is concerned. In light of our analysis here, this should suit the emancipated Jew very nicely. For now, he does not have to pay the price of conversion in order to solve the problem of his full integration; rather, the problem is solved by removing the religious barrier. Rather than him having to adapt to the situation, the situation is adapted to his needs, seeing that the public life-stream where his integration is to take place is cleared of the problem connected with the religious dimension.[10]

Now, this rationale – which accounts for the stance taken by the emancipated Jew in favor of the separation of state and church – will also account for the stance depicted above which he takes with regard to civil religion. For inasmuch as religion in general is viewed as a divisive and excluding factor, and seeing that the very aspiration of the emancipated Jew is to overcome exclusion, it is understandable that the emancipated Jew would prefer to have all religion eliminated from the public life-stream of the host-nation; in other words, it is understandable that optimally the emancipated Jew would prefer to have no civil religion operating in the public life-stream, regardless of what form or content it may have. Still, inasmuch as it is specifically the religion of the host-nation which differentiates him and precludes his full entry into the life-stream of the host-nation, it is understandable that, in the event where the rise of a civil religion is inevitable, the emancipated Jew would prefer that it incorporate as little as possible of the host-religion. For the more removed the civil religion is from the religion of the host-nation the more equalized is the position of the emancipated Jew to that of the host-nation with respect to the religious factor, and consequently the more "neutralized" does the obstructive aspect of the religious factor become. Of course, if the civil religion under these circumstances were in addition to incorporate some elements of the emancipated Jew's own religious heritage, and the more the better, it would be even more congenial to him. But basically, the less the civil religion incorporates historical and doctrinal concreteness and specificity or, in other words, the more abstract and universal it is, the more it becomes the religion of man in general, the less obstructive it is to the entry of the emancipated Jew into the life-stream of the host-nation and consequently the more congenial it becomes for the emancipated Jew to support it. Thus, the rationale for the position of the emancipated Jew vis-à-vis the issue of civil religion as, indeed, vis-à-vis the issue of the separation of state and church is to be understood on the basis of his perception of religion generally (and more specifically, of the religion of the host-nation) as divisive and exclusive, thus serving as a barrier to his full entry into the life-stream of the host-nation.

II

This position, however, of the emancipated Jew as regards the issues of the separation of state and church and of civil religion cannot be automatically taken as representing also the position of Judaism with regard to these issues. Certainly, the rationale operating in the case of Judaism would be different from the rationale operating in the case of emancipated Jewry, i.e., from the rationale depicted above. For while the latter was determined by the desires and interests of the emancipated Jew the former would have to be determined by the requirements and dictates of the structure of faith of Judaism. And it is by no means the case that the interests and desires of the emancipated Jew or, for that matter, of the Jew generally do always coincide with the requirements and dictates of the structure of faith of Judaism. It may be ironic but it is nonetheless the fact that the two often clash – what is good for the Jews is not necessarily always good for Judaism and, conversely, what is good for Judaism is not necessarily always good for the Jews. But if the rationale operating with respect to Judaism is different from the rationale operating with respect to the emancipated Jew then it is quite possible that the position of Judaism with regard to the issues before us would be quite different from the position of the emancipated Jew. We certainly cannot take for granted that the two positions would necessarily be identical,

Indeed, if we examine the structure of faith of Judaism we will see that its inner logic dictates a position towards the issues of the separation of state and church and of civil religion that is diametrically opposed to the position taken by the emancipated Jew. Space does not allow us to present in detail the argument for this claim but the crux of the matter lies in the fact that the structure of faith of mainstream Judaism is such that it requires as a condition *sine qua non* the availability to itself of the social, economic and, ideally, also the political domains of life; namely, it requires what we have called the "horizontal dimension" of life.[11] This is so by virtue of the fact that it is through the full gamut of the relations between man and man – the social, economic and political – that mainstream Judaism responds and witnesses to the divine. The axis of the human-divine relation (the most essential aspect of any structure of faith) is essentially established here through the "horizontal dimension," thus constituting the "horizontal dimension" as the inescapable matrix through which mainstream Judaism must express itself. It clearly excludes the alternative of relegating mainstream Judaism to an exclusive concern with what we may term the "vertical dimension," namely, the direct, inward relation of the individual believer to the divine, thus separating and removing the religious concern from the "horizontal dimension" of life. In mainstream Judaism the religious concern, the relation to the divine, must be mediated through the "horizontal dimension" of life and it is, therefore, no exaggeration to say that without the availability to itself of the "horizontal dimension" mainstream Judaism could not function and would disintegrate.

But if this be the case, then the inner logic of the structure of faith of mainstream Judaism should dictate opposition to the separation of state and church when it signifies the exclusion of religion from the "horizontal dimension" – dictating a more strenuous opposition to the "wall of separation" alternative than to the "line of division" alternative, while within the "line of division" alternative dictating increased opposition as the line is drawn less and less in favor of religion. For clearly the separation of state and church in the context of these significations would deprive Judaism of the availability of the "horizontal dimension," the deprivation being more radical in the "wall of separation" alternative than in the "line of division" alternative while within the "line of division" alternative it becomes more radical as the line is drawn less and less in favor of religion. Seeing that the structure of faith of mainstream Judaism requires the availability of the "horizontal dimension" and must opt to preserve it as much as possible, the rationale for dictating the stance delineated here is evident. Similarly, the inner logic of the structure of faith of mainstream Judaism should dictate opposition to the rise of civil religion, though in the context where civil religion does arise, the closer it is to Judaism the more acceptable it should be. This is so inasmuch as the requirement of the structure of faith of mainstream Judaism for the "horizontal dimension" is tantamount to saying that mainstream Judaism perceives its own vocation to be precisely that of a "civil religion." It itself should fulfill the function of "civil religion" and consequently it must oppose any other formulation which would supplant it in this function.

As such, of course, the stance which the structure of faith of mainstream Judaism dictates is diametrically opposed to the stance taken by emancipated Jewry. For, as we have seen above, the stance of emancipated Jewry supports the separation of state and church – lending its strongest support to the "wall of separation" alternative rather than the "line of division" alternative, while within the "line of division" alternative its support increases as the line is drawn less and less in favor of religion; and as regards the rise of civil religion, though it may prefer, in the last analysis, its exclusion (thus seemingly agreeing in this instance with the stance dictated by the structure of faith of mainstream Judaism),[12] in the context where it does arise, the less the civil religion reflects the traditional religion the stronger is its support for it. This diametrical opposition, however, between the stance taken by emancipated Jewry and the stance dictated by the structure of faith of mainstream Judaism should not really be surprising. Indeed, it is to be expected, seeing that while the inner logic operating in terms of the interests of the emancipated Jew is determined by the desire to *exclude* religion from the "horizontal dimension," the inner logic operating in terms of the structure of faith of mainstream Judaism is determined by the need to *include* religion within the "horizontal dimension."[13]

There is, however, one instance where the interests of emancipated Jewry and the requirements of the structure of faith of mainstream Judaism do converge and dictate the same stance, namely, when the separation of state and church carries its minimal signification, i.e., when it merely signifies the disestablishment of religion and not its exclusion from the "horizontal dimension." For both emancipated Jewry and the structure of faith of mainstream Judaism should favor disestablishment, though the rationale operating in the two cases is quite different and, indeed, as we have seen, so is the religion involved – for emancipated Jewry it is the religion of the other, the religion of the host-nation, while for the structure of faith of Judaism it is its own religion, the religion of Judaism. The rationale for the stance taken by emancipated Jewry has already been elucidated above. The task before us now is to attempt to elucidate the rationale for the stance dictated by the structure of faith of mainstream Judaism.

To begin with, one may first note that there is no rationale flowing from the structure of faith of mainstream Judaism which requires the establishment of religion. For, we as have maintained, the fundamental criterion, the criterion which determines all else in the rationale flowing from the structure of faith of mainstream Judaism and impinging upon the question of the separation of state and church, is constituted by the requirement that the "horizontal dimension" be available to religion, i.e., to Judaism. But this requirement in no way implicates the further requirement that religion, i.e., Judaism, be established. Thus, the all-determining criterion remains neutral to the question of establishment – it does not dictate support for the establishment of religion though it also does not dictate opposition to it. As such, of course, the absence of support for establishment or, to put the matter conversely, the absence of opposition to disestablishment may be taken as tacit support for disestablishment.

But the rationale can be established, it seems to us, more directly and explicitly. It can be established on the ground that the structure of faith of mainstream Judaism belongs to the "prophetic" rather than to the "priestly" type of faith.[14] For as such, we do, indeed, have a direct and explicit rationale seeing that the "prophetic" type does clearly implicate opposition to the establishment of religion. It implicates this opposition because in its perspective the vocation of religion is to be the conscience and critic of society and the state and such a vocation cannot be carried out in the context of establishment. One cannot very well discharge the duties of conscience and critic when one is at the same time supported and maintained by that which is to be criticized – one is not very likely to bite the hand that feeds one. Religion cannot be a function of the state, one of its various departments, and at the same time properly fulfill its task of sitting in judgment over the state. The offices of king and priest may be combined but not the offices of king and prophet. The "prophetic" type has, therefore, a direct and explicit rationale for opposing the establishment of religion and inasmuch as the structure of faith of mainstream Judaism does belong to the "prophetic" type it likewise is led to oppose the establishment of religion by this same direct and explicit rationale.

We should be clear, however, that the whole analysis thus far necessarily implicates a Judaism that operates, so to speak, in its own "home," in its own "backyard," in a situation where its adherents, i.e., the Jewish community, have sovereignty over the "horizontal dimension"; in short, it necessarily implicates the placement of Judaism in the context of a Jewish state. For the analysis here has been based on the claim that the structure of faith of Judaism requires the availability to itself of the "horizontal dimension" and this presupposes a situation in which Judaism can rightfully claim the "horizontal dimension" for itself, i.e., can rightfully appropriate and impinge upon it, a situation which, in turn, can be secured only in the context of sovereignty, i.e., only in the context of Jewish statehood. Thus, strictly speaking, the conclusions of our analysis thus far apply only in the case when Judaism is situated in its own "home," when it is the dominant religion of the community that wields sovereignty over the "horizontal dimension."[15]

But this, of course, is tantamount to saying that the conclusions derived from the analysis thus far have no applicability in the context of diaspora. For clearly in the context of diaspora, Judaism is not situated in its own "home." The only possible implication which the analysis thus far may carry for the diaspora situation (and it is an ancillary consideration at that) is to intimate that it would ill-behoove Judaism to criticize other religions (for example Christianity) for opposing the separation of state and church in the context of their own respective "homes," seeing that it itself when situated in the context of its own "home" pursues the same opposition. If Judaism, as we have argued, must demand the right to impinge in its own "home" upon the "horizontal dimension," it must grant to other religions the right to do the same in their respective "homes" – what is good for the goose is good for the gander.

But not only the conclusions but the very form and substance of the analysis pursued thus far are not to the point as far as the context of diaspora is concerned. For as far as the context of diaspora is concerned the analysis thus far has based itself on the wrong criterion and consequently it has raised the wrong question. Namely, it has based itself on the criterion that the "horizontal dimension" must be available to Judaism and, therefore, its main question centered on how the separation of state and church would impinge on that availability. But in the context of diaspora this criterion and this question are completely beside the point, seeing that Judaism has no rightful claim on the "horizontal dimension" to begin with; it does not make sense to raise the question of whether something is or is not available when that something is in principle absent altogether.

In the context of diaspora, the criterion that is to be applied must be formulated in terms of the viability and survival of Judaism. For in diaspora, Judaism is per force passive – the recipient of the action of others. It is, therefore, not so much the question of what Judaism does and requires as the question of what others (i.e., the host-nations) do and how it affects Judaism that is relevant here; and this is ultimately judged by how it affects the prospects for the viability and survival of Judaism. Thus, specifically with respect to the separation of state and church and to the rise of civil religion, these issues when taking place in diaspora clearly do not involve Judaism but the host religion – it is the host-religion and not Judaism which is to be separated from the state and whose place and function is to be supplanted by the rise of a civil religion. But although these issues do not directly involve Judaism they certainly may affect Judaism as regards its prospects for viability and survival. To determine, therefore, the stance that Judaism in the context of diaspora should take towards these issues we must examine them with a view as to how they impinge upon the prospects of the viability and survival of Judaism in diaspora.

III

In light of this new criterion which is applicable to the context of diaspora it is not too difficult to see that the separation of state and church in all its three significations actually holds a certain advantage for Judaism when placed in diaspora. For in all three significations the act of separation clearly reduces the power and influence of the host-religion (and the more maximal the significations of the separation, the more substantial is the reduction in the power and influence of the host-religion). Given the threat which a host-religion inescapably presents for Judaism when placed in diaspora, such reduction in the power and influence of the host-religion should clearly work to the advantage of Judaism.

Similarly, one can see that the rise of civil religion may well hold a possible advantage for Judaism inasmuch as civil religion is likely to be more neutral and less threatening towards a minority religion than a host-religion which is a traditional religion. A civil religion is likely to transcend the factors that lead to mutual rejection, friction and intolerance between traditional religions. For the intolerance and mutual rejection between traditional religions are due primarily to the doctrinal and historical differences between them. But it is precisely these differences which a civil religion is likely to neutralize or, at least, reduce when (as the case may often be) it is a watered-down version of a traditional religion or, to put the matter differently, when it is a religion grounded in some pervasive humanitarian-ethical precepts or in some aspects of universal human reason and experience. Certainly, a civil religion will not be a religion grounded in doctrinal confessions or symbolic expressions that are determined by revelation or by history and this, after all, is the crux of the matter. Thus, to a considerable extent the rise of civil religion cleans the slate, so to speak, and introduces a new context in which, on the surface at least, Judaism is accorded a more equal footing with the traditional religion of the host-nation and this can certainly be viewed as presenting a more congenial and advantageous situation for Judaism.

It would seem, therefore, that both the separation of state and church and the rise of civil religion are advantageous for Judaism when it is placed in diaspora. A closer and more careful examination would show, however, that they are not purely advantageous, that coupled with the advantages they also present possible disadvantages; that indeed, these possible disadvantages are implicated in every one of the various formulations in which the notions of the separation of state and church and of civil religion express themselves.

Thus, one can argue that the disestablishment of religion presents not only the advantage of reducing the power and influence of the host-religion but also the possible disadvantage that, in all likelihood, Judaism too will be deprived of a measure of recognition and support from the state. For it is a curious fact that by and large the establishment of the host-religion tends to involve the state with the other nonestablished religions in its domain; indeed, when the religious climate is not too intolerant, the tendency is for the state to bestow some measure of formal recognition and support on these nonestablished religions. Now, from a practical vantage point, such recognition and support, though it be minimal and, in a way, given in a lefthanded manner, can nonetheless be very beneficial and helpful to a minority religion such as Judaism. In the adverse conditions of diaspora-existence, where none or, at best, very few of the necessary external props in support of the institution of religion are available, any support or recognition from the state can only be helpful. Such support, however, would be clearly lost in the context of disestablishment.[16]

Likewise, one can argue that in the "wall of separation" formulation where the advantage accrued to Judaism from the elimination of the power and influence of the host-religion is most pronounced, a possible disadvantageous and, indeed, a most seriously disadvantageous situation for Judaism is also present. For granted that the total exclusion of the host-religion from the "horizontal dimension" is to be viewed as a substantial advantage to Judaism, one cannot leave the matter at that – one must inquire as to what would come to take the place of the host-religion in characterizing the "horizontal dimension." It is here that a serious disadvantage for Judaism may arise, seeing that in these circumstances what, in all probability, would take the place of the host-religion would be a thorough-going secularism or, alternatively, in a context where a civil religion has arisen, a civil religion which is some form of neo-paganism, and that these alternatives are potentially much more detrimental to the viability and survival of Judaism than the traditional religion of the host-nation is likely to be, particularly when the latter (as is likely to be the case) is a sister biblical faith (e.g., Christianity). For surely, a thorough-going secularism is more inimical to Judaism than any religion may be (no matter how hostile towards Judaism it may be), while in the whole spectrum of religions no religious formulation is farther removed from Judaism than paganism.[17] Paganism represents the fundamental alternative to biblical faith and consequently it is, in the last analysis, the real antagonist to Judaism, an antagonist which can become most virulent.[18] Thus, commensurate to the pronounced advantage which the "wall of separation" formulation presents to Judaism, the disadvantage which it may also entail is equally of utmost seriousness. Indeed, in the last analysis, the disadvantage may well outweigh the advantage and Judaism may well be placed here in the position of having jumped from the frying pan into the fire.

Finally, one can argue that even in the "line of division" formulation where *on balance*, i.e., when taking both the favorable and unfavorable factors into account, the situation for Judaism is probably most advantageous (seeing that it reduces the power of the host-religion yet avoids thorough-going secularism or, in the context of civil religion, that it fosters watered-down, "neutralized" versions of the traditional religion which may even incorporate elements of Judaism rather than neo-pagan cults), a disadvantageous situation which in certain circumstances may be most threatening is nonetheless also present. For the "line of division" formulation creates a situation that is much more congenial for the assimilation of emancipated Jewry into the environment of their host-nation. This is so not only because the formulation diminishes the presence of the host-religion, but even more pertinently, because the civil religion which it is likely to substitute for the host-religion is far less of a barrier to the process of assimilation. A civil religion which is a watered-down nondescript version of the host-religion, which emphasizes universally accepted ethical principles and suppresses the particularity of history and doctrine (and especially when it may also extend its base to encompass the heritage of Judaism) is much more inviting and much more likely to be embraced by emancipated Jewry than is the traditional religion of the host-nation. For clearly, such a civil religion would mitigate many of the intellectual and psychological barriers which the traditional religion with all its doctrinal, ritualistic and symbolic baggage presents and, as such, it can only enhance the process of assimilation. Now, such assimilation may suit the interests and desires of emancipated Jewry, but it is certainly most threatening to the viability and survival of Judaism. For the viability and survival of Judaism are threatened not only by force and persecution but also, sad and ironic as it may be, by acceptance and assimilation. True, this latter alternative does not inflict the suffering of rejection nor does it threaten Judaism with the painful death of physical extermination. Indeed, if anything, it extends the generosity of embrace. Still, though it be an embrace, it is nonetheless the embrace of death. It may be a painless death but it is death nonetheless – the painless death of spiritual extinction.

Thus, the "line of division" formulation has also its disadvantageous aspect. Indeed, it is a most insidious disadvantageous aspect inasmuch as its threat is not readily apparent. It is delivered, so to speak, concealed, wrapped in a package that is most appealing to the emancipated Jew or, to change the metaphor, its bitter pill comes coated with the most enticing flavor. Furthermore, in the context of the situation which basically prevails today in the West, it represents the more imminent threat, seeing that in an enlightened and tolerant environment – and it is, after all, such an environment which basically characterizes the Western democracies today – the more imminent danger comes from the threat of assimilation rather than from the threat of persecution.

We can see again, therefore, that in this formulation, as in the other two alternative formulations, the stance of Judaism when it is placed in diaspora as regards the issues of the separation of state and church and of civil religion is, in the last analysis, equivocal – one can see advantages but also disadvantages and indeed, the more favorable the advantages, the more serious are the disadvantages.

IV

Thus, we have seen that in attempting to analyze the Jewish position regarding the issues of the separation of state and church and of civil religion, one must actually deal with three different entities – with emancipated Jewry, with Judaism taken in terms of its structure of faith (i.e., when it is placed in the context of its own "home") and with Judaism when it is placed in the context of diaspora. Furthermore, we have also seen that as regards the implication of religion in the issues before us, one is actually confronted with two basically different situations – a situation where the religion implicated is Judaism itself and a situation where it is a host-religion other than Judaism, the former situation being exemplified when one is dealing with Judaism in terms of its structure of faith while the latter situation is exemplified when one is dealing with Judaism in the context of diaspora or when one is dealing with emancipated Jewry. Lastly, and most significantly, we have seen that the Jewish position regarding the issues before us is really comprised of three distinct and different stances; namely, it is comprised of 1) an essentially positive stance when dealing with emancipated Jewry, 2) an essentially negative stance when dealing with Judaism in terms of its structure of faith and 3) an essentially equivocal stance when dealing with Judaism in the context of diaspora. Indeed, given the two former observations, this last observation constituting the very essence of our analysis here should not be surprising. For clearly the stance of Judaism or, for that matter, of emancipated Jewry would be affected by whether the religion implicated in these issues is Judaism or another religion. But even more pertinently, it is clearly and directly affected by the first observation, namely, by the fact that there are three different entities involved here. For, as we have seen, each of these entities implicates a different criterion which, in turn, of necessity determines a different stance. Thus, with respect to Judaism when viewed in terms of its structure of faith, the determining criterion is the availability of the "horizontal dimension;" with respect to Judaism when viewed in the context of diaspora it is the viability and survival of Judaism; and with respect to emancipated Jewry it is integration (i.e., assimilation) into the "horizontal dimension" belonging to the host-nation. Clearly, these criteria are not compatible and consequently it is inescapable that three different and, indeed, contradictory stances would emerge here.

One must conclude, therefore, that the Jewish position towards the issues of the separation of state and church and of civil religion is far from univocal. Certainly, it is not just simply the wholeheartedly supportive position associated here with the stance taken by emancipated Jewry. The Jewish Position, when taken in all its dimensions, is much more equivocal and on balance much less supportive.

Indeed, a good case can be made that even with respect to emancipated Jewry, its position too ought to be less supportive. For one can argue that the wholeheartedly supportive position of emancipated Jewry is due to the fact that its perception of the situation in which it is placed is lacking – it has a blind spot. Namely, as we have seen above, the wholeheartedly supportive position of emancipated Jewry for the issues before us and, indeed, for these issues in their maximal signification, flows from the fact that emancipated Jewry perceives the host-religion as the ultimate barrier to its full integration. Now, there can be no denying that the host-religion does, indeed, serve as a barrier and consequently the inner logic underlying the position of emancipated Jewry is quite valid as far as it goes. But here lies the rub – it does not go far enough. For there is another factor, we would submit, that serves as a barrier to the full integration of emancipated Jewry. This factor is the ethnic factor; namely, the Jew is set apart not only by his religion but also by his ethnicity. Indeed, the ethnic factor is a more obdurate and pernicious barrier to integration than is the religious factor. It is the ethnic rather than the religious factor, particularly in the circumstances of the modern world, which really stresses and aggravates the exclusion of the Jew. Emancipated Jewry, however, fails to take account of this factor in formulating its position towards the issues before us. It fails to see that even if the host-religion and, indeed, all religion are totally removed, it would still be excluded from full integration by the ethnic factor. Here lies the blind spot in emancipated Jewry's perception of its situation.[19]

But if the ethnic factor is brought into the picture then the position taken by emancipated Jewry, specifically its wholehearted support for the "wall of separation" formulation and its corresponding civil religion, must be reassessed. For, as we have noted above, one must ask in these circumstances as to what comes to take the place of the host-religion and the answer in connection with the "wall of separation" formulation is that it is most likely a thoroughgoing secularism or a civil religion that is some form of neo-paganism. But both secularism and neo-paganism are much more likely to bring to the fore and stress the factor of ethnic differentiation than is a host-religion that is a biblical faith. As such, in light of this consideration and our observation above regarding the pernicious nature of the ethnic factor, the "wall of separation" formulation should be really viewed as a hindrance rather than as an opening towards the integration of emancipated Jewry. By its very inner logic, determined as it is by the criterion of seeking full integration, emancipated Jewry should view, therefore, the "wall of separation" formulation as being more inimical to its interests than the presence of the host-religion.

Thus, the position of emancipated Jewry when it is based in reality and not in illusion, namely, when it takes into account the ethnic factor, is brought somewhat closer to the position of Judaism when placed in the context of diaspora. At least with regard to the "wall of separation" formulation, the position of emancipated Jewry should now be much closer to the position of Judaism when placed in the context of diaspora (and it is, after all, with respect to this formulation that the most telling difference between the two positions was previously precipitated). Of course, this is by no means to say that the difference between the two positions is removed altogether. Indeed, with regard to the other two formulations, i.e., the "line of division" formulation and the "disestablishment" formulation, the difference delineated above remains, seeing that these formulations are not really affected by considerations of the ethnic factor and consequently the position of emancipated Jewry with respect to them is not changed. That a difference between the two positions remains should not, however, be surprising. For, in the last analysis, there is no escape from the fact that the criterion determining the position of emancipated Jewry, i.e., the criterion of full integration into the "horizontal dimension" of the host-nation, and the criterion determining the position of Judaism when placed in the context of diaspora, i.e., the criterion of the viability and survival of Judaism, are in conflict. Integration into a "horizontal dimension" that is not Jewish necessarily signifies a weakening of the viability and a threat to the survival of Judaism. Indeed, this is in a nutshell the fundamental problem which the Emancipation precipitates for Judaism. Fortunately for us, however, the analysis of this problem goes beyond the parameters of our topic in this paper and we need not pursue it here.

---

[1] These distinctions and indeed the characterizations of "wall of separation" and "line of division" are derived from John F. Wilson's perceptive and judicious book *Public Religion in American Culture,* Temple University Press, 1979.

[2] Since, as we have noted, it is mainly in the United States that the issues of the separation of state and church and of civil religion arise most poignantly, it is inevitable that an analysis of the stance taken by Jewry vis-à-vis these issues should draw its data primarily from the position taken by American Jewry. But as will become clear in the course of our analysis below, with regard to these issues American Jewry really depicts the position of a predominant segment of diaspora Jewry worldwide and consequently one can legitimately talk of the position of Jewry in modern times without any further qualifications.

[3] There are, however, indications that of late this position has been undergoing re-examination in some quarters of the community. In part, this may be due to purely utilitarian-pragmatic

considerations brought about by new institutional vested interests (e.g., the desire to receive governmental support for religious day-schools). But also, and much more laudably, it may be due to a growing appreciation of the role of religion in the social-political domain, on the one hand, and of the threat of Judaism that secularism may present, on the other. Indeed, this paper may be seen as reflective of this trend of thought.

[4]Of course, this is not to say that the religion of the host-nation is necessarily deprived in this context of all special power and is thus placed on an equal footing with the other religions that may be present. On the contrary, it may still retain considerable pervasive power by virtue of the fact that it is the religion of the majority. But, at least, when separated from the state, it is deprived of overt and direct power.

[5]See, for example, the position taken by Count Clermont-Tonnere, Robespierre, Count Mirabeau, Dohm, Herder.

[6]Or as Count Clermont-Tonnere put it, "The Jews should be denied everything as a nation, but granted everything as individuals," quoted in *The Jew in the World,* edited by P. Mendes-Flohr and J. Reinharz, Oxford University Press, 1980, p. 104.

[7]For a fuller analysis of the problem that the Emancipation presents to the Jew and to Judaism see my article "The Dilemma of Identity for the Emancipated Jew" reprinted in *New Theology* No. 4, edited by Martin E. Marty and Dean G. Peerman, Macmillan Co., N.Y., 1967.

[8]Indeed, this was clearly seen very early in the process of the Emancipation. See, for example, the open letter sent by David Friedlaender to the Protestant minister W. A. Teller quoted in *ibid.,* pp. 95-99.

[9]As quoted in *ibid.,* p. 223.

[10]The religious dimension can, of course, continue to operate in this context as long as it is confined to being a private and inward affair of the individual. But as such, this means that the religious dimension may still function as a divisive factor, albeit not formally as a stated public policy which continues to impose disabilities upon the emancipation of the Jew. Indeed, in view of this it is understandable that many emancipated Jews are drawn to a more sweeping secularism, to a secularism that wishes to eradicate religion altogether, not only from the public domain but from the private domain as well. They come to hate religion generally with a vengeance, seeing it as a pernicious, divisive factor that can only lead to discrimination and discord among men. Still, interestingly enough, this general hatred is focused in particular against their own religion, i.e., against Judaism; for after all, Judaism does not only share, *qua* religion, in the guilt of religion generally for introducing discrimination and hatred, but, given the circumstances of Jewish existence, i.e., the circumstances of diaspora-existence, it is responsible for making them the *victims* (rather than the perpetrators) of such discrimination and hatred; namely, it is responsible for making them pay the price, i.e., bear the suffering of such discrimination and hatred.

[11]This point has been made by a number of people. For an excellent analysis of the link between the need of Judaism for the "horizontal dimension" and the problem precipitated by the Emancipation see Max Wiener, *Judische Religion in Zeitalter der Emancipation.*

[12]But this opposition to the rise of civil religion manifested in some circles of emancipated Jewry is not to be equated with the opposition dictated by the structure of faith of mainstream Judaism. The similarity is only on the surface – both oppose the rise of civil religion. The respective reasons, however, which lead to this stance are diametrically opposed. The opposition of the emancipated Jew is because he does not want to have any religion, not even a civil religion, in the "horizontal dimension." The opposition of the structure of faith of mainstream Judaism, on the other hand, is because it requires the presence of Judaism in the "horizontal dimension" and cannot accept, therefore, its being supplanted by a civil religion. Thus, beneath the superficial similarity the fundamental opposition between the stance of emancipated Jewry and the stance of the structure of faith of mainstream Judaism is just as acute also here.

[13]We should note, however, that the religion referred to in connection with the structure of faith of mainstream Judaism is specifically and exclusively Judaism while the religion referred

to in connection with emancipated Jewry is the religion of the host-nation or religion in general. As such, our comparison between the stance taken by emancipated Jewry and the stance dictated by the structure of faith of mainstream Judaism is not quite legitimate, seeing that the two stances do not refer to the same entity but to different entities. Indeed, our analysis below will be adjusted so as to take care of this discrepancy.

[14]Evidently, we cannot go here into a detailed justification of this claim. It may suffice, however, if we point rather briefly and somewhat dogmatically to the fact that an essential distinguishing mark of the "prophetic" type, in contra-distinction to the "priestly" type, is its requirement for religion to be involved in the "horizontal dimension." But if this be the case, then the structure of faith of main-stream Judaism clearly belongs to the "prophetic" type, seeing that it requires, by its very essence, the involvement of religion in the "horizontal dimension."

[15]Indeed, in the re-established state of Israel where Judaism is in its "home" there is no separation of church and state or civil religion. Furthermore, the right and propriety of Judaism's involvement in the "horizontal dimension" is accepted by Jewry almost universally. For there is no denying that the vast majority of Jewry desires and, indeed, considers it essential and right that the state be specifically a Jewish state and not only a state where Jews live. This clearly means, however, that Judaism's impingement on the "horizontal dimension" must be accepted and validated, for without such impingement the state cannot really be a Jewish state. Thus, when Judaism is the dominant religion, as is the case in the state of Israel, there is really no opposition to having religion involved in the "horizontal dimension."

True, there is among Jews a lot of unhappiness with and opposition to the religious situation prevailing in the state of Israel. But this, we would submit, is due specifically to the fact that Judaism here utilizes the power of the state to impose itself on the community, that it is constituted as the established religion. Furthermore, for some, though by no means all, there is the further consideration which has nothing to do with the *status* of religion, i.e., Judaism, but which rather impinges on the *kind* of Judaism involved. Namely, we would suggest that the unhappiness and opposition is also due, at least in part, to the fact that the Judaism established here is a Judaism in its expression of Orthodoxy and that it is, therefore, not even the aspect of establishment but specifically the aspect of Orthodoxy which presents the real problem. Indeed, a case can be made that while Orthodoxy was a most suitable expression for diaspora-existence, it is not a suitable expression for existing in a re-established state and that consequently its imposition in the context of the re-established state is bound to cause conflict and opposition. But be this as it may, these considerations, i.e., the consideration that Judaism is constituted as an established religion and that its expression is Orthodoxy, in no way countermand the claims of our analysis above (if anything, the opposition to establishment actually conforms with the analysis above). What would have presented a serious problem is an opposition to Judaism's impingement upon the "horizontal dimension" but this, we would submit, is by and large not the case.

[16]It would be interesting to compare in this connection how Judaism fares, both in the short and in the long run, in such countries as, for example, Great Britain and the United States.

[17]By the way, secularism and paganism are not all that different. At bottom, they are actually quite similar – they are really two sides of the same coin in the sense that ultimately both establish their universe on blind power as its ultimate principle. One may perhaps say that paganism is the imaginative-mythical expression while secularism is the rational-scientific expression. But both are expressions of what ultimately is the same *Weltanschauung*, i.e., a *Weltanschauung* in which blind power is the ultimate principle. Thus, it should not be surprising that secularism and neo-paganism go hand in hand together here as the two alternative substitutes. There is a consistent inner logic which dictates this.

[18]Indeed, a good case can be made that the specially virulent anti-Judaism strain within Christianity is due to its paganization, namely, that it expresses itself essentially in Hellenistically-grounded Christianity rather than in Hebraically-grounded Christianity. As such, here too one really encounters, in the last analysis, paganism.

[19]That the emancipated Jew is inclined to overlook the factor of ethnic differentiation is actually quite understandable. For the factor of ethnic differentiation, in contrast to the factor of religious differentiation, is a "given" that neither he nor anyone else can do anything about. It is, indeed, ultimate in the sense that it cannot be removed – it is inextricable. As such, however, it is understandable that the emancipated Jew in his desire for full integration would be inclined to ignore or even deny the reality of this factor. One is inclined to ignore or deny uncomfortable realities. Still, this does not change the fact that the factor of ethnic differentiation exists. The emancipated Jew lives, therefore, in an illusory world when he believes and acts on the supposition that it is only the religious factor which differentiates him from his host-nation and that if the religious factor were to be removed, the road to full integration would become wide open.

Chapter Thirteen

The Social Dimension of the Structure of Faith of Judaism in its Phenomenological and Historical Aspects

The purpose of this paper is to examine the stance that Judaism takes with respect to the political dimension in life. We should note, therefore, at the very start that we are concerned here with the stance that *Judaism* takes rather than with the stance that *Jews* may or may not take towards the political dimension. It is important to note this as it is by no means the case that the stance which Jews may take is always and necessarily the same as the stance which Judaism may dictate. The needs and requirements of the former are by no means always and necessarily identical with those of the latter. Indeed, the whole history of Judaism and of the Jewish people (and it is rather a long history) bears witness to the continuous tension between the two. What Jews *qua* human beings wish and require is not necessarily what Judaism wishes and requires for them. Conversely, therefore, it also follows that what is good for the Jews is not necessarily good for Judaism, and, vice versa, what is good for Judaism is not necessarily good for the Jews. As stated, this ironic discrepancy characterizes the situation throughout Jewish history but it certainly comes to the fore and is most pronounced in the modern era in the context of the Emancipation. There can be no denying that in this context the interests and needs of the emancipated Jew often collide head-on with the interests and needs of Judaism. Thus, what we may claim on behalf of Judaism may not at all be what the emancipated Jew would want to claim as his position. But be this as it may, our concern is with the position of Judaism and not with the position of Jewry, specifically, emancipated Jewry. Namely, we are not concerned with the historical, sociological or psychological analysis of the attitude taken by a certain collectivity of people but rather with the philosophical analysis of a certain *Weltanschauung*, i.e., a certain view of the world and man's place and vocation in it, which we call Judaism; or rather, as we would be inclined to say, we are concerned with a philosophical analysis of the structure of faith which constitutes Judaism.

We must realize, however, that Judaism in its historical manifestation as, indeed, all other historical religions, encompasses a number of structures of faith. It is not monolithic; rather, it is a mixture of different structures of faith held together by shared symbols, rituals and institutions. Thus, we should specify that our intention is to deal exclusively with these structures of faith that can be encountered in the prophetic strand of the Bible and in the nonmystical halachic strand of Rabbinic Judaism and that we do not propose to deal here with those structures of faith which may manifest themselves, for example, in the priestly strand or the wisdom strand of the Bible or in the mystical or hasidic strand of Rabbinic Judaism. Had we dealt with these latter strands the picture that would have emerged regarding our topic would have been quite different. Our choice to deal with the former strands, i.e., the prophetic and nonmystical halachic strands, is not, however, completely arbitrary. For we would want to argue that these strands represent the mainstream expression in the historical manifestation of Judaism and, what is even more significant, that they represent the *distinctive* expression of Judaism. (Indeed, no less significantly, though on a different level, a case can be made that it is by virtue of the structures of faith encountered in these strands that Judaism could survive through millennia of years of diaspora-existence.) But whether or not one accepts the validity of these justifications, it is important that we are clear about the parameters of our investigation, namely that when we refer to Judaism in this paper we have in mind the prophetic and nonmystical halachic strands of Judaism.

Lastly, in the way of clarification, we should specify that the notion of "political dimension" involved in our discussion here is used in its broadest sense, namely, as the dimension which encompasses not only the political (now, in the narrower sense) relations but also the social and economic relations; in short, the notion is used here to signify what we may call the "horizontal dimension" of life in its totality.

Thus, the task before us in this paper is to examine in what way (and if at all) the structure of faith of Judaism (specifically, of the prophetic and halachic strands) implicates involvement in the horizontal dimension of life. Namely, is involvement in the horizontal dimension of life a necessary, essential and inextricable aspect of the religious life or is it of no real consequence? And if the former, in what sense does it constitute the religious vocation for Judaism?

We can answer this central question in a very straightforward and unqualified way: our thesis is that the structure of faith of Judaism necessarily implicates, as an essential and inextricable act, its involvement within the horizontal dimension of life in all its aspects, i.e., the social, economic and political. Take away the possibility of involvement in the horizontal dimension of life and the very structure of faith of Judaism (i.e., of prophetic and non-mystical halachic Judaism) disintegrates. The task before us now, of course, is to justify and explain this claim.

To justify this claim should not, in our judgement, be too difficult. For it can hardly be denied that Biblical prophecy by its very essence is deeply involved in the horizontal dimension of life. Take away the critique of social injustice, of economic oppression, the involvement in international politics, and what is left of Biblical prophecy? And isn't the distinctive and imposing feature of the *halacha* the fact that it encompasses an all-comprehensive civil, political and criminal law in addition to the ritual law, thus encompassing the totality of the horizontal dimension of life? The point, I think, needs no further elaboration. Indeed, biblical and rabbinic scholarship has almost universally recognized and acknowledged this point. To quote at random only a few sources: "the justice of the prophets is social justice. They demand not only a pure heart but also just institutions. They are concerned for the improvement of society even more than for the welfare of the individual ...";[1] "the Hebrews were the first who rebelled against the injustice of the world ... Israel demanded social justice";[2] "our social legislation is derived from the spirit of the prophets. Also in the future will the spirit of Israel remain the instigator and awakener of social reforms";[3] "the basis of Judaism is ethics";[4] "the idea of the inseparateness between religion and ethical life arose for the first time in Judaism ... this idea of the unity of ethics and religion passes through the whole Bible ... and this applies equally to rabbinic literature";[5] "in any reading of Judaism the ethical dimension is of supreme importance. Judaism has always taught that God wishes man to pursue justice ... to make his contribution towards the emergence of a better social order. This is a constant theme in the Bible and in the Rabbinic literature."[6] To further buttress this assertion here, therefore, is not really called for; what is called for, however, is to try and explicate why and how this is so. This is the intriguing and challenging task which we will try to pursue in the remainder of this paper.

We would submit that the key to the understanding of why the structure of faith in these strands of Judaism necessarily and essentially implicates the involvement within the horizontal dimension of life lies in the fact that the very structure of faith here formulates itself from the ethical perspective rather than from the ontological perspective. What do we mean by this? We mean that the fundamental predicament of man is not perceived here to lie in the way man is constituted but rather in the way in which he expresses and realizes himself within the possibilities and limitations of his given ontological constitution. The fact that man is constituted, to use Buberian terms, as an It-Thou being, as body and soul, as material and spiritual, as divine and earthly – as the bearer of the divine image and a being of nature, a member of the animal kingdom – is not perceived to constitute the fundamental predicament. There is nothing wrong with the way man was created; by and large, there is no pessimism or desperation about this – the judgment about creation is positive, that it was good. Rather, where the fundamental predicament, the problem, is perceived to lie is in the balance which man all to often strikes between these two dimensions in the way he expresses and realizes himself. The problem lies in the fact that man all too often realizes and expresses himself as a beast – albeit a sophisticated beast but therefore also, all too often, as a very mischievous beast – rather than as the bearer of the divine image. To use Buberian terms again, the predicament lies in the fact that man, all too often, acts and relates to others in the I-It rather than in the I-Thou context. Commensurately, therefore, the salvation that is envisioned and yearned for does not involve the ontological transformation of man, the new creation of man as a "new being," but rather the steadfastness of man in striking and maintaining the proper balance between the two dimensions constituting his being – indeed it is a redemption rather than a salvation that is envisaged.

It should be clear that as such the perceived predicament and the envisaged redemption are centered here not on the way man is constituted, on his ontological makeup, but on his actions, on his relations with others. Consequently, the perspective involved here, i.e., the perspective in terms of which the structure of faith formulates itself, is evidently an ethical perspective. For the evaluation of actions and relations, specifically of *man's* actions and relations, is precisely what constitutes the business of ethics.

But a structure of faith that formulates itself from the ethical perspective would necessarily implicate involvement in the horizontal dimension of life. For in being concerned with the proper balancing between the It and the Thou dimension in man's expression and realization of himself in his actions and relations, it must of necessity encompass the action and relations of man with respect to the world, specifically, to the human world, i.e., to the human horizontal dimension of life. The horizontal dimension of life cannot be left out of the picture as inconsequential precisely because the perceived predicament and commensurately the envisioned redemption necessarily involve here (at least in part) man's actions and relations which impinge upon the horizontal dimension of life. Thus, man's actions and relations with respect to the horizontal dimension of life become here an inextricable part in the formulation of the two basic categories of the structure of faith, i.e., of the category of the fundamental predicament and that of redemption.

But even more to our point (and this, indeed, is the very crux of the matter) the very actions and relations of man with respect to God and, conversely, God's actions and relations with respect to man must be "refracted," mediated, here through the horizontal dimension of life. For we must not overlook or forget that the It dimension in man is not to be extirpated, which is tantamount to saying that man is to remain a this-worldly being.[7] But this, in turn, means that all actions involving man, thus including the actions and relations which express the Thou dimension, must inevitably be "refracted" through the It dimension. Thus, even man's action and relation with respect to God which, in terms of God being a pure Thou being (the Eternal Thou), are to belong exclusively to the pure Thou dimension, must be "refracted" here through the It dimension, i.e., through the horizontal dimension, because of the inextricable presence of the It dimension in the constitution of man. This, of course, means that the most fundamental and central aspect of the religious life, namely, the relation between man and the divine, is required here to be mediated through the horizontal dimension. Indeed, in the prophetic and nonmystical halachic strands of Judaism the burden of the expression of the relationship of man to God, namely, the burden of the expression of faith and of worship, is not expressed in direct vertical relationships but rather in indirect relationships, i.e., in relationships which go through the horizontal dimension, specifically, the human horizontal dimension (seeing that man is the only being in nature endowed with the Thou dimension).[8] Or to make the same point, but this time not with respect to man but rather with respect to the divine, it is indeed the case that in the structure of faith of the prophetic and nonmystical halachic strands of Judaism God, who is constituted as a pure Thou and as transcending the world, is nonetheless represented as deeply and essentially involved in the relations of man to the world; again, specifically the social world of man. God, the pure Thou, the transcending God, is affected in the most real and profound sense by what man does or does not do with respect to the world, especially with respect to his fellow-man.[9] Thus, in the prophetic and in the nonmystical halachic strands of Judaism, man can fully witness to God, in the last analysis, only through the world – he can fully establish his relationship to God only through the world, he can work for redemption and redemption can be realized only through and in the world. Take away man's involvement in the horizontal dimension of life and the whole structure of faith collapses. Thus, in the strands of Judaism represented here one cannot separate the vertical from the horizontal, the sacred from the profane, relegating the religious concern, i.e., the faith, exclusively to the former. The religious concern, i.e., the faith, which, of course, must ultimately come to rest in the vertical is nonetheless inextricably intertwined within the horizontal.

But let us be clear about the precise meaning of the relationship that exists here between faith and the horizontal dimension of life. Clearly it is diametrically opposed to the model whereby faith taken as the direct vertical relating of man to the divine, is completely (one is tempted to say hermetically) separated from the horizontal dimension (a model that may be found, for example, in some formulations of German Lutheranism). But let us note what may not at first sight appear so clear, that it also differs from the model whereby faith, still constituted here as the direct vertical relating of man to the divine, is now connected with the horizontal dimension; where faith is brought to bear upon the horizontal dimension, for example, by molding and guiding it or by manifesting its fruit within it (a model that may be encountered, perhaps, in Calvinism or in Catholicism). For in Judaism the very constitution of faith is effected through the horizontal dimension. It is not that faith is constituted here independently as a direct vertical mode of relating which is then brought into relation with the horizontal dimension of life; rather, faith is constituted here as an indirect mode of relating which is refracted through the horizontal dimension of life. Without relating through the horizontal dimension of life there can be no faith. Perhaps, we can put the matter thus: the relation of faith to the horizontal dimension of life is not established in the context of sanctification; it is established in the very context of justification.

But to return to our main line of argument, there is an all-important aspect which the formulation of the structure of faith from the ethical perspective further implicates for the prophetic and nonmystical halachic strands of Judaism. Namely, in implicating the involvement of religion in the horizontal dimension, it also implicates an inextricable bond between religion and the category of the ethnic-national entity. This is to say, it establishes religion as being primarily not the affair of the individual but rather the affair of the collectivity, specifically, of the ethnic-national collectivity. Religion expresses itself primarily in the context of the ethnic-national entity, impinging upon the individual only secondarily and then only by virtue of his membership in the ethnic-national entity. (It is not surprising, therefore, that the human pole in the divine-human relation, both when it is the active agent and when it is the receiving object in the relation, is represented here primarily by the ethnic-national collectivity and not by the individual).

For as regards the claim that religion here must implicate the collectivity rather than the individual as the primary context of its expression, this can be seen in the consideration that inasmuch as religion here formulates itself from the ethical perspective, it impinges not on questions concerning the being of man but rather on questions concerning the actions and relations of man. As such, it cannot impinge exclusively on the individual person but must impinge on man and the object of his actions or on man and his partner in relation. Because of a number of considerations that cannot be elaborated upon here, this partner, this "other," implicated here must be a fellow-man (suffice it to say that inasmuch as the ethical perspective involved here represents an ethic that is grounded in accountability and responsibility, it must impinge on actions and relations that arise exclusively between man and his fellow-man and not upon actions and relations that may arise between man and the inanimate objects of nature). Thus, religion here cannot impinge upon man in his monadic individuality; it must impinge upon both man and his fellow-man. But a twosome, i.e., man and his fellow man, constitute already a collectivity, a human community.

And, as regards the claim that the collectivity implicated here cannot be just any collectivity but must be specifically the ethnic-national collectivity, this can be seen from the consideration that only the ethnic-national collectivity can encompass the full gamut of relations constituting the horizontal dimension of life on which a religion formulating itself from the ethical perspective would ultimately have to impinge. All other subnational or extranational collectivities (as, for example, the family, the clan, or any of the social, cultural, professional, ideological or political associations) can present only some of these relations but never all of them. Thus, if the horizontal dimension of life is to be made available to religion in all its relations – the social, economic and political – the collectivity that is to be implicated here must be specifically the ethnic-national collectivity.

But it must be clear, however, that the ethnic-national entity cannot really fulfill its function optimally with respect to religion, i.e., that it cannot make fully available to religion the horizontal dimension of life, unless it has sovereignty. Namely, the ethnic-national entity must have the power to shape, regulate, and determine the relations constituting the horizontal dimension of life. It must have the power to impose its wishes and judgments with respect to these relations. In other words, it must possess a horizontal dimension – a horizontal dimension must rightfully belong to it. It must be at its disposal freely to determine its destiny.

We have thus far argued, therefore, that the prophetic and nonmystical halachic strands for Judaism in formulating themselves from the ethical perspective implicate an indirect relating to the divine, a relating that is "refracted" through the horizontal dimension of life, thus involving Judaism in a very fundamental and essential way in the matrix of the horizontal dimension of life in all its aspects bar none. We have further argued that this implicates an inextricable bond between Judaism and an ethnic-national entity. And lastly, we have argued that for Judaism to optimally express and realize itself, the ethnic-national entity which is inextricably bound to it must possess sovereignty.

Indeed, in light of these considerations one can come to understand and evaluate the major transformations in Jewish history not only from the vantage point of the fortunes or suffering of Jewry, but from the vantage point of the needs and requirements of the structure of faith of Judaism. Namely, we can gain different insights into the strengths and weaknesses of the major periods in Jewish history – strengths and weaknesses that will be judged now not from the vantage point of how they impinged on the well-being of Jewry but rather from the vantage point of how they impinged on the viability of the structure of faith of Judaism.

Thus, from this vantage point, the essential strength and advantage of the Biblical period lies in the fact that it provided sovereignty and consequently that it could place the horizontal dimension in all its relations at the disposal of Judaism. In such a context Judaism could express itself fully and in this sense it was indeed the fulfillment of the promise. Indeed, the tradition knew this, for its continuous yearning for restoration signified for it not only the liberation from the physical sufferings of exile, but the renewal of the opportunity for Judaism to express itself *fully* (in its language: the renewal of the opportunity to observe *all* of God's commandments). It is not a coincidence that the tradition links its messianic hope to the restoration, making the former contingent upon the latter.

On the other hand, the essential predicament and problem which diaspora-existence presents must be seen to lie principally in the fact that diaspora-existence signifies the abrogation of sovereignty. But more specifically, the problem of sovereignty must be seen here to lie not so much in the scattering of the Jews or in their dependence for their very physical survival on the good graces of others, but in the fact that the abrogation of sovereignty threatened the availability to Judaism of the horizontal dimension of life. For without a horizontal dimension at its disposal Judaism could not survive.[10] Indeed, Judaism managed to survive in diaspora-existence only because it succeeded, partly due to fortuitous circumstances, to establish what has been called "a state within a state," namely, only because it succeeded to create in diaspora, and thus without sovereignty, a portable horizontal dimension that was at its disposal. True, this horizontal dimension provided by "ghettoized" existence was limited and consequently the expression of the structure of faith of Judaism in these circumstances could only be a truncated expression. Still, it evidently was sufficient to allow for the survival of Judaism.

By this very same logic, however, when things are to be viewed from the vantage point of the interests and requirements of the structure of faith of Judaism, the crisis which the Emancipation precipitates in modern Jewish life must be seen now to lie essentially in the fact that the thrust of the Emancipation is to abrogate this limited horizontal dimension which Judaism managed to establish for itself in the context of diaspora-existence. For what the Emancipation really signifies is the exit of Jewry from its "ghettoized" existence and its entry into the life-stream of the host-nation and the real crisis that this represents, when viewed from the vantage point of the structure of faith of Judaism, is the loss of the horizontal dimension to Judaism. For the horizontal dimension, albeit the limited, truncated horizontal dimension, that Judaism managed to constitute for itself in the context of "ghettoized" existence could not be transferred into the life-stream of the host-nation. This meant that to the extent that Judaism did manage to accompany emancipated Jewry, albeit in a restricted and mitigated way, into the life-stream of the host-nation, it was nonetheless, in terms of its structure, made impotent in the process. Thus, from the vantage point of the structure of faith of Judaism the real crisis which the Emancipation precipitates for Judaism must be seen to lie in the fact that the Emancipation abrogates the horizontal dimension that was at the disposal of Judaism and that consequently it necessarily emasculates Judaism and renders it impotent.[11]

Finally, the real significance of the re-establishment of the state of Israel (again, when viewed from the vantage point of the structure of faith of Judaism) must be seen to lie in the fact that it rescues for Judaism the horizontal dimension in terms of emancipated Jewry – and indeed it rescues the horizontal dimension no longer in a truncated form but in its full extension. For only in the context of the reestablished state of Israel can Jewry reenter the lifestream of history, can Jewry be emancipated from its "ghettoized" existence, in a way which allows Judaism to accompany it fully and in a manner that is viable. If Judaism is to survive in the context of the Emancipation, therefore, the reestablishment of the state of Israel becomes a condition *sine qua non*. For only in the context of the reestablished state can the horizontal dimension in terms of emancipated Jewry be placed at the disposal of Judaism. And indeed, because the horizontal dimension is provided here with sovereignty, it not only allows Judaism to survive, namely, to hold the fort and mark time (as the horizontal dimension in the context of "ghettoized" existence did), but it should allow Judaism once more to persue its vocation in full force.

Thus, we have tried to argue that by its very structure of faith, seeing that it formulates itself from the ethical perspective, Judaism must express itself in the horizontal dimension. It must impinge upon the horizontal dimension in all its aspects. The availability, therefore, of the horizontal dimension is essential to Judaism. Without a horizontal dimension at its disposal, Judaism would disintegrate. In no other religion is this requirement to be involved in the horizontal dimension, to impinge upon it in all its aspects, more central or essential as it is in Judaism. But we have also tried to argue that Judaism can impinge upon the horizontal dimension only if the horizontal dimension rightfully belongs to it, only if it possesses sovereignty over it. Namely, it can impinge upon the horizontal dimension only in its own "back yard," in its own "home." But this means that the most that Judaism can do in the context of diaspora-existence is to constitute, if allowed, a limited horizontal dimension, as an enclave separated and isolated from the life-stream of the host-nation, upon which it can impinge. Evidently, it cannot impinge upon the horizontal dimension of the host-nation. No host would allow it and rightly so.

But one may contend that while this argument may be valid with respect to host-nations that are homogenous, it would have to be greatly mitigated if the host-nations constitute pluralistic societies. For shouldn't Judaism in these circumstances have a partial rightful claim on the horizontal dimension of life and shouldn't it therefore be allowed to impinge, at least in part, upon it? Thus, if the Emancipation is to take place in the context of a pluralistic society, shouldn't the problem which it precipitates for Judaism be greatly mitigated? There is no question that at first sight the pluralistic alternative appears very attractive. But on a closer look, we would submit, its attractiveness is greatly diminished. First, there are any number of very difficult practical problems which a pluralistic situation presents. How, for example, would such an arrangement work when there are any number of religions claiming the right to impinge upon the horizontal dimension? Would it work by finding the least offensive common denominator of these religions and allow only it to impinge upon the horizontal dimension, or would the horizontal dimension be partitioned among the various religions allowing each to impinge on only part of it? Clearly, neither of these alternatives would be satisfactory to Judaism nor, I dare say, to any other religion. But as far as Judaism is concerned there is even a more serious problem, not of mere practicality but of substance. To see this we must ask, what kind of pluralism are we talking about? Are we talking of a pluralism that is merely religious or are we talking of a pluralism that is actually ethnic? If it is the former, then Judaism, unlike other religions, may well not be able to avail itself of its opportunities. For, as we have seen above,

Judaism is inextricably bound to a specific ethnic-national entity and it would perforce be excluded by virtue of this ethnic bond. Thus, for pluralism to present meaningful possibilities to Judaism in diaspora-existence, one must envision a pluralism that is specifically ethnic. But given the way the world is, we are not at all convinced that such an ethnic pluralism is feasible. We certainly do not know of any instance of authentic pluralism which is stable and viable and which appears to be a permanent state of affairs (leave alone knowing any instance which would also incorporate Judaism as a full-fledged ethnic partner).[12]

Thus, we must conclude that as far as diaspora-existence is concerned, Judaism, in the context of the emancipation, is not really in a position to impinge upon the horizontal dimension of life (what *emancipated* Jewry does is, of course, quite a different story). This is somewhat ironic because Judaism, perhaps more than any other religion, is a religion which by its very essence requires that it impinge upon the horizontal dimension of life. But then, this is part of the price which diaspora-existence exacts.

---

[1] Julius Wellhausen, *Israelitische und Juedische Geschichte*, W. duGruyter Ausg., Berlin, 1921, p. 114.

[2] Ernest Renan, *Histoire de peuple d'Israel*, vol III, Calmann-Levy, Paris, 1895, pp. VI-VII.

[3] Herman Gunkel, *Deutsche Rundschau*, XI, p. 231.

[4] K. Kohler, *The Ethical Basis of Judaism*, Young Men's Hebrew Association, New York, 1887, p. 143.

[5] I. Epstein, *Emunat Ha-Yahadut*, Mossad HaRav Kook, Jerusalem, 1965, pp. 18-19.

[6] L. Jacobs, *A Jewish Theology*, Behrman House Inc., New York, 1973, p. 231.

[7] See, for example, M. Buber, *I and Thou*, translated by Ronald Gregor Smith, Charles Scribner's Sons, New York, second edition, 1958, pp. 11, 34.

[8] See my essay "The Distinctive Expression of the Category of Worship in Judaism" in *Bijdrachen*, September, 1982.

[9] For a striking description of this aspect of the divine in prophetic literature see A.J. Heschel, *The Prophets*, Harper and Row Publishers, N.Y., 1969 particularly Vol. II, chapters 1, 3 and 4.

[10] For a penetrating analysis of this point see Max Wiener, *Jüdische Religion in Zeitalter der Emanzipation*, translated into Hebrew by Lea Zagagi, Hemed Publishers, Jerusalem, 1974.

[11] For a fuller an analysis of the problem which the Emancipation precipitates for Judaism see my essay "The Dilemma of Identity for the Emancipated Jew" reprinted in *New Theology* No. 4 edited by Martin E. Marty and Dean G. Peerman, The MacMillan Co., N.Y.

[12] For a further critique of the notion of pluralism as it impinges on the state of Judaism and Jewry in diaspora see my review article "The Impact of the Emancipation on Continuity and Change in Judaism" in the *Journal of Religion*, vol. 59, no. 4, October 1979.

Part Four

THE ETHICAL PERSPECTIVE

Chapter Fourteen

Kierkegaard's Teleological Suspension of the Ethical – Some Reflections from a Jewish Perspective

In some manifestations of the religious phenomenon the religious dimension is such that by its very essence it necessarily implicates the inner and inextricable intertwining of the ethical dimension with itself (we would designate these various manifestations of the religious phenomenon as belonging to type I). In other manifestations, however, the religious dimension in no way implicates the ethical dimension – the ethical dimension is constituted here as an independent and separate entity though the religious dimension can be brought from the outside to impinge upon it (and these manifestations we would designate as belonging to type II). Lastly, in still other manifestations even this possibility of having the religious dimension impinge from the outside upon the ethical dimension is excluded, thus leaving the two dimensions closed within themselves in a monadic-like fashion with no linkage or bridging between them (clearly these manifestations also belong to type II). Thus, we would submit that the first instance can be encountered, for example, in prophetic biblical faith and in nonmystical halachic Judaism; that the second instance can be encountered in some strands of Christianity (e.g., in Catholicism or Calvinism); and that the third instance may be encountered in some other strands of Christianity (e.g., in German Lutheranism particularly when associated with the pietistic expression) and in many of the nonbiblical religions (e.g., in Shamanistic primary religions, in Greco-Roman paganism and even in the religions of the Ancient Near East).

Inasmuch as we are mainly concerned in this paper with the religious dimension as it expresses itself in mainstream Judaism (which is to say, in a structure of faith that is constituted by prophetic biblical faith and nonmystcal halachic Judaism), we are evidently concerned with a religion that belongs to the first type of religions delineated above, i.e., to that type in which the religious dimension is by its very essence inextricably intertwined with the ethical dimension (where the very content of the religious act of witnessing is the ethical act and the ultimate signification of the ethical act is its being the fundamental act of religious witnessing). Now it should be quite clear that in such a type of religion the concern with the domain of ethics and religion, i.e., with the domain involved in delineating the relation between ethics and religion, must be central and of great significance. After all, this domain impinges upon the most fundamental and the most sensitive aspect of the structure of faith; to wit, it impinges upon the basic nature of the primary act of religious witnessing.[1] Likewise, it should be equally clear that in the context of this domain, i.e., that in the context of discussing the relation between religion and ethics, the real significant issue, the real problem, which ultimately one must inevitably encounter is the issue of ultimacy and supremacy. Namely, sooner or later one must cope with the question of where ultimacy is being placed – is it to be placed in the ethical or in the religious domain – and commensurate to this ascertain which dimension – the ethical or the religious – is given supremacy over the other.[2]

<h1 style="text-align:center">I</h1>

Now, it is precisely with respect to this issue (an issue that is essential and inescapable for religions of type I as, for example, Judaism) that Kierkegaard's formulation of the teleological suspension of the ethical in *Fear and Trembling* receives its essential signification. For the formulation clearly states that the ethical is to be suspended for the sale of some higher end. As such the formulation clearly implies that ultimacy and supremacy are not vested in the ethical domain but rather in that other domain to which the higher end, the end for whose sake the ethical is to be suspended, belongs; and inasmuch as it is clear from the context that the higher end is none other than the divine will, the formulation clearly places ultimacy and supremacy in the religious domain. Thus, the essential signification of Kierkegaard's formulation cannot be mistaken – it places ultimacy and therefore supremacy in the religious and not in the ethical domain.

But Kierkegaard's formulation has not only the distinct merit of stating its position with respect to the issue before us with great clarity; it has the added important advantage that it expresses itself with unusual force and poignancy. This is derived from the fact that Kierkegaard's formulation of the teleological suspension of the ethical is articulated, as is well known, in intimate conjunction with the biblical story of the binding of Isaac (Genesis 22:1-19). For as such it clearly precipitates the issue before us, i.e., the issue of supremacy between the religious and the ethical domain, in the most radical circumstances. It precipitates the issue in the context where, so to speak, the cards are stacked against the religious domain as far as it is conceivably possible to do – is the religious domain, i.e., is the divine command, to have supremacy and prevail even when it demands the murder of one's son? Here lies the force and poignancy of this formulation. It lies in the fact that it removes any and every subterfuge behind which one could hide and conveniently avoid facing the implications of the issue in all their force. It lies in the fact that the formulation here (i.e., the circumstances in whose context the formulation is articulated) does not allow one to be glib or superficial or less than crystal clear about what implications are contained in one's direction. For clearly it is not so difficult to affirm the supremacy of the religious when such an affirmation does not implicate the negation of the ethical; it is even feasible to affirm the supremacy of the religious without too much constraint when such an affirmation does implicate the negation of the ethical but only in some minor, peripheral and not too significant matters. It is, however, a totally different matter when the affirmation of the supremacy of the religious implicates the negation of the ethical in matters that are fundamental, in matters where the negation of the ethical would prove to be most offensive. Is one still prepared to grant the supremacy of the religious when the religious may demand the murdering of one's child? Yet, if such an affirmation is to be at all serious one must be prepared to accept its implications in all their dire possibilities as, for example, one must be prepared to accept sacrificing one's own son as a possible implication of such an affirmation. It is precisely in the making clear of this point that Kierkegaard's formulation of the teleological suspension of the ethical (taken, of course, in the context of the biblical story of the binding of Isaac) receives its special significance and impact. For clearly, any serious concern with the interrelation between ethics and religion is no longer able now to skirt, i.e., to circumvent or fudge over, the real, fundamental problem which such an undertaking precipitates.

It is true, however, that Kierkegaard does not intend for his formulation of the teleological suspension of the ethical to be taken as an expression of a problem; rather he clearly intends for it to be taken as an expression of a definitive answer. Namely, in the face of the most radical circumstances when the religious runs head on into the very grain of the ethical and contradicts it (i.e., when the religious implicates the murdering of one's son), Kierkegaard does not perceive the precipitation of a fundamental problem but rather the presentation of the optimal situation in which to formulate one's position in full awareness of all its implications, even the most radical and difficult implications. Clearly the teleological suspension of the ethical articulates for him a definitive position rather than a problem – supremacy and ultimacy are accorded to the religious dimension over the ethical dimension in all conceivable instances even when the ethical is countermanded in its most fundamental signification.

That Kierkegaard can take this position, that he can claim through his formulation of the teleological suspension of the ethical the definitive position that the religious supersedes the ethical in all conceivable instances, is in a way not all that difficult to understand if we keep in mind the religious tradition from which Kierkegaard is coming and which he represents. For in coming from the Lutheran tradition Kierkegaard is clearly representing an understanding of religion in terms of the context of type II delineated above, which is to say, that for him the constitution of the religious does not necessarily implicate the ethical - the religious and the ethical are not internally bound and intertwined. Rather, the religious and the ethical are constituted here essentially as independent and separate dimensions, the former being delineated exclusively by the vertical relating while the latter is delineated exclusively by the horizontal relating. But clearly, in such a context where the religious does not necessarily implicate the ethical dimension in its very constitution, claiming supremacy and precedence for the religious dimension over the ethical dimension would not precipitate the problem of internal self-contradiction (the religious does not have to be by its very constitution ethical!). Operating in such a context, therefore, Kierkegaard can clearly assert with no "ifs" or "buts" the supremacy of the religious while at the same time countenancing the possibility that it may well contradict and abrogate the ethical in its most fundamental values.

Indeed, the inner-logic operating here, i.e., the inner-logic operating in the context of those religions belonging to type II of our delineation above, would not only allow but would actually lead one to make such a claim. For inasmuch as salvation is placed, almost by definition, in the religious dimension, i.e., in the relating that is vertical, this means that the religious is invested with a worth and a validity that is supreme and ultimate. But this, on the other hand, also means that inasmuch as the ethical dimension, i.e., the relating that is horizontal, is constituted here as a separate dimension independent of the religious dimension, inescapably there will be here a devaluation in the worth and validity of the relating that is horizontal, i.e., of the ethical dimension. Certainly, one would not be able to have here supreme and ultimate worth and validity vested in the ethical dimension, seeing that this has already been pre-empted by the religious dimension and that there is not internal intertwining, internal coalescence, between the religious and the ethical so that the status accorded to the religious is *ipso facto* shared also by the ethical. As such, it should not be surprising that a contradiction or abrogation of the ethical need not be viewed too seriously in this context. After all, such contradiction or abrogation does not touch the ultimate and supreme value. This is clearly arrogated to the religious dimension. Thus, in this context it is indeed the religious alone which takes precedence to the exclusion of all else (even ethics) and consequently one can acquiesce in what may be offensive to other dimensions (even to the ethical and, indeed, even when it is most offensive to the ethical as, for example, when it demands the murder of one's child) as long as the religious dimension is satisfied. This is the point to which the inner-logic operating here must lead and consequently this is the basic posture which one would ultimately encounter in religions belonging to type II. True, generally one would be more comfortable were the implications not pushed that far or expressed in such blatant and unambiguous terms. One could then extol the supremacy of the religious while conveniently fudging over its implications with regard to a possible contradiction of the ethical. Thus, the significance of Kierkegaard's formulation in this context, i.e., in the context of the religions belonging to type II, is precisely to counteract such fudging over by clearly and uncompromisingly spelling out the implications involved and then in full cognizance of these unpleasant implications proceeding to "bite the bullet."[3]

So, the analysis thus far has established the following: 1) that the teleological suspension of the ethical as formulated by Kierkegaard constitutes a statement which undertakes either to represent a certain state of affairs or to put forth a claim to bring about a certain state of affairs; 2) that Kierkegaard can formulate the teleological suspension of the ethical in this way as a statement is due to the fact that he comes from the Lutheran tradition, namely from a religious expression that belongs to type II; 3) that the formulation of the teleological suspension of the ethical as a statement is indeed feasible only in the context of religious expressions belonging to type II, seeing that the feasibility of such a formulation is contingent on the precondition that the vertical, i.e., the religious dimension be separated in its very constitution from the horizontal, i.e., the ethical, dimension (for only in such a context of separation can the requirements of one dimension, as for example, the religious dimension, consistently go hand in hand with – or, even more poignantly, actually demand – the abrogation of the other dimension) and that, in turn, such separation is the distinctive mark exclusively of the religious expressions belonging to type II.

But in addition to these observations the analysis here clearly portends one further observation and, indeed, a further observation that is all-important. Namely, it portends the further observation that in the center of religious expressions where the religious dimension is not separated from the ethical dimension but rather is internally and inextricably intertwined with it, in other words, that in the context of religious expressions which belong to type I, the formulation of the teleological suspension of the ethical, far from articulating a demand that can be met, articulates in truth a demand that in principle cannot be fulfilled and thus rather than signify a possible state of affairs it signifies a problem. It portends that in the context of religious expressions belonging to type I the teleological suspension of the ethical is no longer a definitive exclamation mark but a big question mark. For by the same token that the analysis above of the factor of separation has shown that only in the context where separation is present, i.e., that only in the context where the religious dimension is separate from the ethical dimension, does the formulation of the teleological suspension of the ethical signify a demand that can be met, it will clearly also show that in a context where separation is not present the formulation of the teleological suspension of the ethical cannot possibly be a bona fide demand, i.e., a demand that can be met. Indeed, it will clearly show the diametrical opposite, i.e., that in a context where the religious is by its very constitution intertwined with the ethical the religious cannot go against the ethical nor conversely the ethical go against the religious. As such, a formulation of the teleological suspension of the ethical, seeing that it signifies the countermanding of the ethical for the sake of the religious, must clearly precipitate a serious problem when it is proposed in the context of religious expressions belonging to type I. For how can one affirm a formulation which by its essence implies a discordance between the religious and the ethical in a context whose very essence signifies a fundamental accord and correspondence between the religious and the ethical?

Indeed, as we have seen, the formulation of the teleological suspension of the ethical arises originally in the context of the religious expressions belonging to type II (we evidently have in mind its formulation by Kierkegaard in the context of Lutheranism) and there its affirmation is quite feasible and understandable. As against this, in the context of the religious expressions belonging to type I the formulation of the teleological suspension of the ethical can only arise as a "transplant" (a transplant from the previous context of religious expressions belonging to type II) and here its affirmation, far from being feasible and understandable, is actually very problematical. Thus, the whole point of our analysis above has been to show that there is such a "transplantation" occurring when one is moving from the context of religious expressions belonging to type II to a context of religious expressions belonging to type I and that in this process of "transplantation" the status of the formulation of the teleological suspension of the ethical changes radically in being transformed from a statement or a command into a big question mark. We would submit, however, that it is precisely as a question mark that the formulation of the teleological suspension of the ethical becomes really interesting. Namely, it is precisely in the context of religious expressions belonging to type I, where the teleological suspension of the ethical no longer signifies the positing of a fundamental principle but rather the precipitation of a fundamental problem, that the analysis should become most intriguing and potentially also most instructive. For the analysis here will have to deal with how the religious expression (more specifically, the religious expression belonging to type I) responds to this problem and attempts to overcome it and in doing this one is pushed *per force* to probing the structure of faith operating here in terms of its most fundamental inner-logic, thus gaining, almost inevitably, a much deeper knowledge and appreciation of the phenomenon. Thus, interesting as the analysis of the teleological suspension of the ethical in the context of type II may well be, its analysis when it is formulated in the context of type I is by far much more interesting and, indeed, much more substantive and challenging.

Indeed, the exemplification of this latter analysis delineated above is precisely the task which this paper set out for itself. This is clearly indicated by the title of the paper when it proposes to reflect upon the teleological suspension of the ethical from a Jewish perspective. For there can be no denying that Judaism (more accurately, mainstream Judaism) is an example *par excellence* of a religious expression that belongs to type I. Thus, to reflect on the teleological suspension of the ethical from a Jewish perspective means reflecting on it from a perspective of a religious expression that clearly belongs to type I and this, in turn, means reflecting on it principally in terms of the fundamental problem which it precipitates in this context. Given this context, therefore, the analysis which faces us in the remainder of this paper will have in the main two objectives: 1) to determine the way and grasp the rationale underlying it in which a religious expression belonging to type I (in our case, mainstream Judaism) responds to the formulation of the teleological suspension of the ethical and 2) to see if and to what extent it can overcome the serious problem which the formulation inevitably must precipitate for it. It is to this task that we must now turn.

II

In addressing ourselves initially to the first objective we must readily admit that we do not have the means by which to determine the attitude of mainstream Judaism to the formulation of a teleological suspension of the ethical in a way that would be acceptable to the social sciences. Namely, we do not have a sufficiently clear-cut criterion by which to determine who does and who does not speak for mainstream Judaism. And even if one could suppose that this difficulty has been overcome, we certainly do not have the data at our disposal to make any definitive statement – no questionnaires were passed among the members and no statistics gathered. Finally, even if one opted to turn away altogether from the preceding, rather "sociological," head-counting approach to an examination of the theological-philosophical literature of Judaism to see what reactions it contains towards the formulation of a teleological suspension of the ethical (viewing the individual spokesmen in this domain as the authentic and legitimate articulators of the stance taken by the tradition – an approach, by the way, that has much to recommend itself), the fact is that there is hardly any explicit, sustained treatment of our topic in the theological-philosophical literature of Judaism. The one notable exception is Buber. And although Buber in this instance does not claim to represent the reaction of Judaism but only his own reaction to Kierkegaard's formulation, we would want to claim that his reaction here does indeed represent an authentic and basic reaction of mainstream Judaism. Of course, this claim of ours, as we conceded above, is based only on personal experiences and impressions; and under these circumstances it would only behoove us to be more careful and modest in our claim – we should not (and indeed we do not!) claim that it represents *the* reaction but only that it represents *a* reaction of mainstream Judaism. Still, Buber does articulate a most intriguing positon and, for whatever it is worth, we do feel strongly that it authentically reflects a basic inclination and orientation within mainstream Judaism. But be this as it may, for better or worse, our analysis is based to a considerable degree on Buber's position and it is, therefore, to it that we must now turn in order to launch our analysis.

Buber's position, i.e., his reaction and attempted response to Kierkegaard's formulation of the teleological suspension of the ethical, is succinctly but forcefully expressed in his essay "On the Suspension of the Ethical."[4]

Turning first to the question of Buber's reaction to Kierkegaard's formulation, it is true that it is not stated explicitly in this essay; but implicitly

Buber conveys his reaction in a way that is quite clear and unmistakable. Indeed, it would seem to us that it could not be denied that throughout the essay Buber's approach to the formulation is thoroughly respectful and serious, that he is even appreciative and admiring of its honesty and incisiveness. Certainly, we do not encounter here any derision or out of hand dismissal of the formulation as if it was an aberration, an expression of abnormal fanaticism. If anything, one gets the feeling that Buber is actually attracted to the formulation. At the same time, however, it cannot be denied that in the last analysis Buber finds the formulation unacceptable and does reject it. Thus, we encounter in Buber a reaction that is twofold, that essentially constitutes itself as a dialectical double movement towards its object, i.e., towards the formulation; it is a reaction that is both a yes and a no, that wants to draw near and is attracted and yet feels constraint to push away and reject.

Of course, in view of our claim above we should not take this reaction merely as Buber's private reaction, as the peculiar response of a certain isolated individual. For, as we have argued above, in this reaction Buber is quite authentic to his Jewish heritage – he is expressing a reaction that would be quite characteristic to mainstream Judaism. Thus, this twofold reaction, this dialectical yes and no, this attraction and rejection is not only Buber's reaction but a reaction authentic to mainstream Judaism, so to speak, a "Jewish reaction." The reaction thus becomes the expression of a much larger constituency and its status is commensurately strengthened. But the most significant advantage is accrued when one moves from the description of the reaction to attempt to provide a rationale for it. For at bottom it is really only in terms of the structure of faith of mainstream Judaism that a rationale can be construed.

Thus, the positive attitude towards the formulation of the teleological suspension of the ethical, i.e., the attitude expressing itself in the respect, seriousness and appreciation shown towards the formulation, receives its rationale, we would submit, from the fact that the very essence and thrust of the formulation lies in its poignant and radical expression of the uncompromised supremacy of the religious and that it is precisely this aspect which constitutes the very heart of the structure of faith of mainstream Judaism (or, for that matter, of any other authentic expression of biblical faith). Namely, what is at stake here is nothing else than the affirmation of the unconditioned, uncompromised, transcendence of the divine over-against any and every other aspect and being – the divine transcends any identification with or limitation by any other aspect or being no matter how elevated or ennobled it may be. This, after all, is what the formulation of the teleological suspension of the ethical is in the last analysis really saying. But this is also precisely what the notion of monotheism essentially signifies. For in clearly affirming the oneness, the singleness, the uniqueness of the divine the notion of monotheism must of necessity also implicate radical transcendence with respect to the divine. To safeguard the uniqueness of the divine, the divine cannot be allowed to be compromised by anything else no matter how elevated or ennobled this thing may be. Thus, both the teleological formulation and the monotheistic notion assert, in the last analysis, the same claim; to wit, they both ultimately assert radical transcendence on behalf of the divine.

Now, there can be no denying that the consensus of opinion will overwhelmingly agree that the notion of monotheism constitutes a fundamental, essential tenet in the structure of faith of mainstream Judaism.[5] And if this be the case then we can now understand why one encounters within mainstream Judaism a reaction to the teleological formulation that is basically sympathetic, respectful and appreciative. For after all, what the teleological formulation expresses, in the last analysis, is nothing else but the same principle which finds expression in a tenet that is essential and fundamental in the structure of faith of Judaism, i.e., the tenet of monotheism. Namely, what mainstream Judaism must encounter in the teleological formulation is the expression of its own most fundamental principle, i.e., the expression of the radical transcendence of the divine; and, indeed, it encounters this principle here when it is expressed in a most forceful and poignant way. In these circumstances how could the reaction of mainstream Judaism to the teleological formulation not be respectful, sympathetic and appreciative? Thus, given the fact that the thrust of the teleological formulation is to express, precisely in the most extreme circumstances, the supremacy of the religious dimension (or, in other words, the radical transcendence of the divine) and to safeguard such supremacy against any compromise, i.e., against any reduction whatsoever (even when the threatened reduction or compromise is to such an appealing dimension as the ethical!), it is quite understandable that the teleological formulation should elicit respect and appreciation when viewed from the perspective of mainstream Judaism.

But valid and significant as the above explication may well be, it is not as yet the whole story. For there is an additional consideration involved here which has not as yet been explicated. And since it is precisely this consideration which establishes the really ultimate and distinctive signification of the structure of faith of mainstream Judaism, it follows that without the explication of this consideration one may not have touched upon the really ultimate and fundamental motivation which directs the reaction of mainstream Judaism to the teleological formulation. Indeed, this consideration arises also in close association with the tenet of monotheism. But while it agrees that the tenet of monotheism is the fundamental and essential tenet in the structure of faith of mainstream Judaism, (thus agreeing that in dealing with any aspect of this tenet one is inevitably touching the very heart of mainstream Judaism) it wants to claim that there is a more fundamental and essential signification borne by the tenet of monotheism than the assertion of radical transcendence with respect to the divine being. Namely, while not denying that the tenet of monotheism does indeed implicate radical transcendence on behalf of the divine being, the consideration here wants to claim that the really fundamental and essential signification of the tenet lies in yet a further implication which the tenet carries; to wit, in its implication that the divine being is by its very essence constituted as a personal being. The fundamental and essential signification of the tenet of monotheism when it is embedded in the context of the structure of faith of mainstream Judaism is to implicate that the divine being is by its very essence constituted not as a being-of-Power, an It-being but as a being-of-Consciousness, a Thou-being. Now, we would submit that a very strong case can be made on behalf of this claim; that indeed, the most distinctive and the most fundamental aspect of mainstream Judaism does lie in its assertion that the divine being is by its very essence constituted as a personal being or, in other words, that ultimacy resides in a being-of-Consciousness, in a Thou-being and not in a being-of-Power, in an It-being; and that is, indeed, the fundamental signification which the tenet of monotheism carries in the context of mainstream Judaism.[6]

But if this be the case, then it follows that when the claim for the supremacy of the religious dimension over the ethical dimension is made in this context, i.e., in the context of the monotheistic expression of mainstream Judaism, then the claim really means to signify, in the last analysis, that supremacy and thus ultimacy are placed in a Thou-being and not in an It-being (in other words, it is placed in a god constituted as a Thou-being and not in a god constituted as an It-being). For in making the claim in any context whatsoever for the supremacy of the religious dimension over the ethical dimension one is really making ultimately the claim for the supremacy of a divine being over any and all ethical maxims and laws. But now, when this claim is made specifically in the context of mainstream Judaism, it is clearly tantamount to claiming supremacy for a Thou-being over an It-being, seeing that the divine being is by its very essence constituted here as a Thou-being and that ethical maxims and laws, no matter how spiritually imposing or uplifting they may be, are clearly impersonal entities, i.e., It-beings. Thus, the really distinctive and fundamental aspect of mainstream Judaism, when one pushes things all the way, lies in its claim that supremacy and ultimacy reside in a Thou-being and not in an It-being, not even when the It-being is represented by the most edifying and inspiring ethical maxims and laws. In other words, the really distinctive and fundamental characteristic of mainstream Judaism lies in the fact that in its context ultimately one encounters a person (i.e., spontaneity, intentionality, contingency) and not a set of maxims and laws (i.e., necessity, detachment, universality) no matter how profound and worthy they may be.

This point may well need stressing because in the way Judaism is usually perceived the distinctive and fundamental characteristic of the tradition is located in its contribution to ethics, in the highly developed and profoundly sensitive sense of social justice which it introduces into the world. Indeed, very often the very essence of the tradition is equated with (in other words, reduced to) the social ethics it constitutes. And, as we shall see below, there is much truth in this. For there is no denying that the very essence of mainstream Judaism is intimately connected with the expression of social ethics. But, and this is the crux of the point we are trying to make here, such an expression of social ethics with which the tradition is so intimately connected is not perceived within the tradition as grounded in itself, namely, as grounded in its own foundational principles which, in turn, are taken either as axioms or as grounded in some universal reason; rather, it is understood within the tradition as ultimately grounded in the personal being of the divine, i.e., in the spontaneous will of the divine, so that ultimately one encounters here neither inherent ethical maxims nor impersonal universal reason but a particular spontaneous will, a specific personal being.[7]

Again, it is to Buber that we are indebted for having perceived and appreciated the significance of this point. For in his essay "Religion and Ethics"[8] where, as the title indicates, he is concerned with the relation between ethics and religion, Buber first suggests that the central issue in this context is the need of the ethical to ground itself in the religious. The way he puts it is that there is a fundamental need "to bind the radical distinction between good and evil to the Absolute."[9] Secondly, Buber further suggests that in the spiritual history of man there were essentially two attempts to do this. The one attempt which appeared rather universally in Oriental and Greek antiquity (and which we would typologize as "pagan") tried to achieve this absolutization of ethical values by making them the expressions of cosmic law, "the moral order is identical with the cosmic."[10] The second attempt, on the other hand, which appeared in a rather isolated manner in Ancient Israel (and which we would typologize as "biblical faith") tried to establish the absolutization of ethical values not by incorporating them into the continuous, constant and all-encompassing cosmic or heavenly order (as the first attempt did) but rather by referring them to a specific being; to wit, by referring them to the "God of Israel" who, on the one hand, is seen as the Absolute while, on the other hand, He is encountered as a "giver and protector of law."[11] Thus, inasmuch as the precepts of the law are promulgated by the divine who is the Absolute, the precepts of the law, i.e., that which constitutes the ethical, are themselves also endowed with Absoluteness. To paraphrase Buber, now it is no longer the cosmic order that is decisive but rather He who is its sovereign, the Lord of heaven and earth.[12]

We need not follow Buber any further in his pursuit of this theme, for the point which is of interest to us here has already been clearly implicated in what he has said thus far. For the exposition above clearly shows that in Buber's judgment the linkage between the religious and the ethical as such is by no means unique to Judaism. In many other traditions is the religious intimately linked to the ethical, seeing that it is the religious which introduces and sustains the universal principle underlying the pattern of right behavior, be it called Tao in China, Rita in India, Urta in Iran or Dike in Greece.[13] Thus, the linkage between the religious and the ethical, indeed the implication of the ethical by the religious, can by no means be as such the distinctive characteristic of Judaism. But this is not to say that for Buber Judaism does not, indeed, have a distinctive characteristic which sets it apart from all other religious formulations. Indeed it does, except that Buber locates this distinctive characteristic not in the mere implication of the ethical by the religious (this is rather widespread) but rather in the nature and status of the ethical thus introduced. Namely, in Judaism the law, being the expression of the ethical, points beyond itself to another being who promulgates it; it does not as in the other religious formulations come to rest within itself as but a particular reflection of its all-encompassing, universal self. Thus, the implication is clear that for Buber the distinctive characterization of Judaism lies not in its introduction of the law *per se* but rather in its introduction of a law-giver. Even more fundamentally, it follows by clear implication from the foregoing, that the distinctive characterization to be attributed to Judaism here lies in the fact that it encounters the ultimate, i.e., the Absolute, not in some immutable universal law (be it the heavenly order or the cosmic order or the world of pure forms) but in a particular law-giver – in Judaism one encounters ultimately not a law but a law-giver. Finally, there is one further implication that can be clearly derived from the foregoing and with it we do indeed come to the very heart of the matter. Namely, it clearly follows from the above that the ultimate which one encounters in Judaism is a personal being, a being-of-Consciousness, a Thou; as against this, the ultimate which one encounters in the other religious formulations is an impersonal entity, a being-of-Power, an It. For clearly, a being that is itself not a law but the giver and protector of law is of necessity a personal being, a Thou.[14] Conversely, there can be no question that when speaking of a cosmic order or a heavenly law or the world of Forms one is inescapably dealing with impersonal entities, with an It, no matter how elevated or edifying they may well be.

Thus, Buber's incisive insight that in Judaism, in contrast to the other religious formulations, one ultimately encounters not a law but a law-giver, carries with it the further all-important and pregnant implication that in Judaism the ultimate being, the Absolute, is constituted as a personal being, as a Thou, while in the other religious formulations it is constituted as an impersonal being, as an It. As such, although Buber is using a different vocabulary, i.e., the vocabulary of law versus law-giver, and although his immediately explicit concern is not with the question of how the ultimate is constituted but rather with the question of how can ethics be best absolutized, Buber nevertheless succeeds, as we have tried to show above, to clearly implicate the most fundamental observation that can be made with respect to Judaism, namely, that in the last analysis, the real decisive, distinctive mark of Judaism lies in the fact that in contrast to the other religious formulations where it is blind Power that is encountered as the ultimate (be it in the benevolent or malevolent manifestation of its brute force or in the necessity and regularity and consequently in the predictability and lawfulness of its expression), in Judaism the ultimate is encountered beyond blind Power in a being that is personal (i.e., in spontaneity, in freedom and in awareness).

But if this be the case, then we can see a second and, indeed, a more profound rationale for why the teleological formulation should be congenial to Judaism. For now it is not only the affirmation of the supremacy of the religious over everything else (even over the ethical) that makes the formulation congenial; it is also the clear implication that the God involved in the formulation, namely the God who supersedes everything else, who can, indeed, suspend the ethical, is a personal being, a Thou. For clearly the fundamental contingency and spontaneity of the act (and in terms of the formulation the suspension is certainly not continuous or necessary), the notion of suspension and most evidently the very notion of a *telos*, of a higher goal, can make sense only with respect to a personal being, to a Thou – with respect to an impersonal being, to an It, they would simply not make sense. Thus, it is understandable that Judaism in clearly sensing that the God implicated in this teleological formulation is a personal being should respond to the formulation with an underlying basic feeling of respect and appreciation.

But if the rationale (actually the twofold rationale) for the positive reaction of mainstream Judaism towards the teleological formulation has been thus far adduced, one hopes, in a manner that is fairly straightforward and convincing, the rationale for the negative reaction of mainstream Judaism towards the formulation, namely, the rationale for the fact that, in the last analysis, mainstream Judaism must reject the teleological formulation, can now be adduced, we would submit, in a manner that is by far more forthright and convincing. For the negative reaction of mainstream Judaism to the teleological formulation follows directly and without ambiguity from the fact that mainstream Judaism belongs to, indeed, is an example *par excellence* of, type I of the religious formulation delineated above; namely, that it belongs to that type of religious formulation in which the religious and the ethical dimensions are inextricably intertwined, to that type of religious formulation in which the religious act (i.e., the vertically-directed act) inescapably expresses itself though the ethical act (i.e., the horizontally-directed act) and, conversely, the ethical act inevitably points beyond itself to the religious act, so much so that at one and the same time the religious act is the ethical act and, vice versa, the ethical act is the religious act. For as such it should be quite evident that in this context, i.e., in the context of the religious formulation belonging to type I, a suspension of the ethical is in principle not feasible – the very option of a suspension of the ethical is not available. For there is no higher end, a further *telos*, that would justify it, seeing that the religious aspect, which really is the only aspect that could have served as the higher end, the further *telos*, for whose sake the ethical could have been suspended, is not available here. And it is not available because in the context of the religious formulation belonging to type I, where the ethical is inextricably part and parcel of the religious and conversely the religious is inextricably part and parcel of the ethical, the suspension of the ethical is *ipso facto* and inescapably at one and the same time also the suspension of the religious and as such nothing is left for whose sake the suspension could have been undertaken and indeed, justified. Suspension is feasible only if that which is to be suspended does not constitute the ultimate; only if beyond it there still exists yet another being which as such constitutes the ultimate and, moreover, which demands its suspension. Suspension is feasible only with respect to a penultimate but never with respect to an ultimate being and then only if the ultimate dictates it. But clearly these two conditions do not obtain with respect to the ethical in the context of the religious formulation belonging to type I. For while, strictly speaking, the ultimate here is indeed constituted by the religious (this being so almost by definition), the ethical, being constituted here as the inextricable expression of the religious, is as such, so to speak, built into the ultimate, certainly to the extent that its suspension cannot be justified, leave alone required, by the ultimate. Thus, any and every religious formulation that belongs to type I – mainstream Judaism being a foremost instance of such a religious formulation – will, in the last analysis, have to reject any claim for the suspension of the ethical.

Indeed, it follows from our analysis above that in the context of the religious formulation belonging to type I, the teleological formulation no longer presents the articulation of the highest truth regarding such a religious formulation (as, indeed, is the case with respect to the religious formulation belonging to type II) but rather it presents the posing of a most fundamental problem. For while with respect to the religious formulation belonging to type II the teleological formulation in its claim for the suspension of the ethical signifies the radical, uncompromised supremacy of the religious dimension over any and every other dimension (including the ethical), and this certainly constitutes the articulation of the highest truth connected with such a religious formulation, with respect to the religious formulation belonging to type I the teleological formulation in claiming the suspension of the ethical is claiming something which is not feasible. For as we have seen above, in the context of the religious formulation belonging to type I the suspension of the ethical is not feasible; and this unfeasibility constitutes a fundamental characteristic of the religious formulation belonging to type I. Indeed, in view of this, one would be inclined to conclude that while the teleological formulation may well apply to the religious formulation belonging to type II, it certainly should not apply to the religious formulation belonging to type I. For it certainly does not make sense to apply demands which by the very nature of things cannot be delivered.

But it is not easy, precisely in the context of the religious formulation belonging to type I, to give up the challenge of the teleological formulation, i.e., the challenge of the suspension of the ethical. For this challenge arises from another, yet equally fundamental, aspect which characterizes the religious formulation belonging to type I; namely, it arises from the aspect that the ultimate encountered in the religious formulation belonging to type I is constituted as a personal being. For as a personal being its very essence lies in its freedom and, being ultimate, this means moreover that its freedom must be absolute which, in turn, would require that it be granted the possibility of suspending any and every thing it chooses including even the ethical. To reject, therefore, the claim of the teleological formulation, i.e., the claim of the suspension of the ethical, is tantamount to rejecting that the ultimate is constituted as a personal being; one may be left with either an ultimate or a personal being but not with both, i.e., with an ultimate that is a personal being. Yet, it is precisely this demand, i.e., the demand for an ultimate that is a personal being, which constitutes the essential, *sine-qua-non* requirement of the religious formulation belonging to type I. Thus, the signification of the challenge presented by the teleological formulation is not peripheral or incidental. It is not as if it arises arbitrarily or superficially, the product of fancy or passing whim carrying no special significance so that it can be removed without any serious consequences. Rather, it arises out of the most fundamental aspect of the religious formulation belonging to type I, i.e., the assertion that the ultimate is constituted as a personal being, and its removal, therefore, since it clearly undermines the validity of this assertion, must of necessity carry the most serious implications. As such, one cannot extricate oneself from the difficulty here by conveniently excluding the teleological formulation from impinging upon the religious formulation that belongs to type I. And if, indeed, there is no escaping the teleological formulation impinging upon the religious formulation that belongs to type I, then there is also no escaping the contradiction and ambivalence which are built into the way by which the religious formulation belonging to type I relates towards the formulation. Namely, on the one hand, one cannot dismiss here the teleological formulation (for that would undercut the assertion essential to such a religious formulation to wit, that the ultimate is constituted here as a personal being); on the other hand, one cannot at the same time really accept it either, for its demand for the suspension of the ethical is not feasible in terms of the religious formulation that belongs to type I.

But this ambivalence and contradiction regarding the status of the teleological formulation here is actually the direct result and, indeed, but the reflection of the signification which the teleological formulation carries when taken in the context of the religious formulation belonging to type I. For what the teleological formulation really signifies in the context, namely, what it really does here is to lay bare the head-on collision, the contradiction, which exists between the two fundamental and essential principles that are necessarily implicated in the religious formulation belonging to type I, to wit, the principle that the ultimate be constituted as a personal being and the principle that the ethical may not be suspended here. Both these principles must be present in the religious formulation belonging to type I and yet their respective implications, as we have tried to show above, are clearly and inescapably contradictory to each other. This inner contradiction and ambivalence which are built into the very structure of the religious formulation belonging to type I are, however, brought to the fore, i.e., are revealed, most poignantly by the teleological formulation precisely by their forcing the issue in pushing the principles all the way with respect to their implications. Thus, in the context of the religious formulation belonging to type I, the teleological formulation, far from making a statement to be proclaimed, is really raising a problem to be overcome. The teleological formulation here does not signify an exclamation mark but a question mark. And as such, the most challenging and fundamental issue here connected with the teleological formulation is the issue of how the religious formulation belonging to type I manages to overcome the problem posed by the formulation, i.e., manages to get around the clash, mitigate its detrimental effects or, indeed, prevent it from actually arising. In conclusion, therefore, let us briefly examine two possible approaches that have been proposed to see how well they succeed in coping with the problem.

III

One of these approaches is very cogently presented by Buber in an article to which we have already had occasion to refer, i.e., in his article "On the Suspension of the Ethical."[15] It is perhaps not too unfair to suggest that the thrust of Buber's strategy here is not to allow the problem delineated above, i.e., the problem precipitated by the clash between the absoluteness of the free will of the divine and the unfeasibility of suspending the ethical, to actually come before us. For clearly if the problem is not before us then no decision and choice between the two contradictory aspects have to be made and consequently neither of the two aspects need be undermined or compromised and this, for all intents and purposes, is tantamount to canceling the problem. Now, Buber accomplishes this goal by introducing and leaving unsolved yet another problem, a problem which logically precedes the problem delineated above and whose solution (and thus removal) is indeed a necessary presupposition for the problem delineated above to arise. Namely, Buber finds another problem on whose solution the actualization of our problem is made contingent, which means, in other words, that he finds another problem which when left unsolved acts as a "repressor" of our problem, and he then proceeds to argue that this problem does indeed remain unsolved for us today and, therefore, we are saved from the necessity of choosing and deciding with respect to our initial problem, thus canceling, for all intents and purposes, its sting.

In translating this strategy into more concrete terms (which means here as it meant all along in connection with this issue a turning to the story of the binding of Isaac), we can put the case as follows: our problem arises from the fact that God's command here (i.e., sacrifice your son) goes against the ethical judgment (i.e., do not murder). For in these circumstances any choice, any decision, that we may make (what Buber refers to as "the decision of faith") is bound to undermine one or the other essential aspect characterizing the religious formulation belonging to type I, i.e., the absoluteness of God's free will (even to the point of commanding the sacrifice of one's son) or the unfeasibility of suspending the ethical (in commanding an act which is deemed by ethical judgment to constitute an act of murder), and in either case a serious problem is necessarily precipitated. That much in the situation seems to be irrefutable and one must resign oneself to accept it.

But then, how is one to extricate oneself from the problem which this situation necessarily precipitates? Well, Buber's strategy is to focus on the point that before one can really be confronted with this problem one must be ready to grant and clearly uphold that the God who is addressing one here is indeed the true, authentic God (and this, of course, even though the address goes against the ethical). For clearly, if the God involved here is not the true, authentic God but only Moloch (for Moloch imitates the voice of God),[16] our problem dissolves of itself. Thus, Buber is shifting, so to speak, the place where the battle is to take place. It is now to take place on the question of whether one can really uphold with surety that the God involved is the true God. Namely, if our problem is to be overcome, it can be overcome not in its own terms but only by being blocked from materialization in the first place by raising the further problem of whether the God involved is the true God. As Buber observed, "the problematics of the decision of faith is preceded by the problematics of the hearing itself. Who is it whose voice one hears?"[17] And again, "where, therefore, the suspension of the ethical is concerned, the question of questions which takes precedence over every other is: Are you really addressed by the Absolute or by one of his apes?"[18]

Now, on the new battlefield Buber can make his move to salvage the situation. In essence his move consists in the claim that in our time one can no longer uphold with surety that the God involved is the true God and not "one of his apes." It is important, however, to note the inclusion of the qualifier "in our time" in the claim. For while Buber readily concedes that it has always been risky to make such claims, that, indeed, the danger of being fooled by an imitator of the true voice is intrinsic to the very relationship that obtains here, he nonetheless suggests that in the past man did possess images of the Absolute which, although inadequate in many ways, could and did function as guides, as reference points, safeguarding man from succumbing "to the deception of the voices."[19] Thus, it should be underlined that the claim here is not made with respect to any feature that is intrinsic and inescapable to the situation which, in turn, would mean that the claim here is not normative but only descriptive. But even further it should be noted that even as mere description the description is by no means universal in its applicability. Buber clearly excludes the past and gives strong intimations that he would also exclude the future – the future in the sense of being messianic, of being the point where "the new conscience of men has arisen."[20] The claim is strictly confined to the present, to the era in which, to use Nietzsche's words, "God is dead," or in other words to the modern era. For it is precisely the death of God, which in Buber's interpretation comes to signify the decline in the image-making power of the human heart, that is responsible for the inability to uphold with surety that the God involved is the true God, seeing that it is the presence of the images of the divine (the Absolute) which allows one to distinguish the voice of the true God from the voice of Moloch, thus allowing one to uphold with surety the voice of the true God, and that it is precisely the weakening and, indeed, disappearance of these images which the death of God phenomenon manifesting itself in the modern era signifies. Thus, it is specifically with respect to our era, to the present (and not with respect to the past or to the future), that Buber puts forth his claim that one cannot take for granted that the voice addressing one is the voice of the true God. Still, this allows Buber, at least as far as the present is concerned, as far as we are concerned, to overcome our initial problem, what he called "the problematics of the decision of faith," by blocking its materialization through the introduction of "the problematics of the hearing itself." For if we cannot be sure that the God involved is the true God, then clearly "the problematics of the decision of faith" is of necessity suspended, so to speak "bracketed," until a time when we can be sure of this.

Now, how are we to react to this approach? Well, first of all it certainly would not have escaped notice that the way in which the approach here is attempting to overcome the problematic is not at all on the theoretical level but exclusively on the practical level. Namely, the logical head-on collision between the implications of encountering the Absolute as a personal being (i.e., as a free and spontaneous being) and the implications of maintaining the unfeasibility of suspending the ethical is in no way overcome. The logical contradiction between the two basic and essential tenets of the structure of faith stays untouched as it was. Rather what this approach offers in the way of overcoming the problem is the removal of the practical consequences that may follow the suspension of the ethical. What constitutes for it the overcoming of the problem is the ability to block from coming to materialization, thus to neutralize, any of the practical consequences that may ensue from the suspension of the ethical (evidently what would constitute the problem here is the constraint to execute a demand for the sacrifice of one's son). That this is so is really not surprising. For it seems to us that there is really no way of removing the logical contradiction. Thus, on the theoretical level there is no escaping the fact that an unerasable tension, dialectic, is built into the structure of faith of the religious formulation belonging to type I. But what is most important to realize is that precisely because we are dealing here with the religious formulation belonging to type I, i.e., with a formulation where the religious by its very essence expresses itself through the ethical domain, it is indeed the practical, concrete act rather than the purely abstract theoretical inconsistency that counts. What offends is the concrete act of murdering one's son (or even of breaking a promise) rather than the logical inconsistency of maintaining both the supremacy of a personal being possessing absolute freedom and the unfeasibility of suspending the ethical. Thus, the approach here is offering after all an authentic overcoming of the problem when it proposes to block the unsavory practical consequences of the suspension of the ethical rather than remove logical inconsistencies. Indeed, it would seem to us, this predilection towards the practical rather than the theoretical would characterize all viable approaches to the problem here, for it is determined by the very nature of the context in which the problem arises. As said, the problem really arises here when one has to act contrary to the ethical and therefore, correspondingly, it is overcome when the possibility for such an act is removed. Thus, far from being a weakness, the predilection towards the practical, the concrete act, is a distinct advantage for this approach.

Secondly, as we have seen, this approach attempts to overcome our initial problem, i.e., "the problematic of the decision of faith," through the agency of "the problematic of hearing" which it introduces into the picture. Now, there can be no denying that when manipulated by a clever and skillful dialectician (and Buber is certainly that!) this strategy appears very attractive and promising. For it is, indeed, the case that the overcoming of "the problematic of the decision of faith" is contingent upon the inability to overcome "the problematic of hearing," and on that basis it is only too clear that the overcoming of "the problematic of the decision of faith" will indeed depend on what results the handling of "the problematic of hearing" may produce. But to produce the right results, the handling of "the problematic of hearing" must be just right – an order that is not so easy to fill. Buber, however, is handling the task with great insight and consequently succeeds in using the agency of "the problematic of hearing" to its greatest effect. Let us briefly point to one or two aspects of this remarkable handling as we understand it.

Thus, for example, Buber very wisely does not hold that "the problematic of hearing" remains unresolved universally; namely, that at no time and under no circumstances was it, is it or will it be possible for man to distinguish between the voice of the true God and the voice of Moloch. He does not hold this position even though holding this position would have clearly insured that "the problematic of the decision of faith" would have been completely neutralized, i.e., overcome, for all times and all circumstances – certainly a most desirable state of affairs.

And let it be known that Buber's basic religio-philosophic stance could have readily provided a convincing rationale for the claim that the irresolution of "the problematic of hearing" is universal, i.e., for the claim that at no time could one uphold with surety that the voice is the voice of the true God and not the voice of one of his apes. For there is no denying that in the context of Buber's religio-philosophic formulation any claim on behalf of the divine is always and inescapably a risk and a gamble that it may be false. After all, there can be no demonstration and no proof with respect to these claims. There can be, therefore, no escape from the possibility that one could be fooled. In the last analysis, uncertainty is built into the very structure of things here and as such it can obviously express itself in the past and in the future just as well as in the present. Now, on this basis, Buber could have easily claimed a universal irresolution of "the problematic of hearing." And it is not that he is unaware of this implication flowing directly from his position. On the contrary, he dwells on it at great length, waxing very dramatic – all relations with the divine are embedded in holy insecurity.

Yet, Buber does not use this basic, ineradicable underlying uncertainty as a spur and a rationale for claiming a universal irresolution of "the problem of hearing." Rather he seems to take this uncertainty as constituting the "normal" substratum underlying the whole of the human-divine realm, the ether, so to speak, engulfing its totality and thus bathing each of its items in this basic modicum of uncertainty and in return demanding the taking of risk, the placing of trust, as the fundamental acts of affirmation. But it would seem that precisely because this uncertainty is perceived as all-pervasive and inescapable that Buber is not inclined to take it as an acceptable spur and rationale for positing the irresolution of "the problematic of hearing." For this an additional factor which can increase the uncertainty would seem to be required. And indeed, Buber does introduce precisely such a factor – the image of the divine which the human soul may cultivate and develop. For no matter how inadequate the image may be, its presence decreases while its absence increases the uncertainty as to whose voice is being heard – the voice of the true God or the voice of one of his apes. (This possible increase or decrease is, however, in terms of that uncertainty that is already beyond the uniform, all-pervasive uncertainty.) Now, it is precisely in terms of this increased uncertainty due to the absence or the weakening of the image rather than in terms of the constitutive all-pervasive uncertainty that Buber opts to posit the irresolution of "the problematic of hearing." But this means of course that he is transforming the kind of cause which is responsible for the irresolution – it is no longer an innate, constitutive cause but an external cultural or historical cause. For clearly, the genesis, the strengthening or the weakening of the image of the divine within us is essentially culturally and historically conditioned. And this, in turn, would further mean that while in terms of the innate, constitutive causation the irresolution of "the problematic of hearing" which is brought about is inescapably necessary and universal, the irresolution which is brought about in terms of cultural and historical causation is inescapably contingent and in all likelihood partial.

In view of the fact that, as we have just seen, a necessary and universal irresolution of "the problematic of hearing" would have provided by far the best means for overcoming "the problematic of the decision of faith" and that a contingent and partial irresolution must be commensurately far less effective, it is interesting to note that Buber's thought follows nonetheless the latter and not the former alternative. Now, in all probability Buber was not concerned with the particular considerations which we have introduced and his thought was motivated and directed by some other considerations. But whether or not he was aware of our considerations, it seems to us that his opting for an irresolution of "the problematic of hearing" which is contingent and partial rather than necessary and universal is, in the last analysis, the right move precisely for the sake of our considerations. For to have opted for an irresolution of "the problematic of hearing" which is necessary and universal would have certainly meant the exclusion of any and every possibility of upholding with surety that a divine communication has occurred, that one could hear and distinguish the voice of the true God. And such a total exclusion would have certainly meant, in turn, the cancellation, i.e., the disintegration, of the religious pole, seeing that the religious phenomenon is by its very essence built on there being a relation, a communication, between the divine and man. Thus, to have taken up this position would have been tantamount to throwing out the baby with the bath water and this would not do. One certainly wants to overcome "the problematic of the decision of faith" but such overcoming would be pointless if in the process the very feasibility of the religious phenomenon is taken away. Buber's restraint, therefore, in not applying the irresolution of "the problematic of hearing" also to the past and to the future is not only not a shortcoming but is a distinct advantage for his approach.

Yet another insightful aspect which emerges from Buber's handling of "the problematic of hearing" lies in the fact that it is precisely to the present and not to some other span of time, as for example the past or the future, that the irresolution of "the problematic of hearing" is confined. For as such, indeed, one is provided with a span of time which in our context proves to be the only suitable span of time, i.e., the only span of time where the real encounter and the real overcoming of "the problematic of the decision of faith" can take place. For after all, since "the problematic of the decision of faith" really precipitates itself, as we have seen, in the concrete choice (even more precisely, in the concrete external act) and furthermore since, commensurate to this, the real overcoming of the problem is likewise with respect to the concrete external act (namely, the rub of the problem lies in the actual carrying out of an act that is contra-ethical and correspondingly the problem is neutralized and overcome when likewise the act is not actually carried out), it should be clear that the real arena for both the encounter and the overcoming of the problem here is the present rather than the past or the future. It is only in the present (not in the past or the future) that concrete choice is presented, that concrete decision can be made and that concrete action can be executed. With respect to the past all is finished and known; with respect to the future all is "iffy" and speculative. It is only in the present that one encounters concreteness and open-endedness which as such call for one's decision, choice and action but also open up the possibility of being thrown into the throes of agony and perplexity if and when confronted by a command coming from the divine yet going against the ethical. Thus, to the extent that one can exclude the possibility of being confronted by "the problematic of the decision of faith" in the present (though leaving intact the possibility of being so confronted with respect to the past and to the future) one has succeeded in safeguarding oneself against the sting of this problem. Indeed, it would seem that this approach, by succeeding in confining the irresolution of "the problematic of hearing" to the present only (but not to the past or the future), succeeds in achieving the enviable feat of eating the cake and having it too. For it can with respect to the past continue to affirm the absolute supremacy of the divine will even when it countermands the ethical and yet at the same time remove the offensive implications of such an affirmation regarding the ethical by excluding with respect to the present the possibility of the divine clashing with the ethical. Thus, with reference to the past (which is the temporal dimension that would be congenial to such expressions) it establishes in abstraction and in theory the supremacy of the divine free will while with reference to the present (which is the temporal dimension where alone such actions count) it safeguards in practice and actuality that the ethical not be suspended.[21]

We should be clear, however, that in Buber's approach (and in clear contradistinction to the immediate foregoing analysis) the terms "past," "present" and "future" are not to be used in their general denotation referring to the abstract categories of time, to the permanent dimensions of temporality, dimensions that inhere in the very nature of things. Rather, they are to be used in a very limited, specific denotation referring to particular, contingent segments of history. Indeed, Buber does not much use in this connection the terms "present," "past" and "future." Instead, he refers to our time or even more precisely to a time whose *geist* is characterized by the "death of God" or the "eclipse of God" syndrome (this span of time so characterized clearly constituting with reference to us the present), to the "biblical period," the "period of the patriarchs and the prophets" (clearly constituting with reference to us the past) or to "a time when the new conscience of men has arisen" (constituting with reference to us the future.)

We would be wrong, however, to dismiss this as an insignificant peculiarity on Buber's part. Rather, it is a reflection of the precision and consistency of his approach. For this usage, it would seem to us, expresses the tendency to get away from universality in the positing of the irresolution of "the problematic of hearing" as far as possible, thus even to the point of trying to get away from the universality implicated in the use of the abstract categories of temporality (i.e., the universality implied in the claim to cover *every* present, *every* past or *every* future). The approach tries to establish as far as it can the contingency and particularity of the irresolution of "the problematic of hearing" which it must claim; it tries to confine and specify as much as it can this necessary irresolution. For as such it can sustain as much as is possible the viability of the religious pole – it can keep open as widely as is possible the potentiality of the divine communication to man. Clearly here, in protecting the viability of the religious pole in such a committed and consistent way, lies the special strength of this approach.

But at this very same point where its maximal advantage is manifested, lies also its gravest shortcoming. For although there can be no denying that it succeeds in safeguarding against the suspension of the ethical by introducing the irresolution of "the problematic of hearing" into our present, this is done so minimally, so stringently and narrowly, that one is not at all sure that the feasibility of safeguarding against the suspension of the ethical is adequately provided. Thus, as we have seen, the irresolution of "the problematic of hearing" and consequently the safeguarding against the suspension of the ethical could be established with respect to our present only because our present is characterized by the "death of God" (or the "eclipse of God") syndrome. Namely, strictly speaking, the irresolution can be established only because of the "death of God" syndrome – the coupling is between the "death of God" syndrome and the irresolution. And from this it follows that only with respect to spans of time that are characterized by the "death of God" syndrome (but then to one and every such span of time) can the irresolution of "the problematic of hearing" be established. But this is evidently much too contingent and limited to adequately protect the interests of the ethical pole, i.e., to adequately safeguard against the suspension of the ethical. For our era, our present, for example, could easily have not been characterized by the "death of God" syndrome and then the irresolution of "the problematic of hearing" could have not been established which, in turn, would have culminated in our being confronted by "the problematic of the decision of faith." Likewise, there is no compelling reason and certainly no guarantee that the "death of God" syndrome would continue in the future, thus providing spans of time, i.e., "presents," which would be characterized by the "death of God" syndrome. And certainly many of the previous "presents" constituting now the past were not characterized by the "death of God" syndrome.

Thus, although a solution with respect to our present situation can be attained on the basis of Buber's approach, namely, although we can establish on the basis of this approach that we can be saved the agony of "the problematic of the decision of faith" and the dread of the suspension of the ethical, the application of the approach is so contingent that it does not really remove sufficiently the possibility of being confronted with "the problematic of the decision of faith" so that one can be comfortable with the approach. Although it is true that in terms of this approach we are spared a direct encounter with the problem, other spans of time in which the problem may well have to be confronted are pressing hard on us from all directions. The dreadful either/or which the problem precipitates for us, although strictly speaking still but a theoretical question, is too close and too real a possibility not to impress itself on us as a concrete problem. We may even feel that the way in which this approach extricates us from this dilemma is rather superficial and unsatisfactory.

As such, one cannot really relate here to "the problematic of the decision of faith" on a purely theoretical level as if it were exclusively hypothetical. This certainly cannot be a reassuring position for the ethical role which is concerned to remove as much as possible the precipitation of a decision. Indeed, given the drift of this approach, the likelihood is that if a decision were to be precipitated it would go for the religious and against the ethical pole.[22]

Thus, there is no question that this approach formulated by Buber acquits itself well with the religious pole. It is a different matter, however, when one views it from the vantage point of the ethical pole. Here it becomes clear that it fails to convincingly provide sufficient protection against the suspension of the ethical. Obviously as such, the religious formulation belonging to type I in any of its manifestations – as, for example, mainstream Judaism – cannot be fully content with the approach formulated by Buber.[23] For it the solution must come from a different approach. Such an approach is, indeed, available and has been embraced, for example, by the fundamental orientation of mainstream Judaism both in the biblical and the post-biblical periods. Let us in conclusion outline in a most schematic way the main thrust of its strategy as it manifests itself in mainstream Judaism.

IV

The essential thrust of the strategy which this second formulation (to which we may refer as the classical prophetic approach) presents may be summarized in the following two statements: 1) the personal being of the divine, thus its spontaneous free will, constitutes here the ultimate and therefore, in the last analysis, the divine free will must prevail in all circumstances; 2) it is taken, however, as an axiomatic act of trust that this divine being by his own free will never suspends the ethical.

Clearly, this formulation should satisfy completely both the religious and the ethical pole. It satisfies the religious pole by asserting with no qualifications whatsoever the absolute supremacy of the divine being in its spontaneous free will in all conceivable circumstances. It satisfies the ethical pole by excluding the possibility that in *practice,* in reality, God would suspend the ethical. And as we have seen, while for the religious pole it is the theoretical affirmation of divine supremacy which is important, for the ethical pole it is rather the practical absence of the counterethical act which is important (rather than any theoretical speculations as to its supremacy).[24] Furthermore, the exclusion of the possibility of the suspension of the ethical is made in this approach completely universal. There is no limitation, no contingency applied here. And obviously, since the exclusion of the suspension of the ethical is attained here by quite different means than was the case in the previous approach formulated by Buber, such universalization carries here no threat whatsoever to the viability of the religious pole (as was the case with the former approach). As such, the approach can satisfy completely again both the ethical pole (by universalizing the exclusion of the suspension of the ethical) and the religious pole (by in no way limiting the possibility of the divine communicating with man).

Evidently, the way this approach is formulated it is tailor-made to the requirement of the religious formulation belonging to type I. It encompasses the tension and contradictory pulls which are built into this formulation and as such, it can fully overcome "the problematic of the decision of faith," seeing that the problem here constitutes itself as nothing else but the laying bare of such tension and contradiction. True, the approach here can attain all this because, in the last analysis, it constitutes itself on an act of trust – it is an act of trust of the believer that God will not act in such a way. Of course, within an act of trust, within an axiom, one can arrange matters to one's satisfaction. Now, an act of trust may not be legitimate or acceptable in the philosophic domain but it is completely legitimate and acceptable in the religious domain. For it is the distinctive characterization of the religious perspective that it recognizes the limitation of all human powers, particularly rationality, and thus opens itself to the going beyond them through the act of trust. In the religious domain, therefore, sooner or later one must come to the act of trust. And inasmuch as we are dealing here with a religious domain, it is perfectly legitimate and acceptable to establish one's strategy by which to overcome "the problematic of the decision of faith" on an act of trust.

Lastly, it becomes clear that the real problem in this context is precipitated if and when our experience contradicts the act of trust which says that God does not suspend the ethical. Namely, in having overcome so nicely and neatly "the problematic of the decision of faith," the problem of holding on to both the supremacy of the personal being of the divine and the unfeasibility of suspending the ethical, we prepared the ground for a new problem to arise – the problem of theodicy. The act of trust allows us to overcome "the problematic of the decision of faith" but it also makes it possible to raise the problem of theodicy.

Indeed, in mainstream Judaism the question of theodicy is the fundamental religious act. Far from being an expression of atheism, a rejection of the divine, it is a question that arises from within the very bosom of religion. True, it is a challenge to the divine (how come this is the case?) and therefore implies a critique. Yet, and much more profoundly, the challenge and critique can be raised only because one first accepts the axiomatic act of trust that God is bound to the ethical and would not act against it. Thus in each challenge one reaffirms the underlying act of trust which makes possible the raising of the challenge. Thus, the challenge of theodicy is at bottom the primary act of religious witnessing, the primary act witnessing to the inextricable bond between the divine and the ethical. It is an act which through the challenge affirms the essential characteristic of the religious formulation belonging to type I, namely the insoluble bond between the divine and the ethical. It is not surprising therefore that throughout its history from Abraham to the post-holocaust era mainstream

Judaism raises and wrestles with the question of theodicy. It may not have the answer but it must raise the question. It is in the raising of the question that the authentic religious orientation expresses itself. Just as the religious formulation belonging to type II (the type in which the religious is *de jure* severed from the ethical) is captured in its very essence by the resignation "Let your will be done!" so the religious formulation belonging to type I is captured in its very essence by the challenge "Is the Judge of all the earth not to do justice?"

---

[1]Something which clearly is not the case with respect to the other types of religion where the religious is essentially separated from the ethical and where, indeed, in consequence the concern with the domain of ethics and religion is much more peripheral and of far less moment.

[2]It may be helpful at this juncture to briefly indicate what the notion of the religious dimension and that of the ethical dimension essentially signify in the context of this discussion. Indeed, we would suggest that "religious" essentially signifies here the reality of the personal being of the divine and its free will while "ethical" signifies the acceptance of a set of maxims or laws as guidelines or criteria by which the desired human action is determined. Thus, in asking whether the religious or the ethical dimension is ultimate and supreme one is really asking whether it is God in his free will or a set of maxims and values which is taken to provide the ultimate and supreme authority and justification for the course of action which man ought to pursue. This, in the last analysis, is the real issue which is at stake in the discussion here.

[3]In all probability, however, there would be some uneasiness and queasiness as to the validity of associating so closely Kierkegaard's teleological suspension of the ethical with expressions of the religions which belong to type II. This uneasiness, in turn, is most probably due to a difference which we have not had occasion to refer to above but which nonetheless does validly obtain between the implications of the inner-logic operating in the context of religious expressions belonging to type II and the situation depicted by Kierkegaard's teleological suspension of the ethical when it is formulated in close conjunction with the story of the binding of Isaac. This difference lies in the fact that in the context of the story of the binding of Isaac the ethical is undermined (the suspension of an evil act, e.g., the murdering of one's son). As against this, in the context of religious expressions belonging to type II, the inner logic operating there can only take one as far as sanctioning acquiescence in the presence of evil but certainly not to the point of prompting the active perpetration of evil. The ethical is countermanded here not by the actual doing of evil but by the absence of active resistance to evil. Thus, we do indeed have here a difference – the difference between activity and passivity, between actively perpetrating evil and passively not resisting its on-going existence.

Of course, in the context of the religious expressions belonging to type II one can argue that underlying these acts of passive acquiescence and, indeed, providing the very possibility for their expression, lies the further act which on the premise of having cut asunder the vertical from the horizontal (excluding the possibility of the former impinging upon the latter or of the latter being at the service of the former) proceeds to renounce and abdicate the horizontal dimension, i.e., the this-worldly dimension. And this act is clearly active and not passive – it does not signify the suffering of a certain state of affairs but the actual bringing about of it. Furthermore, and most importantly, this act is not just one among a great many other run-of-the-mill acts (which in contrast to the others happened to be active rather than passive). No, in the context of the religious expressions belonging to type II this act is the most fundamental act; in this context it is the essential and distinctive act. For inasmuch as it signifies the renunciation and abdication of the horizontal dimension the act in the context of the religious expressions belonging to type II clearly underlies all other possible acts and in this sense constitutes a most fundamental act; and inasmuch as the act not only underlies all the other acts but actually makes their expression possible the act is clearly esential; finally, inasmuch as the act in signifying renunciation and abdication of the horizontal dimension clearly captures the central feature by which the religious expressions belonging to type II are distinguished from all other religious expressions the act is clearly distinctive of this type. Thus, one could argue that in spite of all the passive acts of acquiescence encountered here one can also encounter here an active act and, indeed, encounter it in the very fundamental, essential and distinctive act which underlies all the other acts in this context (all of which, to be sure, being acts that are passive). But this means that, in the last analysis, one would have to concede that the countermanding of the ethical in the context of the religious expressions belonging to type II is achieved ultimately also here by an active rather than a passive act (for after all it is the fundamental act of abdicating the world before the divine which, in the last analysis, is the primary act in the countermanding of the ethical and this act is clearly active) thus equating the situation here with that encountered in the story of the binding of Isaac. Surely, Kierkegaard must have made such an equation in his mind. For he clearly perceives his renunciation of Regina Olson in terms of the sacrifice of Isaac. The renunciation of Regina Olson is also an act of sacrifice. And though there are no doubt any number of similarities between the two instances to justify the equation (as, for example, that in both instances the act is constituted as a rejection of the horizontal dimension for the sake of the vertical dimension, that in both instances the act, i.e., the sacrifice, is brought about because of a demand emanating from the vertical, i.e., from the divine, or that in both instances the act clearly implicates a countermanding of the ethical), the equation would not have held if the two acts were not also perceived as ultimately being constituted as the same kind of act, i.e., as active rather than merely passive acts. Thus, even in the context of the religious expressions belonging to type II, as encountered, for example, in the thought of Kierkegaard who clearly represents the impact of the Lutheran tradition, the countermanding of the ethical does not express itself exclusively in passive acts of acquiescence but ultimately and fundamentally one encounters behind these many and various passive acts of acquiescence an active act of renunciation where the countermanding of the ethical is really effected. Still this argument may not be all that convincing after all. For there is no denying that the overwhelming preponderance of acts in which the ethical is countermanded in the context of the religious expressions belonging to type II are passive acts of of acquiescence. The argument above could point to only one act (albeit a fundamental and essential act but nonetheless numerically speaking only one act) that is an active act of renunciation. As such, one cannot close one's eyes to the fact that in this context the countermanding of the ethical is overwhelmingly associated with passive acts of acquiescence. And with respect to such a context the question may well be raised as to how valid is the application of the teleological suspension of the ethical, seeing that it is formulated in close association with the story of the binding of Isaac and that consequently it establishes only too clearly without any doubt or ambiguity that the countermanding of the ethical is associated specifically with an act that is active. Can it really be meaningfully applied to our context where with one exception (though granted this one exception is constituted by an act that is fundamental, essential and distinctive) the acts involved are passive acts of acquiescence?

Evidently, one must come up with a rationale that would go beyond the rationale offered above; namely, one must come up with a rationale that would go beyond attempting to formulate its justification in terms of the single act of renunciation underlying the multiplicity of the passive acts of acquiescence and would formulate its justification in terms of the very passive acts of acquiescence themselves. Now, it would seem to us that such a rationale is indeed available. For if one were to examine the matter more carefully one would realize, we would submit, that the difference between the active and passive act really receives its significance only when it is assessed from the standpoint of the ethical. Namely, from the standpoint of the question of responsibility or guilt, i.e., the degree of responsibility or guilt implicated, there is indeed a significant difference between the act countermanding the ethical being active and its being passive. Thus, for example, there is clearly a significant difference with respect to the guilt or responsibility incurred between actually murdering someone and failing to take action when seeing someone else murdering someone. In this context the difference between the active and passive act, the difference between the active and passive countermanding of the ethical, is real and significant and must be taken into consideration. As such, indeed, it would be highly problematical, from the perspective of the ethical standpoint, to compare (leave alone equate or transfer) a state of affairs where the countermanding of the ethical is active with a state of affairs where it is passive (it would be like comparing apples and pears). In other words, from the perspective of the ethical standpoint, it is indeed highly problematical to associate the teleological suspension of the ethical in conjunction with the story of the binding of Isaac (where the countermanding of the ethical is active) with the religious expressions belonging to type II (where the countermanding of the ethical is passive.) But the ethical standpoint, i.e., the question of the degree of responsibility or guilt, is not the issue at stake here – it is not the issue that the teleological suspension of the ethical precipitates. The issue at stake here, the issue which the teleological suspension of the ethical precipitates, is the issue of the relation between the religious and the ethical, or more specifically, the issue of the supremacy and ultimacy of the religious over the ethical. And with respect to this issue the difference between the active and the passive act evaporates. For the way the ethical is countermanded, the question of the "how," is really immaterial here. What is significant is the claim that the ethical is countermanded and that it is countermanded because of considerations or dictates brought forth by the religious. For this, and this only, establishes the supremacy of the religious over the ethical. The question of whether the countermanding of the ethical expresses itself in an active or a passive act is beside the point here as it does not affect the question of articulating the supremacy and ultimacy of the religious over the ethical – a passive act of acquiescing in the ongoingness of evil is just as much a countermanding of the ethical as is an active act of perpetrating evil (and as such it is just as much an act establishing the supremacy of the religious over the ethical as is the active act of actually perpetrating evil). Thus, if the issue at stake is indeed the issue of the supremacy of the religious over the ethical then the discrepancy between the active countermanding of the ethical as finding expression in the teleological suspension of the ethical when formulated in conjunction with the story of the binding of Isaac and the passive countermanding of the ethical as finding expression in the preponderance of the religious expressions belonging to type II is not really of any significance. And as such, indeed, the two expressions can be consistently and meaningfully linked, even though in the one expression (i.e., the former expression) the ethical is countermanded by an active act while in the other expression (i.e., the latter expression) it is countermanded by a passive act.

[4]This essay appears in a volume of collected essays by Buber entitled *Eclipse of God* (Harper Brothers, New York, 1952), pp. 115-120.

[5]Indeed, commensurate to this it is now also understandable that in terms of the structure of faith of mainstream Judaism the cardinal sin, i.e., the main and fundamental transgression, is the sin of idolatry. For what, in the last analysis, idolatry really signifies is precisely such a compromise of the radical transcendence of the divine. This can be seen fairly easily. Thus, the usually accepted understanding of idolatry is as follows: idolatry is constituted by an act in which one relates to a non-absolute being (no matter how important, ennobled, powerful or enduring it is) as if it were absolute – the taking of a contingent being as the ultimate being. But clearly, this understanding implies that the act of idolatry is, in the last analysis, but an act compromising the radical transcendence of the divine, i.e., the absolute, being. For in relating to a non-absolute being as if it were an absolute being idolatry constitutes its divine, i.e., absolute, being in terms of a non-absolute being) – in truth, its divine being is a non-absolute being. Thus, idolatry identifies its divine being with a non-absolute being and as such it clearly compromises the radical transcendence of its divine being. It turns out, therefore, that both idolatry and monotheism impinges positively, i.e., affirming and safeguarding the radical transcendence, while idolatry impinges negatively, i.e., compromising and negating the radical transcendence. Idolatry is but the other side of the coin from monotheism. As such, a reverse correspondence between monotheism and idolatry should indeed obtain – the centrality of monotheism should indeed implicate idolatry as the cardinal sin and, vice versa, taking idolatry as the cardinal sin should clearly point to monotheism as the central tenet.

This consideration, however, besides being interesting for its own sake is also relevant to the point we are trying to make here; namely, that the notion of the radical transcendence of the divine is fundamental in the structure of faith of mainstream Judaism. For it follows from the above that this claim can be established not only by the direct observation of the fundamental and central status that the notion of monotheism commands here, but also by the further indirect observation that idolatry is taken here as a cardinal sin. Consequently, the fact that in mainstream Judaism idolatry is indeed taken as a cardinal sin is a further buttressing observation in support of our claim.

[6]For further elaboration on this point see my article "Monotheism" in *Encyclopedia Judaica* and my essay entitled "Some Reflections on the Jewish Idea of God,"*Concilium*, No. 123, March 1977, pp. 57-65.

[7]It is important to note in this connection that the *Halacha*, i.e., the legal formulation, fully reflects this understanding. For in terms of the *Halacha* the authority of the precepts is in the last analysis grounded exclusively in the fact that they are commanded by God. Thus, it is the divine will, i.e., the personal being of the divine, and not the apprehension of any ethical maxim, which constitutes here the ultimate point of reference. Venerable and old as the tradition of trying to find a rationale for the various precepts may well be, the obligation to observe the precepts in no way depends on the availability of such a rationale but exclusively on the fact that they are expressions of the divine will. And to the extent that the *Halacha* expresses the very essence of mainstream Rabbinic Judaism this stance taken by the *Halacha* should, therefore, be most instructive.

[8]This essay appears also in *Eclipse of God* (Harper Brothers, New York, 1952), pp. 95-111.

[9]*Ibid.*, p. 99. Since "the radical distinction between good and evil" clearly signifies the inextricable foundational act on which ethics is constituted and since "the Absolute" is provided only in the domain of religion, the above statement is tantamount to saying that there is the need of grounding (i.e., of binding) the ethical in the religious.

[10]*Ibid.*, p. 99. And after this absolutization is undermined by sophistry *(ibid.,* p. 101) it reasserts itself in Plato by making ethical values the expression of immutable ideal forms *(ibid.,* pp. 101-102).

[11]*Ibid.*, p. 103.

[12]*Ibid.*, p. 104.

[13]*Ibid.*, p. 99.

[14]Indeed, the way in which this being is further depicted by Buber in this essay – as, for example, its depiction as the particular, specific "God of Israel," or as the "Covenantal God," or as the God who teaches man by the example of his own choosing between good and evil – clearly and indubitably establish this being as a personal being, a Thou.

[15]See *op. cit.,* in particular pp. 117-119.

[16]*Ibid.*, p. 118.

[17]*Ibid.*, pp. 117-118.

[18]*Ibid.*, pp. 118-119.

[19]*Ibid.*, p. 119.

[20]*Ibid.*, p. 120.

[21]By the way, this strategy in Buber's approach whereby the intervention of the divine is relegated to the past and future but excluded from the present, namely, where it is determined that the address of the voice of the true God can be upheld with surety with respect to the past or the future but not with respect to the present, readily reminds me of the strategy adopted by the rabbis with respect to revelation. For as is well known, while the rabbis of the Talmud quite clearly accepted the revelation of God in the past, e.g., Sinai, and in the future, e.g., the messianic era, they at the same time just as clearly suspended God's intervention by revelation during the interim period, i.e., during the present. The parallel is quite striking with the difference, of course, that in the case of Buber's approach one is concerned with the question of the conduct of man and the aim is to safeguard the applicability of an independent ethical judgment while in the case of the Talmudic rabbis one is concerned with the question of legislation (or hermeneutics) and the aim is to secure the applicability of independent rationality. The underlying structure, however, is the same. Thus, in both cases the expression of the religious pole, i.e., the expression of the direct impingement of God on

man, is relegated to the past and the future while the expression of the human pole, i.e., the expression of the activity of man, is defended in terms of the present. In view of our analysis above, we should be in a position to better appreciate the tendency towards such an arrangement and the advantages that accrue from it.

[22]Thus, for example, one gets the strong impression from Buber's handling of this issue that when a head-on collision between religion and ethics occurs (as it may well have occurred in the past), the religious pole wins – one is to obey the divine even at the cost of suspending the ethical.

[23]Indeed, in this respect, when the chips were really down, Buber showed himself to be more the existentialist thinker than the representative of mainstream Judaism.

[24]By the way, this should help us to better appreciate the significance of the fact that in such stories as that of the binding of Isaac or of Job the narrative in which one would seem to encounter the suspension of the ethical by the divine is introduced and qualified by the notion of trial – God is merely placing Abraham or Job to a test. For this means that the suspension of the ethical is presented here merely for the sake of the trial but that in reality it has no standing. Thus, since God does not suspend the ethical here in actuality, in practice, once and for all, the sting of the problem is removed or at least greatly mitigated.

Index

Abraham 48, 100, 281, 286

Absolute-Thou 54, 60

Ahad Ha-Am 182, 192, 193

Akiva 22

Albo 36

aliya 216, 218-222

Aristotelianism 8

Baal Ha-Razon 10

Baeck (Leo) 119, 189

being-of-Consciousness 5, 12, 32, 33, 42, 43, 61, 123, 125, 139, 266, 268

being-of-Power 5, 7, 12, 13, 32, 34, 43, 53, 122, 125, 129, 139, 266, 268

Ben Sirach 129

ben Zoma 21-23

Bible 8, 15-17, 19, 20, 65, 116, 126-128, 246, 247

biblical 11, 16, 18-21, 23-25, 31-38, 41, 45, 46, 51, 53, 54, 56, 58-62, 65, 95, 104, 110-112, 116-119, 126-129, 137-139, 142-144, 148, 153, 154, 161, 166, 173, 175-178, 238, 241, 246, 247, 251, 257-259, 264, 267, 278, 280

body 15, 17, 65, 67, 68, 74, 97, 107, 119, 124-126, 128, 130, 131, 133, 134, 136, 139, 173, 183, 226, 247

Buber (Martin) 12, 32, 182, 254, 263, 264, 267, 268, 272-276, 278, 280, 284-286

Buberian 12, 67, 173, 247

Bund 182

Calvinism 249, 257

Christian 84, 165

Christianity 67, 69, 84, 104, 107, 229, 235, 238, 243, 257

church 183, 188, 190, 225-237, 239-241, 243

civil religion 225-229, 231-233, 236-243

Clermont-Tonnere (Count) 242

Cohen (Hermann) 181, 189, 190

Consciousness 4, 5, 12-14, 33, 43, 51-53, 61, 67, 70, 106, 109, 122, 126, 128, 137, 139, 145, 149, 166, 173, 181, 212

Conservative (Judaism) 112

creatio ex nihilo 15-28, 30, 34-39

creation 11, 15-24, 26, 27, 32, 34-40, 68-73, 103, 104, 166, 167, 176, 247, 248

D'vekut 9

Daniel 103, 126-128

David 18, 91, 242

Davidic 18, 210, 212

Day of Judgment 135

death 74, 102, 107, 108, 121-134, 139, 238, 274, 278, 279

deutero-Isaiah 18, 20, 38

diaspora 83, 84, 88, 95, 96, 103, 107, 108, 110-120, 188, 191-193, 198, 200, 203, 206, 209, 211, 213, 217, 219, 221-223, 235-237, 239-241, 252, 254

divine 3, 8-10, 14-16, 20, 22, 26, 29, 31, 32, 34, 35, 37-41, 43-62, 66-69, 72, 74, 110, 149, 153, 155-157, 159-168, 170, 173, 191, 232, 233, 247-249, 251, 254, 258, 264-267, 272, 274-278, 280-286

divine providence 41, 45-47

Dohm 242

Dubnow (Simon) 182, 192

Ecclesiastes 126-128

Ein-Sof 9, 10

emancipated 86, 90-92, 94-96, 105, 106, 109, 112-116, 118-120, 184, 185, 188, 200-203, 213, 220, 221, 223, 230-234, 238-245, 252, 254

Emancipation 89, 91, 95, 96, 105, 109, 112-115, 118-120, 185, 186, 192, 193, 200, 202, 203, 213, 214, 219, 223, 230, 231, 241, 242, 245, 252-254

Enoch 127, 129

Epicureanism 41, 42

Epicurus 41

Epstein (I.) 34, 254

Epstein (Yechezkel) 36

essence 3-6, 8, 11, 12, 14, 15, 19, 25, 35, 37, 38, 40, 42, 49, 52, 53, 55-57, 59, 60, 65-69, 72, 75, 77, 81, 83-88, 90, 93-96, 100, 102, 104, 105, 107, 118, 120, 121, 128, 132, 141, 143-145, 151, 153, 155, 161, 163, 165, 166, 175-177, 183, 186, 190, 191, 201, 203, 206-208, 210-212, 219, 239, 243, 246, 254, 257, 261, 262, 264, 266, 267, 271, 273, 274, 277, 282, 285

Eternal-Thou 38, 54, 58-60, 175, 176, 248

ethic 250

ethical 3, 5, 8, 18, 19, 27, 31, 38, 39, 84, 97, 115, 118, 119, 131-139, 146-154, 160-165, 168-170, 189-192, 212, 238, 247, 248, 250, 251, 253-255, 257-275, 277-286

ethics 28, 134, 136, 147, 184, 189, 191, 247, 248, 257-260, 266-268, 282, 285, 286

ethnic 79, 81-102, 104-108, 110, 113, 114, 120, 183-192, 194, 202, 213, 240, 241, 244, 253, 254

evil 47, 48, 65, 71-73, 138, 168, 178, 267, 282, 284, 285

Ezekiel 138

faith 3, 14-16, 24-29, 31, 34, 36-38, 40-42, 46-49, 53, 54, 61, 62, 71, 73, 77, 81, 84-86, 101, 102, 106, 108, 109, 111, 113, 114, 116, 117, 120, 129, 136, 137, 141-143, 146-149, 152-156, 159, 160, 165-169, 175-177, 197-199, 210, 211, 213, 232-235, 257, 258, 262, 264-267, 272-277, 279-281, 284

First Cause 8

Formstecher 181, 190

Fourth Ezra 127, 129

Freehof (S.) 38

Friedlaender (David) 242

Gamaliel 24

Genesis 14-18, 20, 22, 29, 34, 35, 37, 38, 127, 128, 258, 276

Genesis Rabbah 35

ghetto 95

God 3-6, 8, 10, 11, 14-18, 20, 22-32, 34-39, 41, 42, 45-55, 57, 59-61, 66, 68-74, 109, 127, 132, 143, 164, 165, 167, 169, 176, 177, 195, 203, 212, 247-249, 266, 267, 269, 273-282, 284-286

Gordon (A. D.) 182, 194-196

Greek 25, 37, 38, 130, 267

Gunkel (Herman) 254

Halacha 3, 97, 99-101, 107, 117, 137, 156, 161-164, 168-170, 223, 247, 285

halachic 3, 31, 32, 41, 45, 96-99, 102, 107, 154-165, 168-170, 189, 203, 246, 248-251, 257

Hebrew Scripture 127, 129, 136, 137, 153, 154, 167, 173-177, 179

Heine (Heinrich) 230

Herder 242

Herzl (Theodor) 181, 186, 214, 218

Heschel (A. J.) 43, 254

Hess (Moses) 182, 187, 188, 191

hierocracy 225

Hillel 21

Hirsch (S. R.) 181, 190, 203

history 11, 28, 30, 38, 39, 44-48, 51, 60, 67, 69, 74, 75, 77, 79-81, 84, 86, 87, 94, 95, 105-119, 126, 137, 148, 165, 169, 176, 183, 190, 191, 197, 198, 203, 205, 208, 210, 211, 218, 219, 222, 229, 237, 238, 245, 251, 252, 267, 278, 281

homo religiosus 144, 145

Hutchinson (J. A.) 165

I-It 12-15, 32, 33, 247

I-Thou 12, 15, 32, 33, 247

idealism 8, 67-69, 159

identity 43, 77, 78, 81, 87-89, 92, 94-97, 102-106, 109, 110, 112-115, 119, 120, 132, 133, 184, 200, 202, 223, 231, 242, 254

ideology 205, 206, 209, 210, 215, 216, 218, 220, 222, 223

immigration 216

immortality 121, 123, 124, 126, 129-136, 139

Isaiah 34, 37, 128, 167

Ishmael 22

Islam 24, 25, 107, 229

Israel 38, 45, 47, 48, 69, 83, 103, 104, 106, 108, 110-112, 115-120, 130, 138, 158, 182, 184, 187, 188, 193-197, 201, 203, 205, 206, 209, 211, 243, 247, 252, 267, 285

Israeli 83, 84, 95, 103, 116, 205, 206

Israelite 101

It-being 4, 7-9, 12-15, 27-29, 31-34, 37, 38, 42, 45, 53, 60, 61, 266

It-dimension 33, 61, 62, 67, 156-158

It-domain 53, 54, 59, 61, 62, 154, 168

It-God 4-10, 42, 53-55, 61

It-sphere 152, 153

Itness 150, 151

Jacobs (Louis) 129, 254

Jeremiah 128, 138, 167

Jew 45, 68, 71, 75, 77-86, 89-99, 101-110, 112-116, 119, 120, 159, 186, 192, 195, 200, 213, 214, 216-219, 222, 229-232, 234, 239, 240, 242, 244, 245, 254

Jewish 8, 9, 25, 34, 48, 65, 66, 68, 69, 71, 72, 74, 75, 77-88, 90-109, 111-120, 129, 153, 181-197, 201, 205-223, 229, 230, 235, 239-243, 245, 251, 252, 254, 257, 262, 264, 285

Jewry 77, 78, 83-86, 91, 92, 95, 96, 102-104, 109, 112-116, 118-120, 181, 184, 188, 189, 202, 203, 205, 213, 214, 217, 219, 221-223, 225, 229-234, 238-243, 245, 251, 252, 254

Job 34, 48, 60, 128, 138, 286

Joshua ben Hananiah 21, 22, 36

Judaism 3, 5, 8, 10-15, 21, 24-29, 31, 32, 34, 36-56, 58, 59, 62, 65-75, 84, 85, 93, 95-121, 126, 128-131, 135-139, 141-143, 146, 152-154, 159, 160, 165, 181-203, 206-216, 218-220, 225, 229, 231-243, 245-254, 257, 258, 262-270, 280-282, 284-286

Judith 129

Kavanah 159, 170

Kierkegaard 259-262, 283

Kook (Rav) 182, 194, 195, 254

land 32, 86-91, 94, 95, 104, 105, 120, 181, 182, 184-188, 190-201, 203, 211, 212, 215, 222, 231

Landau (Yechezkel) 38

Law 68, 103, 107, 108, 111, 112, 115-119, 156, 157, 168, 206, 247, 267, 268

Lazarus (Moritz) 181, 190

Lehmann (K.) 165

Leviticus 128

Lutheranism 249, 257, 262

Maharal 195

Maimonides 34, 36, 37

man 3, 4, 6, 8, 11, 13, 14, 19, 24, 27-29, 31-33, 38-40, 42, 44, 45, 56, 59-61, 65-75, 86, 108, 115, 122, 124, 126-129, 133, 134, 138, 139, 141, 144, 145, 147, 148, 155, 161, 164, 166, 167, 170, 173-178, 186, 189, 195, 203, 210, 212, 230-232, 247-250, 267, 273, 275, 277, 278, 281, 282, 285, 286

materialism 67, 68

Mendelssohn (Moses) 185

Mirabeau (Count) 242

monotheism 56, 61, 62, 264-266, 284, 285

monotheistic 15-21, 23, 25-27, 35, 47, 51, 52, 54-56, 100, 265, 266

Moore (George F.) 129

Mosaic covenant 18

Moses 118, 187

mysticism 8, 9, 32, 153, 194

nature 6, 11-17, 25-35, 37-40, 43-47, 56, 60, 68, 69, 71, 74, 87, 88, 100, 111, 113, 115, 117, 119, 129, 131, 148, 154, 164, 167, 169, 173, 177, 179, 181, 185, 188, 195, 198, 213, 241, 247, 249, 250, 258, 268, 270, 275, 278

Nehemiah 23, 111

neo-Platonism 8

Nordau (Max) 181

Olson (Regina) 283

omnipotence 46, 47, 49-51, 72

omnipotent 47, 50, 51, 74

original sin 71

Orthodox (Judaism) 95

pantheism 5-9, 68, 143, 145, 166

Pentateuchal 107, 156, 157, 168

people 59, 69, 83-85, 88, 89, 91, 93, 94, 96, 97, 103, 111-113, 118, 119, 121, 130, 135, 158, 181, 182, 184-188, 190-195, 199, 205, 211-218, 220, 222, 223, 242, 245

Pinsker (Simhah P.) 186

Plato 67, 285

Platonic 25, 34, 35

power 4, 5, 7, 8, 12, 13, 33, 38, 43, 46, 47, 50-55, 57-62, 67, 69, 70, 72, 74, 88, 103, 110, 111, 113, 115, 117, 122, 123, 129, 139, 142, 149, 153, 158, 167, 169, 170, 174, 178, 195, 199, 210, 225, 229, 236-238, 242, 243, 251, 268, 269, 274

prophecy 18, 38, 111, 127, 137, 155, 161, 167, 176, 246

prophetic 31, 41, 45, 154, 155, 157, 159-161, 165, 167, 168, 176, 234, 235, 243, 246, 248-251, 254, 257, 280

providence 8, 41, 45-47, 60, 109, 167

Psalms 34, 35, 128

rabbi 21-24, 35, 36, 38, 39, 91, 118

Rabbinic Judaism 45, 47, 68, 101, 110-112, 114, 116-118, 128-130, 135-137, 154, 182, 202, 203, 215, 246, 285

race 79, 86, 87, 90, 98

racial 87, 88, 105, 195

Rahner (K.) 165

Rav 22, 23, 35, 182, 194, 195

Reconstructionist (Judaism) 112

Redeemer 18

Reform (Judaism) 112

relation 3, 6, 7, 11-15, 27-29, 31-33, 39, 42, 65, 69-71, 88, 90, 104, 133, 136, 147, 148, 150, 176, 177, 225, 232, 233, 248-250, 257, 258, 267, 277, 284

religion 11, 14, 25, 28, 42, 45, 51, 62, 65, 73, 84, 85, 88, 95-98, 100, 101, 104-108, 113, 119-123, 126, 129, 138, 139, 143, 145, 146, 158, 166, 168, 169, 181, 184, 189, 197, 225-243, 247, 250, 251, 253, 254, 257-259, 267, 281, 282, 285, 286

religious 3, 5, 8, 11, 14, 16, 20, 28, 29, 31, 32, 38, 39, 41, 42, 51-53, 56, 59, 65, 79, 81-86, 88, 92, 93, 95-102, 104-110, 112, 114, 116-118, 120, 121, 123-126, 128, 132, 142-148, 155, 164, 166, 168, 170, 175-177, 182-185, 188-192, 194, 197, 199, 202, 203, 207-211, 213, 214, 217, 227, 231, 233, 237, 238, 240, 242-244, 246, 248, 249, 253, 257-274, 277-286

Renan (Ernest) 254

righteous 30, 39, 47, 73, 130, 161, 176, 198, 199, 201

Rosenzweig (Franz) 70, 118, 181, 190, 194, 211

Saadia 36, 37

Samuel I 128

Sarah 100

Saul 128

Savior 18

Scripture 22, 40, 127, 129, 136, 137, 153, 154, 167, 170, 173-177, 179

secular 91, 95, 110, 111, 120, 170, 189, 191, 202, 215, 226, 227

secularist 145, 146, 166, 183, 206-208, 214, 215

sefirot 9, 10

segula 195, 196

Shammai 21

Sheol 127

Shimon Bar Yohai 21

Simeon ben Zoma 21

Sinai 65, 118, 119, 285

Smolensky 185, 192

social action 173, 176, 177

soul 33, 67, 68, 124-126, 128-136, 139, 173, 186, 195, 247, 276

Spirit 8, 53, 65-69, 74, 91, 103, 104, 139, 173, 174, 178, 195, 196, 222, 247

state 17, 18, 34, 35, 37, 57, 79, 89, 90, 102, 103, 110, 111, 115-117, 119, 120, 127, 128, 134, 155, 160, 185, 188, 192, 200, 202, 205-212, 215-219, 221-223, 225-237, 239-243, 252, 254, 261, 275, 282, 283

Steinheim 181, 190

Stoic 34

structure-of-faith 11, 41, 42, 44-52, 55, 58, 59, 61, 181

Syriac Baruch 127, 129

Talmud 21, 39, 134, 170, 285

talmudic 21, 23, 35, 91, 106, 129, 134, 285

Teller (W. A.) 242

theodicy 47-52, 54, 56, 59, 61, 62, 132, 281, 282

Thou 4-6, 12, 29-32, 38, 39, 42, 55, 58-61, 67, 149-154, 167, 169, 173-179, 248, 249, 254, 268, 269, 285

Thou-being 4, 9, 12-14, 27, 29, 32, 33, 37, 42-45, 54, 59-61, 266

Thou-dimension 33, 61, 62, 67, 68, 156, 157, 162

Thou-domain 53, 61, 62, 154, 159, 168

Thou-God 4-10, 42, 53-55, 61

Thou-sphere 152, 153, 167

Thouness 4, 150, 151

Tobias 129

Torah 22, 107, 117, 118, 215

Toynbee (Arnold) 117

Ugandists 187

Upanishads 65

Urbach (E. E.) 24, 35, 36, 129

von Rad (G.) 38

Wellhausen (Julius) 254

Weltanschauung 31, 32, 41, 123, 137, 144, 173, 177, 214, 243, 245

Weltanschauungen 31

Wiener (Max) 242, 254

Wisdom literature 8, 18, 38

Wolfson (H. A.) 34

worship 68, 141-147, 150-155, 160, 161, 165-167, 169, 170, 249, 254

Wright (G. Ernest) 34, 35, 37

Yehoshua 24

Zangwill (Israel) 181

Zimzum 10

Books of Interest
from The Studies in Judaism Series
and University Press of America

Midrash as Literature: The Primacy of Documentary Discourse
Jacob Neusner
New Perspectives on Ancient Judaism, Volume 1—Religion, Literature and Society in Ancient Israel, Formative Christianity and Judaism
Jacob Neusner, Peder Borgen, Ernest S. Frerichs, and Richard Horsley
New Perspectives on Ancient Judaism, Volume 3—Judaic and Christian Interpretation of Texts: Contents and Contexts
Jacob Neusner and Ernest S. Frerichs